Paradigm

Keyboarding & Applications I
SIXTH EDITION

Sessions 1–60

William Mitchell
Patricia King
Ronald Kapper

with Microsoft®
Word 2010

Paradigm PUBLISHING

St. Paul

Managing Editor: Christine Hurney
Developmental Editors: Spencer Cotkin, Cheryl Drivdahl, Brenda Owens
Production Editor: Bob Dreas
Design and Production Specialists: Julie Johnston, Valerie King, Jack Ross
Cover and Text Designer: Leslie Anderson
Copy Editor: Judy Peterson
Proofreader: Buuji, Inc.
Indexer: Terry Casey
Illustrations: Cohographics
VP & Director of Digital Projects: Chuck Bratton
Digital Project Manager: Tom Modl

Care has been taken to verify the accuracy of information presented in this book. However, the authors, editors, and publisher cannot accept responsibility for Web, email, newsgroup, or chat room subject matter or content, or for consequences from application of the information in this book, and make no warranty, expressed or implied, with respect to its content.

Trademarks: Some of the product names and company names included in this book have been used for identification purposes only and may be trademarks or registered trade names of their respective manufacturers and sellers. Microsoft is a trademark or registered trademark of Microsoft Corporation in the United States and/or other countries. The authors, editors, and publisher disclaim any affiliation, association, or connection with, or sponsorship or endorsement by, such owners.

We have made every effort to trace the ownership of all copyrighted material and to secure permission from copyright holders. In the event of any question arising as to the use of any material, we will be pleased to make the necessary corrections in future printings. Thanks are due to the aforementioned authors, publishers, and agents for permission to use the materials indicated.

ISBN 978-0-76384-783-8 (Text)
ISBN 978-0-76384-788-3 (Text and Online Lab)
Internet Resource Center: www.paradigmcollege.net/keyboarding6
Online Lab: snapkey6.emcp.com

© 2013 by Paradigm Publishing, Inc.
875 Montreal Way
St. Paul, MN 55102
Email: educate@emcp.com
Website: www.emcp.com

Printed in the United States of America

21 20 19 18 17 16 15 14 13 12   1 2 3 4 5 6 7 8 9 10

Contents

Preface

Keyboarding and using Microsoft® Word to produce documents are fundamental skills for anyone who plans to work in any type of business environment. These skills are not limited to particular jobs and are required for all kinds of business settings. To be effective in communicating through email, business correspondence, and other types of documents, a person must be able to think and key simultaneously. Keyboarding and document production are no longer nice-to-know skills—they are now essential skills.

Paradigm Keyboarding and Applications I with Microsoft Word 2010: Sessions 1–60, Sixth Edition and the accompanying SNAP Online Lab provide instruction in the basic keyboarding skills needed to key alphabetic, numeric, and special symbol characters on a standard keyboard. The textbook and Online Lab also teach the skills needed to use a 10-key numeric keypad. Furthermore, the textbook and Online Lab provide instruction in the fundamental elements of word processing using Microsoft Word 2010 for document production. Word features are applied to the production of a variety of business documents, including email, memos, business letters, business reports, and manuscripts. Proper formatting is emphasized in the preparation of business documents. No prior experience in keyboarding (or typing) and word processing is required to use this textbook and Online Lab.

The emphasis of the textbook and Online Lab is to develop a student's keyboarding speed and accuracy skills, a firm command of Word features, and the ability to prepare common business documents quickly, accurately, and with correct formatting. After successfully completing a course that uses this textbook and the accompanying Online Lab, students will be able to:

- Key straight-copy alphanumeric material using correct touch techniques at an average rate of 40 words a minute (WAM) with a maximum of one error per minute
- Key numeric copy using correct touch techniques on the 10-key numeric keypad at a rate of 25 WAM with no errors
- Use fundamental Word features such as inserting and deleting text, changing fonts and line spacing, centering and aligning text, checking spelling and grammar, using tabs, formatting bulleted and numbered lists, using headers, inserting and modifying tables, inserting headers and footers, keying footnotes and citations, and others
- Prepare and correctly format common business documents including email, memos, business letters, business reports, and manuscripts
- Compose coherent content at the keyboard at the word, sentence, paragraph, and document levels

Keyboarding Program Overview

The all-new *Paradigm Keyboarding and Applications I with Microsoft Word 2010: Sessions 1–60, Sixth Edition* and the *SNAP Online Lab* provide a streamlined and current approach to mastering life-long keyboarding and word processing skills. In this easy-to-navigate program, students will learn how to key with speed and accuracy by watching key-reach videos, completing drills, taking timings, and preparing correctly formatted business documents.

Paradigm Keyboarding and Applications I with Microsoft Word 2010: Sessions 1–60, Sixth Edition includes the first 60 of the 120 sessions that comprise the Paradigm Keyboarding Series. For additional keyboarding timing practice and further instruction in word processing using Microsoft Word 2010, and instruction and practice in preparing business documents, see *Paradigm Keyboarding and Applications II with Microsoft Word 2010: Sessions 61–120, Sixth Edition*. For a course that focuses on keyboarding skills without instruction in Microsoft Word, see *Paradigm Keyboarding: Sessions 1–30, Sixth Edition*. These titles are available at www.paradigmcollege.com or by calling 800-353-6685.

Textbook and Sessions Features

Paradigm Keyboarding and Applications I with Microsoft Word 2010 is divided into 12 units. Units 1–4 introduce alphabetic, top-row number, and special character keys and the numeric keyboard. Units 5 and 6 emphasize composing at the keyboard and speed and accuracy enhancement. Microsoft Word 2010 is introduced in Unit 7 and used extensively for the balance of the book. In Units 7–11, different types of business documents are discussed and Word features are used to prepare documents. Unit 12 is an end-of-course evaluation and covers the skills learned in Units 7–11.

Each session in Units 1–6 is a coherent lesson with specific objectives that focus on particular keyboarding skills. Students can work at their own pace and can repeat session activities as often as needed. To keep the drill work engaging, session activities vary, but all activities are designed to help the student accomplish the session objectives. For most sessions, students will complete warm-up drills and timings. Sessions also include ergonomic tips and success tips. Additionally, for Units 1–5 students will complete new key drills, reinforcement drills, and thinking drills. Beginning with Unit 7, in addition to demonstrating their improved keyboarding skills, students will complete document activities in which they will apply Word features to prepare a variety of business documents.

Keyboarding skills are developed through practice, and the textbook and Online Lab provide ample practice opportunities for students. All key locations and proper finger positioning and finger reaches are clearly shown with keyboard diagrams, available in the textbook and in the Online Lab. The Online Lab delivers dynamic videos to demonstrate finger technique. Skills are continually reinforced and applied through multiple drills. Drills that are specifically designed to reinforce previously learned skills are identified with the cycle symbol, shown at the left. In addition, the Online Lab incorporates diagnostic software that identifies keys that a student struggles with and provides additional, customized practice activities to help the student improve those key reaches.

Success and Ergonomic Tips provide suggestions to help students work safely and efficiently.

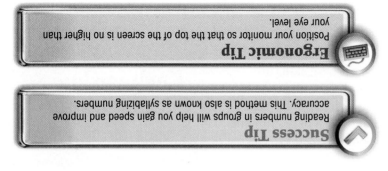

Success Tip

Reading numbers in groups will help you gain speed and improve accuracy. This method is also known as syllabizing numbers.

Ergonomic Tip

Position your monitor so that the top of the screen is no higher than your eye level.

The SNAP Online Lab Features

The SNAP Online Lab is a web-based keyboarding tutor and learning management system that accompanies the textbook. Access the Online Lab at snapkey6.emcp.com. The Online Lab gives students any-time access to their course activities from any web-connected computer running Windows XP, Vista, or 7. Students do not have to synchronize work completed at different computers. Instructors also have access to all student work and scores from any web-connected Windows computer by logging into the Online Lab.

Completing Keyboarding Activities in the SNAP Online Lab

All Online Lab activities are referenced in the textbook, individually numbered, and clearly identified in the left margin of the text. The activities in the Online Lab include exercises, videos, timings, and documents.

Exercises

To keep the drill work interesting, there are a wide variety of exercise types in the SNAP Online Lab. Students will complete activities by either referring to prompts on screen or by keying from drill lines printed in the textbook. The textbook and Online Lab provide clear directions to guide students through the learning experience. Students will not get lost!

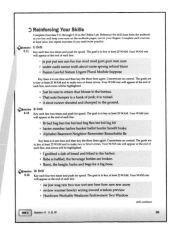

Exercises are used to warm up at the beginning of a session, to learn and practice key locations, to practice responding to questions and composing at the keyboard, and to work on increasing keying speed and improving keying accuracy.

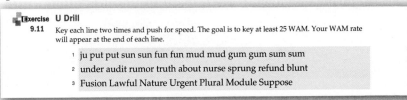

Exercise 9.11 U Drill

Key each line two times and push for speed. The goal is to key at least 25 WAM. Your WAM rate will appear at the end of each line.

1. ju put put sun sun fun fun mud mud gum gum sum sum
2. under audit rumor truth about nurse sprung refund blunt
3. Fusion Lawful Nature Urgent Plural Module Suppose

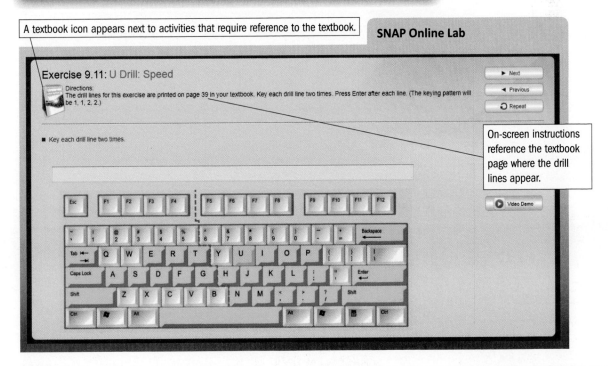

A textbook icon appears next to activities that require reference to the textbook.

SNAP Online Lab

Exercise 9.11: U Drill: Speed

Directions:
The drill lines for this exercise are printed on page 39 in your textbook. Key each drill line two times. Press Enter after each line. (The keying pattern will be 1, 1, 2, 2.)

► Next
◄ Previous
↻ Repeat

■ Key each drill line two times.

On-screen instructions reference the textbook page where the drill lines appear.

▶ Video Demo

Videos

Videos demonstrate correct finger positioning and finger reaches for all keys. Students can use these videos to help develop good keyboarding technique, which is essential for developing speed and accuracy.

Introducing the U, B, and W Keys

Videos 9.1-9.3 The locations of the U, B, and W keys are shown in the following diagram. Watch Videos 9.1 through 9.3 and practice using these new keys.

Exercises 9.2-9.10 Complete Exercises 9.2 through 9.9 to learn these new keys. Also complete the thinking drill, Exercise 9.10. When keying the drill lines, follow the instruction prompts provided in the Online Lab.

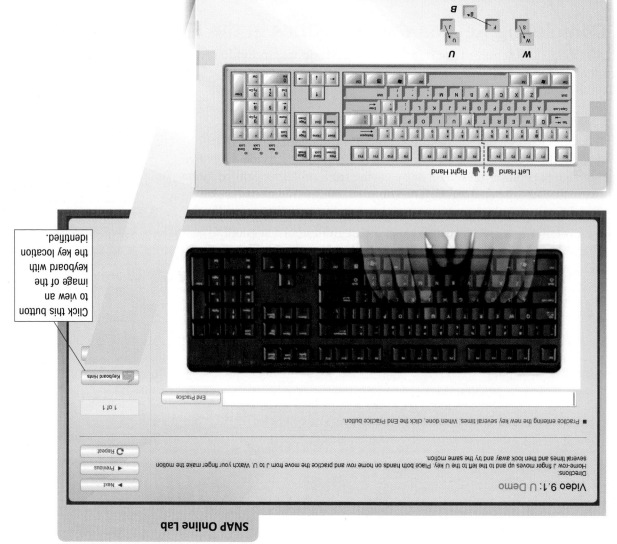

SNAP Online Lab

Video 9.1: U Demo

◀ Next
◀ Previous
↻ Repeat

Directions:
Home-row J finger moves up and to the left to the U key. Place both hands on home row and practice the move from J to U. Watch your finger make the motion several times and then look away and try the same motion.

■ Practice entering the new key several times. When done, click the End Practice button.

1 of 1

End Practice

Keyboard Hints

Click this button to view an image of the keyboard with the key location identified.

Left Hand 🖐 🖐 Right Hand

Timings

Timings are an important tool in assessing keying proficiency and the SNAP Online Lab provides immediate feedback on speed and accuracy for all timings. Timings begin in Session 6, with a 1-minute duration. The first 3-minute timing is introduced in Session 18 and the first 5-minute timing appears in Session 28.

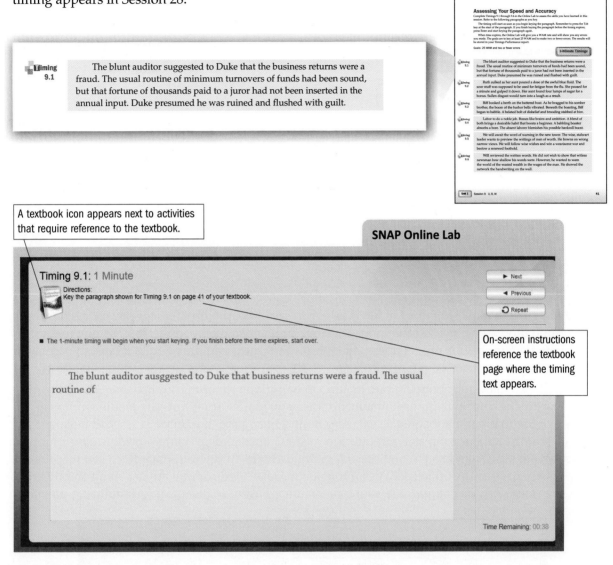

A textbook icon appears next to activities that require reference to the textbook.

SNAP Online Lab

On-screen instructions reference the textbook page where the timing text appears.

Documents

Document activities are completed using Microsoft Word 2010. For each document activity, students launch the activity on the Online Lab, complete the activity as specified by the easy-to-follow, step-by-step instructions in the textbook, and finally submit the document for assessment. Each document activity launch page includes a textbook icon and a reference to the corresponding textbook page numbers.

The Online Lab automatically manages the files for each document activity. When the student clicks the Launch Activity button, the Online Lab opens Word in the Online Lab window and retrieves the base document used in the activity. The Online Lab also automatically saves all files created in the document activities for future reference.

There are three basic types of document activities: checked and timed activities, checked activities that are not timed, and unchecked activities.

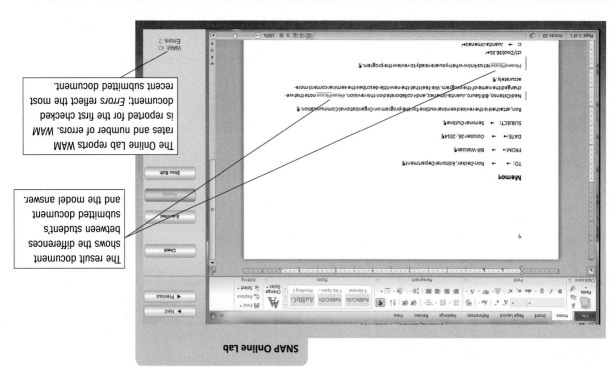

SNAP Online Lab

The Online Lab reports WAM rates and number of errors. WAM is reported for the first checked document. *Errors* reflect the most recent submitted document.

The result document shows the differences between student's submitted document and the model answer.

Checked Document Activities: For most document activities, the Online Lab will report a WAM score and evaluate keying and formatting accuracy. For these types of document activities, when the student has completed the activity and proofread the document, he or she clicks the Check button, which stops the timer, displays the WAM score, and initiates the checking process. While the checking process is occurring, the Result button displays an embedded green progress bar until the Result document is ready for review. The Result document visually indicates any differences (that is, errors) between the student's submitted document and the model answer.

After viewing the Result document, students can then return to the Word document that they generated by clicking the Submitted button. Alternatively, students can view both their submitted document and the Result document by clicking the Show Both button. The Show Both button splits the screen and displays both documents in an over/under format. A student can then make corrections to the submitted document, which can be checked again for errors.

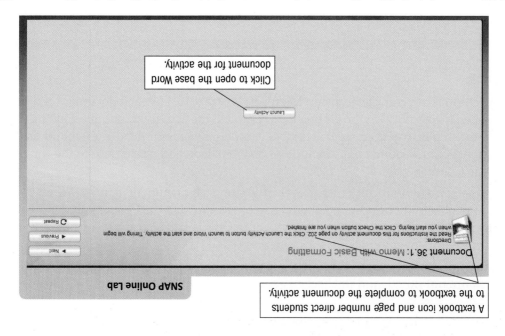

SNAP Online Lab

Document 36.1: Memo with Basic Formatting

Directions
Read the instructions for this document activity on page 202. Click the Launch Activity button to launch Word and start the activity. Timing will begin when you start keying. Click the Check button when you are finished.

Click to open the base Word document for the activity.

A textbook icon and page number direct students to the textbook to complete the document activity.

Checked Document Activities—Focus on Formatting: For some document activities, the Online Lab only evaluates keying and formatting accuracy (that is, the activity is not timed). Mostly, these activities involve editing a pre-existing Word document. When editing is complete, the student clicks the Check button, which initiates the checking process.

Unchecked Document Activities: Unchecked document activities are more open-ended than checked documents. In these types of activities, students compose a document according to the instructions in the textbook. These documents are not intended to match a model answer and are not checked by the Online Lab. When the student finishes the activity, he or she clicks the Upload button. The document is then sent to the Online Lab where the instructor can review it.

Navigating in the SNAP Online Lab

All of the available SNAP Online Lab activities are listed by unit. By clicking the activity name, the student is taken to the Launch page for that activity. At the Launch page, the student either clicks the <u>Attempts</u> link to see all the work he or she has completed on the activity or the student clicks the Launch button to open the activity. Once the student launches an activity, he or she can move to other activities using the Next and Previous buttons. This procedure is described in greater detail on pages 4–5 of Session 1.

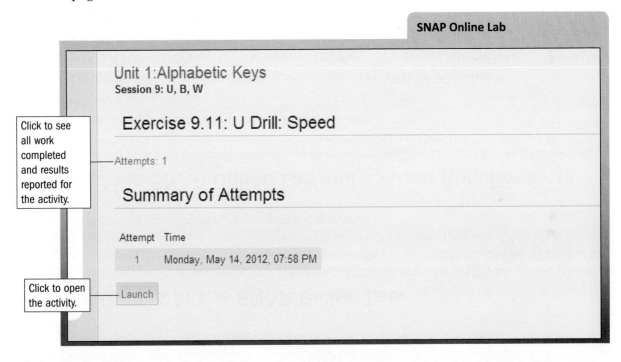

Viewing Activity Results and Reports in the SNAP Online Lab

Students and instructors can view student activity scores and results by clicking the <u>Attempts</u> link on each activity page. This link opens a page that displays all text keyed or documents created by the student for that activity.

In addition to the Attempts report for each activity, the Online Lab provides a number of specialized reports.

Prescriptive Analysis Report

The Prescriptive Analysis report summarizes how successful a student is in learning a particular key reach and suggests reinforcement activities for keys that are difficult for the individual student.

Progress Report

The Progress report lists all the exercises in the Online Lab and applies a check mark next to each activity for which the student has completed all the required work.

Timings Performance Report

The Timings Performance report lists the student's best words-a-minute (WAM) scores for each 1-, 3-, and 5-minute timing activities. The report can be viewed as a table or as a graph.

Average Timings Performance Report

The Average Timings Performance report lists an average WAM rate and error count for the student for all timings taken during the entire course.

Document Performance Report

The Document Performance report lists student WAM and error count scores for checked document activities. These scores reflect the student's initially checked document.

Viewing Grades in the SNAP Online Lab

The Online Lab includes a grade book that automatically documents the grades for all completed timing activities and checked document activities. Instructors can add other activities to the grade book, and then enter grades for those activities. Instructors can also edit grades. All grade data can be easily exported to other learning management systems.

Installing the SNAP Online Lab and System Requirements

Session 1 (page 2) provides detailed instructions in how to install the Online Lab on a computer. Students and instructors go to snapkey6.emcp.com to download and install the Online Lab. If needed, technical support is available at support.emcp.com.

The following are minimum system requirements for using the Online Lab on your computer:

- Operating System: Windows XP (SP3), Windows Vista (SP1), or Windows 7
- Broadband Internet Connection: Minimum 128 kbps connection to the Internet
- Web Browser: Internet Explorer 7 or more recent version (32-bit version only), Firefox 3.6 or more recent version, Chrome 11 or more recent version
- Popup-blocking software disabled for snapkey6.emcp.com
- JavaScript and cookies enabled
- Security: Firewall(s) configured to allow data transfer to and from snapkey6.emcp.com and www.youtube.com
- .Net 4.0 installed: .Net 4.0 is a free Microsoft application that is present on many computers that run Windows. .Net 4.0 is available at www.microsoft.com/en-us/download [search for *Microsoft .NET Framework 4 (Web Installer)*]

Logging into the SNAP Online Lab

Once the Online Lab is installed on a computer, a student simply double-clicks the Launch Online Lab icon on the desktop. A login screen appears. A student receives an enrollment key from his or her instructor and uses it along with the passcode packaged with the textbook to create an account. A student chooses a username and password and will use them to log in. This procedure is described and illustrated in detail on pages 3–4 of Session 1.

Instructor Resources

The SNAP Online Lab is a web-based learning management system that lets instructors easily deliver customized keyboarding courses and efficiently communicate with enrolled students. The SNAP Online Lab includes a grade book for assigning grades, tracking student progress, and downloading results.

Additional instructor support is delivered on CD and includes a sample syllabus, reference material and instructional support for each session, a theory quiz, general suggestions on teaching keyboarding, a set of PowerPoint presentations for student study or classroom instruction, as well as content for pretest and posttest timings. The pretest and posttest timings are completed in the SNAP Online Lab.

The contents of the Instructor Resources CD are also available on the password-protected instructor side of the book-specific website at www.paradigmcollege.net/keyboarding6e.

Acknowledgements

The authors and editors would like to thank the following individuals for their involvement in this project: Jacquelyn McDugle, Blackhawk Technical College, Janesville, Wisconsin; Janet Blum, Fanshawe College, London, Ontario; and Desiree Carvel, Minneapolis, Minnesota.

Putting together an educational package that is enjoyed by students and valued by instructors is a challenging undertaking. Many dedicated instructors participated in this project. Specifically, we would like to express our sincere thanks to the numerous academic colleagues who offered excellent suggestions during the review phase of this project. We greatly appreciate the time, experience, and expertise provided by the following individuals:

Cristina Aguanno
George Brown College

Amy Alegre
George Brown College

Adana Anschultz
Santa Fe College

Kathleen D. Anspach
San Diego Mesa

Karen Antill
Heald College

Zelma Arnold
Wright Career College

Dee Askew
Rowan-Cabarrus Community College

Vickie Axline
Marion Technical College

Louise Balotti
Florence-Darlington Technical College

Melynda Barks
Mineral Area College

Sandy Barnard
Lincoln Land Community College

Terry C. Barton
Jefferson College

MJ Bennett
Pulaski Technical College

Renee Bennett
Pulaski Technical College

Becky Bernard
Vanguard Adult Career Center

Dr. Melba H. Bolling
Virginia Highlands Community College

Carol Bourke
Brevard Community College

Karen Brandt
College of The Albemarle

Nancie M. Brown
Butte College

Terry Butler
Rhodes State College

Bruce Caine
triOS College

Patricia Campbell
Carroll Community College

Francisca Campos
Borough of Manhattan Community College

Gene Carbonaro
Long Beach City College

Dr. Sheri Carder
Florida Gateway College

Patricia Casey
Trident Technical College

Gail Chambers
Southwest Tennessee Community College

Charlene Clark
Gwinnett Technical College

Nancy E. Coleman
Branford Hall Career Institute

Bruce Collins
Davenport University

Jean Condon
North Platte Community College

Carolyn Conley
Milwaukee Area Technical College

Lori Cook
Montcalm Community College

Susan Cooperman
Montgomery College

Jo Cox
Yorktown High School

Patrick Coyle
Everest College

Elizabeth Cranston
Everest College

Amie Crawford
Hinds Community College

Debra Crocco
Newport Business Institute

Christette Cromarty
Selkirk College

Sandy Daniel
Rowan-Cabarrus Community College

Francelle Darris
St. Louis Community College

H. Steven Dashefsky
Norwalk Community College

Jose de la Rua
Everest College

Carol Decker
Montgomery College

Mary Dermody
Chabot College

Judith Dixon
York Technical

Dr. Rosalie Duren
Camden County College

Charlene Dybas
Fulton Montgomery Community College

Margaret Dye
Southwest Virginia Community College

Lynn Dee Eason
Sault College

Albert Eilers
Cincinnati State Technical and Community College

Arlene Eliason
Minnesota School of Business

Paula S. Eller
Wilkes Community College

Jane Ellis
Oakland Community College

Bonnie Errico
Hagerstown Community College

Don Eusey
Flint Hills Technical College

Kim Evans
Ocean Grove Charter School

Rita Farris
Blackhawk Technical College

Donna Fender
Wytheville Community College

Janis Flynn
National College

Aldene Fricks
St. Louis Community College

Vickie Fry
Westmoreland County Community College

Carole Galan
Everest College

Eugina Garrett
Rhodes State College

Joe Gehrke
College of Lake County

Karen Gillgrass
Sault College

Sheila Gionfriddo
Luzerne County Community College

Diane Goetzinger-Pena
Delta College

Vonn Goolsby
Tulsa Community College

Kathleen Gowdey
Berkshire Community College

Summer S. Gowen
Okefenokee Technical College

Pat Granger
Lamar State College-Pt. Arthur

Helen Grattan
Des Moines Area Community College

Nancy Graviett
St. Charles Community College

Jona Green
YTI Career Institute

Edward Grenier
Everest College

Lori Griswold
Hyde Park Middle School

Gail Guarino
Cape Cod Community College

Sue Guerrant
Vance-Granville Community College

Linda Haberaecker
Davenport University

Emmajane Hagenbuch
Northampton Community College

Hilda Hall
Surry Community College

Mary Lou Hall
Desert Oasis High School

Ann W. Handy
Eastern Shore Community College

Winona Hatcher
Aiken Technical College

Bobbie Hawkins
Southwest TN Community College

Marcie Hawkins
Zane State College

Constance Haynes
Schoolcraft College

Susan Heller
Reading Area Community College

Rose Hendrickson
Sheridan College

Pamela Hooper
National College

Sharon Huls
Southeastern Community College

Carol Hulsey
Polk State College

Marilyn Humeston
North Central State College

Antoinette Hutchings
State University of New York

Rhoda A. M. James, Ed.D
Citrus College

Kathleen Jenkins
Luzerne County Community
College

Nancy E. Jobe
Ivy Tech Community College-
Evansville

Darla Johannsen
Owens Community College

Betty Jolly
Caldwell Community College

Judy Jones
Churchland High School

Elizabeth Julian
Augusta Technical College

Lori Kapler
CDI College

Cheryl Kellogg
Marion Technical College

Jacki King, MS, CMT, CCA
Mid-State Technical College

Rosalie King
Prairie State College

Mitzi Kirwan
Western Iowa Tech

Suzanne Krissler
State University of New York

Deborah Kunkle
Blackhawk Technical College

Karen Lankisch
University of Cincinnati
Clermont

Sandi Larson
Minot Public Schools

Wanda Latimer
San Diego Mesa College

Grace Laverdiere
Oakland Community College

Jeanette LeDuke
Conestoga College

Theresa Leflore
Rowan-Cabarrus Community
College

Twila Lehman
Linn-Benton Community
College

Carol Lehrer
Santa Ana College

Mary Liidemann
Sheridan College, Davis
Campus & CDI College,
Mississauga Campus

Michelle Likins
North Georgia Technical College

Lynn Lilly
Nashville State Community
College

Marlene Lucas
Westmoreland County
Community College

Miriam Lynch
Long Beach City College

Linda Maatta
Davis College

Kristy Malacos
Sanford-Brown Cleveland

Sheila Malahowski
Lehigh Carbon Community
College

Terri Maradei
Montgomery College

Ethel Matney
POLYTECH Adult Education

Amie Mayhall
Olney Central College

Lisa McClure
Western Wyoming Community
College

Jacquelyn McDugle
Blackhawk Technical College

Lisa Mendez
Sheridan College

Darrelyn Miller
Grays Harbor College

Dave Miller
Monroe County Community
College

Susan Mitchell
Davenport University

Kimberly Moody
Clark County School District

Kathleen Moore
triOS College

Sherry Morgan
Henry Ford Community College

Carol Mull
Greenville Technical College

Kate Nelson
Everest College

Nancy Nesbit
Willow Creek School

Pauline Newton
Presentation High School

Kathy Nugent
Hillsborough Community
College

Amy O'Geary
Vance-Granville Community
College

Stephen J. O'Leary
Middlesex Community College

Lauren Parrish
Carroll Community College

Joanne S. Patti
Community College of
Philadelphia

Alicia Pearlman
Baker College

Connie Petlack
Butte College

Kathy A. Pillans
Navarro College

Duane Pitchford
St. Louis Community College at
Forest Park

Marcia Polanis
Forsyth Technical Community
College

John Price
Pulaski Technical College

Brian Priscott
Everest College

Darlene Putnam
Thomas Nelson Community
College

Sylvia Ranson
Conestoga College

Ronda Raub
Vernon College

Darlene Redd
Tennessee Technoloby Center

Judy Reiman
Columbia College

Linda Ren
Everest College Kitchener
Canada

Betty Reynolds
Arizona Western College

Turia Richardson
Davenport University

Tracey Riches
Everest Institute-Corinthian Colleges, Inc.

Leslie Ries
Daymar College

J Rigby
Oakland Community College

Teresa Roberts
Wilson Community College

Vicki Robertson
Southwest Tennessee Community College

Marilind Roff
St. Clair County Community College

Sheryl Rossi
Marion Technical College

Cheryl R. Russell
St. Clair County Community College

Nancy Scheffler
Jenks Middle School

Maryann Schiff
Norwalk Community College -

Roger Scott
Chattanooga State

Denise Sebesta
Community College of Allegheny County

Bonnie Shoemaker
Luzerne County Community College

Joan Siepietowski
Luzerne County Community College

Pearl Skewes
Navarro College

Lydia Slater
Rock Valley College

Mary Slaughter
Okefenokee Technical College

Amy Smith
Black Hawk College

Lorraine Smith
Fresno City College

Chris Smith
Northeastern Technical College

Mary Jeanne Sowards
Nashville State Community College

Helen Spain
Wake Technical Community College

Lisa Stark
Florida Gateway College

Sandi Stubbins
Centennial High School

Diane Stumpf
Washburn Institute of Technology

Kathy Taylor
Kirtland Community College

Cindy Thompson
University of Arkansas Community College at Morrilton

Traci Thompson
Kilgore College-Longview

Barbara Tietsort
University of Cincinnati, Blue Ash College

Janine Tiffany
Reading Area Community College

James Trick
Newport Business Institute

Gerrie Trossman
Oakton Community College

Ola Tyler
Davenport University

Karen Waddell
Butler Community College

Jackie Warren
Tidewater Community College

Robin Wehner
Jefferson College

Roberta Whitney
Southeast Career Technical Academy

Virginia Wiley
Raymond Walters College

Maureen Willis
J.L. Stanford Middle School

Dr. Brian Wilson
College of Marin

Michelle Woodruff
SCL Technical College

GeorgeAnn Woodward
South Florida Community College

Bettie Wright
Umpqua Community College

Marilyn Wudarcki
North Idaho College

Kay Young
Moore Norman Technology Center

Sue Youngberg
Bay College-West Campus

Eugene Zailer
Everest College

Mary Zajac
Bucks County Community College

Kathleen Zimmerman
Des Moines Area Community College

Joyce Zweedyk
Kalamazoo Valley Community College

Unit 1 Alphabetic Keys

Home Row, Space Bar, Enter

Session Objectives

- **Access and explore the Online Lab**
- **Identify the home row keys**
- **Practice correct finger positioning for the A, S, D, F, J, K, L, and semicolon (;) keys**
- **Use the space bar and Enter key appropriately**
- **Apply ergonomic principles to your work station**
- **Use corrrect posture when keying**

Getting Started in the Online Lab

You will be using the Online Lab web-based software along with your textbook to complete session activities that will help you develop your keyboarding skills.

Installing the Online Lab Software

If your computer does not already have the Online Lab software, complete the following steps to install it.

1 Connect to the Internet.

2 Launch your Web browser (such as Internet Explorer, Firefox, or Chrome) and then go to snapkey6.emcp.com.

3 Click the Get Started button.

4 Click the Install button to download the Keyboarding Online Labs software.

5 Click the Open or Run button (this will vary based on your browser) and follow the instructions to install the software.

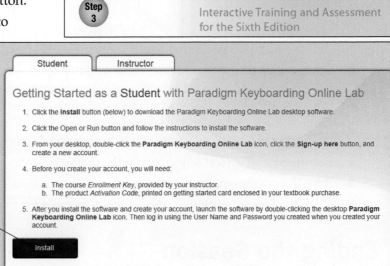

Figure 60.3 Memo Content for Document 60.3—Continued

photographs, charts, and so on. ¶ Providing this depth of information earlier in the career search process weeds out jobs you're not qualified for and establishes virtual rapport with your interviewers. The portfolio concept also helps prove the facts on your resume because it shows and not just tells. Prospective employers and clients want to see that you have solved problems like theirs. ¶ If you say that you have strong presentation skills, post a video clip! Articles, awards, graphs, audio references, white papers, case studies, press releases, and schedules of appearances are just some of the options you have to prove your expertise. ¶ Maybe there will come a time when the web career portfolio is as ubiquitous as the resume; but for now, there is a lot of opportunity to stand out from your competition and be extraordinary by having one. Of course, if the design and content of your portfolio is as unique as you are, that will further differentiate you. And, like any other website, there has to be a compelling reason to drive traffic to it. You must go way beyond the content that is in your resume. ¶ The bottom line? You will be googled, and when the average job lasts about 3.5 years, it certainly makes sense to constantly foster professional visibility both online and offline.

Reinforcing Writing Skills

Now that you have completed this keyboarding course, reflect on what you have learned and on how it was presented by completing the Document 60.4 activity.

 Document 60.4

Evaluating the Course

1. Navigate to the Document 60.4 launch page in the Online Lab and then click the Launch Activity button. The Online Lab will open **Doc060.04** in the activity window.

2. Compose an evaluation of the course and this textbook. Format it as a memo report to your instructor. Use headings to guide your reader through the report. Describe what you have accomplished. Did you meet the learning objectives listed in the preface? If not, why? Discuss the strengths and weaknesses of the textbook and the Online Lab. How could they be improved? Then, pick your favorite session or activity and explain why you liked it.

3. Proofread and correct any errors in the memo report.

4. Save the document.

5. Click the Upload button to upload the document for instructor review.

Ending the Session

The Online Lab automatically saves the work you completed for this session. Congratulations on completing this course!

Enrolling in the Online Lab

Once you have installed the Online Lab software, complete the following steps to enroll in the Online Lab for your Keyboarding course.

1 Double-click the Online Lab icon on your computer desktop.

2 Click the Sign up here button.

3 Fill in the fields on the Student Registration page.

    a Create a username and password that you can remember.

    b In the *Enrollment key* field, key the enrollment key given to you by your instructor for your course.

    c In the *Activation code* field, key the activation code that is printed on the card packaged with your textbook.

    d Click the Create my new account button (Step 3d). You are now enrolled in the Online Lab for your keyboarding course and are returned to the login page.

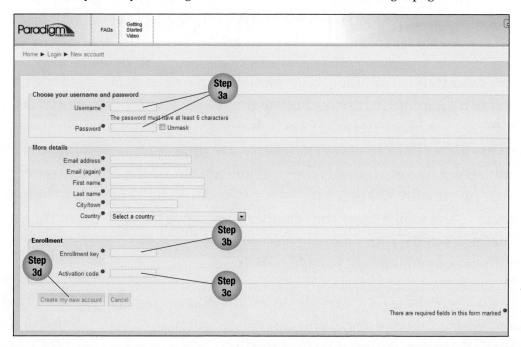

steps continue

Figure 60.3 Memo Content for Document 60.3 —Continued

that you would want potential employers to find as a first impression. • There are quite a few professionally relevant and positive results about you, but these snippets of information make it difficult to get a comprehensive picture. • You have a website that comes up highly ranked in the search results and paints a clear picture of your professional self. ¶ You can guess from these scenarios that everything that you post online or that is written about you becomes a part of your online identity. You'll want to consider the impact, positive or negative, that a comment on someone's blog or online news articles, or a review on a shopping site, will have.

(bf) *Your Own Blog*

One of the easiest and most economical ways to get an online presence that is well-designed and search-engine friendly is to create a professional blog. With WordPress, TypePad, or Blogger, you don't have to know HTML to start posting articles about your area of expertise. Just make sure that your posts are professional and relevant to your target audience. Use this vehicle to demonstrate your knowledge, your experience, and current grasp on happenings in your industry. On your blog, you can make your resume available for download (include text, Word, and PDF versions), link to other relevant sites, and include your career bio on the "about" page.

(bf) *Twitter*

You can establish another professional source of information about yourself online by joining Twitter and using it to tweet about professional issues. You can: ¶ • Share (retweet) the best tips from professionals in your field. • Pass along links to news stories that are important developments in your industry. • Tweet your own helpful job-related tips. • Show just enough of your personality (20 percent of your tweets can be personal) to help people get to know you. • Start conversations with people who tweet things that interest you. ¶ Twitter conversations can also lead to in-person meetings with people who might be able to help you.

(bf) *Online Career Portfolios*

To go beyond the blog and create a more comprehensive picture of yourself and what you have done, you can create an online career portfolio. A web portfolio is the traditional paper portfolio concept reinvented for the online medium with links and multimedia content. Portfolios are more than web-based resumes in that they must contain tangible evidence of your past performance, including work samples, testimonials, articles, videos,

continues

4 Key the user name and password you created when enrolling.

5 Click the LOG IN button.

Navigating in the Online Lab

Once enrolled and logged in to your Keyboarding course in the Online Lab, you will see a page listing the activities in your course. Figure 1.1 shows the Unit Contents page. Click an activity link to go to that activity's View page. Then click the Launch button to bring up that activity.

Figure 1.1 Unit Contents Page in the Online Lab

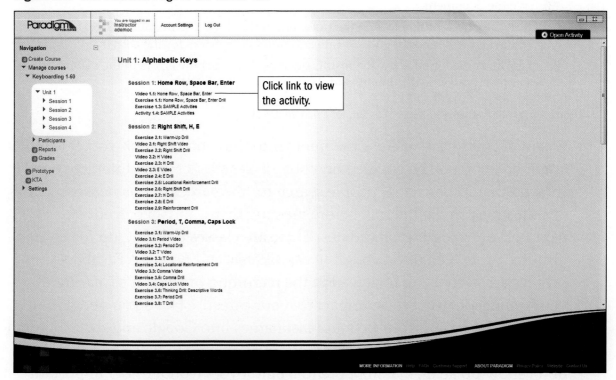

2 Key a memo report with the following guide words and information. *Note: Turn off bold formatting prior to pressing the Tab key.*

TO:	Graduating Students
FROM:	Michael Farr, Student Services
DATE:	March 10, 2014
SUBJECT:	Using the Internet to Go Beyond the Resume

3 Key the body of the memo shown in Figure 60.3, but note the following formatting instructions:

   a Format the bulleted paragraphs in the report. Use solid, circular black bullets, add an extra blank line between bulleted items (press Shift + Enter), and decrease the indent so that the bullets align with the left margin of the document.

   b Key the side headings in bold and turn off bold formatting before pressing the Enter key after keying the headings.

4 Key a vertical-style header for all pages except the first page. The header should begin 1.0 inch from the top of the page. Within the header, there should be a blank line below the header text.

5 Key the initials **tpm** and the document file name at the end of the memo.

6 Proofread the document and correct any errors.

7 Save the document.

8 Click the Check button to stop the timer and upload the document for checking. The Online Lab will report the WAM rate and number of errors for the activity.

9 If errors are reported, view the results document, correct the errors in the submitted document, save the document, and then click the Check button.

Figure 60.3 Memo Business Report Content for Document 60.3

Potential employers will use the Internet to find and research you. ¶ More and more, you will be googled on your job search. A Harris Interactive poll showed that 23 percent of people search for the names of business associates or colleagues on the Internet before meeting them, and 75 percent of recruiters are googling candidates. There are classes popping up for human resource professionals on googling candidates, and people's Facebook profiles are even being reviewed in the recruiting process. It's clear that your online identity has an impact on your career. ¶ Have you googled yourself? Try typing your first and last names into Google and then try them in quotes. When you do, you could discover one of the following: ¶ • You don't show up at all, making potential employers wonder how important you are. • You have a common name, and it's hard to find anything relevant to you. • There are negative results about you (arrests, firings, opinionated comments on nonprofessional blogs, incriminating Facebook photos and comments, or other unflattering information). • Your personal blog or family website comes up high in the search results and it isn't something

continues

Figure 1.2 Online Lab Exercise Activity Screen

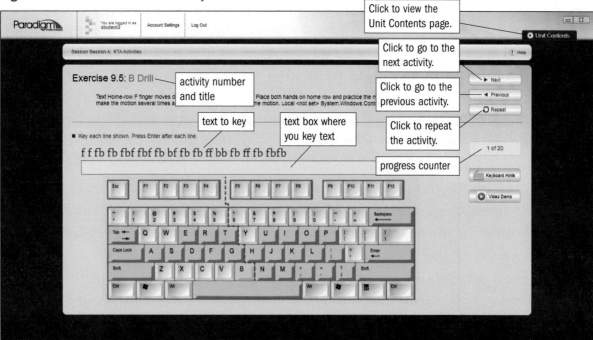

When you click the Launch button, you will see a screen similar to the one shown in Figure 1.2.

To move around the Online Lab, you can click the Next button to go to the next activity, click the Previous button to go to the previous activity or click the Repeat button to return to the beginning of the present activity. To see the list of all activities, grouped by session (as shown in Figure 1.1), click the Unit Contents tab.

Directions for the activity are at the top of the screen. If there is text for you to read as you key, it appears below the instructions. (For many activities, the text to key is in the book.) The insertion point (blinking vertical line) is placed in the text box in which you will key text. Some activities are divided into more than one part. You can check how many parts of an activity you have completed by noting the progress counter on the right side of the screen.

Introducing the Home Row Position

Video
1.1

When you begin to type, you will always start by placing your fingers on the same keys on the keyboard, the home row keys. As shown in the following illustration, when you are in the home-row position, the fingers of your left hand are positioned over the A, S, D, and F keys and the fingers of your right hand are positioned on the J, K, L, and semicolon (;) keys. Either your left or right thumb is positioned on the space bar. As needed, use the little finger of your right hand to press the Enter key. Watch Video 1.1 in the Online Lab and practice the home-row position. *Note: Your keyboard may appear somewhat different than the one illustrated in this book.*

Figure 60.2 Unbound Manuscript Content for Document 60.2

As a student living in a dorm, you will be able to buy a ~~college~~ meal plan. [a student with] A meal plan is a contract with the college's dining service that provides a [^] certain number of meals per week for a set price. For example, one plan may include 10 meals per week, while another may be 19 meals per week. ¶Choose the food plan that best fits your habits and schedule. If you buy a plan with too few meals, you will have to find food off campus or buy a single meal ~~at the commons~~ [on campus], which can be more expensive. If you buy a plan with too many meals, be aware that you likely ~~won't~~ [will not] get a refund for the meals you ~~don't~~ [do not] use. ¶Eating good food at college is essential for both your physical and mental health. ~~U.S.~~ college students are often warned about the "Freshman 15," the amount of weight that many ~~new college~~ students supposedly gain by eating and drinking unhealthy food and beverages during their first year at college. Fortunately, colleges and universities ~~nowadays~~ offer a variety of food to keep you happy and healthy. ¶Yes, you can have your pick of pie, cake, and ice cream, but you will also have healthier ~~options~~ [entrees] such as salad, and cold cuts. Some colleges cater to specific tastes or dietary needs. An example of this would be ~~offering~~ a vegetarian meal plan option. ¶If the types of food ~~that are~~ available to students is important to you, find out if you can buy it nearby. For example, the availability of international food may be limited at some campuses. ¶If you have a refrigerator and/or microwave in your ~~college~~ [if you] dorm room or live off campus, you ~~can~~ [could] make some of your meals at home. Remember to check your dorm's policy about ~~what~~ [the] types of ~~electric~~ kitchen equipment you ~~can~~ [may] use in your room. Your dorm may also have a shared kitchen you can use for cooking and baking. ¶As you decide which college [be sure to] to attend, ask about your ~~college's~~ meal plan options. ~~See for yourself by~~ [Experience a typical] [meal by] eating at a dining hall when you visit the ~~college~~ [campus]. You want college food that fits both your tastes and your budget.

Document Memo Business Report

60.3

1 Read all instructions for this document activity, navigate to the Document 60.3 launch page in the Online Lab, and then click the Launch Activity button. The Online Lab will open **Doc060.03** in the activity window. The timer will start as soon as you begin keying the document.

steps continue

Practice using the home row keys, space bar, and Enter key by completing the drills in Exercises 1.1–1.2 in the Online Lab. All of the work you do in the lab will be saved automatically.

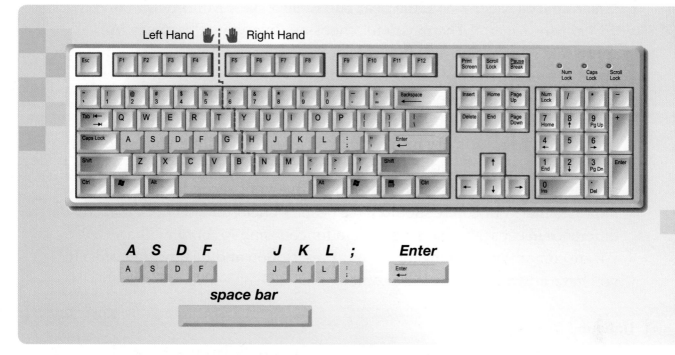

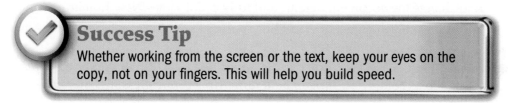

↻ Reinforcing Your Skills

You will continue to practice using the home row keys, space bar, and Enter key in the following drills. Type the following drill lines for Exercises 1.3 and 1.4 in the Online Lab.

> **✓ Success Tip**
> Whether working from the screen or the text, keep your eyes on the copy, not on your fingers. This will help you build speed.

Figure 60.1 Block-Style Letter Content for Document 60.1

Mrs. Kathleen Kiger ¶ 84 Little Bear Hill Road ¶ New Milford, CT 06776 ¶ Dear Mrs. Kiger: ¶ Thank you for choosing Riverview Pharmacy. We appreciate your business, and we are dedicated to providing you with the highest level of prescription service and care. ¶ At the time your prescription was processed, your secondary insurance was not billed. When you picked up your prescription, the pharmacy collected the copay that was indicated by your primary insurance. ¶ As a result of billing your secondary insurance, we determined that you are due a refund based on what you paid at the time of service and the amount that your secondary insurance indicates that your copay should have been. ¶ Enclosed is a check for the difference in copay. ¶ Thank you again for choosing Riverview Pharmacy. We are committed to filling all of your prescription and healthcare needs. If you have any questions, please contact us at (203) 555-4000. ¶ Sincerely,

Document **Unbound Manuscript**

60.2

1   Read all instructions for this document activity, navigate to the Document 60.2 launch page in the Online Lab, and then click the Launch Activity button. The Online Lab will open **Doc060.02** in the activity window. The timer will start as soon as you begin keying the document.

2   Change the document default formatting by completing the following steps:

a   Change the document default font to 12-point Times New Roman.

b   Change the document default line spacing to double spacing with no extra space before or after paragraphs.

3   Key **COLLEGE MEAL PLANS** as the report title. The title should be centered and formatted as bold. *Hint: Turn off bold formatting before pressing Enter after keying the title.*

4   Key the text shown in Figure 60.2, implementing the proofreading marks indicated. Press Tab for each paragraph start.

5   Create a header that prints on the second page of the document. Key the report title in all capital letters at the left margin, press Tab twice to move the insertion point to the right margin, and then insert a plain page number. The header and footer of the first page of the document should be blank.

6   Proofread the document and correct any errors.

7   Save the document.

8   Click the Check button to stop the timer and upload the document for checking. The Online Lab will report the WAM rate and number of errors for the activity.

9   If errors are reported, view the results document, correct the errors in the submitted document, save the document, and then click the Check button.

Exercise 1.3 Home Row Drill

- Key each line one time. Do not key the number at the beginning of each line.
- Press the Enter key quickly at the end of each line.
- Keep your eyes on the copy as you key.
- Repeat the exercise if you need more practice.

1 aaa sss ddd fff jjj kkk lll ;;; sd kl ;
2 aa ss dd ff jj kk ll ;; asdf jkl; af j;
3 a s d f j k l ; aa ss dd ff jj kk ll ;;

4 a ad a ad add add adds adds a ad add ad
5 a as as a ask ask asks asks a all all a
6 ad add as ask a; a; as adds asks a;; ad

7 fads fads fall fall falls falls fad fad
8 lass lass lad lad lads dad dads ask ask
9 falls flask alas fads dads asks all sad

Exercise 1.4 Reinforcement Drill

Key the following drill lines. Press the Enter key quickly after each line. Your words-a-minute (WAM) rate will appear after each line. (In keyboarding, one word equals five keystrokes. Characters, spaces, and Enters are all counted as keystrokes.)

1 all all
2 sad sad dad dad
3 fad fad alas alas

4 fall fall lad lad add add
5 a all all a alas alas a as ad add ask a
6 ask ask asks asks all all alas alas all

7 ad add as ask all alas adds asks all ad
8 dad dad dads dads sad sad fad fad fads
9 flak flak flask flask lad lad lads lads

 Ergonomic Tip
Sit upright in your seat to eliminate lower back pain and strain. Correct posture for keyboarding is illustrated in Figure 1.3.

Ergonomic Tip

When using a mouse, hold it loosely. Click the buttons using a light touch.

Preparing Documents

Now that you have completed the instructional activities for creating emails, memos, letters, reports, and manuscripts, you will be assessed on how quickly and accurately you can format, key, proofread, and correct these documents. In the following document activities, each completed document is to be "mailable," which means that it contains no errors. A document that requires additional corrections is not considered mailable.

Your goals are to key each document in mailable form and at a rate of at least 25 WAM. If your rate is less than 25 WAM or if your document contains uncorrected errors, your instructor may ask you to repeat documents. Be sure to check each document to make sure all parts of the document are included such as dates, file names, and copy notations.

To help you succeed, carefully review the document instructions and the content of each document before keying. Make sure you know the formatting elements and guidelines for each document to be keyed. If you are unsure, check the appropriate sessions in the text for a review of document style and Word features.

Document 60.1 Business Letter

1 Read all instructions for this document activity, navigate to the Document 60.1 launch page in the Online Lab, and then click the Launch Activity button. The Online Lab will open **Doc060.01** in the activity window. The timer will start as soon as you begin keying the document.

2 Key the text shown in Figure 60.1 as a block-style letter.

   a Move the insertion point to 2 inches from the top of the document and then key **September 12, 2014** as the current date.

   b Indicate that the letter is from Kelly Wentworth, and put the department name, Accounts Receivable, under the signature line.

   c Key the reference initials **jmp** and include the file name below the department name.

   d Indicate that an enclosure is included with the letter.

3 Proofread the document and correct any errors.

4 Save the document.

5 Click the Check button to stop the timer and upload the document for checking. The Online Lab will report the WAM rate and number of errors for the activity.

6 If errors are reported, view the results document, correct the errors in the submitted document, save the document, and then click the Check button.

Figure 1.3 Correct Keyboarding Posture

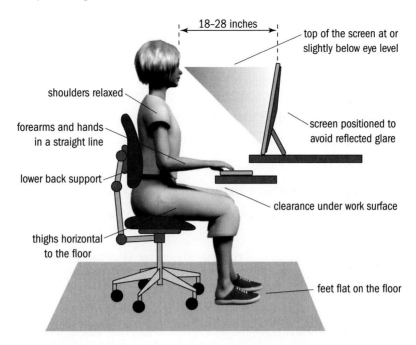

Ending the Session

The Online Lab automatically saves the work you completed for this session. You can continue with the next session or exit the Online Lab and continue later. Instructions for completing these actions follow and are also available in the Online Lab.

Continuing with the Next Session

You can continue to the next session in the Online Lab by clicking the Next button twice. This will take you to Video 2.1. *Note: You will skip Exercise 2.1, a warm-up drill, because by completing Session 1 you are already warmed up.*

Exiting the Online Lab

To exit the Online Lab simply click the Close button in the upper right corner of your screen.

Complete one 5-minute timing on the timing text below.

Goals: 35 WAM and five or fewer errors
SI: 1.61 syllables per word

5-Minute Timing

Timing 60.2

Few employers will hire someone they think will be a problem—even if they have a great background. Poor writing and speaking skills, unfriendliness, dishonesty, and other personality traits are all reasons for being screened out.

One of the most important things an employer will consider is whether someone will be dependable. Most employers will not hire someone unless they think the person will be dependable. This is often true even if the person has a good skills set or training for the job. Being dependable means being on time, having good attendance, and working hard to meet deadlines. It also may mean that you are likely to stay at the job for a while. If you convince an employer that you are dependable and you work hard, you may get the job over someone who has better credentials.

How do employers decide who will be dependable? They look at your past work history as well as your present job. If you have been dependable in the past, they know you are likely to be a good worker in the future. The information you or your references provide about past jobs, schooling, and personal accomplishments will be important in helping an employer decide whether you will be dependable. If employers are not convinced they can depend on you, they probably will not hire you.

Some teachers are grading students on behavior in class. Perfect attendance and promptness are expected by teachers and employers, too. This is just one measure and is often discussed during a check of your background.

Employers expect that employees are able to communicate complex information clearly, concisely, and completely. To prepare for working in an office, students should strive to make written and verbal communication with instructors and peers accurate, concise, appropriate, and effective.

Session 2

Right Shift, H, E

Session Objectives

- Identify the Shift, H, and E keys
- Practice correct finger positioning for the right Shift, H, and E keys
- Learn how to key uppercase letters
- Use words-a-minute (WAM) rate to set speed goals
- Practice WAM rate for the right Shift, H, and E keys

Getting Started and Warming Up

Exercise 2.1 If you exited the Online Lab at the end of Session 1, complete the following steps:

1 At the Windows desktop on your computer screen, double-click the Online Lab icon on your desktop. *Note: If the computer you are using for this session doesn't have an Online Lab icon, see the instructions on page 2 for installing the Online Lab software, or if you are in a school computer lab, contact your instructor.*

2 Key your user name and password.

3 Click the LOG IN button.

4 At the Unit Contents page, click <u>Exercise 2.1: Warm-Up Drill</u>.

5 Warm up by completing Exercise 2.1.

steps continue

Complete one 3-minute timing on the timing text below.

Goals: 40 WAM and three or fewer errors
SI: 1.51 syllables per word

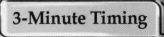
3-Minute Timing

Timing 60.1

Nature lovers cannot find words that describe the strange beauty of a coral reef. These fragile and dainty aquatic kingdoms have been compared to colorful gardens; the sea animals are the flowers of this classic garden. The strangely eerie sights beneath the waters of the seas have made scientists gasp at the exquisite coral reef beauty.

Some reefs contain hundreds of varieties of coral. The warm and clear water is ideal for the continued healthy existence of all those small stony coral polyps. They are the architects of the coral reef. Others who live in this ocean world are countless invertebrates and a number of different species of fish. The creatures are beautiful and sometimes bizarre in appearance and can be seen in almost every shape and color to be imagined.

Each of the tiny creatures has a different and unique form of protective gear. The sea urchin is well fortified with an arsenal of rock-like, blunt spines. The lionfish exudes some of the most powerful and poisonous venom in the world. The stonefish is a near-perfect replica of a rock; but when an unsuspecting fish is nearby, it is quickly captured by the stonefish.

6 Follow the directions at the top of your screen. When you are finished warming up, click the next button.

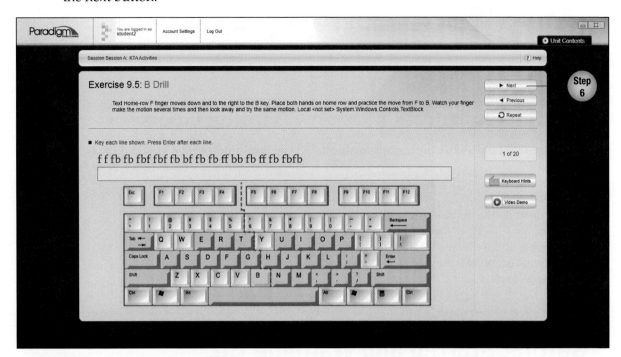

Introducing the Right Shift, H, and E Keys

Videos 2.1–2.3 The locations of the right Shift, H, and E keys are shown in the following diagram. In this and subsequent keyboard diagrams new keys are shown in yellow and previously introduced keys are shown in blue. *Remember: The right Shift key is used to make uppercase letters that are keyed with the left hand.* Watch Videos 2.1 through 2.3 and practice using these new keys.

Exercises 2.2–2.5 Complete Exercises 2.2 through 2.5 to learn these new keys. When keying the drill lines, follow the instruction prompts provided in the Online Lab.

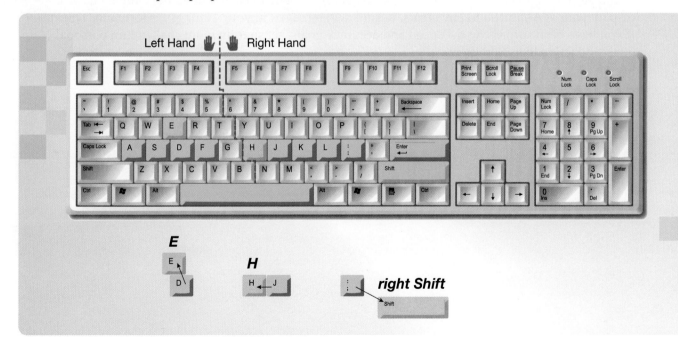

Document Preparation Productivity Check

Session Objectives

- Demonstrate the ability to format a business letter
- Demonstrate the ability to format an unbound manuscript
- Demonstrate the ability to format a memo report
- Compose an assessment of this course
- Produce documents at a rate of 25 WAM and in mailable form

Timing Goals

- 3 minutes: 40 WAM and three or fewer errors
- 5 minutes: 35 WAM and five or fewer errors

Getting Started and Warming Up

Exercise 60.1 If you are continuing immediately from Session 59, you can skip the Exercise 60.1 warm-up drill. However, if you exited the Online Lab at the end of Session 59, warm up by completing Exercise 60.1.

Exercise 60.2 Begin your session work by completing Exercise 60.2, a timed short drill, in the Online Lab.

Assessing Your Speed and Accuracy

Complete Timings 60.1 and 60.2 in the Online Lab. At the end of each timing, the Online Lab will display your WAM rate and any errors. Results will be saved in your Timings Performance report. If you have been surpassing the speed and accuracy goals, set slightly more challenging personal goals and strive to exceed them.

↻ Reinforcing Your Skills

Complete Exercises 2.6 through 2.9 in the Online Lab. Reference the drill lines from the textbook as you key and keep your eyes on the textbook pages, not on your fingers. Key each line once and press the Enter key quickly at the end of each line. Complete each exercise at least once, but repeat exercises if you need more practice.

> ✓ **Success Tip**
> Your wrists should hover above the keyboard. Do not rest them while you key.

Exercise 2.6 **Right Shift Drill**

Key each drill line one time. Press the Enter key after each line.

1 Ad All Asks Adds Alas All Ask As Add Ad
2 Fad fad Falls falls Fall fall Fads fads
3 Sad All Asks Dads Fads Alas Flask Falls

Exercise 2.7 **H Drill**

Key each drill line one time. Press the Enter key after each line.

1 jh hall hall hall sash sash has sash hash
2 half half half lash lash lash half lash
3 Dads sash Falls Shall Shall Flash Flash

Exercise 2.8 **E Drill**

Key lines 1–2 for speed. Key each line two times. In other words, key line 1, press Enter, key line 1 a second time, and then press Enter. Continue this pattern when you key line 2. Try to make your fingers go faster as you key each line a second time.

1 deal dead deaf fade led lead lease lake
2 she she ale ale elf elf elk elk heal heal fake fake

Key lines 3–5 one time and then key the three lines again. As you key these lines, slow down a bit and concentrate on control.

3 deal deal ease ease else else desk desk fell fell
4 fade fade feel feel dead dead head head heal heal
5 Elk Elk Else Ease Ed Elf Else Ease Ed Ed

Unit 12

Productivity Measurement Part I

Session 60

Document Preparation Productivity
Check

Reinforcement Drill

Key the following drill lines one time. Press the Enter key after each line. Your words-a-minute (WAM) rate will appear after each line. Repeat this exercise if you would like more practice.

1 lad lad lads lads Flak Flak Flask Flask

2 fall hall alas dash half

3 flash flash shall shall

4 half half

5 Sad Dad Add Ask Fad Salad Flak Dads All

6 Dads Ask lad Ask dad lads lass lass Add

7 jh has had has had has had has had lash

8 ha has ash Ash Ash had ash ash hall Flash

9 eel deed eel she see she see ale elf ale fee

10 ease deal ease deal else desk else desk fell

11 fade feel fade feel dead head dead head heal

12 Else Elk Ease Ed Elf Else Ease Ed Elf Ed

Ergonomic Tip
To avoid strain or potential long-term pain, just tap the keys lightly when keying.

Ending the Session

The Online Lab automatically saves the work you completed for this session. You can continue with the next session or exit the Online Lab and continue later. If you need to review the procedures for continuing to the next session or exiting the Online Lab, refer back to Session 1, page 8.

Figure 59.3 Report Content for Document 59.2—Continued

~~systems house~~ *developers,* for technical support, training, and sometimes on-site troubleshooting. ~~Even if the system was designed in house, the responsible department often operates as an independent entity—sometimes even charging the department acquiring the system.~~ The support stage continues until a new information system is proposed and developed, usually years later. At that point, the existing system is retired and no longer used.

Figure 59.4 Source Content for Document 59.2

First Citation

Type of Source: Article in a Periodical

Author: Kolstad, Diana

Title: Developing an MIS Project Plan

Periodical Title: Project Planning Monthly

Year: 2014

Month: March

Day: 11

Pages: 35-49

Medium: Print

Second Citation

Type of Source: Book

Author: Kessler, Mark R.

Title: Implementing Change

Year: 2014

City: West Allis

Publisher: Chalmers Press

Medium: Print

Ending the Session

The Online Lab automatically saves the work you completed for this session. You may continue with the next session or exit the Online Lab and continue later.

Session 3

Period, T, Comma, Caps Lock

Session Objectives

- Identify the period (.), T, comma (,), and Caps Lock keys
- Practice correct finger positioning for the period (.), T, comma (,), and Caps Lock keys
- Create simple responses to statements or questions while keying
- Build keyboarding speed

Getting Started and Warming Up

Exercise 3.1 If you are continuing immediately from Session 2, you may skip the Exercise 3.1 warm-up drill. However, if you exited the Online Lab at the end of Session 2, warm up by completing Exercise 3.1. Refer to page 9 of Session 2 for instructions on logging on to the Online Lab and navigating to the appropriate exercise.

Introducing the Period, T, Comma, and Caps Lock Keys

Videos 3.1–3.4 The locations of the period (.), T, comma (,), and Caps Lock keys are shown in the following diagram. Watch Videos 3.1 through 3.4 and practice using these new keys.

Exercises 3.2–3.6 Complete Exercises 3.2 through 3.5 to learn these new keys. Also complete the thinking drill, Exercise 3.6. When keying the drill lines, follow instruction prompts shown in the Online Lab.

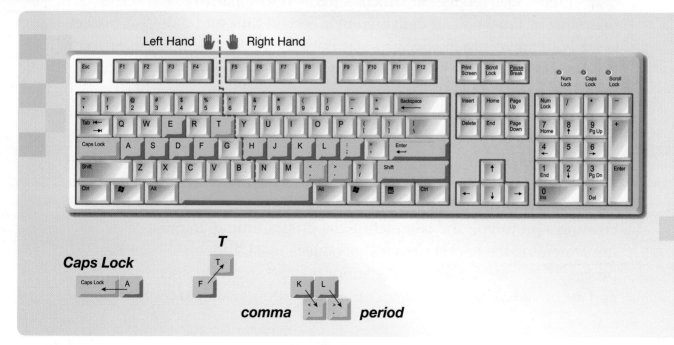

8 Insert a Works Cited page at the end of the document by completing the following steps:

   a Place the insertion point at the end of the document and then insert a hard page break.

   b Center the insertion point and key **Works Cited** and then press Enter.

   c Change the text alignment to align at the left margin.

   d Click the Bibliography button in the Citations & Bibliography group on the References tab and then click *Insert Bibliography*.

9 Proofread the document and correct any errors.

10 Save the document.

11 Click the Check button to stop the timer and upload the document for checking. The Online Lab will report the WAM rate and number of errors for the activity.

12 If errors are reported, view the results document, correct the errors in the submitted document, save the document, and then click the Check button.

Figure 59.3 Report Content for Document 59.2

Identifying and assembling a team of employees with the required skills and expertise is ~~a necessary~~ *the first* step in developing a new in-house information system. A management group may be involved in both answering questions and providing information in the early ~~planning~~ phases of the project, but programmers and/or software engineers handle the design and implementation of any new system. ¶ The first step in the system development life cycle is planning. The planning step involves preparing a needs analysis and conducting feasibility studies. Because of their large size, information systems require the creation of a project team. The project plan, developed by the project team, includes an estimate of how long the project will take to complete, an outline of the steps involved, and a list of deliverables. Deliverables are "documents, services, hardware, and software that must be ~~finished~~ *completed* and delivered by a certain time and date." ¶ A project is ready to move into the design stage once the project team has approved the plan, including the budget. The design process begins with ~~the~~ writing of the documentation, ~~which~~ cover*ing* functional and design specifications. In most cases, the project team creates ~~the~~ functional specifications, *which* describing what the system must be able to do. ¶ The project can move into the next phase, implementation, once the development team and the systems ~~house~~ *group* develop the design specification*s* and approve the plans. This step is where the actual work of putting (the system together) is completed, including creating a prototype and completing the programming. In most cases, implementing the new system is the longest, most difficult step in the process. ¶ A system goes into the support stage after it has been accepted and approved. A support contract normally allows users to contact the

(margin note: Kolstad citation, page 36)

(margin note: Kessler citation, page 173)

continues

↻ Reinforcing Your Skills

Complete Exercises 3.7 through 3.12 in the Online Lab. Reference the drill lines from the textbook as you key and keep your eyes on the textbook pages, not on your fingers. Complete each exercise at least once, but repeat exercises if you need more practice.

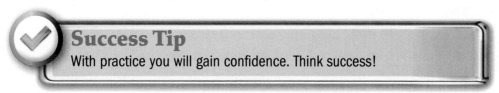

Success Tip
With practice you will gain confidence. Think success!

Exercise 3.7 · Period Drill

Key each drill line one time. Tap the space bar only once after the period at the end of a sentence. If a period ends a line, tap Enter immediately. Do not press the space bar first.

1 All lads shall dash. A lad shall fall.

2 Ask a sad lad. Sad lads fall. Ask Al.

3 Add Jake as last dads. Hats stall a test.

Exercise 3.8 · T Drill

Key each drill line one time.

1 ft at hat hats sat sat tall tall data data

2 fast fast slat slat halt halt last last fat fat

3 test eat the there that steed staff sat set heat

Exercise 3.9 · Comma Drill

Key each drill line one time. Do not insert a space before a comma. Be sure to insert one space after a comma.

1 That tall, fat, fast lad shall ask dad.

2 A flat, half lath falls; all lads halt.

3 Fasted at Tea Lake, left felt hats, sat aft safe seat.

Exercise 3.10 · Caps Lock Drill

Key each drill line one time. Remember that the home-row A finger reaches to tap the Caps Lock key to type a series of words in uppercase. Tap the Caps Lock key again to return to lowercase letters.

1 TALK AT A FAST LAD; A SAD LAD HAS A FALL.

2 DAD HALTS A TALL LAD. A SAD LAD HALTS.

3 JED HAD LEAD FEET. LATHE AT SHADE DEAD.

Exercise 3.11 · Speed Drill

Your mind controls your fingers, so think *speed*. After you practice setting your mental goal several times, you should find that your mind eventually controls your fingers automatically.

Figure 59.1 Report Content for Document 59.1—Continued

might be asked to help redesign the company's website. Along the way, he ∧ *or she* might learn something that ~~he can~~ use ∧*d* down the road—~~if he starts his own~~ ∧*when starting a* business, for example. *may be*

Being open to change also means understanding that your career will likely be made up of several jobs, some of them quite different. But all of those jobs are steps toward your larger goals. The key is to be flexible with (*Insert Footnote 2*) your goals and especially with how you reach them, ∧Take advantage of the opportunities that come along so ∧*;* that you can gain the skills and experience you'll need to find success.

Figure 59.2 Footnote Content for Document 59.1

Footnote 1: Pamela Lochwood, "Revisiting Lifelong Learning," *Employment Monthly*, October 2014, 19.

Footnote 2: "Keeping Goals Real," *Goal Setting 101*, accessed June 18, 2014, http://www.emcp.net/goalsetting101.

Document 59.2 Unbound Manuscript in MLA Style with In-text Citations and a Works Cited Page

1 Read all instructions for this document activity, navigate to the Document 59.2 launch page in the Online Lab, and then click the Launch Activity button. The Online Lab will open **Doc059.02** in the activity window. The timer will start as soon as you begin keying the document.

2 Format the document as follows:

   a Change the document default line spacing to double spacing with no extra spacing before or after paragraphs.

   b Change the document default font to 12-point Palatino Linotype.

3 Set the document style reference to *MLA Seventh Edition*.

4 Insert a *Plain Number 3* in the header, following the last name of the manuscript author, Van Brocklin.

5 Key the information about the manuscript at the top of the document. The information should indicate that the manuscript is being prepared by Megan Van Brocklin for her instructor Gary Stapleton for the course MIS 101. The paper date is 10 May 2014. The title of the report is Developing an Information System. **Hint: Reference Figure 57.1 for formatting of this information.**

6 Key the text in Figure 59.3, implementing the proofreading marks indicated in the text. **Hint: Begin paragraphs with a 0.5-inch tab indent.**

7 Key the source information shown in Figure 59.4, locating the citation references in the document according to the placement instructions in Figure 59.3. Include page references for the in-text citations according to the proofreading marks.

steps continue

Key each line two times. Press the Enter key after each line. (Follow the keying pattern 1, 1, 2, 2, 3, 3.) Try to make your fingers go faster as you key each line a second time.

1 Talk at a fast lad; a sad lad has a hat.

2 A lad talks; the dad talks; a dad talks.

3 Dad halts the sad lad. A sad lad halts.

Exercise 3.12 **Reinforcement Drill**

Key the following drill lines one time. Press the Enter key after each line. Your words-a-minute (WAM) rate will appear after each line. Repeat this exercise if you are hesitating while you key the drill lines.

1 The lads dash. A dad asks the lads.

2 Feds dash. Dads dash. Dads ask the sad lads.

3 Ask Al. Sad lads halt. Ask a sad lad.

4 data data data slat slat slat jet jet jet

5 that that that task task task talk talk talk

6 salt salt salt flat flat flat lath lath lath

7 A flat atlas; a flat hat; a flat flask.

8 A half a flask; a half lath; half a slat.

9 A sad lad halts. Dale halts a fat lad.

10 A sad lad has a hat. Talk at a fast lad.

11 A half lath; half a flask; half a slat.

12 The fat lads talked fast. A dad talks fast.

13 Dash, Al, flat, half, lath, head, heat,

14 A fat, sad, flat, hall shaft has the lead.

15 Dale asked Al. Dad asked the lads.

Ergonomic Tip

The top of the computer screen should be at eye level or slightly below. If you wear bifocal or multifocal glasses, however, the screen should be low enough so that you do not have to tip your head up to read it. You can adjust your monitor or chair to the correct position.

Ending the Session

The Online Lab automatically saves the work you completed for this session. You can continue with the next session or exit the Online Lab and continue later. If you need to review the procedures for continuing to the next session or exiting the Online Lab, refer back to Session 1, page 8.

6. Format the page numbers in the document by completing the following steps:

   a. Format the document so that it has a different first page footer.

   b. On the first page, insert a *Plain Number 2* style page number at the bottom of the page.

   c. On the second page, insert a *Plain Number 3* style page number at the top of the page.

7. Proofread the document and correct any errors.

8. Save the document.

9. Click the Check button to stop the timer and upload the document for checking. The Online Lab will report the WAM rate and number of errors for the activity.

10. If errors are reported, view the results document, correct the errors in the submitted document, save the document, and then click the Check button.

Figure 59.1 Report Content for Document 59.1

(Tab) Setting goals can help you plan for the future and even overcome obstacles along the way, but not everything will go according to plan. Changes in your lifestyle, such as getting married or starting a family, can cause you to rethink your goals. Over time your interests and values might change. You might decide to go back to school or move to a different part of the country or even a different part of the world.

Some changes are choices you make; some changes are outside of your control. Companies shut down, jobs get moved overseas, and customer needs shift. Every day new technology changes the way we work. This technology often leads to greater opportunities, but sometimes it results in lost jobs. The job market is constantly evolving. If you keep an open mind, you *may be able to* take advantage of those changes to get ahead.

Individual jobs can evolve as well. Most of today's in-demand jobs are *challenging*, requiring workers to multitask and adapt, taking on more and more responsibilities. In nearly every industry, new technology forces workers to learn new skills just to keep up: Nurses learn about new medications, construction workers learn how to operate a new *equipment* machine, and office workers learn how to use a new piece of software. Lifelong learning—always updating your knowledge and skills—is *becoming* more and more important for workers in every field. (*Insert Footnote 1*)

To reach your goals, you *must* need to be willing to change with the times and to grow with your job. That might mean taking on some tasks or projects outside of your job description. This can be a learning experience that will make you a more valuable worker. For example, a salesperson

continues

N, Left Shift, Colon

Session Objectives

- Identify the N, left Shift, and colon (:) keys
- Practice correct finger positioning for the N, left Shift, and colon (:) keys
- Use correct technique to make uppercase letters and colons

- Use 10-second timings to build keyboarding speed
- Employ critical thinking when keyboarding

Getting Started and Warming Up

Exercise 4.1 If you are continuing immediately from Session 3, you may skip the Exercise 4.1 warm-up drill. However, if you exited the Online Lab at the end of Session 3, warm up by completing Exercise 4.1. Refer to page 9 of Session 2 for instructions on logging on to the Online Lab and navigating to the appropriate exercise.

Introducing the N, Left Shift, and Colon Keys

Videos 4.1–4.2 The locations of the N, left Shift, and colon (:) keys are shown in the following diagram. Watch Videos 4.1 and 4.2 and practice using these new keys.

Exercises 4.2–4.8 Complete Exercises 4.2 through 4.7 to learn these new keys. Also complete the thinking drill, Exercise 4.8. When keying the drill lines, follow the instruction prompts provided in the Online Lab.

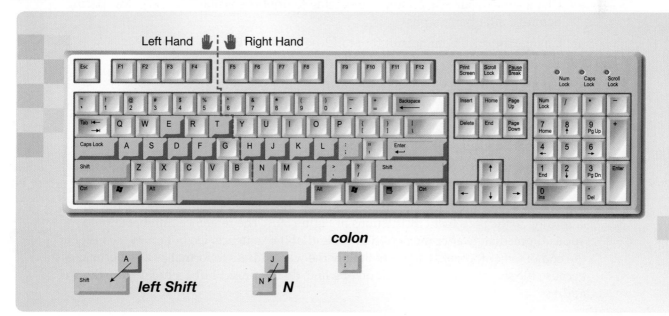

Ergonomic Tip

Take a short break at least once an hour to move your joints through a range of motion. First, flex your wrists gently up and down as far as possible, and then circle your hands in one direction and then the other before returning to the keyboard.

Checking Production Progress: Manuscripts

Sessions 55–58 discussed the procedures for preparing and formatting manuscripts and research papers. In this session, you will be assessed on how quickly and accurately you can key these types of documents. In the following document activities, each completed document is to be "mailable," which means that it contains no errors. A document that requires additional corrections is not considered mailable.

Your goals are to key each document in mailable form and at a rate of at least 25 WAM. If your rate is less than 25 WAM or if your document contains uncorrected errors, your instructor may ask you to repeat documents. To help you succeed, carefully review the document instructions and the content of each document before keying. *Note: Before you begin these documents, if necessary, review the content of Sessions 55 to 58 if you are unsure how to complete a specific formatting or software task.*

Document 59.1

Unbound Manuscript in CMS Style with Footnotes

1. Read all instructions for this document activity, navigate to the Document 59.1 launch page in the Online Lab, and then click the Launch Activity button. The Online Lab will open **Doc059.01** in the activity window. The timer will start as soon as you begin keying the document.

2. Format the document as follows:
   a. Change the document default line spacing to double spacing with no extra spacing before or after paragraphs.
   b. Change the document default font to 12-point Cambria.

3. Key the main heading of the document by completing the following steps:
   a. Set the text to center align and then turn on bold formatting.
   b. Key **GOAL SETTING WITH AN OPEN MIND**, turn off bold formatting, and then press Enter.
   c. Set the text to align at the left margin.

4. Key the text in Figure 59.1, implementing the proofreading marks indicated in the text. *Hint: Begin paragraphs with a 0.5-inch tab indent.*

5. Key the footnotes shown in Figure 59.2, locating the reference numbers in the document according to the placement instructions in Figure 59.1. The reference number should appear immediately after the period at the end of the sentence. Do not press the Enter at the end of either footnote and do not allow the web address to format as a hyperlink. Also, because the second footnote will fit on one line, do not press Shift + Enter before the web address.

steps continue

⟳ Reinforcing Your Skills

Complete Exercises 4.9 through 4.11 in the Online Lab. Reference the drill lines from the textbook as you key and keep your eyes on the textbook pages, not on your fingers.

To increase your keyboarding skills, you must key without watching your fingers. Concentrate on keeping your eyes on the copy whether it is on the screen or in the text. When keying at a controlled rate or for accuracy, concentrate on making the correct reaches. When pushing for speed, concentrate on making your fingers move faster.

Complete each exercise at least once, but repeat exercises if you need more practice.

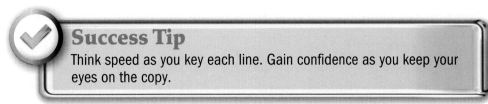

Success Tip
Think speed as you key each line. Gain confidence as you keep your eyes on the copy.

Exercise 4.9 **N Drill**

Key each line two times and push for speed. Remember to press Enter at the end of each line.

1 an an and and land land sand sand
2 then then than than thank thank

Key lines 3–5 one time and then key the three lines again. Concentrate on control.

3 Jan shall hand a sad lad an atlas fast.
4 Hal shall thank that tall and lank lad.
5 Hats and sandals shall stand as fads.

Exercise 4.10 **Left Shift and Colon Drill**

The shift of the semicolon (;) key produces a colon (:). When keying documents, space once after a colon that follows a word. Practice using these keys by keying the following drill lines one time.

1 jJ kK lL ;: Jj Kk Ll ;: JL; jK lL :;:; KL: hH:
2 Had; Lad; Has; Lass; Half: Lads: Hall: Jade:
3 Lass Lad Lads Head: Halt: Lead: Lads: Jet:

Complete one 5-minute timing on the timing text below.

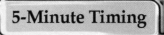
Timing 59.3

After proofreading a document, take another look at it for its overall appearance. Print Preview works well for this. Are some of the lines of text considerably shorter than others? If so, Word's hyphenation feature can help minimize a ragged margin by either automatically dividing or by providing suggestions for dividing a word at the end of a line.

While dividing words can make a document's appearance more attractive, too many divided words may make reading the document confusing to the reader. Finding the proper balance and dividing at logical places within words is key to producing an attractive, easy-to-read document.

Many experts agree that there are basic rules that must be followed when dividing words. Divide words only between syllables, for example. Words pronounced as one syllable should not be divided. Do not divide abbreviations such as WAM or LPN.

Contractions such as aren't or wasn't should not be divided between lines. Only divide words that have at least six characters including the hyphen. To avoid having a document's right margin looking like a ladder, do not hyphenate more than two lines in a row.

Word's automatic hyphenation feature inserts hyphens where needed based on either default settings or settings you select. These word division hyphens are also called "soft" or "optional" hyphens. If text is either added or deleted after hyphenation, the lines of text in edited paragraphs will reflow and line endings may change. If a previously hyphenated word no longer needs hyphenation, Word will not print the hyphen or split the word. Hyphenation features and options are located in the Page Setup group on the Page Layout tab. Here you can specify not to divide words in all capital letters and to limit the number of consecutive lines to be hyphenated.

When manual hyphenation is selected, Word suggests possible places (syllable breaks) within a word to hyphenate. When using Manual Hyphenation, be sure to apply the basic rules of word division as agreed upon by experts.

Exercise 4.11 Reinforcement Drill

Key the following drill lines one time. Press the Enter key after each line. Your WAM rate will appear after each line. Repeat this exercise if you are not reaching 25 WAM.

1   land land than than flank flank tan tan slant slant

2   thank thank nest nest and Dan Dan Landers Landers

3   A tan shaft lands and halts that task.

4   As a fad, hats and sandals shall stand the sand.

5   Del and Dana shall stand and talk last.

6   flash: flash: half: half: sand: sand: hand: hand:

7   Jean shall sell the saddle, jeans, and seashells.

8   Handle the fat kettle that leaks; taste the tea.

9   The fat hen left the lake. She landed at a nest.

10 Dad and the ten lads halted a theft. Dad felt tense.

Ergonomic Tip
Use only finger, not wrist, movements to tap the keys.

Ending the Session

The Online Lab automatically saves the work you completed for this session. You can continue with the next session or exit the Online Lab and continue later. If you need to review the procedures for continuing to the next session or exiting the Online Lab, refer back to Session 1, page 8.

Complete one 3-minute timing on the timing text below. Note that with this session, the WAM goal for 3-minute timings has been increased by 5 WAM.

Goals: 40 WAM and three or fewer errors
SI: 1.57 syllables per word

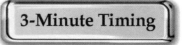

Timing 59.2

Today, the social Web can be accessed by a many types of devices such as cell phones and gaming devices. These allow people to connect with their social sites so as to post text, video, and photos as well as to interact with their friends on the go.

If you perform a search for the social Web, you will see a wide variety of sites and apps that you can use. The function of these sites is as varied as the single users and groups who use them. Social causes use the social Web to muster support in times of crisis, such as raising money to help victims of natural disasters. Businesses use social marketing, driving their branding and sales messages to the public by using all kinds of social networking sites. Harvard and other schools host courses in virtual worlds like Second Life. Office holders use online dialog to discuss political and social issues to gather votes and support. Artists create visual and musical pieces by sharing media and building new pieces of art with input from many people.

The social Web is growing and evolving rapidly, with changes happening daily. Functions and features of the social websites overlap, making it hard to define the technologies precisely. However, grouping them broadly provides a way to study them and understand their value in our digital world. These categories include blogging, social networking, bookmarking, wikis, and media sharing.

Session 5

I, G, Tab Defaults, Word Wrap

Session Objectives

- Identify the I, G, and Tab keys
- Practice correct finger positioning for the I, G, and Tab keys
- Employ preset tabs and word wrap

- Use 15-second timings to build keyboarding speed and accuracy

Getting Started and Warming Up

Exercise 5.1

If you are continuing immediately from Session 4, you may skip the Exercise 5.1 warm-up drill. However, if you exited the Online Lab at the end of Session 4, warm up by completing Exercise 5.1. Refer to page 9 of Session 2 for instructions on logging on to the Online Lab and navigating to the appropriate exercise.

Introducing the I, G, and Tab Keys

Videos 5.1–5.3

The locations of the I, G, and Tab keys are shown in the following diagram. Watch Videos 5.1 through 5.3 and practice using these new keys.

Exercises 5.2–5.9

Complete Exercises 5.2 through 5.8 to learn these new keys. Also complete the thinking drill, Exercise 5.9. When keying the drill lines, follow the instruction prompts provided in the Online Lab.

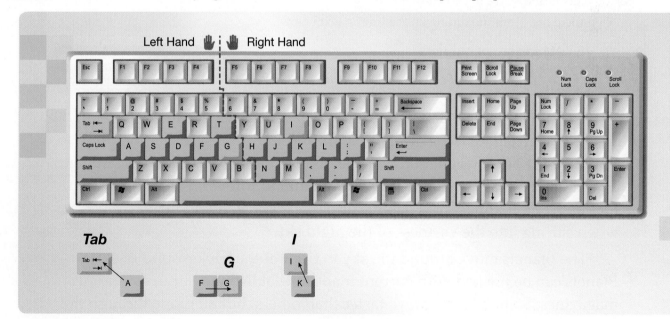

Session 59

Production Progress Check: Manuscripts and Research Papers Part I

Session Objectives

- Review and practice word processing features presented in Sessions 55–58
- Demonstrate formatting of manuscripts
- Produce documents at a rate of 25 WAM and in mailable form

Timing Goals

- 1 minute: 45 WAM and one or no errors
- 3 minutes: 40 WAM and three or fewer errors
- 5 minutes: 35 WAM and five or fewer errors

Getting Started and Warming Up

Exercise 59.1 If you are continuing immediately from Session 58, you may skip the Exercise 59.1 warm-up drill. However, if you exited the Online Lab at the end of Session 58, warm up by completing Exercise 59.1.

Exercise 59.2 Begin your session work by completing Exercise 59.2, a timed short drill, in the Online Lab.

Assessing Your Speed and Accuracy

Complete Timings 59.1 through 59.3 in the Online Lab. At the end of the timing, the Online Lab will display your WAM rate and any errors. Results will be saved in your Timings Performance report. If you have been surpassing the speed and accuracy goals, set slightly more challenging personal goals and strive to exceed them.

Complete one 1-minute timing on the timing text below.

Goals: 45 WAM and one or no errors
SI: 1.40 syllables per word

[**1-Minute Timing**]

Timing 59.1

Learning the constellations in the sky is a great way to spend a clear evening. Starting with the brightest stars and the clearest formations, you can learn to spot constellations such as the Big Dipper or Orion the Hunter, constellations that have been known to mankind forever. The sky has been mapped, and if you learn the patterns of the stars, you will never feel lost when staring into the vastness of the night sky.

The planets move around the sky in front of the background of stars. Planets can be tracked with current maps available online or in astronomy magazines. Some planets move faster than others, but all move through the same constellations as the sun. This path across the sky is called the ecliptic, and all of the constellations of the Zodiac are in this path.

↻ Reinforcing Your Skills

Complete Exercises 5.10 through 5.14 in the Online Lab. Reference the drill lines from the textbook as you key and keep your eyes on the textbook pages, not on your fingers. Complete each exercise at least once, but repeat exercises if you need more practice.

> ✓ **Success Tip**
> Keeping your eyes on the copy will help your speed. If you look away, you will waste time finding your place again.

Exercise 5.10 **I Drill**

Key each line two times and push for speed.

1 if it in it it in kid kid his this fail fine file find
2 The kid thinks I had the idea that he did finish.

Key lines 3–5 one time and then key the three lines again. Concentrate on control. Try to make fewer than two errors on each line.

3 Ill Inside Indeed If Illness Island Indeed Inside
4 She is a skilled athlete and likes little detail.
5 He did ski that hill. That is indeed a sad test.

Exercise 5.11 **G Drill**

Key each line two times and push for speed.

1 gal gal gas gas get get sag sag egg egg glee glee
2 Dennis and Gene nailed a slat in the fallen gate.

Key lines 3–5 one time and then key the three lines again. Concentrate on control and try not to make errors.

3 Giant Giggle Glide Gentle Gene Gain Gift Glad Get
4 The endless agenda had eight legal details added.
5 Al tested his stiff leg. He gnashed his big teeth.

Figure 58.6 Table Content for Document 58.3—Continued

	Becomes public record when maker dies	Remains private after death of maker
Tax savings	Same as with trust	Same as with will
Asset management	Uses a power of attorney or conservatorship to manage assets	Trustor manages trust assets as long as willing and able; identifies successor to trustor to take over when necessary
Costs	Less to prepare than a trust, but probate costs can be substantial	More to prepare, fund, and manage than a will but avoids probate costs if all assets are held by the trust

Reinforcing Writing Skills

Practice your summarizing (paraphrasing) skills by creating an abstract for a report created in a previous session.

Document
58.4

Writing an Abstract

1 Navigate to the Document 58.4 launch page in the Online Lab and then click the Launch Activity button. The Online Lab will open **Doc058.04** in the activity window.

2 Center the insertion point, key **Abstract**, press Enter, and then move the insertion point to the left margin.

3 Key a one-paragraph summary of the main ideas of the report shown in Figure 55.4, report keyed for Document 55.2. *Note: The content of this report is the same content used in the writing activity for Session 57.* When keying the paragraph, do not press the Tab key at the start of the paragraph and key only one space after each sentence within the paragraph.

4 Use Find and Replace to replace the single spaces after the sentences within the paragraph to double spaces.

5 Proofread the document and correct any errors.

6 Save the document.

7 Click the Upload button to upload the document for instructor review.

Ending the Session

The Online Lab automatically saves the work you completed for this session. You may continue with the next session or exit the Online Lab and continue later.

Exercise 5.12 · Reinforcement Drill

Key the following drill lines one time. Press the Enter key after each line. Your WAM rate will appear after each line. Repeat this exercise if you are not reaching 25 WAM.

1 His skin is thin; he is ill; he feels faint; see, he is ill.

2 He thinks it is a fad. I dislike that snide kid.

3 The kitten is a little lifeless and is an infant.

4 She shall indeed need that inside aid as enlisted.

5 His knife slid inside as the ill thief listened.

6 As the sled glides, the infant giggles in delight.

7 She disliked it. The kitten tangled that tinsel.

8 Jake, the gentle giant, giggled at Gina, the elf.

9 As she dashed ahead in glee, Leslie sang a jingle.

10 If he skis at night, Dad needs a light flashlight.

Exercise 5.13 · Tab Drill

The first line of a paragraph is commonly indented 0.5 inch from the left. Microsoft Word and many word processing programs have a default or preset tab stop every 0.5 inch across the page.

In this exercise you will practice the Tab key reach and will see how the preset tabs work. Practice keying the following five columns of names in the Online Lab. Key the first word in the first column (**Len**), and then press Tab. Key the first word in the second column (**Edna**) and press Tab, key **Dale** and press Tab, key **Nina** and press Tab, and then key **Danita**. Press Enter to move to the next line. Repeat the process for the remaining lines.

1 Len → Edna → Dale → Nina → Danita

2 Jen → Tina → Dane → Dean → Thane

3 Tad → Ed → Gina → Kade → Neal

Introducing Word Wrap

Word wrap is a feature whereby text is continued on a new line when one line is full. The next word is automatically moved or "wrapped" to the next line. When you key paragraphs of text (for example, in a letter or report), you do not need to press Enter at the end of each line. Be sure to press Enter to end a paragraph because word wrap is a default setting.

   d   Change the line spacing to single spacing with no extra space between paragraphs.

   e   Insert a table with three columns and one row.

   f   Key the information shown in Figure 58.6. Press Tab at the end of each row to create a new row. Do not press Tab or Enter at the end of the table. *Note: Do not press Enter at the end of each line; let the lines wrap. Your lines will not wrap the same as they do in Figure 58.3.*

11   Format the table by completing the following steps:

   a   Adjust the column widths so that the first column is 1.2 inches, the second column is 2.42 inches, and the third column is 3.04 inches.

   b   Format the table style to *Light List*.

   c   Confirm that the *Header Row* and *First Column* options in the Table Styles Options group on the Table Tools Design tab are the only selected table style options. **Hint: Remove the check mark in the Banded Rows check box.**

   d   Add an extra row after each current row (including the last row) by completing the following steps:

      1)   Turn on the display of nonprinting characters if it is not already turned on.

      2)   Position the insertion point outside of the right margin of the table, next to the cell that contains *Not subject to probate*, and then press Enter.

      3)   Position the insertion point outside of the right margin of the table, next to the cell that contains *Out-of-state property not subject to probate*, and then press Enter.

      4)   Continue inserting blank rows in the table, including after the *Costs* row.

12   Proofread the changes made to the document and correct any errors.

13   Save the document.

14   Click the Check button to stop the timer and upload the document for checking. The Online Lab will report the WAM rate and number of errors for the activity.

15   If errors are reported, view the results document, correct the errors in the submitted document, save the document, and then click the Check button.

Figure 58.6 Table Content for Document 58.3

Item	Will	Trust
Probate	Subject to probate	Not subject to probate
	Out-of-state property subject to probate in that state also	Out-of-state property not subject to probate
	Court supervision provided for beneficiary challenges and creditor disputes	No automatic court supervision to handle disputes

continues

Exercise 5.14 Word Wrap Drill

Key the two following paragraphs in the Online Lab. Press the Tab key to indent the first line of each paragraph and let word wrap move text to the next line automatically. Press Enter at the end of each paragraph.

1 → An idle lad finishes last. He is shiftless as he sits and tells his tales. He needs an insight in the elegant things in life. An idle lad finishes last. He is shiftless as he sits and tells his tales.

2 → Allan is attaining a skill in legal defense. The giant task is thankless. He insists that all the details heighten his thinking. Allan is attaining a skill in legal defense.

Ergonomic Tip

Periodically rest your eyes by focusing for a short time on an object 20 or more feet away.

Ending the Session

The Online Lab automatically saves the work you completed for this session. You can continue with the next session or exit the Online Lab and continue later. If you need to review the procedures for continuing to the next session or exiting the Online Lab, refer back to Session 1, page 8.

b Click the Insert Citation button in the Citations & Bibliography group on the References tab.

c Click *Add New Source.*

d In the Create Source dialog box, click the *Type of Source* down arrow and change the type of source to *Book Section.*

e Key the following source information, being careful to key the spaces, punctuation, and capitalization as shown below:

> *Author:* **Northworth, Karl**
>
> *Title:* **Wills and trusts simplified**
>
> *Book Author:* **Tokheim, Judith; Voiers, Michael**
>
> *Book Title:* **Simplify your life**
>
> *Year:* **2014**
>
> *Pages:* **60-66**
>
> *City:* **Baltimore**
>
> *Publisher:* **Wipperfurth Publishing**

f Proofread the source information and then click OK.

8 Add references to the existing sources by completing the following steps:

a Move the insertion point just before the period in the sentence that begins *Simple wills, oral wills* (the sentence just before the *Trusts* heading on page 4), click the Insert Citation button, and then click *Northworth, Karl* in the source list.

b Move the insertion point just before the period in the sentence that begins *A trust is a legal entity* (the sentence just after the *Trusts* heading), click the Insert Citation button, and then click *Ernst, Lynda D, Kolbinger, Susan M* in the source list.

c Move the insertion point just before the period in the sentence that begins *A will is a document* (the sentence just after the *Wills* heading on page 3), click the Insert Citation button, and then click *Merrier, Jan, Wissen, Renee* in the source list.

d Move the insertion point just before the period in the sentence that begins *Table 1 summarizes* (at the end of the document), click the Insert Citation button, and then click *Cooper, Jolene* in the source list.

9 Create a References page by completing the following steps:

a Move the insertion point to the end of the document (Ctrl + End) and then insert a page break (Ctrl + Enter).

b Center the insertion point and then key **References**.

c Press Enter and set the text alignment to be left aligned.

d Click the Bibliography button in the Citations & Bibliography group on the References tab.

e Click *Insert Bibliography.*

10 Create a page for the table by completing the following steps:

a Move the insertion point to the end of the document (Ctrl + End) and then insert a page break (Ctrl + Enter).

b At the left margin, key **Table 1** and then press Enter.

c At the left margin, turn on italic formatting, key **Comparison of Wills and Trusts**, turn off italic formatting, and then press Enter.

steps continue

Session 6

Skills Reinforcement and Proficiency Exercises: Sessions 1–5, Error Correction

⏱ Session Objectives

- Review and practice correct finger positioning for the keys introduced in Sessions 1–5
- Achieve words-a-minute (WAM) rate with two or fewer errors
- Take 10-second, 15-second, 20-second, and 1-minute timings
- Use timings to assess and reinforce keying speed and accuracy
- Differentiate between the Backspace and Delete keys
- Learn how to correct errors with the Backspace and Delete keys

Timing Goals

- 1 minute: 25 WAM and two or fewer errorrs

Getting Started and Warming Up

Exercises 6.1–6.2 The first two exercises in this session are more than just warm-up drills. Exercise 6.1 is a speed timing drill and Exercise 6.2 is an accuracy timing drill. Complete these exercises even if you are continuing directly from Session 5.

The purpose of this session is to reinforce the keyboarding skills you have developed in the previous sessions. The timings in this session will help you to determine where you are in your skill development. The exercises in the session provide you with the opportunity to further work on improving your speed and accuracy, if you have not reached the target goals.

This session also includes an introduction to the Backspace and Delete keys.

Assessing Your Speed and Accuracy

Complete Timings 6.1 and 6.2 in the Online Lab using the paragraph at the top of the next page. In the Online Lab, you will start with a practice screen which you can use to practice keying the timing text without the timer running. When you have completed your practice, prompt the Online Lab to begin Timing 6.1. Both timings will use the same paragraph. Once you are on an active timing screen, the timing will start as soon as you begin keying.

Remember to press the Tab key at the start of the paragraph, and do not press Enter at the end of each line, but only at the end of the paragraph. If you finish keying the paragraph before the timing expires, press Enter and start keying the paragraph again.

When time expires, the Online Lab will give you a WAM rate and highlight any errors you made. The goals are to key at least 25 WAM and to make two or fewer errors.

5 Add the second source and in-text citation by completing the following steps:

  a In the first paragraph on page 3, locate the sentence that begins *The reasons for estate planning* and position the insertion point at the end of the sentence before the period and after the words *management plan*.

  b Click the Insert Citation button in the Citations & Bibliography group on the References tab.

  c Click *Add New Source.*

  d In the Create Source dialog box, click the *Type of Source* down arrow, scroll down the list, and then click *Document From Web site.*

  e Key the following source information, being careful to key the spaces, punctuation, and capitalization as shown below:

    Author: **Merrier, Jan; Wissen, Renee**

    Name of Web Page: **Estate planning checklist**

    Name of Web Site: **Merrier & Wissen, PC**

    Year: **2014**

    Month: **October**

    Day: **8**

    URL: **http://www.emcp.net/merrierandwissen/checklist**

  f Proofread the source information and then click OK.

6 Add the third source and in-text citation by completing the following steps:

  a In the second paragraph on page 3, locate the sentence that begins *Attorneys continue to use* and position the insertion point at the end of the sentence before the period and after the words *of the words*.

  b Click the Insert Citation button in the Citations & Bibliography group on the References tab.

  c Click *Add New Source.*

  d Click the *Show All Bibliography Fields* check box to insert a check mark.

  e In the Create Source dialog box, click the *Type of Source* down arrow and change the type of source to *Journal Article.*

  f Key the following source information, being careful to key the spaces, punctuation, and capitalization as shown below:

    Author: **Cooper, Jolene**

    Title: **Guidelines for estate planning**

    Journal Name: **Legal Assistants Today**

    Year: **2014**

    Month: **April**

    Pages: **22-27**

  g Proofread the source information and then click OK.

7 Add the fourth source and in-text citation by completing the following steps:

  a In the second paragraph on page 3, locate the sentence that begins *Creating or making a will* and position the insertion point at the end of the sentence before the period and after the words *have children*.

steps continue

Timings 6.1–6.2

That gallant knight led the detail. A tall, thin lad assisted at the flank. The knight failed the task and feels the defeat. A sadness sifts in as his shield falls.

Viewing the Timings Performance Report

The Online Lab provides a report showing the results of all of the document activities completed in the Online Lab. To view your Timings Performance report, complete the following steps:

1 Click the Unit Contents tab to open the Online Lab Unit Contents page.

2 Click *Reports* in the navigation pane.

3 Click *Timings Performance* to open the report. The report displays the results of all paragraph timings you have attempted. If you have attempted a timing more than once, the attempt with the highest WAM rate is shown.

4 Click *Attempts* to view results for all attempts and the text you keyed with errors marked.

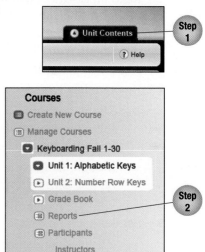

↺ Reinforcing Your Skills

The following speed and accuracy drills provide additional practice on the keys you have learned in Sessions 1–5. If you successfully keyed Timings 6.1 and 6.2 with a 25 WAM or greater and with two or fewer errors and you do not hesitate while keying, proceed to the video introduction of the Backspace and Delete keys and the corresponding exercises in the Online Lab. However, if your WAM and error rates do not match these goals, the speed and accuracy drills in this section will give you the opportunity for further practice.

If you have not mastered a key reach (you hesitate before striking the key) or if you are not keying at least 25 WAM, key the speed drills, Exercises 6.3 and 6.4. If you are making more than two errors per minute, key the accuracy drills, Exercises 6.5 and 6.6.

Speed Drills

For the speed drills, key each line one time as quickly as you can. After practicing the speed drills, either continue by completing the accuracy drills or go directly to Timing 6.3 to see if your speed has improved.

> **Success Tip**
>
> If you need to make a correction to a source that has been keyed into a document, click the Manage Sources button in the Citations & Bibliography group on the References tab, click the source in the *Current List* list box, and then click the Edit button. If the References list was created before the edit was made to the source, right click the list and click *Update Field*.

Document Headings, In-text Citations, References, and Table Pages

58.3

1 Read all instructions for this document activity, navigate to the Document 58.3 launch page in the Online Lab, and then click the Launch Activity button. The Online Lab will open **Doc058.03** in the activity window. The timer will start as soon as you begin keying the document. *Note: The document default line spacing and font size have been set and the title page, abstract page, and headers have already been keyed in this document.*

2 Key two headings in the document by completing the following steps:

  a Move the insertion point to the end of the first paragraph on page 3 of the document following the period after the words *estate planning law*, press Enter, set the alignment to center, turn on bold formatting, and then key **Wills**.

  b Move the insertion point to the end of the paragraph on page 4 that begins *Different types of wills* following the period after the words *wills are examples*, press Enter, set the alignment to center, turn on bold formatting, and then key **Trusts**.

3 Set the document style reference to *APA Sixth Edition* by completing the following steps:

  a Click the References tab.

  b Click the *Style* list box down arrow in the Citations & Bibliography group.

  c Click *APA Sixth Edition*.

4 Add the first source and in-text citation by completing the following steps:

  a In the first paragraph on page 3, locate the sentence that begins *Estate planning is a set* and position the insertion point at the end of the sentence before the period and after the words *estate taxes*.

  b Click the Insert Citation button in the Citations & Bibliography group on the References tab.

  c Click *Add New Source*.

  d In the Create Source dialog box, click the *Type of Source* down arrow and click *Book* to change the type of source.

  e Key the following source information, being careful to key the spaces, punctuation, and capitalization as shown below:

  > *Author:* **Ernst, Lynda D; Kolbinger, Susan M**
  >
  > *Title:* **Legal editing and proofreading**
  >
  > *Year:* **2012**
  >
  > *City:* **St. Paul**
  >
  > *Publisher:* **Paradigm Publishing, Inc.**

  f Proofread the source information and then click OK.

steps continue

Exercise 6.3 — Balanced-Hand Words Drill

Balanced-hand words contain letters that require switching back and forth from your left to right hand to key the letters.

1. and the ant sit ale elf end hen she end sigh sign
2. aid fit sit did tie die dig fig and the hang then
3. halt than hand lens lake lane then than sign fish

4. idle lens lane sigh then dish disk sign half lake
5. shake snake title aisle angle fight handle island
6. angle sight digit gland eight slant height sleigh
7. signal giant tight an he if it and elf the and he

Exercise 6.4 — Letter Combinations Drill

The following combinations focus on common letter sequences found in many words.

1. de den dead deal desk denial dense deft dental
2. di dig dish dial digest dislike dine dike disk
3. I dislike the heat dial that fits the dental fan.

4. fi fish final fine finish fight find fig field finale
5. ga gal gas gag gale gait gallant gasket gadget
6. Gale finished the gasket at the gas gadget gate.

7. ha hate halt half hash hang hand handle hat had
8. ki kite kindle kilt kiln king kink kit kind
9. That hanging kite tail has halted the hail.

10. le lest left lead lend ledge least leaf lean lease
11. li lid lie lied line link linking linkage like
12. At least link the left lid and let the length stand.

13. sa sad sat safe sake sale said sang Sal saline
14. si sit site sitting signal sighted sill silken siding
15. Sad Sal sang a signal as she sighted a safe site.

16. st stead steal steadiness stateside stag state
17. ta tag talk take tale taste task tan tall tail
18. Steadfast Stella stands and talks and then sits.

drill continues

Figure 58.5 Report Content for Document 58.2—Continued

dies without a will. As mentioned previously, this can cause problems if the decedent has children and there is no other surviving parent. Dying without a will can also cause issues if the decedent has considerable assets. When a person dies intestate, the court will apply statutes intended to pass property and other assets on to legal heirs. The court will also appoint a guardian for minor children. This may be a problem when the legal heirs or appointed guardians are not those whom the decedent would have chosen.

The person making the will is referred to as the *testator*. The testator will choose an *executor* or *personal representative* to be responsible for carrying out the directions in a will. The executor or personal representative is a fiduciary in the management of an estate. A *fiduciary* is a person who has been chosen by another to make financial decisions on behalf of that person.

Different types of wills are available depending upon the situation such as simple wills, oral wills, joint wills, and conditional wills.

A *trust* is a legal entity that holds assets for the benefit of another. The person who provides property and creates a trust is called a *trustor*, sometimes referred to as a trust maker, grantor, donor, or settlor. The trustor appoints a trustee, who holds legal title to property or money and has broad powers over its maintenance and investment. Sometimes the trustee is a person or corporation (such as a bank) or a combination of both. A beneficiary to a trust is the person who receives the benefits or advantages (such as income) of a trust either during the lifetime or after the death of the trustor.

Trusts can be either revocable or irrevocable. A *revocable trust* is sometimes called a *living trust*. A revocable trust is one that can be changed after the trust is created. Life circumstances change and a revocable trust gives the maker the ability to make changes to the trust as necessary. On the other hand, an *irrevocable trust* is one that, once made, cannot be changed.

A trust is a different option from a will. However, both wills and trusts are legal tools a person can use to distribute an estate after death. An attorney can assist in evaluating the advantages and disadvantages of each option to help a client decide on one form or the other. Table 1 summarizes the differences between a will and a trust with regard to probate, tax savings, management of assets, and costs.

19 te tea test tenth tend tenant tease teak tent

20 th then that than thing this theft thin thesis

21 Then that tested tenant, Ted, did a tenth test.

Accuracy Drills

For the following accuracy drills, key each group of lines one time. Concentrate on control as you key. After practicing the accuracy drills, go directly to Timing 6.3 to see if your accuracy has improved.

> ### ✓ Success Tip
> Concentrate on keying with control for accuracy as you type the lines in the accuracy drills. Remember that your mind controls your fingers!

 Exercise 6.5 **Double-Letter Words Drill**

These words require you to key the same letter twice in a row. Your finger does not need to return to the home row between identical letters.

1 see glee needs indeed feeling needless teens seed

2 egg sell sniff haggle falling eggshell stall eggs

3 eel keen sheen needle fiddles seedling sleek deed

4 add kiss stiff assist endless lifeless still hill

5 fee need sheet seeing dissent likeness steed heel

6 add fell skill allied skilled settling shell tell

7 see feel teeth indeed gallant sledding sleet knee

8 all hall shall little install knitting stall tall

9 Sadness is a feeling I assess as an alleged need.

10 Assist the skiing attendant and lessen all falls.

11 The sleek kitten shall flee the illegal attendants.

12 Haggling is a senseless dissent that is needless.

13 Flatten the stiff fiddle and install the tassels.

7 Save the document.

8 Click the Check button to stop the timer and upload the document for checking. The Online Lab will report the WAM rate and number of errors for the activity.

9 If errors are reported, view the results document, correct the errors in the submitted document, save the document, and then click the Check button.

Success Tip

According to APA style, key journal article titles with only the first word capitalized but key journal titles with main words capitalized.

Figure 58.5 Report Content for Document 58.2

Estate planning is a set of procedures intended to manage an individual's assets in the event of incapacitation or death, including the giving of assets to heirs and the settlement of estate taxes. *Heirs* are the persons who are entitled by law to the estate if the decedent died without a valid will; they may include a surviving spouse, children, and possibly more remote descendants. Most estate plans are set up with the help of an attorney experienced in estate planning law. The reasons for estate planning include protecting assets from taxes, making sure that survivors are properly cared for, and establishing a wealth-management plan.

A *will* is a document spelling out what is to be done with a person's assets after he or she has died. This document has no force while the person is alive and may be altered or revoked at any time. The will becomes applicable at the time of the person's death and applies to the estate as it is at the time of death. "Last will and testament" is a fancy and redundant way of saying *will*. Attorneys continue to use this phrase because they and clients like the formal sound of the words. The words *will* and *testament* actually mean the same thing. A document will be the "last" will if the maker of it dies before writing another one. Creating or making a will usually does not cross young people's minds until they are married and/or have children. If parents were to die with minor children and no will, the court would decide where the children would live and who would care for them. Parents usually want to be the ones who decide these important details, and a will is the legal document through which to make those decisions known.

When a person dies and has completed a valid will, he or she is said to have died *testate*. The term *intestate* describes a situation where a person

continues

Exercise 6.6 Longer Words Drill

Longer words require more concentration and that leads to better accuracy. Keep your eyes on the copy as you key.

1 endless athlete flatten inflated install disliked
2 lenient distant delighted heading inkling digital
3 A lenient athlete has inflated the flattened keg.

4 hesitating likeness indefinite alkaline initiated
5 heightened stealing gaslight lengthened delegates
6 The hesitating delegate is stealing the gaslight.

7 landslide skinflint stateside essential legislate
8 negligent lightness sightless delighted attendant
9 tasteless steadfast defendant thankless seashells
10 Seashells in the landslide delighted a skinflint.

Assessing Your Speed and Accuracy

Now that you have practiced the appropriate speed and accuracy drills, complete two 1-minute timings using the following paragraph. (This is the same text keyed for Timings 6.1 and 6.2.)

Each timing will begin as soon as you begin keying the paragraph. Remember to press the Tab key at the start of the paragraph. If you finish keying the paragraph before the timing expires, press Enter and start keying the paragraph again.

When time expires, the Online Lab will give you a WAM rate and will show you any errors you made in the keyed text.

The results of all of your timings will be stored in your Timings Performance report. Compare your rates from Timings 6.3 and 6.4 to your rates from Timings 6.1 and 6.2. Has your speed improved? Do you have fewer errors? If you are not reaching at least 25 WAM with two or fewer errors, repeat Sessions 1–5.

Goals: 25 WAM and two or fewer errors

1-Minute Timings

Timings 6.3–6.4

That gallant knight led the detail. A tall, thin lad assisted at the flank. The knight failed the task and feels the defeat. A sadness sifts in as his shield falls.

   h   Click the Close Header and Footer button in the Close group or double-click in the body of the document.

7   Proofread the document, checking the format against the format shown in Figures 58.1 and 58.2.

8   Save the document.

9   Click the Check button to stop the timer and upload the document for checking. The Online Lab will report the WAM rate and number of errors for the activity.

10   If errors are reported, view the results document, correct the errors in the submitted document, save the document, and then click the Check button.

Figure 58.4 Abstract Content for Document 58.1

Different options exist for planning the distribution of property and possessions after death. Terminology used in estate planning is identified. A will is a document that identifies what is to be done with a person's assets after death. A trust is a legal entity that holds assets for the benefit of another. Trusts can be either revocable or irrevocable. With a revocable trust, changes in life's circumstances (such as the birth of a child or divorce) allow the maker of the trust to change the provisions of the trust. Wills and trusts are compared with regard to probate, tax savings, asset management, and costs. An attorney can assist in selecting the option that best fits the client's needs.

Document 58.2

Research Paper Body in APA Style

1   Read all instructions for this document activity, navigate to the Document 58.2 launch page in the Online Lab, and then click the Launch Activity button. The Online Lab will open **Doc058.02** in the activity window. The timer will start as soon as you begin keying the document. *Note: The document default line spacing and font size have been set and the title page, Abstract page, and headers have already been keyed in this document. However, there is only one space after sentences in the abstract paragraph. The space after sentences will be adjusted in Step 5 below.*

2   Move the insertion point to the end of the document (Ctrl + End) and then insert a page break (Ctrl + Enter).

3   Change the text alignment to center, key **An Overview of Estate Planning**, press Enter, and then change the text alignment to left alignment.

4   Key the text shown in Figure 58.5. The text includes several italicized terms. When formatting these words, do not italicize the space or punctuation following the term. When two consecutive words are set in italic (such as *personal representative*), set the space between the words in italic. Also, remember to press the Tab key at the start of each paragraph. *Note: Key only one space after sentences, except the last sentence in a paragraph, and do not press Enter at the end of the last sentence.*

5   Since the APA style specifies that sentences end with two spaces after a period, use the Find and Replace feature to insert the double spaces. *Note: Make sure the author's name on the title page is not reformatted with two spaces after the middle initial.*

6   Proofread the document and correct any errors.

steps continue

Introducing the Backspace and Delete Keys

Videos 6.1–6.2 The locations of the Backspace and Delete keys are shown in the following diagram. Watch Videos 6.1 and 6.2 and practice the reaches for these new keys.

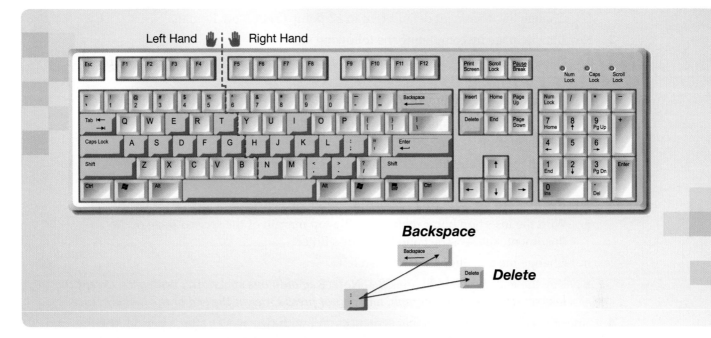

Backspace

Delete

The Backspace and the Delete keys are both used to correct text. However, they produce corrections in different ways.

Pressing the Backspace key will delete the character to the left of the insertion point. In other words, the Backspace key deletes backwards from the insertion point. The Backspace key is a good choice to use if you immediately realize you have tapped the wrong character key when keying text.

Pressing the Delete key will delete the character to the right of the insertion point. In other words, pressing the Delete key deletes forward from the insertion point. To make a correction in text using the Delete key, use the arrow keys or mouse to position the insertion point immediately to the left of the character to be deleted, press the Delete key to remove the incorrect character, and then tap the correct character key.

Complete Exercises 6.7 and 6.8 in the Online Lab, but follow the step instructions shown in the textbook.

Exercise 6.7 Backspace Drill

To practice correcting with the Backspace key, complete the following steps in Exercise 6.7 in the Online Lab. The steps will direct you to key intentional errors and then will direct you to fix them using the Backspace key.

1 Key the following:

> The hesitatint

2 Press the Backspace key to delete the letter *t* in the keyed line. The text should read *The hesitatin*.

3 Press the G key so the text reads *The hesitating*.

drill continues

2 Change the document default formatting by completing the following steps:

    a Change the document default line spacing to double spacing with no extra spacing before or after paragraphs. *Hint: Click the Set As Default button in the Paragraph dialog box and apply the default to this document only.*

    b Change the document default font to 12-point Times New Roman.

3 Key the title page by completing the following steps:

    a Press the Enter key three times to move the insertion point close to 2 inches from the top of the document.

    b Change the text alignment to center.

    c Key the title of the report, **Estate Planning**, and then press Enter.

    d Key the author's name, **Suzanne Kitts**, and then press Enter.

    e Key the school affiliation, **Rhode Island College**, and then insert a page break (Ctrl + Enter).

4 Key the Abstract page by completing the following steps:

    a With the insertion point centered at the top margin of the second page of the document, key **Abstract** and then press Enter.

    b Change the text alignment to flush left.

    c Key the text shown in Figure 58.4. *Note: Key only one space after sentences, except the last sentence in the paragraph, and do not press Enter at the end of the last sentence.*

5 Since the APA style specifies that sentences end with two spaces after a period, use the Find and Replace feature to insert the double spaces by completing the following steps:

    a Move the insertion point to the beginning of the document (Ctrl + Home).

    b Click the Replace button in the Editing group on the Home tab.

    c Key a period and one space in the *Find what* text box.

    d Key a period and two spaces in the *Replace with* text box.

    e Click the Find Next button and then the Replace button until all instances are replaced.

    f Click OK and then close the Find and Replace dialog box.

6 Insert the headers in the document by completing the following steps:

    a Double-click in the header area of the first page of the document to open the header and display the Header & Footer Tools Design tab.

    b Click the *Different First Page* option in the Options group to insert a check mark.

    c With the insertion point at the left margin of the first page header, key **Running head: ESTATE PLANNING** and then press Tab two times.

    d Click the Page Number button in the Header & Footer group on the Header & Footer Tools Design tab, point to *Current Position*, and then click *Plain Number*.

    e Click the Next button in the Navigation group on the Header & Footer Tools Design tab to move to the second page header.

Step 6e

    f With the insertion point at the left margin of the second page header, key **ESTATE PLANNING** and then press Tab two times.

    g Click the Page Number button in the Header & Footer group on the Header & Footer Tools Design tab, point to *Current Position*, and then click *Plain Number*.

steps continue

4 Press the space bar and then key the following:

delegate is te

5 Press the Backspace key two times to delete *te*. The text should read *The hesitating delegate is*.

6 Key the following:

stealing the gas l

7 Press the Backspace key two times to delete *l* and the space after *gas*.

8 Key the following:

light.

9 Proof your final line to make sure it reads *The hesitating delegate is stealing the gaslight*.

Exercise 6.8 Delete Drill

To practice correcting with the Delete key, complete the following steps in Exercise 6.8 in the Online Lab. The steps will direct you to key intentional errors and then will direct you to fix them by positioning the insertion point using the arrow keys or the mouse and the Delete key.

1 Key the following:

That tenant, Ted, did the alleged deed.

2 Position the insertion point immediate to the left of the *T* in *Ted*.

3 Press the Delete key three times, one time for each character in the name *Ted*. This action will delete the name from the sentence.

4 Key the following:

Dale

5 Proof the text to confirm that it reads *That tenant, Dale, did the alleged deed*.

6 Position the insertion point immediately to the left of the *a* in *That*.

7 Press the Delete key two times to delete the letters *a* and *t*.

8 Key the following:

e

9 Proof the text to confirm that it reads *The tenant, Dale, did the alleged deed*.

Ergonomic Tip
If your mouse is separate from your keyboard, keep the mouse at the same height and distance from you as the keyboard.

Ending the Session

The Online Lab automatically saves the work you completed for this session. You can continue with the next session or exit the Online Lab and continue later. You can also review the results of the timings completed in the Online Lab by reviewing your Timings Performance report.

Success Tip

Although it is important to note the heading level formatting requirements for APA, not all of these levels are used in the documents keyed in this session.

Figure 58.3 Sample Headings in APA Format   *Note: Do not key this document.*

planning law. The reasons for estate planning include protecting assets from taxes, making sure

that survivors are properly cared for, and establishing a wealth-management plan.

Common Estate Planning Documents — first-level heading: centered, bold, and main words capitalized

There are two typical estate planning documents; however, each type has a variety of

options and specialty clauses.

Types of Wills — second-level heading: aligned at left margin, bold, and main words capitalized

Different types of wills are available depending on the personal circumstances of the

individual making the will.

third-level heading: aligned at the paragraph start, bold, only first word capitalized, ends with a bold period

 Simple will. A simple will leaves the entire estate (the testator's property covered by the

will) to one or more named beneficiaries.

 Joint or mutual will. A joint will (also called a mutual will) distributes the property of

The space following the heading's period is not bold.

two or more people. A joint will is a single document signed by each testator and leaving all

assets to the other. It stipulates what will happen with the assets when the second person dies.

In the following document activities you will apply the APA style to a report. In the first document activity, you will key the title page and Abstract page. In the second document, you will key the body of a research paper. In the third document, you will add headings, in-text citations, generate and format a References page, and prepare a table for a report.

Document 58.1

Title Page and Abstract in APA Style

1 Read all instructions for this document activity, navigate to the Document 58.1 launch page in the Online Lab, and then click the Launch Activity button. The Online Lab will open **Doc058.01** in the activity window. The timer will start as soon as you begin keying the document.

steps continue

P, R, Question Mark

Session Objectives

- Identify the P, R, and question mark (?) keys
- Practice correct finger positioning for the P, R, and question mark keys
- Take 15-second and 1-minute timings to build keyboarding speed and accuracy
- Explore common keyboarding errors

Timing Goals

- 1 minute: 25 WAM and two or fewer errors

Getting Started and Warming Up

Exercise 7.1 If you are continuing immediately from Session 6, you may skip the Exercise 7.1 warm-up drill. However, if you exited the Online Lab at the end of Session 6, warm up by completing Exercise 7.1.

Introducing the P, R, and Question Mark Keys

Videos 7.1–7.3 The locations of the R, P, and question mark (?) keys are shown in the following diagram. Watch Videos 7.1 through 7.3 and practice using these new keys.

Exercises 7.2–7.7 Complete Exercises 7.2 through 7.6 to learn these new keys. Also complete the thinking drill, Exercise 7.7. When keying the drill lines, follow the instruction prompts provided in the Online Lab.

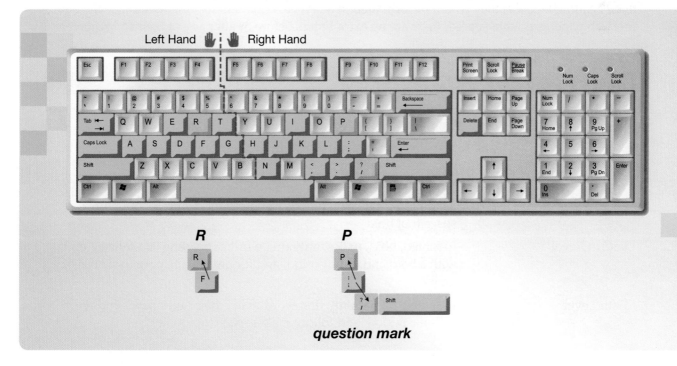

question mark

Figure 58.2 Abstract Page Using APA Style

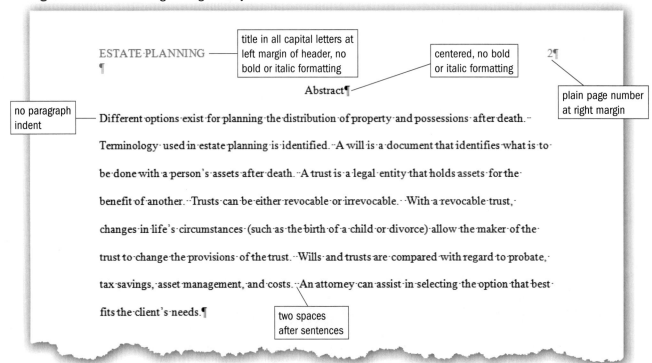

Formatting Headings in APA Research Papers

As mentioned in previous sessions, the main purpose of headings in a report, manuscript, or research paper is to help readers find the important ideas in the document. The APA style identifies formatting for five levels of headings. These should be applied in the order listed even when a report does not use all five heading levels.

Table 58.2 shows how each type of heading is formatted. Figure 58.3 shows examples of the first three heading levels as they would be formatted in an APA-formatted document. Because the entire research paper is double-spaced, there are no extra Enters before or after any of the heading levels.

Table 58.2 APA Heading Formatting Styles

Heading Level	Formatting Style
First Level	Centered, bold, main words in the heading capitalized, press Enter once before and after
Second Level	Left align, bold, main words in the heading capitalized, press Enter once before and after
Third Level	Indented on paragraph indent (0.5 inch), bold, only first word of heading capitalized, end with a bold period, and follow with a space (not bold)
Fourth Level	Indented, bold, italics, only first word of heading capitalized, end with a bold and italic period, and follow with a space (not bold or italic)
Fifth Level	Indented, italics, only first word of heading capitalized, end with an italic period, and follow with a space (not italic)

↻ Reinforcing Your Skills

Complete Exercises 7.8 through 7.11 in the Online Lab. Reference the drill lines from the textbook as you key and keep your eyes on the textbook pages, not on your fingers. Complete each exercise at least once, but repeat exercises if you need more practice.

Exercise 7.8 **P Drill**

Key each line two times and push for speed. The goal is to key at least 25 WAM. Your WAM rate will appear at the end of each line.

1 ;p pan pat pea peg pen pep pet pie pig pin pit pails
2 ;p ship tape pink skip slap taps gaps pest sap paste
3 Peasant Pennant Pitfall Patient Pheasant Pleasant Philadelphia

Key lines 4–6 one time and then key the three lines again. Concentrate on control. The goals are to key at least 25 WAM and to make two or fewer errors. Your WAM rate will appear at the end of each line, and errors will be highlighted.

4 A tall, split, peeling aspen sapling is diseased.
5 Pat speaks and pleads and defends the plaintiffs.
6 Did Jane tape that splint and dispense the pills?

Exercise 7.9 **R Drill**

Key each line two times. Push for speed the first time you key a line and concentrate on control the second time. The goal is to key at least 25 WAM. Your WAM rate will appear at the end of each line.

1 fr rain rare real rink rake rage rear ripe rip rage rigid
2 stare there their after pride tired far her press jar tear
3 Refrain Repress Release Retreat Resident Register Reap

Exercise 7.10 **Question Mark Drill**

Tap the space bar only once after the question mark (?) at the end of the sentence. This rule applies to all end-of-sentence punctuation. When a question mark ends a line in the drill, tap Enter immediately. Do not tap the space bar first.

Key lines 1–3 and then key the lines again. Concentrate on control. The goal is to key at least 25 WAM. Your WAM rate will appear at the end of each line.

1 Is Jennie ahead? Is Dennis safe? Is Allen late?
2 Is Ken late? Is Dale fit? Is Neil in his teens?
3 Did she dine? Did the leaf fall? Did Jane flee?

Table 58.1 APA Formatting Guidelines for Research Papers—Continued

Paper Element	Formatting Guidelines
Abstract	A brief summary of the research paper. Appears on page 2 and includes required header. The heading *Abstract* is centered at the top margin in plain text (no bold or italic formatting). Do not tab indent the abstract paragraph (see Figure 58.2).
Citations	In-text and include author and date
References	Begin on a separate page at the end of the document. The heading *References* is centered at the top margin in plain text (no bold or italic formatting). Allow Word to automatically generate from in-text citation sources. The list should be double-spaced with no extra spaces between entries and with a hanging indent.
Tables	When included, tables are placed on separate pages after the References page (unless requested before the References page by the instructor assigning the paper or the journal editor requesting manuscripts for publication).

Success Tip

Rather than trying to key two spaces after every period when keying a document for the APA style, use the Find and Replace feature to replace all periods followed by one space with a period followed by two spaces.

Figure 58.1 Report Title Page Using APA Style

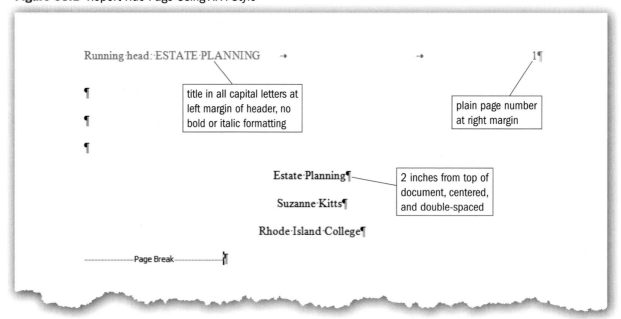

Key lines 1–3 one time and push for speed. The goal is to key at least 25 WAM. Your WAM rate will appear at the end of each line.

1 In the sleet, a sheep passed the pines and plants.

2 In his pastel sedan, Jake passed that fast jeep.

3 His left thigh is gashed; the patient is in pain.

Success Tip

Think control as you key each line. If you make more than two errors on a line, repeat it. Keep your eyes on the copy in the text as you key.

Key lines 4–9 one time. Concentrate on control. The goals are to key at least 25 WAM and to make two or fewer errors. Your WAM rate will appear at the end of each line, and errors will be highlighted.

4 rest tree trip hire ring fire earn hard dirt fair

5 range ridge raise reign rinse art jar rinse right

6 eager fir ran after heart large dress greed green

7 Shall I still slide in the infield if Jake faints?

8 Has she hit? Has the thief left? Has he landed?

9 Is Dale fit? Is Neil in his teens? Is Ken late?

Identifying Common Keyboarding Errors

Some errors affect only the appearance of a document. On the other hand, certain keyboarding errors can have a drastic effect on the message being communicated. Consider the result of transposing two numbers in a customer's invoice, such as keying $19 instead of $91. Following is a list of some common keyboarding mistakes. Reviewing this list will help you be aware of possible errors as you complete timings and later as you prepare letters and other documents.

- Keying wrong words
- Transposing numbers
- Placing extra spaces between words or numbers
- Placing a space before a punctuation mark
- Not capitalizing a proper noun or the first word of a sentence
- Capitalizing a word in a sentence that should not be capitalized
- Placing too many spaces after a punctuation mark or between paragraphs
- Using improper left, right, top, or bottom margins
- Not indenting properly
- Being inconsistent in vertical spacing
- Using incorrect punctuation

Formatting in APA Style

The *Publication Manual of the American Psychological Association* (APA) provides a guide for writers, editors, students, and educators writing for the social and behavioral sciences. There are two types of papers: (1) a review of the academic and other literature on a particular topic and (2) a report on an experimental or other scientific research project. The second type of paper should include the topic and its importance to a specific scientific discipline, specific questions that were evaluated by the research, the researcher's strategy or experimental design, results of the research, and the author's interpretation of the results. Each report type has unique requirements. The APA style includes an easy-to-use reference and citation system as well as guidance for using headings, tables, and figures for both types of reports.

The APA style requires a title page and, commonly, an abstract. The abstract is a summary of the key points included in the paper. The abstract should contain just one paragraph double-spaced (but no tab indent at the start) and there should be a separate page immediately after the title page.

The format used in this session will be for a literature review research paper containing an abstract and a table along with in-text citations and a References page. The formatting guidelines are from the *Publication Manual of the American Psychological Association*, *Sixth Edition*. Table 58.1 provides some key formatting guidelines for the APA style. Figure 58.1 shows an example of a title page and Figure 58.2 shows an example of an Abstract page, both applying the formatting guidelines listed in Table 58.1. You will create these pages in the Document 58.1 activity.

Table 58.1 APA Formatting Guidelines for Research Papers

Paper Element	Formatting Guidelines
Text Alignment	Left aligned, paragraphs begin with 0.5-inch tab (except Abstract page)
Font	12-point, serif font such as Cambria, Bookman Old Style, Times New Roman, or Palatino Linotype
Margins	Default: 1-inch top, bottom, left, and right margins
Line Spacing	2.0 line spacing (with 0 points extra spacing before and after paragraphs) throughout document
Spacing after Sentences	Two spaces at the end of each sentence (see Figure 58.2)
Title Page	Includes title of research paper, author's name, and institutional affiliation double-spaced in the top half of the page. Text is centered and title is positioned 2 inches from top of document. Include header as specified in this table (see Figure 58.1).
Header/Page Numbers	
Title Page	Header is set 0.5 inch from the top of the document and includes the text *Running head: TITLE OF RESEARCH PAPER* (in plain text, no bold or italic formatting) beginning at left margin; the page number (digits only) is set at right margin (see Figure 58.1).
Remaining Pages	Header is set 0.5 inch from the top of the document that includes *TITLE OF RESEARCH PAPER* in plain text (no bold or italic formatting) beginning at left margin; the page number (digits only) is set at right margin.

continues

Assessing Your Speed and Accuracy

Complete Timings 7.1 and 7.2 in the Online Lab to assess the skills you have learned in this session. Refer to the following paragraphs as you key. The timing will start as soon as you begin keying the paragraph. Remember to press the Tab key at the beginning of all paragraphs in timings. If you finish keying a paragraph before the timing expires, press Enter and start the paragraph again.

If you are not reaching 25 WAM on your recent drills, push for speed when you key these timings. If you are keying at least 25 WAM but are making more than two errors per minute, concentrate on accuracy. When time expires, the Online Lab will give you a WAM rate and will show you any errors you made. The results will be stored in your Timings Performance report.

Goals: 25 WAM and two or fewer errors

1-Minute Timings

Timing 7.1
Jane prepares legal papers and letters. She prefers reading ledgers and graphs. It is tiring and drains her. If she falters at the start, Jane is risking a defeat. The stern leader sees her stress and praises her spirit.

Timing 7.2
Print the paragraph in large letters. Raise the title and delete the digraphs. Insert three fresh phrases at the end. It is all right if Dane deletes that first phrase. It is a danger and a threat. Perhaps the ending is right.

Ergonomic Tip
Your hands are to float or glide above the keyboard, not rest on it.

Ending the Session

The Online Lab automatically saves the work you completed for this session. You can continue with the next session or exit the Online Lab and continue later.

Complete two 5-minute timings on the timing text below. Timings 58.3 and 58.4 use the same paragraphs.

Goals: 35 WAM and five or fewer errors
SI: 1.50 syllables per word

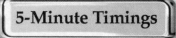

Timings 58.3–58.4

If you work with a computer, you should develop the habit of backing up your critical files. Computers have a tendency to develop problems caused by viruses or even complete failure of the hard drive. Virus problems can be minimized by subscribing to a good anti-virus protection program and scheduling regular automatic updates for it. Although becoming more unusual, your computer's hard drive may work fine one day but not start at all the next.

Most people don't understand how important a good system backup is to the user. Losing a week's (or even a day's) work due to operator error, a fire, an earthquake, or water damage can be catastrophic for a business. As a student, think about the impact of losing your research paper that is due tomorrow. You probably will only have to have that happen once to realize the importance of backing up your important files!

When a backup for a computer system is done, the files and data from the computer's hard drive are copied to a location that is separate from the main computer. In the event an original file is damaged or lost, the backup file can be accessed--if one exists, of course. Flash drives, CDs, DVDs, external hard drives, and cloud storage are all potential locations for backup files.

What types of files should be backed up? Think for a minute what you have on your computer that means the most to you. Most users would not want to lose their documents, email, photos, and music.

Microsoft Windows operating system comes with Backup and Restore to simplify the entire backup process. With its easy-to-follow-steps and prompts, the user decides the files or folders to back up and how often. Go to the Control Panel today to get started!

Ergonomic Tip
While sitting, occasionally straighten and stiffen each leg to the front and push the heel away so the back of the leg is stretched. This will help relax leg muscles and joints.

Session 8

M, O

Session Objectives

- Identify the M and O keys
- Practice correct finger positioning for the M and O keys
- Build keyboarding speed and accuracy with timings
- Spell words correctly when keyboarding

Timing Goals

- 1 minute: 25 WAM and two or fewer errors

Getting Started and Warming Up

Exercise 8.1 If you are continuing immediately from Session 7, you may skip the Exercise 8.1 warm-up drill. However, if you exited the Online Lab at the end of Session 7, warm up by completing Exercise 8.1.

Introducing the M and O Keys

Videos 8.1–8.2 The locations of the M and O keys are shown in the following diagram. Watch Videos 8.1 and 8.2 and practice using these new keys.

Exercises 8.2–8.8 Complete Exercises 8.2 through 8.7 to learn these new keys. Also complete the thinking drill, Exercise 8.8. When keying the drill lines, follow the instruction prompts provided in the Online Lab.

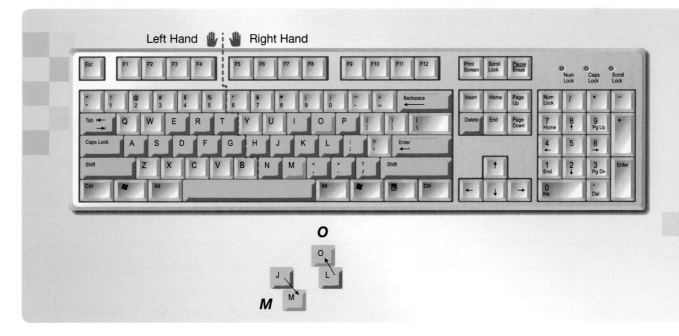

Preparing Manuscripts in APA Style

Session Objectives

- **Format a manuscript according to APA style**
- **Format a title page and an abstract page**
- **Format headings in a report**
- **Insert sources and in-text citations in a manuscript**
- **Create a References page**
- **Format a table in a report**
- **Compose an abstract**

Timing Goals

- **1 minute: 45 WAM and one or no errors**
- **5 minutes: 35 WAM and five or fewer errors**

Getting Started and Warming Up

Exercise 58.1 If you are continuing immediately from Session 57, you may skip the Exercise 58.1 warm-up drill. However, if you exited the Online Lab at the end of Session 57, warm up by completing Exercise 58.1.

Exercise 58.2 Begin your session work by completing Exercise 58.2, a timed short drill, in the Online Lab.

Assessing Your Speed and Accuracy

Complete Timings 58.1 through 58.4 in the Online Lab. At the end of each timing, the Online Lab will display your WAM rate and any errors. Results will be saved in your Timings Performance report. If you have been surpassing the speed and accuracy goals, set slightly more challenging personal goals and strive to exceed them.

Complete two 1-minute timings on the timing text below. Timings 58.1 and 58.2 use the same paragraphs.

Goals: 45 WAM and one or no errors
SI: 1.53 syllables per word

> **1-Minute Timings**

Timings 58.1–58.2
If you are thinking about setting up an office in your home, you must think about the legal aspect of your new venture. Zoning, insurance, and taxes may all impact your home office plans.

All cities have some type of zoning law. You must be sure that you know and comply with all laws for the area in which you live. You must also change your personal home insurance policy to include your new business venture. Although the insurance premium will increase, it is essential to insure equipment and protect yourself against any potential claims.

↻ Reinforcing Your Skills

Complete Exercises 8.9 through 8.11 in the Online Lab. Reference the drill lines from the textbook as you key and keep your eyes on the textbook pages, not on your fingers. Complete each exercise at least once, but repeat exercises if you want to improve your WAM rate or accuracy.

Exercise 8.9 **M Drill**

Key each drill line two times and push for speed. The goal is to key at least 25 WAM. Your WAM rate will appear at the end of each line.

1 jm am am him him man man mad mad jam jam me me mean

2 might might metal metal dream dream ram ram made made

3 Mashed Mean Mailed Minted Melted Makes Melt Might Mild

Key lines 4–6 one time and then key the three lines again. Concentrate on control. The goals are to key at least 25 WAM and to make two or fewer errors. Your WAM rate will appear at the end of each line, and errors will be highlighted.

4 Mike is making a frame; he needs ample sandpaper.

5 Did Mamie transmit the message after amending it?

6 Did Sammie eliminate all mistakes in the message?

Exercise 8.10 **O Drill**

Key each drill line two times and push for speed. The goal is to key at least 25 WAM. Your WAM rate will appear at the end of each line.

1 lo do go no to of on or doe off one too mom dot not for ton

2 roof look room toot noon foot food soon moon doom root

3 Order Older Folder Online Option Model Morning Oasis Operate

Key lines 4–6 one time and then key the three lines again. Concentrate on control. The goals are to key at least 25 WAM and to make two or fewer errors. Your WAM rate will appear at the end of each line, and errors will be highlighted.

4 Does Norman Olson look for those options noted on the form?

5 The golf pro told the people to look for good golf partners.

6 The donations for the top ten projects are right on target.

Reinforcing Writing Skills

Headings allow readers to grasp the organization of written material. When readers easily grasp the organization of a manuscript or other type of document, there is a very good chance that they will retain the information. Wherever possible, use headers in the document you produce.

Practice adding headings to a report that is formatted in MLA style in the following document activity.

Document **Adding Headings to a Report**

57.2

1. Navigate to the Document 57.2 launch page in the Online Lab and then click the Launch Activity button. The Online Lab will open **Doc057.02** in the activity window.

2. Add four side headings to this document. Insert each at the left margin with one return before and after. Key each in regular text, capitalizing the first word and all other major words in the heading. Read the document to determine locations for the suggested headings and then insert them. The headings to insert are listed in no particular order below:

   - Mental Interface
   - Natural-Language Interface
   - Speech Recognition
   - Virtual Reality

3. Proofread the document and correct any errors. Do not allow headings to print at the bottom of the page, separated from the following paragraph. *Note: Use the Keep with next feature. Do not insert a hard page break.*

4. Save the document.

5. Click the Check button to upload the document for checking. The Online Lab will report the number of errors for the activity.

6. If errors are reported, view the results document, correct the errors in the submitted document, save the document, and then click the Check button.

Ending the Session

The Online Lab automatically saves the work you completed for this session. You may continue with the next session or exit the Online Lab and continue later.

Reinforcement Drill

Key the following drill lines one time. Press the Enter key after each line. The goals are to key at least 25 WAM and to make two or fewer errors. Your WAM rate will appear at the end of each line, and errors will be highlighted.

1 The malt that Pam made had milk and mint in it.

2 The fine farm animal, Sandman, had a marked limp.

3 Mail the letter at midnight and add ample stamps.

4 Is that smashed metal mass a damaged helmet, Jim?

5 As her mind dimmed, Minne missed the main message.

6 In April, Tonia Jones took her first plane ride to a remote island.

7 She told those on the longest list to find roommates for ten months.

8 Look for people that are doing the right things for the team.

9 The Golden Age is something to look for in their lifelong plans.

10 Look for the person that likes to do things that are not right.

Assessing Your Speed and Accuracy

Complete Timings 8.1 through 8.6 in the Online Lab to assess the skills you have learned in this session. Refer to the folowing paragraphs as you key.

The timing will start as soon as you begin keying the paragraph. Remember to press the Tab key at the start of the paragraph. If you finish keying the paragraph before the timing expires, press Enter and start keying the paragraph again.

When time expires, the Online Lab will give you a WAM rate and will show you any errors you made. The goals are to key at least 25 WAM and to make two or fewer errors. The results will be stored in your Timings Performance report.

Goals: 25 WAM and two or fewer errors

1-Minute Timings

Timing 8.1
Marna smelled the simmering meat. The steam permeated the air. She managed a small taste and smiled. The meat and milk might help that little girl and ease her pain.

Timing 8.2
As he firmed the damp earth at the tree, the miser imagined he heard a small sigh. Mirages in the misted marsh alarmed him. Grim fears emerged as his mindless tramping faltered.

Timing 8.3
Make that simple diagram first and then send a message in the mail. Tell that salesman that his latest remarks made the manager mad. The meeting impaired the imminent merger.

Figure 57.3 Report Content for Document 57.1—Continued

government controls of some type are enforced, rapid changes in technology will probably allow their circumvention. In the future, the questions of what should be done to control unacceptable internet content and who should undertake such control will continue to be widely discussed.

Figure 57.4 Source Content for Document 57.1

First Citation

Type of Source: Journal Article
Author: Kaplan, Jayne
Title: Computer Ethics: Facts, Figures, Ideas, and Influences
Journal Name: New Computing
Year: 2014
Pages: 34-42

Second Citation

Type of Source: Conference Proceedings
Author: Blumenfeld, Morry S.
Title: Robotic Development Update
Pages: 47-52
Year: 2014
Conference Publication Name: Engineering 2014 Conference
City: Milwaukee
Publisher: GEMS Publishing
Medium: Document

Third Citation

Type of Source: Document From Web site
Author: Sears, Kevin
Name of Web Page: Robots Making Robots
Name of Web Site: Lance Robotics
Year: 2014
Month: March
Day: 24
Year Accessed: 2014
Month Accessed: November
Day Accessed: 11

Timing 8.4 More and more people are looking for homes that are near shopping areas, homes with ample parking spots, and good mortgage rates. Realtors are eager to help people find their dream home.

Timing 8.5 Those people that are doing things to help others represent feelings that are not forgotten. The time spent doing things for others is one of the easier things to do that makes one feel good. It is important to help others.

Timing 8.6 Those people who fish together are often times looking for other lakes to get the fish that dreams are made of. These people tell great stories from their past fishing trips. Their trophies are important to them.

> **Ergonomic Tip**
> Position your monitor so that the top of the screen is no higher than your eye level.

Ending the Session

The Online Lab automatically saves the work you completed for this session. You can continue with the next session or exit the Online Lab and continue later.

Figure 57.3 Report Content for Document 57.1—Continued

The first generation of avatars, digital representations that look and talk like ordinary people, has already appeared. [insert Blumenfeld citation, page 47] Given the rapid advances in technological capabilities and artificial intelligence, predicting that avatars in the future will be indistinguishable from real human beings is not farfetched. This eventuality will pose a rash of ethical dilemmas. For example, should computer users necessarily be warned when they are dealing with an avatar and not a human being? Should avatars be prevented from emulating certain behaviors? In what ways might avatars be used by some for criminal activities, and how can such behavior be prevented? These are just a few of the numerous ethical questions arising from future developments in artificial intelligence.

Self-Replicating Robots

We already know that robots can be created to create other robots. [insert Sears citation] Such self-replication of technology has great potential to get out of hand, and it thus poses numerous ethical concerns. For instance, have we created a technology that might someday displace, dominate, or even eliminate humans? How can we know? These are some of the ethical questions concerning robots that will be debated in the near future.

Narrowing the digital Divide

While the digital divide between developed countries is narrowing, the gulf between developed and underdeveloped nations is still vast. Debate over how this gap is to be narrowed will continue. Should poorer nations be encouraged to concentrate on gaining basic needs, such as adequate electricity, communications, and health care infrastructures, or should they be encouraged to use available resources to develop digital technologies in order to "catch up" with developed nations? Will computer technologies truly benefit less developed societies and, if so, how? What role should developed nations play in providing and monitoring the dispersal of such technology?

Governmental Control of Internet content

Many people today are concerned about some of the content available on the internet. Children and vulnerable adults are especially at risk. Some governments, worried about losing control over what information their citizens can access, have already placed severe restrictions on Internet access and content. The question of whether or not the government should control internet content remains a topic of lively debate. The truth is that even if

continues

Session 9

U, B, W

Session Objectives

- Identify the U, B, and W keys
- Practice correct finger positioning for the U, B, and W keys
- Apply critical thinking quickly while keyboarding

Timing Goals

- 1 minute: 25 WAM and two or fewer errors

Getting Started and Warming Up

Exercise 9.1 If you are continuing immediately from Session 8, you may skip the Exercise 9.1 warm-up drill. However, if you exited the Online Lab at the end of Session 8, warm up by completing Exercise 9.1.

Introducing the U, B, and W Keys

Videos 9.1–9.3 The locations of the U, B, and W keys are shown in the following diagram. Watch Videos 9.1 through 9.3 and practice using these new keys.

Exercises 9.2–9.10 Complete Exercises 9.2 through 9.9 to learn these new keys. Also complete the thinking drill, Exercise 9.10. When keying the drill lines, follow the instruction prompts provided in the Online Lab.

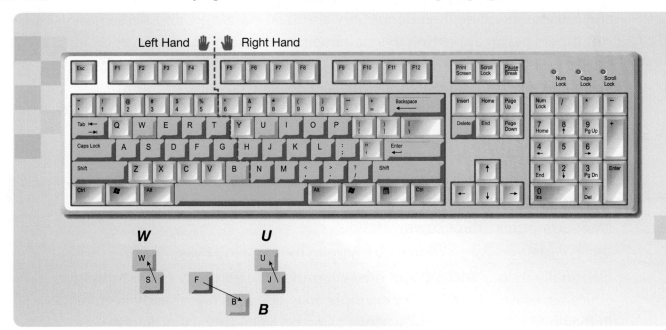

8 Insert a Works Cited page at the end of the document by completing the following steps:

   a Place the insertion point at the end of the document (Ctrl + End) and then insert a hard page break (Ctrl + Enter).

   b Center-align the insertion point and then key **Works Cited**.

   c Press Enter and set the text alignment to left aligned.

   d Click the Bibliography button in the Citations & Bibliography group on the References tab.

   e Click *Insert Bibliography.*

9 Proofread the document and correct any errors.

10 Save the document.

11 Click the Check button to stop the timer and upload the document for checking. The Online Lab will report the WAM rate and number of errors for the activity.

12 If errors are reported, view the results document, correct the errors in the submitted document, save the document, and then click the Check button.

Figure 57.3 Report Content for Document 57.1

Audrey Lopez

Amanda Schoen, MS

English 201

22 December 2014 (Enter)

Future of Computer Ethics (Enter)

(Tab) Computers and the transformations they engender have only recently entered into most people's lives. Large mainframes used by the government and businesses made their debut only about 50 years ago, and personal computers began appearing in small businesses and homes as recently as the early 1980s. While the precursor of the internet was created nearly 30 years ago, widespread use of the Internet and the creation of the world wide Web occurred during the past twenty years. The field of computer ethics has been developed to address ethical problems arising from new technologies. While accurately predicting the direction of such ethical considerations in the future is impossible, some general speculations can be made on emerging trends.

New Computer Ethics Laws

   Legislation is often slow to catch up to the reality of *daily* everyday life. Eventually it does catch up and this will prove true for many of the computer ethics issues we face today. For example, may attempts hae already been made in the united States to draft laws increasing personal privacy protection.

Artificial Intelligence and Avatars

continues

↺ Reinforcing Your Skills

Complete Exercises 9.11 through 9.14 in the Online Lab. Reference the drill lines from the textbook as you key and keep your eyes on the textbook pages, not on your fingers. Complete each exercise at least once, but repeat exercises if you need more practice.

Exercise 9.11

U Drill

Key each line two times and push for speed. The goal is to key at least 25 WAM. Your WAM rate will appear at the end of each line.

1 ju put put sun sun fun fun mud mud gum gum sum sum

2 under audit rumor truth about nurse sprung refund blunt

3 Fusion Lawful Nature Urgent Plural Module Suppose

Key lines 4–6 one time and then key the three lines again. Concentrate on control. The goals are to key at least 25 WAM and to make two or fewer errors. Your WAM rate will appear at the end of each line, and errors will be highlighted.

4 Just be sure to return that blouse to the bureau.

5 That auto bumper is a hunk of junk; it is ruined.

6 A stout runner shouted and slumped to the ground.

Exercise 9.12

B Drill

Key each line two times and push for speed. The goal is to key at least 25 WAM. Your WAM rate will appear at the end of each line.

1 fb bad bag ban bar bat bed beg Ben bet bid big bit

2 barter member harbor banker ballot border benefit brake

3 Alphabet Basement Neighbor Remember Remarkable Be

Key lines 4–6 one time and then key the three lines again. Concentrate on control. The goals are to key at least 25 WAM and to make two or fewer errors. Your WAM rate will appear at the end of each line, and errors will be highlighted.

4 I grabbed a dab of bread and biked to the harbor.

5 Babe is baffled; the beverage bottles are broken.

6 Barni, the beagle, barks and begs for a big bone.

Exercise 9.13

W Drill

Key each line two times and push for speed. The goal is to key at least 25 WAM. Your WAM rate will appear at the end of each line.

1 sw jaw wag raw two war wet saw hew how new sew snow

2 review warmer bowler wiring inward wisdom preview

3 Hardware Workable Weakness Endowment Two Window

drill continues

2 Change the document default formatting by completing the following steps:

   a Change the document's default line spacing to double spacing with no extra space before or after paragraphs. *Hint: Click the Set As Default button in the Paragraph dialog box and apply to this document only.*

   b Change the document default font to 12-point Times New Roman.

3 Create a header on all pages of the document by completing the following steps:

   a Click the Insert tab.

   b Click the Page Number button in the Header & Footer group.

   c Point to *Top of Page* and then click *Plain Number 3.*

   d With the insertion point immediately to the left of the plain page number, key **Lopez** and then press the space bar.

   e Double-click in the document to make the document active.

4 Set the document's style reference to *MLA Seventh Edition* by completing the following steps:

   a Click the References tab.

   b Click the *Style* list box down arrow in the Citations & Bibliography group.

   c Click *MLA Seventh Edition.*

5 Key the proofread report shown in Figure 57.3, implementing the proofreading marks. As you key the body of the report, key the source content shown in Figure 57.4. Insert the first citation and key the source information into the document by completing the following steps:

   a Place the insertion point in the first paragraph, after *as the early 1980s* and before the period at the end of the sentence.

   b Click the Insert Citation button in the Citations & Bibliography group on the References tab.

   c Click *Add New Source.*

   d In the Create Source dialog box, click the *Type of Source* down arrow and then click *Journal Article.*

   e Key the information for the first citation shown in Figure 57.4 in the fields in the *Bibliography Fields for MLA Seventh Edition* section of the Create Source dialog box.

   f Proofread the keyed information and then click OK.

   g Insert the page reference for the Kaplan citation by completing the following steps:

      1) Click the Kaplan citation in the document.

      2) Click the down arrow on the citation placeholder and then click *Edit Citation.*

      3) Key **36** in the *Pages* text box.

      4) Click OK.

6 Insert the second and third citations into the document, using the location information shown in Figure 57.3 and the source content shown in Figure 57.4. For the second citation, include the page reference *47*. There is no page reference for the third citation.

7 Set the heading *Governmental Control of Internet Content* to keep with the following paragraph.

steps continue

Key lines 4–6 one time and then key the three lines again. Concentrate on control. The goals are to key at least 25 WAM and to make two or fewer errors. Your WAM rate will appear at the end of each line, and errors will be highlighted.

4 Wear a warm gown if it snows; the weather is raw.

5 The new lawn will grow when watered well at dawn.

6 It is wise to wire the news to the waiting woman.

Exercise 9.14 Reinforcement Drill

Key lines 1 and 2 one time for speed. The goal is to key at least 25 WAM. Your WAM rate will appear at the end of each line.

1 ju put put sun sun fun fun mud mud gum gum sum sum

2 vault audit rumor truth about nurse sprung refund blunt

Key line 3 one time. Concentrate on control. The goal is to key at least 25 WAM. Your WAM rate will appear at the end of each line.

3 Fusion Lawful Nature Urgent Plural Module Suppose

Follow the previous procedures and key lines 4 and 5 one time for speed. Key line 6 one time for speed, while also concentrating on control.

4 Beneath the bridge in the brook, the bears bathed.

5 He is bitter and bleak; the dark banjo is broken.

6 A nimble rabbit blinks and nibbles bean blossoms.

Follow the previous procedures and key lines 7 and 8 one time for speed. Key line 9 one time for speed, while also concentrating on control.

7 Will Marlow wash in warm water that wool sweater?

8 With a white towel, Warren wiped the jeweled bowl.

9 If Win washes the new window, is he wasting water?

Exercise 9.15 Thinking Drill

Using the following initial letters, key as many words as you can think of that begin with the letters given.

bu   bi   wo   wh

Key the words in a list. Key all the "bu" words first, and then go to the next set of letters. Try to think of at least 10 words. If you can think of 20 to 30 words, that's great.

Figure 57.2 Completed Report for Document 57.1

Lopez 3

Governmental Control of Internet Content

Many people today are concerned about some of the content available on the Internet. Children and vulnerable adults are especially at risk. Some governments, worried about losing control over what information their citizens can access, have already placed severe restrictions on Internet access and content. The question of whether or not the government should control Internet content remains a topic of lively debate. The truth is that even if government controls of some type are enforced, rapid changes in technology will probably allow their circumvention. In the future, the questions of what should be done to control unacceptable Internet content and who should undertake such control will continue to be widely discussed.

Lopez 4

Works Cited

Blumenfeld, Morry S. "Robotic Development Update." *Engineering 2014 Conference*. Milwaukee: GEMS Publishing, 2014. 47-52. Document.

Kaplan, Jayne. "Computer Ethics: Facts, Figures, Ideas, and Influences." *New Computing* (2014): 34-42.

Sears, Kevin. "Robots Making Robots." 24 March 2014. *Lance Robotics*. 11 November 2014.

Lopez 1

Audrey Lopez

Amanda Schoen, MS

English 201

22 December 2014

Future of Computer Ethics

Computers and the transformations they engender have only recently entered into most people's lives. Large mainframes used by the government and businesses made their debut only about 50 years ago, and personal computers began appearing in small businesses and homes as recently as the early 1980s (Kaplan 89). While the precursor of the Internet was created nearly 30 years ago, widespread use of the Internet and the creation of the World Wide Web occurred during the past twenty years. The field of computer ethics has been developed to address ethical problems arising from new technologies. While accurately predicting the direction of such ethical considerations in the future is impossible, some general speculations can be made on emerging trends.

New Computer Ethics Laws

Legislation is often slow to catch up to the reality of daily life. Eventually it does catch up and this will prove true for many of the computer ethics issues we face today. For example, many attempts have already been made in the United States to draft laws increasing personal privacy protection.

Artificial Intelligence and Avatars

The first generation of avatars, digital representations that look and talk like ordinary people, has already appeared (Blumenfeld 47). Given the rapid advances in technological capabilities and artificial intelligence, predicting that avatars in the future will be

Lopez 2

indistinguishable from real human beings is not farfetched. This eventuality will pose a rash of ethical dilemmas. For example, should computer users necessarily be warned when they are dealing with an avatar and not a human being? Should avatars be prevented from emulating certain behaviors? In what ways might avatars be used by some for criminal activities, and how can such behavior be prevented? These are just a few of the numerous ethical questions arising from future developments in artificial intelligence.

Self-Replicating Robots

We already know that robots can be created to create other robots (Sears). Such self-replication of technology has great potential to get out of hand, and it thus poses numerous ethical concerns. For instance, have we created a technology that might someday displace, dominate, or even eliminate humans? How can we know? These are some of the ethical questions concerning robots that will be debated in the near future.

Narrowing the Digital Divide

While the digital divide between developed countries is narrowing, the gulf between developed and underdeveloped nations is still vast. Debate over how this gap is to be narrowed will continue. Should poorer nations be encouraged to concentrate on gaining basic needs, such as adequate electricity, communications, and healthcare infrastructures, or should they be encouraged to use available resources to develop digital technologies in order to "catch up" with developed nations? Will computer technologies truly benefit less developed societies and, if so, how? What role should developed nations play in providing and monitoring the dispersal of such technology?

Success Tip

A quick way to insert a hard page break in a document (such as at the end of a report, just before the Works Cited page) is to press Ctrl + Enter.

Document **Report with Citations and Works Cited Page in MLA Style**

57.1

1 Read all instructions for this document activity, navigate to the Document 57.1 launch page in the Online Lab, and then click the Launch Activity button. The Online Lab will open **Doc057.01** in the activity window. The timer will start as soon as you begin keying the document.

steps continue

Assessing Your Speed and Accuracy

Complete Timings 9.1 through 9.6 in the Online Lab to assess the skills you have learned in this session. Refer to the following paragraphs as you key.

The timing will start as soon as you begin keying the paragraph. Remember to press the Tab key at the start of the paragraph. If you finish keying the paragraph before the timing expires, press Enter and start keying the paragraph again.

When time expires, the Online Lab will give you a WAM rate and will show you any errors you made. The goals are to key at least 25 WAM and to make two or fewer errors. The results will be stored in your Timings Performance report.

Goals: 25 WAM and two or fewer errors

1-Minute Timings

Timing 9.1

The blunt auditor suggested to Duke that the business returns were a fraud. The usual routine of minimum turnovers of funds had been sound, but that fortune of thousands paid to a juror had not been inserted in the annual input. Duke presumed he was ruined and flushed with guilt.

Timing 9.2

Ruth sulked as her aunt poured a dose of the awful blue fluid. The sour stuff was supposed to be used for fatigue from the flu. She paused for a minute and gulped it down. Her aunt found four lumps of sugar for a bonus. Sullen disgust would turn into a laugh as a result.

Timing 9.3

Biff booked a berth on the battered boat. As he bragged to his somber brother, the boom of the harbor bells vibrated. Beneath the boasting, Biff began to babble. A belated bolt of disbelief and brooding stabbed at him.

Timing 9.4

Labor to do a noble job. Bosses like brains and ambition. A blend of both brings a desirable habit that boosts a beginner. A babbling boaster absorbs a bore. The absent laborer blemishes his possible bankroll boost.

Timing 9.5

We will await the word of warning in the new tower. The wise, stalwart leader wants to preview the writings of men of worth. He frowns on wrong narrow views. We will follow wise wishes and win a wearisome war and bestow a renewed foothold.

Timing 9.6

Will reviewed the written words. He did not wish to show that witless newsman how shallow his words were. However, he wanted to warn the world of the wasted wealth in the wages of the man. He showed the network the handwriting on the wall.

Creating a Works Cited Page According to MLA Style

Once the citations and source information are entered for a report, Word provides tools to help you compile the cited sources to list at the end of the document. In Session 56, you created a bibliography according to *The Chicago Manual of Style, Sixteenth Edition's* format. In this session, you will create a listing of sources according to the MLA style. According to MLA style, the bibliography listing is placed on a separate page at the end of the paper and is titled *Works Cited*. The title is centered and like the other headings in the report, the title is not set in bold. Also, the text of the Works Cited page is double-spaced with no extra spaces after paragraphs, to match the format of the body of the report.

To create the Works Cited page for a report that contains citations, complete the following steps:

1 Place the insertion point at the end of the document (Ctrl + End) and then insert a hard page break (Ctrl + Enter).

2 With the insertion point at the top of the new page, center-align the insertion point (press Ctrl + E) and then key **Works Cited**.

3 Press Enter and then set the text alignment to left aligned (press Ctrl + L).

4 Click the References tab.

5 Click the Bibliography button in the Citations & Bibliography group.

6 Click *Insert Bibliography*.

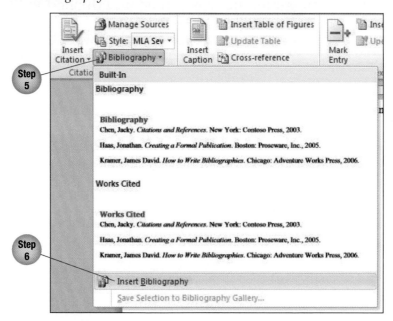

If the document default line spacing has been changed to double spacing with no additional space following paragraphs, then the references list that Word generates from the document's sources will have the same line spacing. In the following document activity, you will key a report, add citations and sources, and then use Word to generate the Works Cited page listing the sources at the end of the document. Figure 57.2 shows a thumbnail of the final document. Notice that the author's name and a page number appear on all of the pages of the document.

Ergonomic Tip

Experiment with your foreground and background screen colors to find the combination that is most comfortable for you. Avoid using light-colored characters on the screen. Instead, use dark characters on a light-colored background.

Ending the Session

The Online Lab automatically saves the work you completed for this session. You can continue with the next session or exit the Online Lab and continue later.

4 Click the Insert Citation button in the Citations & Bibliography group on the References tab.

5 Click *Add New Source* to open the Create Source dialog box.

6 Click the *Type of Source* list box down arrow and then click the type of source from the drop-down list.

7 Key the necessary information in the *Bibliography Fields for MLA Seventh Edition* section of the Create Source dialog box. If necessary, click the *Show All Bibliography Fields* check box to expand the Create Source dialog box and display more fields for the source.

8 Click OK.

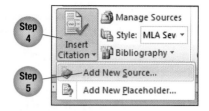

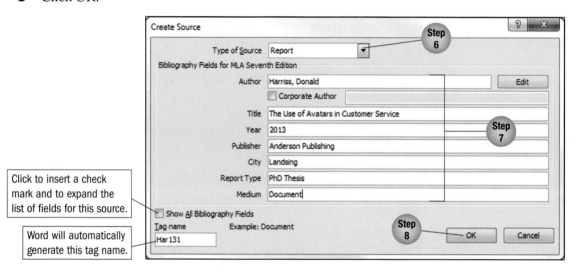

Click to insert a check mark and to expand the list of fields for this source.

Word will automatically generate this tag name.

Once a citation and the corresponding source information have been entered into the Create Source dialog box, add a page reference to the in-text citation by completing the following steps:

1 Click on the citation reference in the document to highlight the field code.

2 Click the down arrow and then click *Edit Citation*.

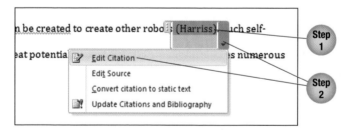

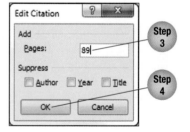

3 Key the page reference in the *Pages* text box in the *Add* section of the Edit Citation dialog box.

4 Click OK.

After completing these steps, the citation will appear in the body of the document, with no comma between the author's last name and the page reference, according to MLA style.

If after creating a citation and inserting source information, you find that a change or correction is needed to the source, click the citation to make it active, click the citation down arrow, and then click *Edit Source* to open the Edit Source dialog box. The previously keyed source information displays and can be edited.

Session 10

Skills Reinforcement and Proficiency Exercises: Sessions 1–9

☽ Session Objectives

- Review and practice correct finger positioning for the Sessions 1–9 keys
- Employ successful keyboarding skills to build speed and accuracy

Timing Goals

- 1 minute: 25 WAM and two or fewer errors

Getting Started and Warming Up

Exercise 10.1

If you are continuing immediately from Session 9, you may skip the warm-up drill at the start of this session. However, if you exited the Online Lab at the end of Session 9, warm up by completing Exercise 10.1.

The purpose of this session is to reinforce the keyboarding skills you have developed in the previous sessions. The timings in this session will help you to determine where you are in your skill development, and the exercises in the session provide you with the opportunity to further work on improving your skill and accuracy, if you have not reached the target goals.

Assessing Your Speed and Accuracy

Complete Timings 10.1 and 10.2 in the Online Lab using the paragraph below. In the Online Lab, you will start with a practice screen that you can use to practice keying the timing text without the timer. When you have completed your practice, prompt the Online Lab to begin Timing 10.1. Both timings will use the same paragraph. Once you are on an active timing screen, the timing will start as soon as you begin keying.

Remember to press the Tab key at the beginning of the paragraph. Also, do not press Enter at the end of each line, but only at the end of the paragraph. If you finish keying the paragraph before the timing expires, press Enter and start keying the paragraph again.

When time expires, the Online Lab will give you a WAM rate and will show you any errors you made. The goals are to key at least 25 WAM and to make two or fewer errors. The results of both timings will be stored in your Timings Performance report.

Goals: 25 WAM and two or fewer errors

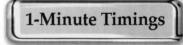
1-Minute Timings

Timings 10.1–10.2

When the winter snow thaws, warm rain washes the world. Wild flowers begin to flutter in a slow swing with the wind. Whiffs of a meadow awakened swirl down at the dawn. The dew is a rainbow and twinkles as a jewel. Winter has blown onward.

Figure 57.1 First-Page Formatting of a MLA Report   *Note: Do not key this document.*

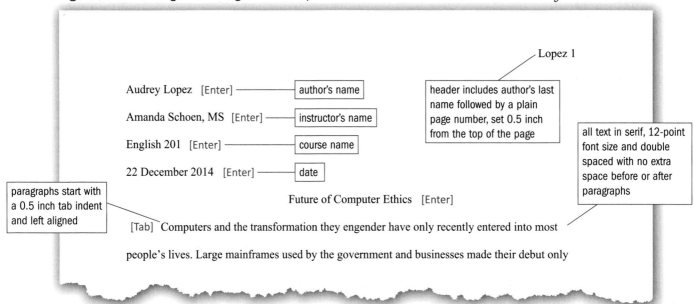

Audrey Lopez [Enter] ——— author's name

Amanda Schoen, MS [Enter] ——— instructor's name

English 201 [Enter] ——— course name

22 December 2014 [Enter] ——— date

Lopez 1

header includes author's last name followed by a plain page number, set 0.5 inch from the top of the page

all text in serif, 12-point font size and double spaced with no extra space before or after paragraphs

paragraphs start with a 0.5 inch tab indent and left aligned

Future of Computer Ethics [Enter]

[Tab] Computers and the transformation they engender have only recently entered into most

people's lives. Large mainframes used by the government and businesses made their debut only

Inserting In-Text Citations According to MLA Style

When using MLA style for in-text citations, the citations should include the author's last name and the page number where the information occurs in the source. The author's name might appear either in the sentence itself or in parentheses following the quote or paraphrase, but the page number(s) should always be in the parentheses rather than in the text of a sentence. A corresponding complete reference should also appear on the Works Cited page at the end of the manuscript or research paper.

Word automates the formatting process for inserting in-text citations and allows you to use these citations at the end of the report in a Works Cited page. To insert an initial in-text citation for a source that is in a report using MLA Seventh Edition style, complete the following steps:

1   Click the References tab.

2   Click the *Style* list box down arrow and then click *MLA Seventh Edition* from the drop-down list of styles.

3   Place the insertion point in the report, where you want the citation to be placed. For example, place the insertion point just before the period at the end of the sentence that is being credited.

steps continue

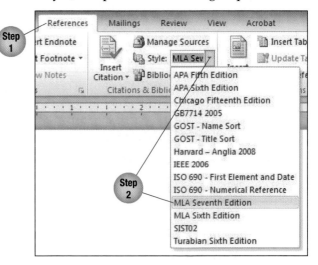

⟳ Reinforcing Your Skills

The following speed and accuracy drills provide additional practice on the keys you have learned in Sessions 7–9. If you successfully keyed Timings 10.1 and 10.2 with a 25 WAM or higher and with two or fewer errors and you do not hesitate while keying, proceed to Session 11. However, if your WAM and error rates do not match these goals, the speed and accuracy drills in this section will give you the opportunity for further practice.

If you have not mastered a key reach (you hesitate before striking the key) or if you are not keying at least 25 WAM, key the speed drills, Exercises 10.2 through 10.4. If you are committing more than two errors per minute, key the accuracy drills, Exercises 10.5 and 10.6.

Speed Drills

For the speed drills, key each line one time and try to make your fingers go faster as you key the lines. After practicing the speed drills, either continue by completing the accuracy drills or go directly to Timing 10.3 to see if your speed has improved.

Exercise 10.2 Keys Review Drill

Key each line one time. Focus on speed.

1 asdf jkl; ;p; frf jmj fbf lol fbf sws pr mt db wm

2 p pad pan peg pen pin pit pie plan phase pledge plane

3 r rap ran red rip rent rests real repels refers roam rope

4 m ham hem men him mate mind mesh manage mandate

5 u up upper under urge utmost unit utter until untold umpire

6 o oh or odd old one oaf opens omit ogle order of oblong

7 b bad beg bid bop brag blend board brake better bowl

8 w was wed who win woe were when went where with

9 Shannon Olan Bronson George Janet Kent Martin John

Exercise 10.3 Balanced-Hand Words Drill

Key each line one time. Focus on speed.

1 lamb blend bland blame amble emblem problem bible

2 lap nap pen paid pane flap span pale spent dispel

3 air pan sir risks lair heir pair hair flair widow

4 map maid mane melt sham lame mend firm make flame

5 due burn turn dug fuel tug rug Bud bug gut guru bus rub tub

6 fog sod oak rod foam fork form foam odor soak rod

drill continues

Formatting in MLA Style

The reports created in this session will follow the format outlined according to the *Modern Language Association (MLA) Handbook*. Table 57.1 and Figure 57.1 provide some key formatting guidelines for the MLA style.

Table 57.1 MLA Formatting Guidelines for Research Papers

Paper Element	Formatting Guidelines
Text Alignment	Left aligned, paragraphs begin with 0.5-inch tab (see Figure 57.1)
Font	12-point, serif font such as Cambria, Bookman Old Style, Times New Roman, or Palatino Linotype (see Figure 57.1)
Margins	Default: 1-inch top, bottom, left, and right margins
Line Spacing	2.0 line spacing (with 0 points extra spacing before and after paragraphs) throughout document, including Works Cited page (see Figure 57.1)
Title Page	Not used. Instead, the information is included on the first page of the report.
First Page of Report	Includes author's name, instructor's name, course name, and date, each on one line and flush left (see Figure 57.1)
Report Title	Begins one Enter after the date, center in plain text (no bold or italic formatting) and key the title capitalizing the first letter of each major word. Press Enter once.
Header/Page Numbers	Header is set 0.5 inch from the top of the document and at the right margin and includes the writer's last name followed by one space and the page number (digits only, see Figure 57.1). Numbering the first page may be optional, depending on guidelines provided by the person requesting the manuscript or research paper.
Side Headings	Not required by the MLA style, but may be used to increase the document's readability. When headings are included, it is important to use consistent formatting throughout the document.
Long Quotations	Quotes longer than four lines should be introduced with a colon and indented one inch from the left margin.

7 bow wig wow vow down gown wisp with wish when wit

8 Did the lame lamb amble down to the big pale oak?

9 The pale widow paid for the vivid gown and a wig.

10 When did Bob mend the pair of problem emblems?

Exercise 10.4 · Two-Letter Combinations Drill

Key each line one time. Focus on speed.

1 pe peg pen pest pets pert peso petite petition

2 pi pin pie piles pipes pink pine pig piston pilot

3 That petite person with pets had piles of pinkish pills.

4 ra ran rap ranks rake rates raised range rapid random

5 ri rid rip rises ripe right ridges rigid rinse rigs rim

6 Rapid Red ran to the raised ridges on that range.

7 ma man mat math make mail marsh manager margin

8 mi mid mild mind mint midst might misting mire mite

9 The manager might mail the mild mints to the man.

10 bu bud bus bun burn bust butter bullet build button builder

11 du due duke dust dull dud dues dumb dusk duo dunk dug

12 The bus tour took us to Utah to see multiple mountain ranges

13 oa oak oats oath oatmeal load toad roast float oasis

14 The oath at the oak tree oasis was about oats.

15 ba bad bag bail balk bath badge barks bandages bald

16 bl blade bleak blast blank blight blind blinks blow

17 The bat blinked at a baboon blinded in bandages.

18 wa was war wag wade wait wane wash waste warm want

19 wi win wit wig wide wipe will wise wield wiper window

20 Winna washed and wiped her window; she wasted water.

Complete two 5-minute timings on the timing text below. Timings 57.3 and 57.4 use the same paragraphs.

Goals: 35 WAM and five or fewer errors
SI: 1.40 syllables per word

5-Minute Timings

Timings 57.3–57.4

Do you use the Quick Access Toolbar in Microsoft Office? Save, Undo, and Redo are the default commands that appear when Microsoft Office is installed. Are you aware that you can add commands that you use frequently? For example, you might consider adding the Open and Close commands to avoid having to access the File tab each time you want to open or close a document.

To add a command to the Quick Access Toolbar, click the tab or group to display the command you want to add. Right-click the command and then click Add to Quick Access Toolbar from the shortcut menu. It is really as easy as that! Removing commands is even quicker. Just right-click the button to delete and choose Remove from Quick Access Toolbar from the shortcut menu.

You may want to rearrange the items on that toolbar. To do so, right-click anywhere on the Quick Access Toolbar and click Customize the Quick Access Toolbar. Under Customize Quick Access Toolbar on the right side of the dialog box, select the command you want to relocate, and then click the Move Up or Move Down arrow to position it where you want.

Perhaps you find that the Quick Access Toolbar's original location next to the program icon is too far from the document area to be convenient. If so, you might want to move it closer. Right-click anywhere on the toolbar and select Show Quick Access Toolbar Below the Ribbon. Try that for a few days before forming an opinion. Some users feel that putting this toolbar below the ribbon takes away room from the work area. Because it is so easy to change its location, you can move it when you feel it necessary.

Ergonomic Tip
Check your posture periodically. Relax the muscles in your forearms, shoulders, and neck by sitting straight up or leaning back in your chair. Stand up and stretch every 20 minutes.

Accuracy Drills

For the accuracy drills, key each line one time and concentrate on control as you key. After practicing the accuracy drills, go directly to Timing 10.3 to see if your accuracy has improved.

Exercise 10.5 **Double-Letter Words Drill**

Key each group of lines one time.

1 slipping sipping happen flipping appease shipping
2 terriers irritates terrains follow all twitter
3 dimmer dinners hammering manners immense immerges

4 moon roof pool hood hook loot took mood root door
5 gobble rabble hobble babble pebble nibbles rabbit
6 of off offers offends offset offense offering offside

7 Janelle slipped the irritated terrier in the door.
8 That immense rabbit followed and nibbled a bottle.
9 She will be shipping the poor winter winner soon.

Exercise 10.6 **Longer Words Drill**

Key each group of lines one time.

1 elephant dependent safekeeping plaintiff pipeline
2 standard registrar parenthesis telegrams resident
3 That resident registrar sends standard telegrams.

4 familiar eliminate sentimental dependent estimate
5 immigration minimum fumigate memorial intimidated
6 Eliminate that sentimental, familiar newspaper.

7 rational tradition imagination negotiate international
8 ambition elaborate independent establish possible
9 stalwart knowledge handwriting wholesale whenever
10 Establish rational imagination when possible.

Preparing Manuscripts in MLA Style

Session Objectives

- Format a manuscript according to MLA style
- Insert source information and in-text citations in a manuscript
- Create a Works Cited page
- Add headings to a report

Timing Goals

- 1 minute: 45 WAM and one or no errors
- 5 minutes: 35 WAM and five or fewer errors

Getting Started and Warming Up

Exercise 57.1 If you are continuing immediately from Session 56, you may skip the Exercise 57.1 warm-up drill. However, if you exited the Online Lab at the end of Session 56, warm up by completing Exercise 57.1.

Exercise 57.2 Begin your session work by completing Exercise 57.2, a timed short drill, in the Online Lab.

Assessing Your Speed and Accuracy

Complete Timings 57.1 through 57.4 in the Online Lab. At the end of each timing, the Online Lab will display your WAM rate and any errors. Results will be saved in your Timings Performance report. If you have been surpassing the speed and accuracy goals, set slightly more challenging personal goals and strive to exceed them.

Complete two 1-minute timings on the timing text below. Timings 57.1 and 57.2 use the same paragraph.

Goals: 45 WAM and one or no errors
SI: 1.40 syllables per word

1-Minute Timings

Timings 57.1–57.2

In Australia's Northern Territory, it may appear that an 18-foot-long snake is undulating across the desert. In reality it may be a trail of more than 100 caterpillars lined up head to tail, marching endlessly over the sand. When the food supply runs low, the insects strike out in single file to find another source of food. Traveling mostly at night, the insects march in a straight line seeming never to stop. They have little to fear.

Assessing Your Speed and Accuracy

Now that you have practiced the appropriate speed and accuracy drills, complete two 1-minute timings using the following paragraph. Note that this is the same text keyed for Timings 10.1 and 10.2.

Each timing will start as soon as you begin keying the paragraph. Remember to press the Tab key at the start of the paragraph. If you finish keying the paragraph before the timing expires, press Enter and start keying the paragraph again.

When time expires, the Online Lab will give you a WAM rate and will show you any errors you made in the keyed text.

The results of your timings will be stored in your Timings Performance report. Compare your rates from Timings 10.3 and 10.4 to your rates from Timings 10.1 and 10.2. Has your speed improved? Do you have fewer errors? If you are not reaching at least 25 WAM with two or fewer errors, repeat Sessions 7–9.

Goals: 25 WAM and two or fewer errors

1-Minute Timings

Timings 10.3–10.4

When the winter snow thaws, warm rain washes the world. Wild flowers begin to flutter in a slow swing with the wind. Whiffs of a meadow awakened swirl down at the dawn. The dew is a rainbow and twinkles as a jewel. Winter has blown onward.

Success Tip
As noted, repeat Sessions 7–9 if you did not reach 25 WAM with two or fewer errors. Without these skills, it will take you longer to master keyboarding.

Ergonomic Tip
Focus directly on your paper copy by placing it on a copyholder rather than flat on the work surface.

Ending the Session

The Online Lab automatically saves the work you completed for this session. You can continue with the next session or exit the Online Lab and continue later.

3   Key the citation information presented in Figure 56.6. The information for each entry is listed in the correct sequence, but it should be formatted according to the guidelines provided in Table 56.5.

4   Proofread and correct any errors in the document.

5   Save the document.

6   Click the Check button to upload the document for checking. The Online Lab will report the number of errors for the activity.

7   If errors are reported, view the results document, correct the errors in the submitted document, save the document, and then click the Check button.

Figure 56.6 Bibliography Content for Document 56.4

Web Page
Julie Bellman-Lancaster
My Teaching Experience in Saudi Arabia
Overseas Teaching, Inc.
Accessed November 12, 2014
www.emcp.net/teachingoverseas/opportunities.html

Periodical
Lisa Skarlupka
Dealing with Difficult People
Today's Administrative Assistant
October 2013

Book
Ron Tunby and Duane Cooper
Work for the United States Postal Service
Rochester, New York
ABC Publishing
2013

Ending the Session

The Online Lab automatically saves the work you completed for this session. You may continue with the next session or exit the Online Lab and continue later.

V, Z, C

Session Objectives

- Identify the Z, C, and V keys
- Practice correct finger positioning for the V, Z, and C keys
- Explore using the correct -ed and -ing endings for verbs while keyboarding

Timing Goals

- 1 minute: 25 WAM and two or fewer errors

Getting Started and Warming Up

Exercise 11.1 If you are continuing immediately from Session 10, you may skip the Exercise 11.1 warm-up drill. However, if you exited the Online Lab at the end of Session 10, warm up by completing Exercise 11.1.

Introducing the V, Z, and C Keys

Videos 11.1–11.3 The locations of the V, Z, and C keys are shown in the following diagram. Watch Videos 11.1 through 11.3 and practice using these new keys.

Exercises 11.2–11.10 Complete Exercises 11.2 through 11.9 to learn these new keys. Also complete the thinking drill, Exercise 11.10. When keying the drill lines, follow the instruction prompts provided in the Online Lab.

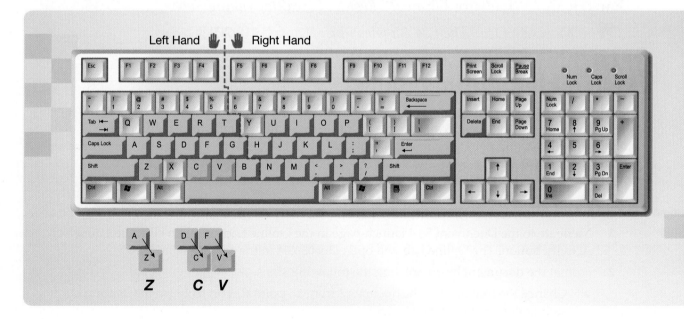

4 Key the text in Figure 56.5. *Note: In order for the Hanging Indent feature to work properly, do not press the Enter key at the end of each line to match the word wrap in Figure 56.5. Rather, let the lines wrap automatically. Your lines will wrap differently than they do in Figure 56.5.*

   a To ensure consistency in the document checking, do not apply italic formatting to the punctuation following an italic title or to the space following the title.

   b Do not format the web address as a hyperlink.

5 Proofread the document and correct any errors. With Show/Hide ¶ on, check the spacing after punctuation marks and confirm that the punctuation mark formatting is correct.

6 Save the document.

7 Click the Check button to stop the timer and upload the document for checking. The Online Lab will report the WAM rate and number of errors for the activity.

8 If errors are reported, view the results document, correct the errors in the submitted document, save the document, and then click the Check button.

Figure 56.5 Bibliography Content for Document 56.3

Bouchard, Mary Lou. "Writing a Research Paper." *Everything You Should Know about Reporting Research*. Accessed July 14, 2015. [Shift + Enter] http://www.emcp.net/researchforstudents/writing-a-research-paper.html.

Livingston, Alexandra R. *Living Your Values*. Denver: Marchant Publishing International, 2013.

Mitchell, William, Patricia King, and Ronald Kapper. *Keyboarding & Applications I*. St. Paul: Paradigm Publishing, Inc., 2012.

Pauk, Jean. "What's for Dinner?" *Fast and Healthy Family Foods*, June 2015.

"Time Marches On." *The Los Angeles Flyer*, March 10, 2013.

Reinforcing Writing Skills

In addition to the challenge of researching and writing research papers, actually keying them is also challenging, especially because of the attention to detail needed when creating the bibliography. In the following document activity, you will take a list of source citation information for a research paper about careers and key it into a bibliography document using the style guidelines presented in the *Preparing a Bibliography* section of this session.

Document 56.4

Editing and Keying a Bibliography Page

1 Navigate to the Document 56.4 launch page in the Online Lab and then click the Launch Activity button. The Online Lab will open **Doc056.04** in the activity window.

2 Format the document by completing the following steps:

   a Change the font used in the document from 11-point Calibri to 12-point Cambria by setting the document default font.

   b Set a hanging indent at the default 0.5 inch.

   c Center-align and bold the correct heading.

steps continue

↻ Reinforcing Your Skills

Complete Exercises 11.12 through 11.15 in the Online Lab. Reference the drill lines from the textbook as you key and keep your eyes on the textbook pages, not on your fingers. Complete each exercise at least once, but repeat exercises if you want to improve your WAM rate or accuracy.

Exercise 11.11

V Drill

Key each drill line two times and push for speed. The goal is to key at least 25 WAM. Your WAM rate will appear at the end of each line.

1 vi vim vigor vital vault vain prove provide various volume
2 love Viking violent van vote viable prove Vivian leave
3 Vermont Marvel Vernon Vitamin November Paved

Key lines 4–6 one time and then key the three lines again. Concentrate on control. The goals are to key at least 25 WAM and to make two or fewer errors. Your WAM rate will appear at the end of each line, and any errors will be highlighted.

4 Vernon voted for the woman from Nevada in November.
5 Violet varnished twelve Vermont made shelves in five hours.
6 Nevada living is interesting, invigorating, and motivating.

Exercise 11.12

Z Drill

Key each drill line two times and push for speed. The goal is to key at least 25 WAM. Your WAM rate will appear at the end of each line.

1 az maze maze doze doze raze raze zip zebra zest
2 seize breeze amaze razor hazel zombies wizard zing zane
3 Trapeze Zealous Pretzel Horizon Zealous Zenith

Key lines 4–6 one time and then key the three lines again. Concentrate on control. The goals are to key at least 25 WAM and to make two or fewer errors. Your WAM rate will appear at the end of each line, and any errors will be highlighted.

4 Liz seized that sizzling pizza and ate with zeal.
5 Minimize the hazard and stabilize that bulldozer.
6 Zeb baked a dozen pretzels in the sizzling blaze.

Exercise 11.13

C Drill

Key each drill line two times and push for speed. The goal is to key at least 25 WAM. Your WAM rate will appear at the end of each line.

1 ca calk cane case calf camp carp cave cede cad came
2 camera notice impact circle decide zinc clock corner
3 Compare Produce Consult Service Council Enclosure Carl

drill continues

Table 56.5 Bibliography Citations According to *The Chicago Manual of Style*, *Sixteenth Edition*

Books

Author Last Name, Author First Name. *Book Title*. City of Publication: Publisher, Year.

Example of single-author book:

    Livingston, Alexandra R. *Living Your Values*. Denver: Marchant Publishing International, 2013.

Example of multiple-author book (only first author's name is reversed):

    Mitchell, William, Patricia King, and Ronald Kapper. *Keyboarding & Applications I*. St. Paul: Paradigm Publishing, Inc., 2012.

Articles from Magazines

Author Last Name, Author First Name. "Article Title." *Name of Magazine*, Month Year.

Example of single-author article:

    Pauk, Jean. "What's for Dinner?" *Fast and Healthy Family Foods*, June 2015.

Example when no author is listed:

    "Time Marches On." *The Los Angeles Flyer*, March 10, 2013.

Web Pages

Author Last Name, Author First Name. "Web Page Title." *Name of Website*. Accessed Date. [Shift + Enter] http://www.address.

Example:

    Bouchard, Mary Lou. "Writing a Research Paper." *Everything You Should Know About Reporting Research*. Accessed July 14, 2014. http://www.emcp.net/researchforstudents/writing-a-research-paper.html.

 Success Tip

Being able to follow detailed formatting directions will make it easy for you to adapt to any writer's reference or style manual procedures.

Document

56.3

Bibliography Page

1. Read all instructions for this document activity, navigate to the Document 56.3 launch page in the Online Lab, and then click the Launch Activity button. The Online Lab will open **Doc056.03** in the activity window. The timer will start as soon as you begin keying the document.

2. Format the document by completing the following steps:

    a. Change the font used in the document from 11-point Calibri to 12-point Bookman Old Style. Make this setting the default for only this document.

    b. Set a hanging indent at the default 0.5 inch.

3. Type the title of the document by completing the following steps:

    a. Center-align the insertion point, turn on bold, and then key **BIBLIOGRAPHY**.

    b. Turn off bold formatting and then press Enter.

    c. Change text alignment to left aligned.

steps continue

Key lines 4–6 one time and then key the three lines again. Concentrate on control. The goals are to key at least 25 WAM and to make two or fewer errors. Your WAM rate will appear at the end of each line, and any errors will be highlighted.

> 4 Carlton, the cat, curled in comfort in the chair.
>
> 5 Chris decided to purchase a record and a picture.
>
> 6 Cecelia consumed a rich chocolate ice cream cone.

Exercise 11.14

Reinforcement Drill

Key lines 1 and 2 one time for speed. The goal is to key at least 25 WAM. Your WAM rate will appear at the end of each line.

> 1 She loves violet vases in various rooms and on her veranda.
>
> 2 Voices were overheard coming from the five oval offices.

Key line 3 one time. Concentrate on control. The goals are to key at least 25 WAM and to make two or fewer errors. Your WAM rate will appear at the end of each line. Any errors will be highlighted.

> 3 Victor was a victim of violent actions by Marv and Vernon.

✓ Success Tip

When keying for control, try to make fewer than two errors in a line. Be sure to keep your eyes on the copy in the textbook as you key.

Follow the previous procedures and key lines 4 and 5 one time for speed. Key line 6 one time for speed, while also concentrating on control.

> 4 Hazel won the prize as Buzz gazed with amazement.
>
> 5 The freezing drizzle glazed the bronze zinnias.
>
> 6 Hal has been penalized after embezzling a zillion.

Follow the previous procedures and key lines 7 and 8 one time for speed. Key line 9 one time for speed, while also concentrating on control.

> 7 With tonic and citric acid, can Carrie cure colds?
>
> 8 Could the clever client conceal crucial evidence?
>
> 9 A crow circled the cottage as Vivian watched with caution.

Guidelines for Formatting the Bibliography Page

The format for entries in a bibliography may vary slightly from one research style manual to another. Organizations, educational institutions, or instructors may require a very specific format. Always consult your employer or instructor for the preferred style to be followed.

When setting up a bibliography listing for documents in this unit, use the following guidelines:

- Use default margins, line spacing, and paragraph spacing.
- Use the same font as the body of the research paper.
- Set a 0.5-inch hanging indent so that the second and additional lines of a bibliography entry will be indented from the left margin.
- Center and key the title *BIBLIOGRAPHY* in bold text at the top of the document page.
- Begin each entry at the left margin.
- List bibliography entries alphabetically, according to the author's last name.
- Use standard spacing after punctuation marks—space once after periods, question marks, and colons.
- End each entry with a period and press Enter once before beginning the next entry.

Guidelines for Listing Sources in a Bibliography

There are many different types of sources that may be used in the development of a manuscript or research paper. Table 56.4 lists examples of sources that may be included in a bibliography.

Bibliographic details for the sources listed in Table 56.4 may vary, but each entry should include the author, title, and publication facts for the resource. List the sources on the bibliography page alphabetically by the author's last name. If no author is listed, use the first word in the title for alphabetizing.

When formatting titles of publications, follow the same guidelines as stated previously for footnotes:

- Use italic formatting to indicate an entire publication such as a book, newspaper, or periodical.
- Use quotation marks around the name of a chapter, article, short story, essay, or poem to indicate a source contained within another publication (such as a book).

The writing style manual required or recommended for a research paper will include very specific details for listing nearly every imaginable resource. In this session, you will be using only books, periodicals, and web pages. Study the examples shown in Table 56.5 to guide your formatting of bibliography references when using *The Chicago Manual of Style* as your style guide.

Table 56.4 Types of Sources to Be Referenced in a Bibliography

Art, sound recording	Electronic source
Article in a periodical	Film or video
Blog	Interview
Book	Journal or periodical article
Book section	Patent
Case	Performance
Conference proceedings	Report
Document from a website	Website

Assessing Your Speed and Accuracy

Complete Timings 11.1 through 11.6 in the Online Lab to assess the skills you have learned in this session. Refer to the following paragraphs as you key.

The timing will start as soon as you begin keying the paragraph. Remember to press the Tab key at the start of the paragraph. If you finish keying the paragraph before the timing expires, press Enter and start keying the paragraph again.

When time expires, the Online Lab will give you a WAM rate and will show you any errors you made in the keyed text. The goals are to key at least 25 WAM and to make two or fewer errors. The results will be stored in your Timings Performance report.

Goals: 25 WAM and two or fewer errors

1-Minute Timings

Timing 11.1
Traveling in this vast native land is a near marvel. The savage rivers and various paved miles are impressive. Vivid sights revive the mind and lift spirits. Villages reveal veiled vestiges; a dividend is derived.

Timing 11.2
Even if Gavin is vain, she has avid fans and attentive friends. Her singing is sensitive; she reveals her vast talent. She deserves lavish and vivid praise. Her versatile verses are a massive advantage and elevate her fevered fans.

Timing 11.3
Zeb zipped to that zoo with zest and nuzzled the zebras. He sneezed in the breeze and went to see the lizards. He wants to be a zoologist when he gets older. He knows a zillion things and his dazed and puzzled parents are amazed.

Timing 11.4
Zelda gazed in amazement as Zip, the wizard, seized a wand. It was ablaze with a maze of fire and lights. He did dozens of hazardous feats and puzzled all at the bazaar. He also was a trapeze whiz and dazzled folks.

Timing 11.5
A cookout on the beach could include cheese, carrots, meat sandwiches, and cold juice. If the chill of the ocean is too much, hot chocolate and hot coffee can chase the cold chills. The decent lunch and a chat with chums can enrich affection.

Timing 11.6
An office clerk who lacks basic ethics could become the subject of scorn. Those persisting in cruel and careless attacks on certain new workers can cause havoc. It is logical to follow strict, concise rules concerning office tact. Choose the right track and be sincere.

heading from being cut off from its following paragraph, the heading can be formatted to force Word to keep it with the following text. Most often, the Keep with next formatting will move the heading to the following page.

To format a heading so it stays with the next paragraph, complete the following steps:

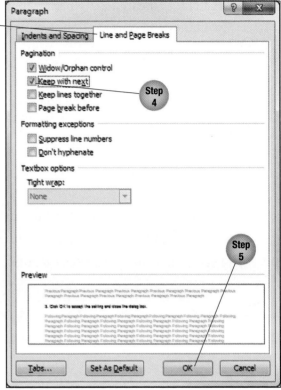

1   Click anywhere within the heading.

2   Click the Paragraph dialog box launcher in the Paragraph group on the Home tab.

3   Click the Line and Page Breaks tab.

4   Click the *Keep with next* check box in the *Pagination* section to insert a check mark.

5   Click OK to accept the setting and close the dialog box.

Practice controlling the pagination of a document in the following document activity.

Document 56.2

Unbound Manuscript with Font and Pagination Changes

1   Read all instructions for this document activity, navigate to the Document 56.2 launch page in the Online Lab, and then click the Launch Activity button. The Online Lab will open **Doc056.02** in the activity window.

2   Change the font used in the document from Cambria to Bookman Old Style by setting the document default font. *Note: It is not necessary to select all of the text to change the document default font.*

3   Format the *Procedure* heading so that it stays with the following paragraph by applying the *Keep with next* option on the Line and Page Breaks tab in the Paragraph dialog box.

4   Confirm that the font formatting and pagination changes are correctly set in the document.

5   Save the document.

6   Click the Check button to upload the document for checking. The Online Lab will report the number of errors for the activity.

7   If errors are reported, view the results document, correct the errors in the submitted document, save the document, and then click the Check button.

Preparing a Bibliography

A **bibliography** is a formal listing of all the sources used in a research paper. This includes any sources from which you quoted or paraphrased material as well as other sources that were consulted or provide further information about the topic. The bibliography is placed on a separate page at the end of the resource paper and may be titled *BIBLIOGRAPHY*, *REFERENCES*, or *WORKS CITED*.

Ergonomic Tip
Position your copyholder about the same distance from your eyes as the screen to avoid refocusing for different distances.

Ending the Session

The Online Lab automatically saves the work you completed for this session. You can continue with the next session or exit the Online Lab and continue later.

Figure 56.3 Research Paper Content for Document 56.1—Continued

Rising Time. Fast-rising yeast rises more quickly in warmer temperatures but also is more sensitive to temperature extremes.

Texture. Breads made with fast-rising yeast have a slightly more open texture than those made with regular yeast. The resulting breads and rolls, however, don't appear to differ significantly.

Impact of Bread Machines

What crockpots did to pot roasts is what the bread machine has done to baking bread—just add the ingredients and check back later. Fleischmann's Bread Machine Yeast is an instant yeast designed for mixing directly with other dry ingredients before use. Rising time is reduced by as much as 50 percent by eliminating the first rise. This yeast may be used in all recipes calling for instant yeast.

Bread machine mixes allow the user to create bakery-fresh bread at home by just adding water and letting the bread machine do the rest. Fleischmann's Bread Machine Mixes come in a variety of flavors including Country White, Stoneground-Wheat, Italian Herb, and Sourdough, while online stores offer more than 100 different bread mix varieties.

 While bread machines offer freshly baked bread at the push of a button, some people have baked more "hockey pucks" or "mushroom loaves" than they'd care to admit. Carefully read the manufacturer's directions and follow instructions for adding and layering ingredients.

Figure 56.4 Footnote Content for Document 56.1

Footnote 1: Mollie Ryan, "Yeast Breads on the Rise," *American Baker*, December 2011, 42.

Footnote 2: "Bread Machine Tips," The Food Guru, accessed June 24, 2014, [Shift + Enter] http://www.emcp.net/foodguru/bread-machine-tips.

Controlling Pagination of Headings

One way to control where text ends on a page is with the Widow/Orphan control, which is in the Paragraph dialog box. As explained in Session 49, the Word Widow/Orphan control feature prevents the first line of a paragraph from being left at the bottom of one page (called an orphan) and the last line of a paragraph beginning a new page (called a widow). By default, this feature is active when a new document is opened in Word.

Word treats headings as single-line paragraphs; therefore, they are not affected by the Widow/Orphan feature. The most logical placement of a heading is on the same page as the paragraph that follows it. Sometimes, however, Word will end a page immediately after a heading. To prevent a

Y, X, Q

Session Objectives

- **Identify the Y, X, and Q keys**
- **Practice correct finger positioning for the Y, X, and Q keys**

Timing Goals

- **1 minute: 25 WAM and two or fewer errors**

Getting Started and Warming Up

Exercise 12.1 If you are continuing immediately from Session 11, you may skip the Exercise 12.1 warm-up drill. However, if you exited the Online Lab at the end of Session 11, warm up by completing Exercise 12.1.

Introducing the Y, X, and Q Keys

Videos 12.1–12.3 The locations of the Y, X, and Q keys are shown in the following diagram. Watch Videos 12.1 through 12.3 and practice using these new keys.

Exercises 12.2–12.10 Complete Exercises 12.2 through 12.9 to learn these new keys. Also complete the thinking drill, Exercise 12.10. When keying the drill lines, follow the instruction prompts provided in the Online Lab.

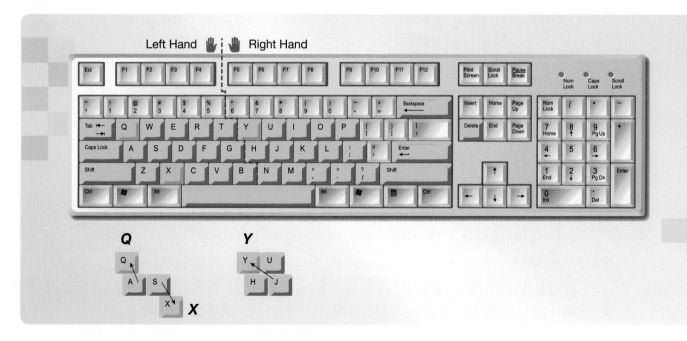

Figure 56.3 Research Paper Content for Document 56.1

Most people bake breads for the process as much as for the product. Mixing the ingredients and kneading the warm dough by the centuries-old rhythm of push-and-pull followed by fold-and-press are the first two steps. Watching through the window as the bread rises in a warm oven almost gives one the feeling of creating a living thing more than making something to eat.

Nearly one-third of all people who like to cook also bake yeast breads. Of those people, nearly half are workers with jobs outside the home, according to Syndicated Research Data. And most of that baking takes place on weekdays.

insert footnote 1

Saving Time

The nation's leading yeast producers say there's one aspect of the bread baking process that home cooks would rather do without. That's the time it takes to let yeast dough rise. Most recipes require at least one rising of an hour or longer; many recipes require a second rising.

Both the major yeast companies, Fleischmann's and Red Star, have come out with fast-rising yeast that can cut in half the amount of time a home cook spends waiting for breads to rise.

The fast-rising yeasts have finer grain than regular dry yeast. The firms say the finer grain adapts well to a quick-mixing technique that allows cooks to save additional time.

Procedure

According to industry literature, the technique involves setting aside one cup of flour and then mixing the yeast directly into the remaining dry ingredients. Then the dry ingredients are combined with the liquid and fat, heated to 125 to 130 degrees, and kneaded with the remaining flour.

Both companies say the fast-rising yeasts also may be rehydrated like regular yeast by dissolving them directly in water heated to 105 to 115 degrees before mixing with the remaining ingredients.

Characteristics

Good bakers are aware of several differences between regular yeast and the fast-rising varieties that make a difference in the baked bread.

Odor. The fast-rising product gives off more yeasty odor while proofing or rising.

continues

⟳ Reinforcing Your Skills

Complete Exercises 12.11 through 12.14 in the Online Lab. Reference the drill lines from the textbook as you key and keep your eyes on the textbook pages, not on your fingers. Complete each exercise at least once, but repeat exercises if you want to improve your WAM rate or accuracy.

Exercise 12.11   Y Drill

Key each drill line two times and push for speed. The goal is to key at least 25 WAM. Your WAM rate will appear at the end of each line.

1 jy yard play yowl very yolk away lazy sly yield you tube

2 spray dairy entry handy lucky staying yonder young

3 Yearn Decay Empty Forty Hurry Lousy Playing Yale Taylor

Key lines 4–6 one time and then key the three lines again. Concentrate on control. The goals are to key at least 25 WAM and to make two or fewer errors. Your WAM rate will appear at the end of each line, and any errors will be highlighted.

4 The kitty and the puppy may not enjoy happy play.

5 It is only your duty to obey every law of safety.

6 Billy is ready to carry the heavy load Wednesday.

Exercise 12.12   X Drill

Key each drill line two times and push for speed. The goal is to key at least 25 WAM. Your WAM rate will appear at the end of each line.

1 sx axle next exam flex text hoax apex expedite fix fox

2 deluxe excise expand export prefix excite text messaging

3 Explode Exhaust Examine Anxiety Exporting X ray Expert

Key lines 4–6 one time and then key the three lines again. Concentrate on control. The goals are to key at least 25 WAM and to make two or fewer errors. Your WAM rate will appear at the end of each line. Any errors will be highlighted.

4 Did excess oxygen explode during that experiment?

5 Explain the context and expedite that experiment.

6 Fix the exhaust and examine the axle of the taxi.

Exercise 12.13   Q Drill

Key each drill line two times and push for speed. The goal is to key at least 25 WAM. Your WAM rate will appear at the end of each line.

1 aq quote quire squid quiet squaw query qualify quite

2 quench equate squeak equity squelching quit quartz

3 Squire Quarry Quaver Quorum Quartering Requesting

drill continues

1. Read all instructions for this document activity, navigate to the Document 56.1 launch page in the Online Lab, and then click the Launch Activity button. The Online Lab will open **Doc056.01** in the activity window. The timer will start as soon as you begin keying the document.

2. Format the document as follows:

   a. At the Paragraph dialog box with the Indents and Spacing tab selected, change the line spacing to double spacing with no extra spacing after each paragraph. Make this setting the default for only this document.

   b. At the Paragraph dialog box with the Line and Page Breaks tab selected, confirm that the Widow/Orphan control is activated.

   c. At the Font dialog box with the Font tab selected, change the font to 12-point Cambria and set the font style as the default for only this document.

3. Type the main heading of the document by completing the following steps:

   a. Set the text to center align and then turn on bold formatting.

   b. Key **YEAST BREADS RISING TO THE OCCASION**, turn off bold formatting, and then press Enter.

   c. Set the text to align at the left margin.

4. Key the text in Figure 56.3, and format the side and paragraph headings according to the style directions outlined in Table 56.3.

5. Key the footnotes shown in Figure 56.4, locating the reference numbers in the document according to placement instructions in Figure 56.3. Do not press the Enter key at the end of either footnote and do not allow the web address to format as a hyperlink.

6. Format the page numbers in the document by completing the following steps:

   a. Double-click in the bottom margin of the first page of the document to open the footer.

   b. Click the *Different First Page* check box in the Options group on the Header & Footer Tools Design tab to insert a check mark.

   c. Click the Page Number button in the Header & Footer group, point to *Bottom of Page*, and then click *Plain Number 2*.

   d. Move the insertion point to the header of the second page.

   e. Click the Page Number button in the Header & Footer group, point to *Top of Page*, and then click *Plain Number 3*.

   f. Double-click in the body of the document to make it active.

7. Proofread the document and correct any errors.

8. Save the document.

9. Click the Check button to stop the timer and upload the document for checking. The Online Lab will report the WAM rate and number of errors for the activity.

10. If errors are reported, view the results document, correct the errors in the submitted document, save the document, and then click the Check button.

Key lines 4–6 one time and then key the three lines again. Concetrate on control. The goals are to key at least 25 WAM and to make two or fewer errors. Your WAM rate will appear at the end of each line, and any errors will be highlighted.

4 Do that quotient; it is a frequent quiz question.

5 Ducks squirmed and quacked in the squalid quarry.

6 Does the quitter frequently squabble and quibble?

Exercise 12.14

Reinforcement Drill

Key lines 1 and 2 one time for speed. The goal is to key at least 25 WAM. Your WAM rate will appear at the end of each line.

1 In a sunny yard, the sassy gray puppy plays daily.

2 The friendly young boy, Gary, annoys silly Sally.

Key line 3 one time. Concentrate on control. The goals are to key at least 25 WAM and to make two or fewer errors. Your WAM rate will appear at the end of the line. Any errors made will be highlighted.

3 A hungry baby in the subway was eyed by a sentry.

Success Tip

When keying for control, try to make fewer than two errors in a line. Remember to keep your eyes on the textbook as you key.

Follow the previous procedures and key lines 4 and 5 one time for speed. Key line 6 one time for speed, while also concentrating on control.

4 Examine her next; Maxine was exposed to smallpox.

5 The new relaxing exercise was explained in the textbook.

6 Is the lynx a vexing jinx or is it an exotic pet?

Follow the previous procedures and key lines 7 and 8 one time for speed. Key line 9 one time for speed, while also concentrating on control.

7 The unique antique aquarium had a thick lacquer on it.

8 In the old square, the quake left a queen in a quagmire.

9 The queasy squirrel was quarantined in the square box.

Formatting Headings in Research Papers

The main purpose of headings in a manuscript or research paper is to call the reader's attention to the important ideas and sections in the document. Heading formats vary according to the number of heading levels and by the style manual you are using. Whatever style is used, it is important to be consistent throughout the document.

Table 56.3 lists the styles for the heading levels to be used in document activities for this session. Figure 56.2 shows examples of the three heading levels formatted in a document.

Table 56.3 CMS Heading Formatting Styles

Heading Level	Formatting Style
Main/First Level	Centered, bold, all letters capitalized, press Enter once after
Side/Second Level	Aligned at the left margin, bold, main words capitalized, press Enter once before and after
Paragraph/Third Level	Run in with paragraphs and begin where other paragraphs begin (for example, on a tab indent), bold, main words capitalized, end with a bold period, and follow with a space (not bold)

Figure 56.2 Headings Formatted in a CMS Research Paper   *Note: Do not key this document.*

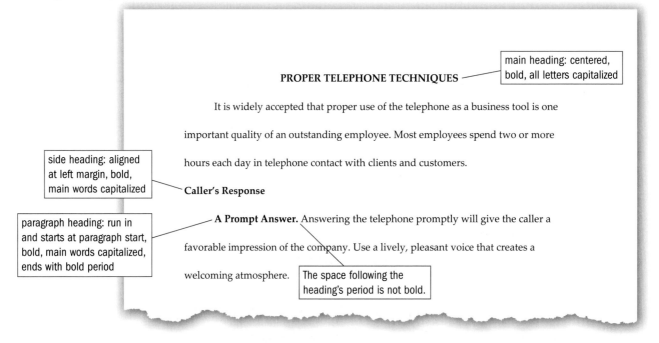

Success Tip

To increase your WAM scores, be sure to review or practice the software features discussed in this session before beginning the timed document activity.

Assessing Your Speed and Accuracy

Complete Timings 12.1 through 12.6 in the Online Lab to assess the skills you have learned in this session. Refer to the following paragraphs as you key.

The timing will start as soon as you begin keying the paragraph. Remember to press the Tab key at the beginning of the paragraph. If you finish keying the paragraph before the timing expires, press Enter and start keying the paragraph again.

When the time expires, the Online Lab will give you a WAM rate and will highlight any errors you made in the keyed text. The goals are to key at least 25 WAM and to make two or fewer errors. The results will be stored in your Timings Performance report.

Goals: 25 WAM and two or fewer errors

1-Minute Timings

Timing 12.1
Basically, employers like a loyal employee. Honesty and courtesy always pay off in any job or duty. Apathy and sloppy typing are always likely to be very costly to a company. Any employee who displays a steady style will be properly rewarded and enjoy a fairly large salary.

Timing 12.2
There is simply no key to easy money. A bad agency may say that you are lucky and a legacy of wealthy glory is yours. Yet, if you try fancy or phony schemes, you will be mighty sorry. Steady, weekly saving is the thrifty means to easy money. Lay a penny away a day and be happy.

Timing 12.3
An extra exercise to help your mind relax is inhaling and exhaling deeply. It extends all the oxygen capacity before it is expelled. Choose an exact time each day to expedite an extra relaxing exertion. Your anxieties and vexations disappear and you relax. Try this exciting experience.

Timing 12.4
Exercise an extreme caution before investing in an old duplex. Have an expert examine all the existing details and explain them to you. It may be easier to buy a luxurious and deluxe apartment house. An experienced land expert knows if it is an expensive venture.

Timing 12.5
The quick squad conquered the unique quintet without question. The quarterback squelched most questions about technique or quality of the team. If they qualify for the trophy, will they quietly squash the next team or will the coach require an extra practice session?

Timing 12.6
Angelique might request a price quotation on an exquisite antique quilt. She acquired it from a queen in a quaint town near the equator. Quiet inquiries have arisen from qualified buyers. The question is, should she keep the quality quilt or sell it quickly as requested?

2 Click the References tab.

3 Click the Insert Footnote button in the Footnotes group. Clicking the Insert Footnote button will insert a superscript number in the document and will insert a separator line at the bottom of the page with a corresponding superscript number below it.

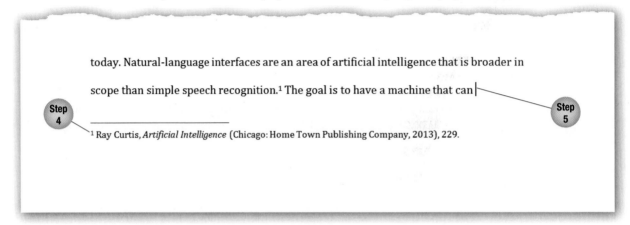

4 Click to the right of the superscript number below the separator line and key the footnote entry. Do not press Enter at the end of the footnote text.

5 Click in the body of the research paper to continue keying the paper.

today. Natural-language interfaces are an area of artificial intelligence that is broader in scope than simple speech recognition.[1] The goal is to have a machine that can

_____

[1] Ray Curtis, *Artificial Intelligence* (Chicago: Home Town Publishing Company, 2013), 229.

Formatting Research Papers Using CMS

The format used in this session is simplified from *The Chicago Manual of Style* to provide experience in following that specific format for the body of a research paper. Table 56.2 identifies the formatting guidelines to be used in this session.

Table 56.2 CMS Formatting Guidelines for Research Papers

Paper Element	Formatting Guidelines
Text Alignment	Left aligned, paragraphs begin with 0.5-inch tab
Font	12-point, serif font such as Cambria, Bookman Old Style, Times New Roman; footnotes should use the same font but in 10-pt size (Word will change automatically.)
Margins	Default: 1-inch top, bottom, left, and right margins
Line Spacing	2.0 line spacing (with 0 points extra spacing before and after paragraphs) except in footnotes (Word will change automatically.)
Report Title	Begins at top margin, centered, bold, all capital letters, followed by one Enter
Page Numbers	First page: Plain number (digits only) centered in the footer
	Second and subsequent pages: Plain number (digits only) at the top right of the header

Ergonomic Tip

Adjust the brightness and contrast controls on the screen to sharpen images.

Ending the Session

The Online Lab automatically saves the work you completed for this session. You can continue with the next session or exit the Online Lab and continue later.

Table 56.1 Footnote Entries According to *The Chicago Manual of Style, Sixteenth Edition*

Books

[1] Author First Name Author Last Name, *Book Title* (City of Publication: Publisher, Year), Page Number.

Example of single-author book:

> [2] Alexandra R. Livingston, *Living Your Values* (Denver: Marchant Publishing International, 2013), 271.

Example of multiple-author book:

> [3] William Mitchell, Patricia King, and Ronald Kapper, *Keyboarding & Applications I* (St. Paul: Paradigm Publishing, Inc., 2012), 247.

Articles from Magazines

[4] Author First Name Author Last Name, "Article Title," *Name of Magazine*, Month, Day, Year, Page Number.

Example of single-author article:

> [5] Jean Pauk, "What's for Dinner?," *Fast and Healthy Family Foods*, June 2015, 45.

Example when no author is listed:

> [6] "Time Marches On," *The Los Angeles Flyer*, March 10, 2013, 29.

Web Pages

[7] Author First Name Author Last Name, "Web Page Title," *Name of Website*, accessed Date, [Shift + Enter] http://www.address.

Example:

> [8] Mary Lou Bouchard, "Writing a Research Paper," *Everything You Should Know about Reporting Research*, accessed July 14, 2014,
> http://www.emcp.net/researchforstudents/writing-a-research-paper.html.

Figure 56.1 Footnotes for a Book and a Journal Article Following *The Chicago Manual of Style*

---

[1] James L. Johnson, *All You Wanted to Know About the Moon* (Tucson: Minute Publishing Co., 2012), 117.
[2] John Dane, "Document Storing Alternatives," *Communications Monthly*, September 2012, 19.

The **Insert Footnote feature** is a tool to help you format footnotes in a research paper. The feature automatically inserts a superscript (raised) number after the quoted or paraphrased text, adds the horizontal line separating the text from the footnote, and numbers the footnotes in order. If a footnote is later added or deleted, Word will automatically renumber the footnotes to accommodate the change. Each footnote entry begins at the left margin in a font size smaller than the body of the text. The footnote appears above the document's footer. Figure 56.1 shows a book and a journal article source following *The Chicago Manual of Style* formatting guidelines placed at the bottom of a page in a research paper.

To create a footnote, complete the following steps:

1   Place the insertion point in the text, at the end of the content that is to be referenced, for example, after a period at the end of the paraphrased text or immediately after the quotation mark at the end of the quote.

steps continue

Skills Reinforcement and Proficiency Exercises: Sessions 1–12

🔄 Session Objectives

- Review and practice correct finger positioning for the Sessions 1–12 keys
- Assess and reinforce keyboarding speed and accuracy with timings
- Utilize drills to practice alphabetic keying

Timing Goals

- 1 minute: 25 WAM and two or fewer errors

Getting Started and Warming Up

Exercise 13.1 If you are continuing immediately from Session 12, you may skip the warm-up drill at the start of this session. However, if you exited the Online Lab at the end of Session 12, warm up by completing Exercise 13.1.

The purpose of this session is to reinforce the keyboarding skills you have developed in the previous sessions. The timings in this session will help you to determine where you are in your skill development and the exercises in the session provide you with the opportunity to further work on improving your skill and accuracy, if you have not reached the target goals.

Assessing Your Speed and Accuracy

In Sessions 7–9 and 11–12, you completed a series of 1-minute timings. The speed and accuracy goals were presented at the beginning of each set of timings. Check your scores by accessing your Timings Performance report.

Using your scores for the timings in Sessions 7–9 and 11–12 as benchmarks, complete Timings 13.1 and 13.2 in the Online Lab using the paragraph at the top of the next page. If you did not reach at least 25 WAM in the previous timings, push for speed. If you reached 25 WAM but had more than two errors, work for accuracy. If you achieved both speed and accuracy goals, push for even greater speed.

In the Online Lab, you will start with a practice screen, which you can use to practice keying the timing text without the timer. Prompt the Online Lab to begin Timing 13.1 when you have completed your practice. Both timings will use the same paragraph. Once you are on an active timing screen, the timing will start as soon as you begin keying.

Remember to press the Tab key at the start of the paragraph, and do not press Enter at the end of each line, but only at the end of the paragraph. If you finish keying the paragraph before the timing expires, press Enter and start keying the paragraph again.

When the time expires, the Online Lab will give you a WAM rate and highlight any errors you made in the keyed text. Again, the goals are to key at least 25 WAM and to make two or fewer errors. The results of both timings will be stored in your Timings Performance report.

Types of Citations

There are several methods for identifying the sources used to develop a research paper. When you quote directly or paraphrase from another source, identify the non-original content with in-text citations, footnotes, or endnotes.

In-Text Citations

In-text citations are brief parenthetical references to the source of an indirect or direct quotation. A text note includes the author's last name and a page number from the work cited, for example, (Updike 25). The works cited are then listed in a more complete form at the end of the report on a separate page titled *Works Cited* or *Bibliography*.

Footnotes

Footnotes are numbered references that appear at the foot (or bottom) of the page. A footnote usually includes the author's last name, publication title, place of publication, publisher, date of publication, and the page numbers of the information cited. The information cited is followed by a superscript number (a raised number immediately following a word in the text), and the information source (which is identified with the same number) is listed at the "foot" or bottom of the page. Footnotes may also be used to offer additional explanation of cited material in the text of a research paper rather than to put that explanation in the body of the paper.

Endnotes

Endnotes are similar to footnotes with the difference being in their placement. Whereas footnotes appear at the bottom of the relevant page, endnotes appear at the end of a report. Endnotes are placed on a separate page before the *Works Cited* or *Bibliography* page. Footnotes are more likely to get your reader's attention, but endnotes result in a less cluttered appearance.

Guidelines for Inserting Footnotes

Footnotes can be used to provide commentary on the text discussion or can inform the reader of the exact source of your quoted or paraphrased material and where additional information can be found. The content of footnotes can differ slightly, depending on the type of source used.

The style guide used for the research paper will govern the presentation of the footnote content such as punctuation and use of italics. In general, the following style rules apply:

- Use italic formatting to indicate an entire publication such as a book, newspaper, or periodical (magazine).
- Use quotation marks around the name of a chapter, article, short story, essay, or poem to indicate a source contained within another publication (such as a book, newspaper, or magazine).

Table 56.1 shows formatting guidelines for formatting footnotes when using *The Chicago Manual of Style*.

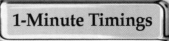

Timings 13.1–13.2

It is good to have honest goals. Nothing is gained if one goes forth in pointless roaming. A major effort is needed to prosper. Isolate those foolish errors and avoid them. Hold to a strong, firm hope and move along.

↺ Reinforcing Your Skills

The following key location, speed, and accuracy drills provide additional practice on the keys you have learned in the previous sessions. If you successfully keyed Timings 13.1 and 13.2 with a 25 WAM or higher and two or fewer errors and you do not hesitate while keying, proceed to Session 14. However, if your WAM and error rates do not match these goals, the drills in this section will give you the opportunity for further practice.

If you have not mastered a key reach (you hesitate before striking a key), practice the alphabetic key location drills, Exercises 13.2 through 13.4. If you are not keying at least 25 WAM, key the speed drills, Exercises 13.5 through 13.7. If you are committing more than two errors per minute, key the accuracy drills, Exercises 13.8 and 13.9.

Alphabetic Key Location Drills

Practice the following drills to help reinforce your keying of the alphabetic characters. Repeat these exercises as often as you like to help you increase both your speed and accuracy.

Exercise 13.2 **Key Positioning Drill**

Practice the correct finger position on the home row keys by keying each letter of the alphabet twice (aa bb cc dd and so on).

Exercise 13.3 **Key Positioning Thinking Drill**

Develop your critical thinking skills when keyboarding by keying the alphabet backwards (z y x and so on).

Exercise 13.4 **Alphabetic Characters Sentence Drill**

Key the following sentence three times to practice keying all of the letters of the alphabet.

1 The quick brown fox jumped over the lazy dogs.

Speed Drills

For the speed drills, key each line one time. After practicing the speed drills, either continue by completing the accuracy drills or go directly to Timing 13.3 to see if your speed has improved.

Ergonomic Tip

Keep the angle between your calf and thigh greater than 60 degrees when seated. This angle relieves the build-up of pressure and cramping in your legs from your thighs resting too heavily on the chair.

Citing Sources in Research Papers

Research papers are created in all types of business and educational institutions. Writing style organizations such as the Modern Language Association (MLA) and the American Psychological Association (APA) provide guidelines for formatting research papers and citing sources used in the research. *The Chicago Manual of Style* (CMS, also referred to as Chicago) is a third popular resource. The method for citing sources may be determined by the style guidelines of your workplace, by your publisher or instructor, or by your preference if none other is stated. In the later sessions in this unit, you will work with each of the above style guides for identifying sources. Research papers in this session will use the footnote and bibliography format from *The Chicago Manual of Style, Sixteenth Edition.*

When to Cite Sources

An important part of the research writing process is crediting the source of ideas or information you have used to create your research document. This process also shows evidence of research you conducted. An advantage of citing sources is that your readers can find and evaluate the quality of your references, if they choose to do so. It does not matter the type of source—it could be printed matter, the Internet, or a conversation. To use another writer's words or ideas without giving credit is called *plagiarism*, which in all cases is unethical and, in some cases, illegal. You must give credit to another individual if you use his or her ideas.

You need to cite sources (show evidence of research and give credit to others) when you directly quote an individual or when you paraphrase from a source.

- **Direct quotation:** When you use another person's exact words or ideas, enclose the information in quotation marks. Here are two examples of a direct quote, formatted in two different ways:

> Dane stated, "If current trends continue, the cost of filing just one document could rise to $2."
> "If current trends continue," stated Dane, "the cost of filing just one document could rise to $2."

- **Paraphrased quotation:** If you paraphrase (do not quote the words exactly), you do not use quotation marks. However, you must still give credit for the idea by using a source note. Below is an example of a paraphrased quote:

> One expert indicated that if trends continue, the cost of storing just one document could rise to $2.

When directly quoting, you may wish to omit one or more words. In those instances, use an **ellipsis**, a series of three evenly spaced periods (. . .). Press the space bar once *before* and *after* each of the three periods when an ellipsis is used within a sentence. When an ellipsis appears at the end of a statement, four periods are used (....).

Exercise 13.5 Balanced-Hand Words Drill

Key each line one time. Focus on speed.

1 sign and the sigh ant sit ale elf hen end she and
2 then hang the and fig dig die tie did sit fit aid
3 fish sign than then lane lake lens hand than halt

4 lake idle half lens lane sign dish sign then disk
5 aisle island handle fight angle title shake snake
6 gland sleigh height fight slant digit angle eight

7 he and the elf and it if he an tight giant signal
8 amble bible problem blame bland blend lamb emblem
9 gown wig bow wow vow down wit when wish with wisp

10 flap pane paid pale spent dispel lap nap pen paid
11 foam fork form foal odor soak rod fog sod oak rod
12 heir lair risks sir pan air widow flair hair pair

13 pelvis disown pens laps vie via pair vivid flames
14 map mane maid melt sham lame mend firm make disks
15 The pale maid paid for the vivid title and a wig.

16 Did the pale lamb amble down to the big bland pen?
17 When did Bob sign the pair of problem emblems?

Exercise 13.6 Letter Combinations Drill

Key each line one time. Focus on speed.

1 ta tall tan task taste tale take talk tag talent
2 th thesis thin theft this think than that then throw
3 te tenant tend tell tenth test tea tenor team text

4 st stead steal steadiness stateside stag steam
5 sa sad saline Sal sang said sale sake safe sat sake
6 si since simple sinker sit single sift sip sin siphon

7 pe pets pest pen peg pea peat penguin pension
8 pi pine pink pipes piles pie pin pious pint

drill continues

Complete two 5-minute timings on the timing text below. Timings 56.3 and 56.4 use the same paragraphs.

Goals: 35 WAM and five or fewer errors
SI: 1.45 syllables per word

Timings 56.3–56.4

Have you really looked at your laptop lately? Can you see dust and fingerprints lurking in every corner? If someone comes near you while you are working at your computer, do you begin wiping away dust and fingerprints? Computer keyboards are also the perfect breeding area for germs. This is especially true on a computer used by more than one individual. An uncontaminated computer is better for you and for the laptop. It's time to buck up and clean it!

Special cleaning solutions and cleaning cloths may be purchased, but the right household items can be used instead. Prepare a solution of half isopropyl alcohol (70 percent) and half distilled water. Dampen a nonabrasive, lint-free textile. Paper towels, depending on the brand, may leave lint or actually scratch the screen. An old cotton T-shirt works well, but it should not be entirely wet or dripping.

To begin the cleaning process, turn off the computer. If you are using a special spray cleaner or have put your household solution into a spritzer, spray the cloth instead of spraying the laptop. Never spray the laptop directly. Using the damp cloth, wipe the laptop's exterior with circular motions proceeding from top to bottom and from left to right to eliminate dust or fingerprints or whatever else may be there.

Clean the display with the same fabric or use a fresh one if the original one seems too dirty. Wipe the screen the same way you did the exterior with circular motions going from top to bottom, from left to right. Do not use much pressure or touch the screen with your fingertips. If the screen looks streaky, repeat the process. A spotless display is easier on your eyes.

To clean between the keys, use either a can of compressed air or a computer vacuum. A regular vacuum may have too much suction and could cause damage. You may want to turn the keyboard upside down first and shake out those "remains" (over a wastebasket, please!). When using compressed air, do not tilt the can. Do not spray into the vents, speakers, or ports. The last step for cleaning the keyboard is to wipe it down with the damp cloth or a pretreated wipe.

9 li like linkage linking link lien lied lie lid lime

10 le leaf least ledge lend lead left lest leap legacy

11 bl blade bleak blast blank blinds blind blight blog

12 ba bandages barks badge bath balk bail bag bad band

13 mi mire misting might midst mint mind milk mid

14 ma margin manager marsh mail make math mat man

15 oa float roast toad load oatmeal oath oats oak boat

16 ri rinse rigid ridges right ripe rises rip rid rice

17 ra rapid range raised rates rake ranks rap ran rayon

18 vi vintage vital visits vine vile vise vim vie viable

19 va vanish varied valid vast vases vane vat van varnish

20 wa waves waste wane wait wade wag war was wash wand

21 wi wiper wield wise will wipe wide wig wit win window

Exercise 13.7 Sentences with Letter Combinations Drill

Key each line one time. Focus on speed.

1 Janie washed and wiped her wig; she wasted water.

2 The boy blinked at a baby bound in bandages.

3 Those offensive oats floated off of that oatmeal.

4 The vital vintage vases vanished from a vast van.

5 The manager might mail the mild mints to the man.

6 Rapid Red ran to the raised ridges on that range.

7 That person had piles of pipes for them.

8 Then that steady tenant, Ted, did a tenth strength test.

9 Steadfast Stacy talks a lot and stands as she talks.

10 Sad Sal sang a signal as she sighted a safe date.

11 At least lower the left lid and shorten the length.

12 That hanging kite tail brings the person around.

13 Gal, finish the gasket for the gas gadget game.

14 I dislike the heat dial that fits the dental fan.

Formatting Footnotes, Research Papers, and Bibliographies in CMS Style

Session Objectives

- Cite sources in a research paper
- Insert footnotes in a research paper
- Format a research paper
- Control page breaks
- Prepare a bibliography

Timing Goals

- 1 Minute: 45 WAM and one or no errors
- 5 Minutes: 35 WAM and five or fewer errors

Getting Started and Warming Up

Exercise 56.1 If you are continuing immediately from Session 55, you may skip the Exercise 56.1 warm-up drill. However, if you exited the Online Lab at the end of Session 55, warm up by completing Exercise 56.1.

Exercise 56.2 Begin your session work by completing Exercise 56.2, a timed short drill, in the Online Lab.

Assessing Your Speed and Accuracy

Complete Timings 56.1 through 56.4 in the Online Lab. At the end of each timing, the Online Lab will display your WAM rate and any errors. Results will be saved in your Timings Performance report. If you have been surpassing the speed and accuracy goals, set slightly more challenging personal goals and strive to exceed them.

Complete two 1-minute timings on the timing text below. Timings 56.1 and 56.2 use the same paragraph.

Goals: 45 WAM and one or no errors
SI: 1.46 syllables per word

1-Minute Timings

Timings 56.1–56.2
Your computer desktop is like home base for your computer. From here, you use a text or graphic menu to run programs and work with files. You can open more than one window at a time; for example, one window may show your web browser open to surf the Internet at the same time that another window displays your email. Switching from one window or application to another is as easy as clicking its program button on the taskbar. You can also customize your desktop to use a different background image or color, or change the color scheme for all your desktop elements.

Accuracy Drills

For the accuracy drills, key each line one time and concentrate on control as you key. After practicing the accuracy drills, go directly to Timing 13.3 to see if your accuracy has improved.

Exercise 13.8 **Double-Letter Words Drill**

Key each line one time. Focus on accuracy.

1 seed teens needless feeling indeed needs glee see
2 tall stall knitting install little shall hall all
3 heel steed likeness dissent seeing sheet need fee

4 see feel teeth indeed gallant sledding sleet knee
5 hill still lifeless endless assist stiff kiss add
6 eggs stall eggshell falling haggle sniff sell egg

7 tell shell settling skilled allied skill fell add
8 deed sleek seedling fiddles needle sheen keen eel
9 rabble rabbit gobble nibbles pebble babble hobble

10 narratives all follow terrains irritates terriers
11 door root mood took loot hook hood pool roof moon
12 immerges immense manners hammering dinners dimmer

13 shipping appease flipping happen sipping slipping
14 of offensive offense offset offends offers off of
15 She will be stalling the nice contest winner now.

16 That immense rabbit emerged and nibbled a carrot.
17 Tu Wee slipped the irritated kitten into the house.

Exercise 13.9 **Longer Words Drill**

Key each line one time. Focus on accuracy.

1 negative retrieve primitive privilege advertising
2 estimate familiar eliminate dependent sentimental
3 Eliminate that sentimental, familiar advertising.

4 resident standard telegrams registrar parenthesis
5 pipeline elephant dependent plaintiff safekeeping
6 That resident registrar sends standard telegrams.

drill continues

"The purpose of this manuscript is to…." Unimaginative statements such as these tend to turn off the reader immediately. Instead, use one of the following "hooks":

- A surprising statistic or unusual fact
- A colorful example
- A quotation
- A question
- A comparison
- A joke or humorous statement

If you cannot think of a good hook to use, beginning with the thesis statement is acceptable. In fact, this straightforward approach is quite common in work-related writing.

Document 55.4 ## Composing a Manuscript Introduction

1. Navigate to the Document 55.4 launch page in the Online Lab and then click the Launch Activity button. The Online Lab will open **Doc055.04** in the activity window.

2. Using a research subject or topic that you have completed in another course or the thesis statement "Public tax dollars are necessary to support major sports teams," compose an introductory paragraph for a manuscript on the subject. The introduction is to be a paragraph of 50 to 100 words (Word Count will help with this). When you have finished, edit your document for clear sentences, effective word choices, and correct punctuation, grammar, and capitalization.

3. Proofread and correct any errors in the letter.

4. Save the document.

5. Click the Upload button to upload the document for instructor review.

Ending the Session

The Online Lab automatically saves the work you completed for this session. You may continue with the next session or exit the Online Lab and continue later.

7 initiated hesitating alkaline likeness indefinite

8 delegates heightened lengthened stealing gaslight

9 The hesitating delegate is stealing the gaslight.

10 digital lenient distant inkling heading delighted

11 disliked endless athlete install flatten inflated

12 A lenient athlete has inflated the flattened keg.

13 whenever stalwart wholesale handwriting knowledge

14 renovate negotiate imagination tradition rational

15 possible establish observation elaborate ambition

16 Establish rational imagination whenever possible.

17 seashells tasteless steadfast thankless defendant

18 attendant delighted sightless lightness negligent

19 legislate essential stateside skinflint landslide

20 Seashells in the landslide delighted a skinflint.

Assessing Your Speed and Accuracy

Now that you have practiced the appropriate drills, complete two 1-minute timings using the following paragraph. Note that this is the same text keyed for Timings 13.1 and 13.2.

Each timing will begin as soon as you begin keying the paragraph. Remember to press the Tab key at the start of the paragraph. If you finish keying the paragraph before the timing expires, press Enter and start keying the paragraph again.

When time expires, the Online Lab will give you a WAM rate and will highlight any errors you made.

The results of all of your timings will be stored in your Timings Performance report. Compare your rates from Timings 13.3 and 13.4 to your rates from Timings 13.1 and 13.2. Has your speed improved? Did you make fewer errors? If you are not reaching at least 25 WAM with two or fewer errors, repeat Sessions 11–12.

Goals: 25 WAM and two or fewer errors

1-Minute Timings

Timings
13.3–13.4

It is good to have honest goals. Nothing is gained if one goes forth in pointless roaming. A major effort is needed to prosper. Isolate those foolish errors and avoid them. Hold to a strong, firm hope and move along.

Document **Manuscript Title Page with a Hyperlink Removed**

55.3

1   Read all instructions for this document activity, navigate to the Document 55.3 launch page in the Online Lab, and then click the Launch Activity button. The Online Lab will open **Doc055.03** in the activity window. The timer will start as soon as you begin keying the document.

2   Set the insertion point to center align text (press Ctrl + E).

3   Key the title page content shown in Figure 55.6.

   a   Remove the hyperlink from the author's email address.

   b   Do not press Enter after the last phone number.

4   Insert a header using the *Blank* header option and key **Running Head: ADVANCES IN WIND POWER** in the text placeholder.

5   Proofread the document and correct any errors.

6   Save the document.

7   Click the Check button to stop the timer and upload the document for checking. The Online Lab will report the WAM rate and number of errors for the activity.

8   If errors are reported, view the results document, correct the errors in the submitted document, save the document, and then click the Check button.

Figure 55.6 Title Page Content for Document 55.3

ADVANCES IN WIND POWER [Enter]

Total Word Count: 625 [Enter]

[Enter]

Isabella A. Kurt [Shift + Enter]

6229 Schumacher Street [Shift + Enter]

Parker, TN 37504 [Shift + Enter]

615.555.4243 [Shift + Enter]

ikurt@emcp.net [Enter]

[Enter]

Eastern Chaparral College [Shift + Enter]

8426 Lost Canyon Drive [Shift + Enter]

Parker, TN 37501 [Shift + Enter]

615.555.8400

Reinforcing Writing Skills

Even with a complete outline of the ideas and information to be covered in a manuscript, many writers have a difficult time writing the first paragraph, which introduces the topic and states the main point, or *thesis*. An effective introduction opens with a few sentences that "hook" the reader's interest. It concludes with a statement of the main point of the manuscript. Above all, do not make the mistake of beginning your paper with the words "I am writing this manuscript because…" or

Ergonomic Tip

To minimize eye strain, align the monitor and keyboard directly in front of you.

Ending the Session

The Online Lab automatically saves the work you completed for this session. You can continue with the next session or exit the Online Lab and continue later.

Figure 55.5 Word Count Dialog Box

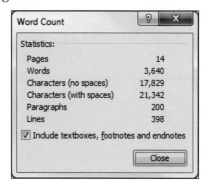

Determining Word Count

Publishers commonly specify the length of articles to be published, and a submitted manuscript must meet those guidelines to be considered for publication. For this reason, word count information is commonly included on the title pages of submitted manuscripts.

Word makes identifying the length of a document easy with its Word Count feature. As you key a document, Word automatically counts the number of pages and words and displays the information on the Status bar at the bottom of the document screen. The page count will indicate where the insertion point is within the document following the word *Page:* For example, if the insertion point is on page 12 of a 14-page document, it will read *Page: 12 of 14.* The word count appears after the word *Words:* on the Status bar. For more information about the document statistics, open the Word Count dialog box by clicking the Words button in the Status bar. You can also open the Word Count dialog box by clicking the Word Count button in the Proofing group on the Review tab. Figure 55.5 shows the Word Count dialog box for a sample document. Click the Close button or the red X to close the dialog box and return to the document.

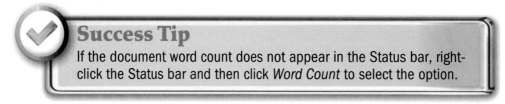

Success Tip

If the document word count does not appear in the Status bar, right-click the Status bar and then click *Word Count* to select the option.

Removing a Hyperlink

Word automatically formats website addresses and email addresses keyed in documents as hyperlinks. When the document is viewed electronically, the recipient can click the hyperlinked website address to go directly to that site. Clicking an email address opens a new email already addressed with the hyperlinked address.

The title page formatted in the next document activity should not include a hyperlink to the author's email address.

To remove a hyperlink immediately after it has been formatted by Word, press Ctrl + Z to undo the formatting. Alternatively, you can remove the formatting by right-clicking on the hyperlink and then clicking *Remove Hyperlink* from the shortcut menu.

Unit 2 Number Row Keys

Figure 55.4 Manuscript Content for Document 55.2—Continued

Programmers can look forward to human language computer interfaces. With better interfaces, programmers may be able to describe what they want using natural (human) language, rather than writing programs in the highly restrictive and rather alien programming languages. Natural-language interfaces are an area of artificial intelligence that is broader in scope than simple speech recognition. The goal is to have a machine that can read a set of news articles on any topic and understand what it has read. Ideally, it could then write a report summarizing what it learned from the articles.

Virtual reality (VR) describes the concept of creating a realistic world within the computer. Online games with thousands of interacting players already exist. In these games people can take on a persona and move about a virtual landscape, adventuring and chatting with other players. The quality of a virtual reality system is typically characterized in terms of its immersiveness, which measures how real the simulated world feels and how well it can make users accept the simulated world as their own and forget about reality. With each passing year, systems are able to provide increasing levels of immersion. Called by some the "ultimate in escapism," VR is becoming increasingly common—and increasingly real.

Although still in the experimental phase, a number of interfaces take things a bit further than VR, and they don't require users to click a mouse, speak a word, or even lift a finger. Mental interfaces use sensors mounted around the skull to read the alpha waves given off by our brains. Thinking of the color blue could be used to move the mouse cursor to the right, or thinking of the number seven could move it to the left. The computer measures brain activity and interprets it as a command, eliminating the need to manipulate a mouse physically to move the screen cursor. While this technology has obvious applications for assisting people with disabilities, military researchers are also using it to produce a superior form of interface for pilots.

Creating a Manuscript Title Page

As with the report title page formatted in Session 52, a manuscript title page will contain important information about the document and the author of the document. Typically, information about the author is not included on the manuscript pages. The contents of a manuscript title page will need to be adapted to meet the style of a specific publisher. Typically, the content of the title page will be keyed in regular text and will appear at the top of the page. The title page created in the next document activity is for a publisher who has requested that the title page include information about the content of the running heads within the manuscript, the word count, and the author contact and affiliation information.

Session Objectives

- **Explore the number row**
- **Identify the 1, 2, and 3 keys**
- **Practice correct finger positioning for the 1, 2, and 3 keys**
- **Read and key numbers as syllables or groups**

Timing Goals

- **1 minute: 30 WAM and two or fewer errors**

Getting Started and Warming Up

Exercise 14.1 If you are continuing immediately from Session 13, you may skip the Exercise 14.1 warm-up drill. However, if you exited the Online Lab at the end of Session 13, warm up by completing Exercise 14.1.

Introducing the 1, 2, and 3 Keys

This is the first session that provides experience with keying the number row, which is located just above the alphabetic keys on the keyboard. Because numbers are used frequently with the alphabetic keys and many of the symbols (for example, the percent sign), developing equal skills with numbers, symbols, and letters is important.

Whether you keyboard for personal or business use, you will frequently key numbers. Some of the numbers that occur regularly in textual material include social security, telephone, address, ZIP code, postal zone, age, weight, height, credit card, and driver's license numbers.

Videos 14.1–14.3 The locations of the 1, 2, and 3 keys are shown in the following diagram. Watch Videos 14.1 through 14.3 and practice using these new keys.

Exercises 14.2–14.5 Complete Exercises 14.2 through 14.5 to learn these new keys. When keying the drill lines, follow the instruction prompts provided in the Online Lab.

As you complete these exercises, keep in mind these important guidelines when keying numbers.

- Use the home-row method. In other words, anchor the left hand on ASDF and the right hand on JKL;.
- Whenever possible, think of numbers in groups of two or three digits. For example, as you key 11, think *eleven*. As you key 111, think *one eleven*.
- When letters and numbers are combined, think of the letter(s) plus a two- or three-digit number. For example, as you key a111, think *a-one, eleven*.

3 Type the title of the manuscript by completing the following steps:

    a Click the Center button in the Paragraph group on the Home tab (or press Ctrl + E) to center the title.

    b Key **Natural Interface Applications**.

    c Press Enter.

    d Click the Align Text Left button (or press Ctrl + E) to turn off the centering formatting.

4 Key the content of the manuscript shown in Figure 55.4. Press the Tab key at the start of each paragraph.

5 With the insertion point in the second page of the document, insert a header that does not print on the first page. The header should include the title of the manuscript (keyed in all capital letters) flush to the left margin and a plain page number flush to the right margin. *Hint: Use the* **Blank** *header option and press the Tab key two times before inserting the* **Plain Number** *option.*

6 Proofread the document and correct any errors.

7 Save the document.

8 Click the Check button to stop the timer and upload the document for checking. The Online Lab will report the WAM rate and number of errors for the activity.

9 If errors are reported, view the results document, correct the errors in the submitted document, save the document, and then click the Check button.

Figure 55.4 Manuscript Content for Document 55.2

Creating a more natural interface between human and machine is the goal in a major area of artificial intelligence. Currently, computer users are restricted in most instances to using a mouse and keyboard for input. For output, they must gaze at a fairly static, two-dimensional screen. Speakers are used for sound, and a printer for hard copy. The user interface consists of keying, pointing, and clicking. New speech recognition and natural-language technologies promise to change that soon.

One of the most immediately applicable improvements in technology comes in the area of speech recognition. Rather than keying information in the computer, users can direct the computer with voice commands. A computer that can take dictation and perform requested actions is a real step forward in convenience and potential. Speech recognition technology has developed rather slowly, mainly because until recently, the typical computer did not have the necessary speed and capacity.

Computers that are able to communicate using spoken English, Japanese, or any of the hundreds of other languages currently in use around the world, would certainly be helpful. In the not-so-distant future, computers will most likely be able to read, write, speak, and understand many human languages. Language translators already exist, and they are getting better all the time.

continues

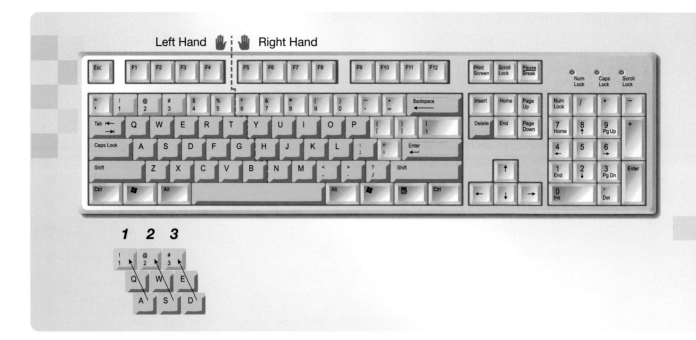

Left Hand   Right Hand

1   2   3

↺ Reinforcing Your Skills

Complete Exercises 14.6 through 14.12 in the Online Lab. Reference the drill lines from the textbook as you key and keep your eyes on the textbook pages, not on your fingers. Complete each exercise at least once, but repeat exercises if you want to improve your WAM rate or accuracy.

Exercise 14.6

1 Drill

Key line 1 one time for speed. Your WAM rate will appear at the end of the line.

Key line 2 one time for control. The goals are to key at least 25 WAM and to make two or fewer errors. Your WAM rate will appear at the end of the line, and any errors will be highlighted.

1   a1 1a1 a111 a1 a1 a11 a111 a1 11a11 a1 1a1 a11 a1

2   a11 a111 11a a1 1a1 a11 111a 111 11a 11 a1 11a 1a

Exercise 14.7

2 Drill

Key line 1 one time for speed. Your WAM rate will appear at the end of the line.

Key line 2 one time for control. The goals are to key at least 25 WAM and to make two or fewer errors. Your WAM rate will appear at the end of the line, and any errors will be highlighted.

1   1 2 1 21 221 122 121 221 2 1 212 112 1 12 21 21 2

2   a12 2a1 112a 12a12 21a1 122a a11 a2a 12a 1a2a 122

✓ Success Tip

When keying the number 21, think *twenty-one*, not *two one*. When keying 221, think *two, twenty-one*. When keying 112a, think *one, twelve-a*.

Figure 55.2 Outline Content for Document 55.1—Continued

[Enter]
[Tab] [Tab] A.[Tab] Definite need [Enter]
[Tab] [Tab] B. [Tab] Post-secondary education

Figure 55.3 Final Formatted Outline for Document 55.1

THE ADMINISTRATIVE MANAGER

I.   NEED

   A. Rapid growth of business
   B. New type of employee

II.   CHANGES

   A. Rising financial costs
       1. Increased paperwork
       2. Inflation
   B. Staffing challenges
       1. Retiring workers
       2. Lack of skills
       3. Technology

III. CAREER OPTIONS

   A. Definite need
   B. Post-secondary education

Document 55.2 **Unbound Manuscript with Changes to the Default Font**

1   Read all instructions for this document activity, navigate to the Document 55.2 launch page in the Online Lab, and then click the Launch Activity button. The Online Lab will open **Doc055.02** in the activity window. The timer will start as soon as you begin keying the document.

2   Change the document default formatting by completing the following steps:

   a   Change the document default line spacing to double spacing with no extra space before or after paragraphs.

   b   Change the document default font to 12-point Times New Roman.

steps continue

Exercise 14.8 — Numbers with Four Digits Drill

When working with groups of numbers having four digits and no natural break, think of the numbers as two pairs. For example, the number 1221 is read as *twelve, twenty-one*.

Key lines 1 and 2 one time for speed. Read the numbers in pairs to gain speed while keying.

1 1221 1112 1221 1112 2112 2112 1122 1122 1221 2221

2 a1122 a1221 1112a 1212a a1112 a2112 a1212 a1221a2

Exercise 14.9 — Numbers with Five or More Digits Drill

Use a 2-3-2 reading pattern when keying number groups with more than four digits and no natural breaks such as spaces, commas, or decimals. For example, read the number 21221 as *twenty-one, two twenty-one*. For the number 2121221, think *twenty-one, two-twelve, twenty-one*.

Key lines 1–5 one time. Mentally pronounce the number combinations as you key them. The goals are to key at 25 WAM and to make two or fewer errors. Your WAM rate will appear at the end of each line, and any errors will be highlighted.

1 21 221 21 221 21 221 a21 212a 12 11a 2121 a121 a2

2 21221 21121 21221 a21112 a12212 a12121 21212 a122

3 a2112121 22 1 21a 2122121 12221 a212a 1221a 12221

4 12 12 12 12 121 121 121 121 a2a a221 a221 2a211 1

5 212a1 121221a 12122a1 22221a 12212a 221221a 21a22

> **Success Tip**
>
> Keep your fingers on the home row and reach from that position to key a particular number or several numbers. Return your finger to the home-row position after keying a number.

Exercise 14.10 — 3 Drill

Key lines 1–2 one time for speed. Your WAM rate will appear at the end of lines 1 and 2.

Key line 3 one time for control. The goals are to key at least 25 WAM and to make two or fewer errors. Your WAM rate will appear at the end of the line, and any errors will be highlighted.

1 332 32 213 231 12 1321 231 32 231 2312 232 1213 3

2 a33 a3 a32 a321 a233 a3232 a132 13232 3223212 a23

3 a323 a3212321 a13231a a1 231a a123 232 32 332 a13

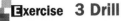

6 Type the title of the outline by completing the following steps:

    a Click the Center button in the Paragraph group on the Home tab (or press Ctrl + E) to turn on centering.

    b Turn on bold formatting, key **THE ADMINISTRATIVE MANAGER**, and then turn off bold formatting.

    c Press Enter.

    d Turn off the centering formatting.

    e Press Enter two times.

7 Key the outline text shown in Figure 55.2.

8 Proofread the document and correct any errors. Check that the Roman numerals, letters, and Arabic numbers are properly aligned, and compare the layout to the document shown in Figure 55.3.

9 Save the document.

10 Reactivate the automatic number formatting feature in Word.

11 Click the Check button to stop the timer and upload the document for checking. The Online Lab will report the WAM rate and number of errors for the activity.

12 If errors are reported, view the results document, correct the errors in the submitted document, save the document, and then click the Check button.

Figure 55.2 Outline Content for Document 55.1

[Tab] I. [Tab] NEED [Enter]

[Enter]

[Tab] [Tab] A. [Tab] Rapid growth of business [Enter]

[Tab] [Tab] B. [Tab] New type of employee [Enter]

[Enter]

[Tab] II. [Tab] CHANGES [Enter]

[Enter]

[Tab] [Tab] A. [Tab] Rising financial costs [Enter]

[Tab] [Tab] [Tab] 1. [Tab] Increased paperwork [Enter]

[Tab] [Tab] [Tab] 2. [Tab] Inflation [Enter]

[Tab] [Tab] B. [Tab] Staffing challenges [Enter]

[Tab] [Tab] [Tab] 1. [Tab] Retiring workers [Enter]

[Tab] [Tab] [Tab] 2. [Tab] Lack of skills [Enter]

[Tab] [Tab] [Tab] 3. [Tab] Technology [Enter]

[Enter]

[Tab] III. [Tab] CAREER OPTIONS [Enter]

continues

Exercise 14.11 · Sentences Drill

Note: If you are learning to key numbers before letters and therefore have not completed Sessions 1–13, skip this exercise.

Key each drill line two times and push for speed. The goal is to key at least 25 WAM. Your WAM rate will appear at the end of each line.

1 Jean shall sell the 321 seashells and 212 stones.
2 Taste the lean tea; handle the kettle that leaks.
3 The 11 attendants halted a ring of thieves. They felt proud.

Key lines 4–6 one time and then key the three lines again. Concentrate on control. The goals are to key at least 25 WAM and to make two or fewer errors. Your WAM rate will appear at the end of the line, and any errors will be highlighted.

4 See, he is ill; his skin is flushed; he feels faint.
5 Enlist the 13 students to help with the many tasks.
6 She is a skilled athlete who strives for perfection.

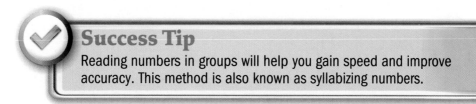

Success Tip
Reading numbers in groups will help you gain speed and improve accuracy. This method is also known as syllabizing numbers.

Exercise 14.12 · Reinforcement Drill

As you key the following drill, remember to mentally read numbers with two or more digits in groups.

Key lines 1 and 2 one time for speed. Your WAM rate will appear at the end of the lines.

1 2 21 21 12 1 112 212 1 2 221 121 121 221 21 1 2 1
2 222 222 22 222 2 222 222 22 2 2 222 222 22 22 2 2

Key line 3 one time for control. The goals are to key at least 25 WAM and to make two or fewer errors. Your WAM rate will appear at the end of the line, and any errors will be highlighted.

3 3 3 3 33 33 33 33 33 333 33 33 3 3 3 33 33 33 3 3 3

Follow the previous drill instructions and key lines 4 and 5 one time for speed. Key line 6 one time for control.

4 1231 3323 321 13 33212 323321 233 23 231 13 233 3
5 a22132213 a21321 2331 2a 22312a 231132a 323132112
6 3112 1232 3321 2311 3122 1312 3222 3221 1223 1233

drill continues

Developing an Outline

Developing an outline is similar to creating a map to a specific location—its purpose is to plan how you are going to get to your destination. When writing a manuscript, developing an outline helps you plan the order and content for major points and subpoints to be included in the manuscript.

An outline may or may not be requested by a publisher. Unless specified differently, format a manuscript outline similar to the outline created in Session 52. In the Document 55.1 activity, you will key an outline for a manuscript.

In the Document 55.2 activity, you will key an unbound manuscript and will format it by following specific formatting guidelines.

Document 55.1 **Manuscript Outline with Changes to Default Line Spacing**

1   Read all instructions for this document activity, navigate to the Document 55.1 launch page in the Online Lab, and then click the Launch Activity button. The Online Lab will open **Doc055.01** in the activity window. The timer will start as soon as you begin keying the document.

2   Before keying any text, check that the automatic list numbering feature is turned off. *Hint: If necessary, review the directions for turning off the automatic list numbering feature in Session 50.*

3   Change the document default line spacing to single spacing with no additional spacing after paragraphs. *Hint: In the Paragraph dialog box, change the spacing settings and then click the Set As Default button. At the message box, make sure the* **This document only?** *option is selected and then click OK.*

4   Set the following tabs in the document:

  a   Set a right tab at 0.5 inch on the horizontal Ruler.

  b   Set left tabs at 0.75 inch, 1.0 inch, and 1.25 inches on the horizontal Ruler. *Hint: See Session 51 to review directions for setting tabs, if necessary.*

5   With the vertical position from top of page measurement added to the Word Status bar, press Enter as needed to move the insertion point 2 inches from the top of the page. (The Status bar should read *At: 2.1".*) *Hint: Review Session 52 if you need help completing this step.*

steps continue

Follow the previous drill instructions and key lines 7 and 8 one time for speed. Key line 9 one time for control.

₇ 23 3231 2231 123 121 233 32 12131 221312 31131 12

₈ 3123 123212 133132 123 321233 3112 32 132 1132 21

₉ 32 321 33312 12 3 23222123 1122331 12 1223 311132

Assessing Your Speed and Accuracy

Complete Timings 14.1 and 14.2 in the Online Lab to assess the skills you have learned in this session. Refer to the following paragraphs as you key. Note that with this session, the WAM goal has increased to 30 WAM. *Note: Do not complete these timings if you have not first completed Sessions 1–13.*

The timing will start as soon as you begin keying the paragraph. Remember to press the Tab key at the start of the paragraph. If you finish keying the paragraph before the timing expires, press Enter and start keying the paragraph again.

When time expires, the Online Lab will give you a WAM rate and will highlight any errors you made. The results will be stored in your Timings Performance report.

Goals: 30 WAM and two or fewer errors

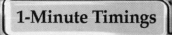 1-Minute Timings

 Timing 14.1
When business is weak, there is not a lot of demand for money. So savings are invested in the stock market. The prices of stocks and bonds go up and interest rates go down. When business is strong, the demand for loans goes up to expand production, and consumers buy cars and homes. This pushes interest rates up.

Timing 14.2
The blunt auditor suggested to Duke that the business returns were a fraud. The usual routine of minimum turnovers of funds had been sound, but that fortune of thousands paid to the 12 jurors had not been inserted in the annual input. Duke presumed he was ruined and flushed with guilt.

 Ergonomic Tip
Sit in a slightly reclined position with your thighs parallel to each other. In other words, do not cross your legs, as it decreases circulation.

Ending the Session

The Online Lab automatically saves the work you completed for this session. You can continue with the next session or exit the Online Lab and continue later.

2 At the Font dialog box, click the Font tab if it is not selected.

3 Scroll down the *Font* list box and then click *Times New Roman*.

4 Click *12* in the *Size* list box.

5 Click the Set As Default button.

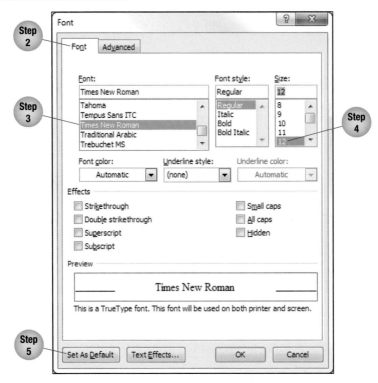

6 At the message box, make sure the *This document only?* option is selected and then click OK. *Note:* **The This document only?** *option will apply the formatting to all of the text keyed in the current document, including headers, page numbers, and other areas of the document.*

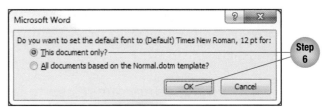

Changing the Default Line Spacing in a Document

As you reviewed the illustration of an unbound manuscript in Figure 55.1, you may have noticed that the text is double-spaced. By default, the line spacing of a blank Word document is 1.15 spacing with 10 points extra space after paragraphs. To change the line spacing in a new document, make the line spacing formatting change before keying the file. You can change line spacing in an already keyed document by selecting all of the content (Ctrl + A) and then changing the formatting.

As you learned in Session 52, change paragraph formatting using the settings in the Paragraph dialog box, which is available by clicking the Paragraph dialog box launcher in the Paragraph group on the Home tab. Make this new line spacing format the default for the document by clicking the Set As Default button in the Paragraph dialog box and then in the message box that opens, make sure *This document only?* is selected before clicking OK to accept the change.

Session 15

4, 5, 6

Session Objectives

- **Identify the 4, 5, and 6 keys**
- **Practice correct finger positioning for the 4, 5, and 6 keys**

Timing Goals

- **1 minute (numeric): 25 WAM and two or fewer errors**
- **1 minute (alphabetic): 30 WAM and two or fewer errors**

Getting Started and Warming Up

Exercise 15.1 If you are continuing immediately from Session 14, you may skip the Exercise 15.1 warm-up drill. However, if you exited the Online Lab at the end of Session 14, warm up by completing Exercise 15.1.

Introducing the 4, 5, and 6 Keys

Videos 15.1–15.3 The locations of the 4, 5, and 6 keys are shown in the following diagram. Watch Videos 15.1 through 15.3 and practice using these new keys.

Exercises 15.2–15.7 Complete Exercises 15.2 through 15.7 to learn these new keys. When keying the drill lines, follow the instruction prompts provided in the Online Lab.

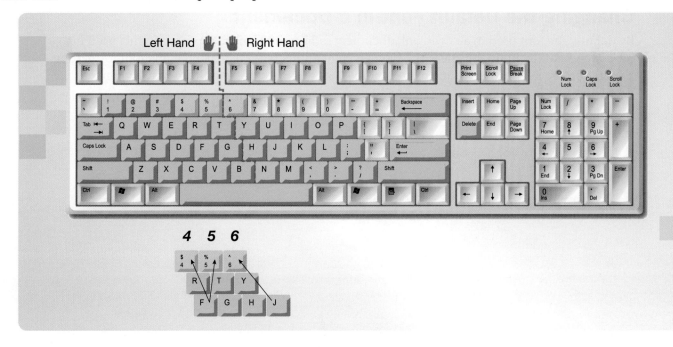

Figure 55.1 Unbound Manuscript Sample   *Note: Do not key this document.*

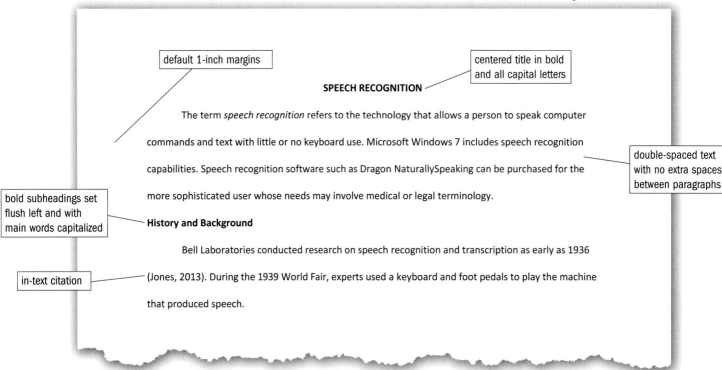

To identify sources of information or ideas, in-text citations (indicating the author's name and resource, publication year, and sometimes page number) are used.

Changing the Default Font in a Document

By default, the font used in a new blank document is 11-point Calibri. To change fonts used in a new document (including the headers, footers, page numbers, etc.), make the line font formatting changes before keying the document and set the formatting as the default for that document.

To change all of the fonts used in a blank document to 12-point Times New Roman, complete the following steps:

1 Click the Font dialog box launcher in the Font group on the Home tab.

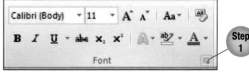

steps continue

⏱ Reinforcing Your Skills

Complete Exercises 15.8 through 15.12 in the Online Lab. Reference the drill lines from the textbook as you key and keep your eyes on the textbook pages, not on your fingers. Complete each exercise at least once, but repeat exercises if you want to improve your WAM rate or accuracy.

Exercise 15.8   **4 Drill**

Key lines 1 and 2 one time for speed. You will key faster if you think of the numbers in groups. The goal is to key with at least 25 WAM. Your WAM rate will appear at the end of each line.

1   14 134 1431 2343 343123 43 334 3 3421 23214 432442

2   a14 a4231 24 4a24 1432a 34 a4321 a4323 a431 a342 a

Key line 3 one time and concentrate on control. The goals are to key at least 25 WAM and to make two or fewer errors. Your WAM rate will appear at the end of the line, and any errors will be highlighted.

3   4343213413 34343213311 4323412341 3431233 44342 43

Exercise 15.9   **5 Drill**

Key lines 1 and 2 one time for speed. The goal is to key with at least 25 WAM. Your WAM rate will appear at the end of each line.

1   11 55 a55 11 55 a55 11 55 55 11 51 a51 15 15 15 5

2   55 44 a45 54 14 15 24 25 34 35 53 43 52 42 51 41a

Key line 3 one time and concetrate on control. The goals are to key at least 25 WAM and to make two or fewer errors. Your WAM rate will appear at the end of the line, and any errors will be highlighted.

3   15115 15115 a55151 a55151 15 5151 151 a155 a51151

Exercise 15.10   **6 Drill**

Key lines 1 and 2 one time for speed. The goal is to key at least 25 WAM. Your WAM rate will appear at the end of each line.

1   11 a66 11 66 11 66 11 66 11 66 a66 11 66 11 66 61

2   166 166 a661 661 161 161 a611 661 661 116 11 a666

Key line 3 one time and concentrate on control. The goals are to key at least 25 WAM and to make two or fewer errors. Your WAM rate will appear at the end of the line, and any errors will be highlighted.

3   11666 16661 61 66 66 111 666 661 1166 16661 61 61

Ergonomic Tip
Keep your head up! Your ears should be in line with your shoulders, and your neck should be straight. Don't lean into the computer or tilt your head to look at the screen.

Preparing Manuscripts

A **manuscript** is a document that is prepared for publication purposes. It might be published as a magazine or journal article, a research report, a newsletter, or even a book. Manuscripts are usually multiple-page documents, but a manuscript can be one page.

In an educational setting, documents that are completed for course assignments may also be referred to as manuscripts. In later sessions, you will be formatting educational manuscripts that include research sources according to nationally recognized style guides.

Manuscripts may be bound or unbound, depending on their length. Unbound manuscripts are generally short—one to four pages. Bound manuscripts are usually five or more pages and typically include a title page, an abstract, the body of the document, and references.

The most efficient method of preparing a manuscript for possible publication is to divide the process into the steps outlined in Table 55.1.

Most publishers require authors to submit a manuscript both as hard copy and electronically as an email attachment. Manuscripts are prepared using a specific format. The format must be consistent, with careful attention to details such as spacing, punctuation, and order or sequence. There are various formats for manuscripts. When manuscript submission guidelines are provided by the magazine, journal, or other publications, you should follow those formatting directions exactly.

It is not intended that you memorize a manuscript format, but rather that you are able to format a manuscript according to the directions or guidelines. In this session, document instructions for margins, spacing, fonts, and font sizes have been used from actual manuscript preparation guidelines for a journal article.

Figure 55.1 illustrates the first page of the body of an unbound manuscript. This format uses double spacing for the text and headings, which provides room for comments by the editor. Although the use of headings is optional, they are helpful to both the writer and the reader.

Table 55.1 Steps for Preparing a Manuscript for Publication

1. Identify the topic.
2. Research the topic for background information.
3. Take notes on cards or in some type of electronic format such as Microsoft OneNote. Include the source of the information (title, author, publisher, publication date, page numbers).
4. Prepare an outline of the major ideas using your computer. Edit and revise the outline.
5. Compose a rough draft of the report using your computer. Include quotations from source notes or other information obtained from your research sources.
6. Revise the writing and edit the document for punctuation, spelling, and capitalization.
7. Prepare an abstract of the manuscript.
8. Prepare a bibliography.

Success Tip

Do not touch the key between the home row and the number key you are entering. This would slow you down. In addition, all keyboards do not have the same alignment.

 Exercise 15.11 **Reinforcement Drill**

Key lines 1 and 2 one time for speed. The goal is to key at least 25 WAM. Your WAM rate will appear at the end of each line.

1 44 44 444 44 44 44 4 4444 44 4 4 444 444 44 44 4 4

2 334 44 343 22343 3443 23423 3422 4321 343 344 43 4

Key line 3 one time and concentrate on control. The goals are to key at least 25 WAM and to make two or fewer errors. Your WAM rate will appear at the end of the line, and any errors will be highlighted.

3 43 44342 3431233 4323412341 34343213311 4343213413

Follow the previous speed instructions for lines 4–5 and 7–8. Follow the previous control instructions for lines 6 and 9.

4 151 51 55 51 55 15 51 15 15 15 5 5 5 55 55 55 5 5

5 51 15115 155 151 51511 15 55151 55151 15115 15115

6 123 a15a a15a a321 a321a21515 a21515 15115 15115

7 6 61 61 61 61 61 666 666 6 6 6 6 66 66 66 66 6 6 6

8 a666 111 116 661 661 a611 161 161 661 a661 166 166

9 61 61 16661 1166 661 666 111 66 66 61 16661 11666

Exercise 15.12 **Sentences Drill**

Note: If you are learning to key numbers before letters and therefore have not completed Sessions 1–13, skip this exercise.

Key lines 1–10 one time for speed. The goal is to key at least 30 WAM. Your WAM rate will appear at the end of each line.

Key lines 1–10 again. This time, focus on control. The goals are to key at least 30 WAM and to make two or fewer errors. Your WAM rate will appear at the end of each line, and any errors will be highlighted.

1 Dennis and Gene nailed 16 boards onto the old gate.

2 Helen had seen the 12 lighted signs shining at night.

3 Anne and Bill ate a salad and 15 figs and a big steak.

drill continues

Complete two 5-minute timings on the timing text below. Timings 55.3 and 55.4 use the same paragraphs.

Goals: 35 WAM and five or fewer errors
SI: 1.47 syllables per word

Timings 55.3–55.4

Do you know about Windows Live SkyDrive? It is a free online storage service from Microsoft Windows Live. If you use Hotmail, Messenger, or Xbox Live, you already have a Windows Live ID. If you don't have one, you can quickly create one on the sign-in page for Windows Live.

What does SkyDrive do? It allows you to create, edit, and store your documents, spreadsheets, presentations, or notes on a server located "in the clouds." This process is referred to as cloud computing.

Although these servers are not literally in the clouds, cloud computing allows the user to create, access, and modify documents anytime from anywhere on any device that can access the Web. That means you or anyone you designate can view, share, and work on documents using a device connected to the Internet.

Your documents are just like web pages because they're stored on a website and displayed in a web browser. The documents look the same in the browser as they do in the Office programs even if they include pictures, borders, text effects, and so on. To view a document, you click it; to share with others, you can send a link or grant them access. With Excel and OneNote, you can even work with others on the same document at the same time.

How do you get your documents into SkyDrive? With Office 2010 you can choose to save directly to SkyDrive through an option in the Save and Send command. While that option is not included with earlier versions of Office, you can upload files the same way you upload other files. Even if you don't have Word, you can create documents in the browser for viewing, editing, and sharing using Office Web Apps.

Office Web Apps are "light" versions of Microsoft Word, Excel, PowerPoint, and OneNote that offer a way to store your documents so that they can be viewed in a web browser. Office Web Apps are available for personal use in Windows Live SkyDrive. It is probably more efficient to create your files on your computer and then save them to SkyDrive. However, you can edit a file easily in a web browser rather than having to open and edit it in the original application and then save and upload the document again.

4 Leslie sang a tiny jingle as she dashed ahead in glee.

5 When Tom tested his stiff ankle, he gnashed his teeth.

6 Please appease that helpless, pleading, pious plaintiff.

7 A tall, split, peeling aspen sapling is plainly diseased.

8 Pat speaks and pleads and defends the three plaintiffs.

9 Did Tim tape that splint and dispense the correct pills?

10 The spaniel has 134 bites and needs some skilled help.

Assessing Your Speed and Accuracy

Complete Timings 15.1 through 15.5 in the Online Lab to assess the skills you have learned in this session. Timings 15.1 and 15.2 are timings on lines of numbers and Timings 15.3 through 15.5 are text-based paragraphs, which include numbers. Refer to the following text you key.

The timing will start as soon as you begin keying. If you finish keying before the timing expires, press Enter and start keying the timing text again.

When time expires, the Online Lab will give you a WAM rate and will highlight any errors you made. The goals for Timings 15.1 and 15.2 are 25 WAM with two or fewer errors and for Timings 15.3 through 15.5 are 30 WAM with two or fewer errors. The results will be stored in your Timings Performance report.

Hint: For the number timings, Timings 15.1 and 15.2, press Enter at the end of each line.

Goals: 25 WAM and two or fewer errors

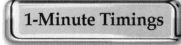

1-Minute Timings

Timing 15.1

333 333 333 444 444 444 555 555 555 666 666 666 56
333 333 444 444 555 666 666 111 111 222 222 123 45
12223 12224 13335 13336 14442 14443 12224 12225 16
32221 42221 53331 63331 24441 34441 42221 52221 63

Timing 15.2

26 35 346 34 45 46 251 2346 235 325 625 463 51616 2
6242 4621 31446 51432 51431 4265 4261 5431 5421 6
16 61 61 31 31 31 3655 66 16 62 5661 6546 665 566 2
16 661 626 365 4466 1263 4565 16 15 1615 26 62 54 3

Session 55

Developing Manuscripts, Outlines, and Title Pages

Session Objectives
- Prepare a manuscript
- Change the default font in a document
- Change the default line spacing in a document
- Key an outline
- Prepare a title page
- Determine word count
- Remove a hyperlink
- Compose a manuscript introduction

Timing Goals
- 1 minute: 45 WAM and one or no errors
- 5 minutes: 35 WAM and five or fewer errors

Getting Started and Warming Up

Exercise 55.1 If you are continuing immediately from Session 54, you may skip the Exercise 55.1 warm-up drill. However, if you exited the Online Lab at the end of Session 54, warm up by completing Exercise 55.1.

Exercise 55.2 Begin your session work by completing Exercise 55.2, a timed short drill, in the Online Lab.

Assessing Your Speed and Accuracy

Complete Timings 55.1 through 55.4 in the Online Lab. At the end of each timing, the Online Lab will display your WAM rate and any errors. Results will be saved in your Timings Performance report. If you have been surpassing the speed and accuracy goals, set slightly more challenging personal goals and strive to exceed them.

Complete two 1-minute timings on the timing text below. Timings 55.1 and 55.2 use the same paragraph.

Goals: 45 WAM and one or no errors
SI: 1.56 syllables per word

1-Minute Timings

Timings 55.1–55.2   Planning flower displays is a time-consuming, but rewarding, task. For example, a mass of brilliant colors and textures could brighten a dark corner or highlight darker foliage and shrubs. Some annuals are better suited for border planting or edging. Others that grow quite tall can be used for unique backgrounds or screening. There are many annuals that make gorgeous bouquets of cut flowers. The gardener can enjoy the fruits of his or her labor with vases of beautiful blossoms placed all around the house. Having your own garden is a benefit you will appreciate time and again. Your friends and relatives will thank you for having a green thumb.

If you are learning to key numbers before letters and therefore have not completed Sessions 1–13, do not complete Timings 15.3 through 15.5. *Note: Do not complete these timings if you have not first completed Sessions 1–13.*

Goals: 30 WAM and two or fewer errors

1-Minute Timings

Timing 15.3

During the winter the jet stream migrates north. For the northern Midwest, this is observed as cold and dry air. It is not unusual for temperatures to plunge well below zero. Any precipitation is usually in the form of snow. Because the air is dry, snowfall amounts are generally not large. However, when weather fronts travel from the south, the collision of these moist systems with cold northern air can produce very large snowfalls of 10 or 20 inches.

Timing 15.4

Muffin is a genuine bulldog. Although he weighs 64 pounds, he bounds about with a flourish. It is fun to see him plunge around, indulging in the pure pleasure of running. He huffs and puffs and slumps to the ground. No doubt, he will jump and lunge again after a pause and find trouble.

Timing 15.5

Thomas bought a used car from a dealer at 16532 Halsted Street. Although the bumper and the trunk were ruined, he assumed that it would run. If he would flush the rust from the lumbering hulk of junk, he might be able to use it. His woeful anguish spurred a new thought; perhaps it was useless.

Ergonomic Tip
Keep both feet flat on the floor or on a footrest to minimize fatigue.

Ending the Session

The Online Lab automatically saves the work you completed for this session. You can continue with the next session or exit the Online Lab and continue later.

Unit 11 Manuscripts and Research Papers Part I

Session 16 — 7, 8, 9, 0, Comma, Decimal Point

Session Objectives

- Identify the 7, 8, 9, and 0 keys
- Practice correct finger positioning for the 7, 8, 9, and 0 keys
- Explore using the comma and decimal keys

Timing Goals

- 1 minute (numeric): 25 WAM and two or fewer errors
- 1 minute (alphabetic): 30 WAM and two or fewer errors

Getting Started and Warming Up

Exercise 16.1 If you are continuing immediately from Session 15, you may skip the Exercise 16.1 warm-up drill. However, if you exited the Online Lab at the end of Session 15, warm up by completing Exercise 16.1.

Introducing the 7, 8, 9, and 0 Keys

Videos 16.1–16.4 The locations of the 7, 8, 9, and 0 keys are shown in the following diagram. Watch Videos 16.1 through 16.4 and practice using these new keys.

Exercises 16.2–16.6 Complete Exercises 16.2 through 16.6 to learn these new keys. When keying the drill lines, follow the instruction prompts provided in the Online Lab.

Figure 54.4 Model Outline for Document 54.3

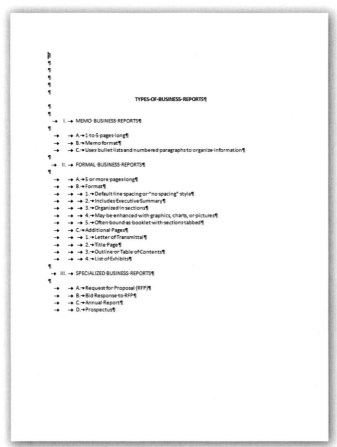

Ending the Session

The Online Lab automatically saves the work you completed for this session. You may continue with the next session or exit the Online Lab and continue later.

↻ Reinforcing Your Skills

Complete Exercises 16.7 through 16.16 in the Online Lab. Reference the drill lines from the textbook as you key and keep your eyes on the textbook pages, not on your fingers. Complete each exercise at least once, but repeat exercises if you want to improve your WAM rate or accuracy.

Exercise 16.7 **7 Drill**

Key lines 1–2 one time for speed. Anchor the ; (semicolon) finger on the home row. The goal is to key at least 25 WAM. Your WAM rate will appear at the end of each line.

1 a55 77 66 76 57 57 a76 77 777 677 a555 76 6 a755a a755a

2 767 767 5767 5757 a576 7675a 7675a 77 777 666 555 a75a

Key line 3 one time and concentrate on control. The goals are to key at least 25 WAM and to make two or fewer errors.

3 a576a 76a5a 6675a 6675 5667 777 a65a7 5672 a7765 a575a

Exercise 16.8 **1–7 Drill**

To develop speed keying the numbers 1–7, see how quickly you can complete the following:

1 Key the numbers 1 through 7 three times. Space once between numbers and press Enter at the end of each number set. Keep your eyes on the screen.

2 Reverse the order and key the numbers 7 down through 1 three times. Space once between numbers and press Enter at the end of each number set. Again, keep your eyes on the screen.

✓ Success Tip
After keying the numbers 7 down to 1, proofread. If you have any errors, repeat the drill until you can key the numbers without error.

Exercise 16.9 **8 Drill**

Key lines 1 and 2 one time for speed. Anchor either the J or the ; (semicolon) finger on the home row when keying 8. The goal is to key at least 25 WAM. Your WAM rate will appear at the end of each line.

1 88 11 588 11 88 11 88 11 88 11 688 11 88 11 8 8823 1482

2 8182 81828 2845 6817 71882 6818 2238 885 888 288 388

Key line 3 one time and concentrate control. The goals are to key at least 25 WAM and to make two or fewer errors. Your WAM rate will appear at the end of the line, and any errors will be highlighted.

3 557 8283 38482 78681 11812 8823 28 28 888 321 854 488

Exercise 16.10 **1–8 Drill**

Complete the following drill to develop speed and concentration.

1 Key the numbers 1 through 8 three times. Space once between numbers and press Enter at the end of each number set. Keep your eyes on the screen.

2 Reverse the order and key the numbers 8 down through 1 three times. Space once between numbers and press Enter at the end of each number set. Again, keep your eyes on the screen.

Figure 54.3 Outline Content for Document 54.3

I.   MEMO BUSINESS REPORTS
    A.   1 to 5 pages long
    B.   Memo format
    C.   Uses bullet lists and numbered paragraphs to organize information

II.   FORMAL BUSINESS REPORTS
    A.   5 or more pages long
    B.   Format
        1.   Default line spacing or "no spacing" style
        2.   Includes Executive Summary
        3.   Organized in sections
        4.   May be enhanced with graphics, charts, or pictures
        5.   Often bound as booklet with sections tabbed
    C.   Additional Pages
        1.   Letter of Transmittal
        2.   Title Page
        3.   Outline or Table of Contents
        4.   List of Exhibits

III. SPECIALIZED BUSINESS REPORTS
    A.   Request for Proposal (RFP)
    B.   Bid Response to RFP
    C.   Annual Report
    D.   Prospectus

Exercise 16.11 — 9 Drill

Key lines 1–2 one time for speed. Anchor the J finger on the home row as the L finger keys 9. Remember to read the numbers as groups. The goal is to key at least 25 WAM. Your WAM rate will appear at the end of each line.

1   8489 19891 1919 1891 9981 19867 183218 189 19 698 98

2   99 88 589 998 998 888 991 999 498 98 99 88 94 32989 29

Key line 3 one time for control. The goals are to key at least 25 WAM and to make two or fewer errors. Your WAM rate will appear at the end of the line, and any errors will be highlighted.

3   23 1989 2239 39823 59891 123 698 92919 9812 375 688 9

Exercise 16.12 — 1–9 Drill

Complete the following drill to develop speed and concentration.

1   Key the numbers 1 through 9 three times. Space once between numbers and press Enter at the end of each number set. Keep your eyes on the screen.

2   Reverse the order and key the numbers 9 down through 1 three times. Space once between numbers and press Enter at the end of each number set. Again, keep your eyes on the screen.

Exercise 16.13 — 0 (Zero) Drill

Anchor the J finger on the home row as the ; (semicolon) finger keys 0. *Note: Be sure to use the zero key, not the capital O.*

Key the following line for speed. The goal is to key at least 25 WAM. Your WAM rate will appear at the end of each line.

Key the line again for control. The goals are to key at least 25 WAM and to make two or fewer errors. Your WAM rate will appear at the end of the line, and any errors will be highlighted.

10 20 30 40 50 60 70 80 90 a10 a20 a30 240 250 10 115 619 057

Exercise 16.14 — 1–100 Drill

Key the numbers from 1 to 100. Space once between numbers.

Exercise 16.15 — Twos Drill

Key the numbers 2 to 200 by twos (that is, key only even numbers). Space once between numbers and do not look at your fingers as you key.

Exercise 16.16 — Number Concentration Drill

Key lines 1–5 one time for control. Concentrate on reading the numbers in groups. The goals are to key at least 25 WAM and to make two or fewer errors. Your WAM rate will appear at the end of the line, and any errors will be highlighted.

1   11201 1316 14037 22304 3405 4506 35607 6708 78092 1415

2   6816z 62317 73218 2219 32206 8782 19222 90234 1929 3030

3   45317 7932 34332 13476 9535 87369 1370 1743 37744 7645

4   2674 65647 1674 84859 34750 25151 23270 45524 8910 573

5   91524 7853 85426 1927 52938 22304 11201 78092 7753 361

Figure 54.2 RFP Content for Document 54.2—Continued

4.2.1.2   The availability of food service management staff throughout the entire catered event.

4.2.1.3   The use of uniformed wait staff with levels of service agreed to prior to the event.

4.2.1.4   Appropriate training for all catering staff, including student staff, prior to being assigned to any catering service.

4.2.2   <u>Pricing and Portions</u>. Any changes in catering prices or portions must be approved by the College.

Document Outline

54.3

1   Read all instructions for this document activity, navigate to the Document 54.3 launch page in the Online Lab, and then click the Launch Activity button. The Online Lab will open **Doc054.03** in the activity window. The timer will start as soon as you begin keying the document.

2   Before keying any text, confirm that the automatic list numbering feature is turned off.

3   Change the format of the document to single spacing with no additional spacing after paragraphs.

4   Set a right tab at 0.5 inch and left tabs at 0.75 inch, 1.0 inch, and 1.25 inches.

5   With the vertical position from top of page measurement added to the Word Status bar, press Enter as needed to move the insertion point 2 inches from the top of the page. (The Status bar should read *At: 2.1"*.)

6   Type the title of the outline by completing the following steps:

   a   Turn on bold and center alignment formatting and then key **TYPES OF BUSINESS REPORTS**.

   b   Turn off bold formatting and press Enter.

   c   Change the alignment to left-aligned and then press Enter two times.

7   Key the outline text shown in Figure 54.3. Figure 54.4 shows the tab and line spacing formatting that should be applied to the document.

8   Proofread the document and correct any errors.

9   Save the document.

10   Reactivate the automatic number formatting feature in Word.

11   Click the Check button to stop the timer and upload the document for checking. The Online Lab will report the WAM rate and number of errors for the activity.

12   If errors are reported, view the results document, correct the errors in the submitted document, save the document, and then click the Check button.

Introducing the Comma and Decimal Point Keys

You have now been introduced to all ten digits and are ready to review other areas of the keyboard. Two symbols used frequently with numbers are the comma (,) and the decimal point (.). The decimal point is also used as a period at the end of a sentence. These keys were presented in Session 3, but because they are used frequently with numbers, more practice is offered here. If you are learning the number keys before the alphabetic keys, the comma and decimal point are new to you.

Videos 16.5–16.6   The locations of the comma and decimal keys are shown in the following diagram. Watch Videos 16.5 through 16.6 and practice using these new keys.

Exercises 16.17–16.20   Complete Exercises 16.17 through 16.20 to learn to use these keys with numbers. When keying the drill lines, follow the instruction prompts provided in the Online Lab.

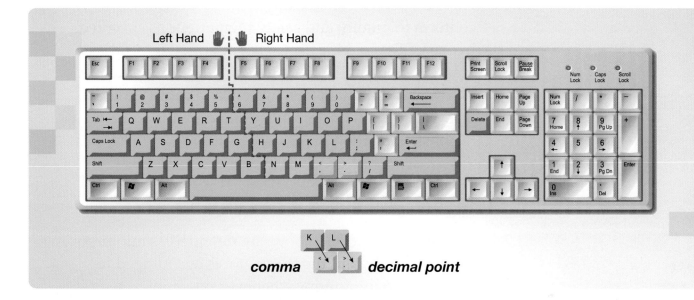

⟳ Reinforcing Your Skills

Complete Exercises 16.21 through 16.24 in the Online Lab. Reference the drill lines from the textbook as you key and keep your eyes on the textbook pages, not on your fingers. Complete each exercise at least once, but repeat exercises if you want to improve your WAM rate or accuracy.

When numbers are separated by commas, decimals, spaces, letters, or other symbols, use those division points as natural breaks between groups of numbers. For example, 5,134 would be read as *five, comma, one thirty-four.*

Exercise 16.21   **Comma Drill**

Key lines 1–2 one time for speed. Concentrate on grouping the numbers by division points. The comma is keyed with the middle finger of the right hand. Reach down from the K key. The goal is to key at least 25 WAM. Your WAM rate will appear at the end of each line.

1 1,368 16,434 92,860 58,167 34,511 76,924 6,331 21,468

2 38,107 48,243 1,509 5,114 15,816 6,184,336 98,165,225

Figure 54.2 RFP Content for Document 54.2—Continued

4.1.2.1   All meats shall be inspected by official inspectors of the U.S. Department of Agriculture and/or the local health department. Meats and deli meats (corned beef brisket, bologna, liverwurst, pastrami, etc.) shall be of the grades and types that will produce high quality finished products. Such items as steaks and roasts shall be prime or choice grade.

4.1.2.2   All fresh and frozen fish and seafood purchases should conform to quality and safety regulations as specified by the USDA, paying particular attention to product identification and labeling information. Any purchase of fresh raw shellfish (i.e., oysters and clams) must be from certified dealers as specified by the National Shellfish Sanitation program.

4.1.2.3   All poultry shall be inspected by official inspectors of the USDA and shall be Grade A or better.

4.1.2.4   The Grades indicated above are intended as minimum standards only, and the contractor is encouraged to exceed these minimums whenever possible.

4.1.3   <u>Low-Fat Products</u>. The contractor shall use natural, low-fat products whenever possible. Natural, low-fat, processed cheeses may be used for cooking purposes. Non-processed cheeses shall be used for catering unless processed cheeses are specifically requested. Tropical oils may not be used by the contractor for cooking purposes.

4.2   Catered Services

4.2.1   <u>Minimum Standards for Catered Services</u>.

4.2.1.1   The use of table linen service when requested by the College or other groups.

continues

Key line 3 one time for control. The goals are to key at least 25 WAM and to make two or fewer errors. Your WAM rate will appear at the end of the line, and any errors will be highlighted.

3   4,408,452 251,145 12,259 1,259 159,467 43,410 875,243

Exercise 16.22 Decimal Point Drill

Key lines 1–2 one time for speed. Concentrate on reading numbers by division. The goal is to key at least 25 WAM. Your WAM rate will appear at the end of each line.

1   41,345.51 15,378.78 31,428.27 89,261,500.68 59.63 61.3

2   91,007.23 851,267.18 109.01 13.17 8.43 4.40 596.27 39.8

Key line 3 one time and concentrate on control. The goals are to key at least 25 WAM and to make two or fewer errors. Your WAM rate will appear at the end of the line, and any errors will be highlighted.

3   990.85 67,349.34 23,265.08 186.84 4.23 .87 8,582 13.455

Exercise 16.23 Reinforcement Drill

Key lines 1 and 2 one time for speed. The goal is to key at least 25 WAM. Your WAM rate will appear at the end of each line.

1   77 77 7 7777 7777 777 777 77 77 7 7 7777 777 77 7

2   6 76 a555 677 777 77 a76 57 57 76 66 77 a55 75 75

Key line 3 one time and concentrate on control. The goals are to key at least 25 WAM and to make two or fewer errors. Your WAM rate will appear at the end of the line, and any errors will be highlighted.

3   4651 1234 3467 461234 3457 56712 62345 5671 71234

Follow the previous speed instructions for lines 4–5, 7–8, and 10–11. Follow the previous control instructions for lines 6, 9, and 12.

4   88 88 88 88 88 888 888 88 88 8 8 8 88 88 88 8 8 8

5   8 11 88 11 688 11 88 11 88 11 88 11 588 11 88 411

6   88 2238 6818 71882 6817 2845 81828 8182 1482 8823

7   91 999 99 9 999 9 99 99 99 91 91 91 99 9 999 9 99

8   19 189 183218 19867 9981 1891 1919 19891 8489 989

9   92919 698 123 59891 39823 2239 1989 2923 32989 94

10 10 20 30 40 50 60 70 80 90 a10 a20 a30 240 250 10

11 6,151 6,719 1,438 4,497 5,313 7,893 38,751 45,134

12 .87 4.23 186.84 23,265.08 67,349.34 990.85 596.27

    g   Type the introductory text for 4.1.2, applying the appropriate formatting according to the text for 4.1.1, and then press Enter twice.

    h   Increase the indent, key **4.1.2.1**, press Tab, and then key the paragraph. At the end of the paragraph, press the Enter key twice.

    i   Key paragraphs 4.1.2.2 through 4.1.2.4 following the procedure outline above. After keying paragraph 4.1.2.4, press Enter twice.

    j   Decrease the indent by one level.

    k   Key the rest of the report and increase and decrease the indentation of the text when necessary.

4   Number all pages *except* the first page by inserting a plain page number at the right margin of the header.

5   Proofread the document and correct any errors.

6   Save the document.

7   Click the Check button to stop the timer and upload the document for checking. The Online Lab will report the WAM rate and number of errors for the activity.

8   If errors are reported, view the results document, correct the errors in the submitted document, save the document, and then click the Check button.

Figure 54.2 RFP Content for Document 54.2

SECTION 4. OTHER MANDATORY REQUIREMENTS

Each of the requirements must be responded to in the format and order presented in each section even if the answer is simply yes or no.

4.1   Food and Supplies

    4.1.1 <u>Compliance with U.S. Grades</u>. All food and supplies purchased shall be in conformance with the specified minimum U.S. Standards for Grades. In the absence of grade labeling, the contractor shall provide the College with packers' labeling codes or an industry-accepted grade equivalent standard to verify the minimum grades specified as being provided. The College shall periodically, or as deemed necessary, inspect the contractor's inventory of food and supplies to determine that purchase standards are maintained.

    4.1.2 <u>Grade Minimum for Food Items Shall Be</u>:

continues

Exercise 16.24 — **Sentence Drill**

Note: If you are learning to key numbers before letters and therefore have not completed Sessions 1–13, skip this exercise.

Key lines 1–10 one time for speed. The goal is to key at least 30 WAM. Your WAM rate will appear at the end of each line.

Key lines 1–10 again. This time, focus on control. The goals are to key at least 30 WAM and to make two or fewer errors. Your WAM rate will appear at the end of each line, and any errors will be highlighted.

1 Of the 15,220 rangers, 170 sprained their ankles last year.

2 Dirk did the drills first and drank the delicious tea later.

3 Take 12 or 13 fresh, green grapes as your dessert treat.

4 He risks great danger if he departs after the dinner.

5 The 14 interns gratefully lingered in the green garden.

6 The meat manager made a simple remark and smirked.

7 Did Mary send the 380 messages after amending them?

8 Pam had made some malts with milk, mint, and mango.

9 The firefighters attempted an immense task and missed.

10 Did Sammie eliminate the 16 mistakes in the message?

Assessing Your Speed and Accuracy

Complete Timings 16.1 through 16.6 in the Online Lab to assess the skills you have learned in this session. Timings 16.1 through 16.3 will be timings on lines of numbers and Timings 16.4 through 16.6 will be text-based paragraphs, which include numbers. Refer to the following text as you key.

The timing will start as soon as you begin keying. If you finish keying before the timing expires, press Enter and start keying the timing text again.

When time expires, the Online Lab will give you a WAM rate and will highlight any errors you made. The results will be stored in your Timings Performance Report.

Hint: For the number timings, Timings 16.1 through 16.3, press Enter at the end of each line.

Goals: 25 WAM and two or fewer errors

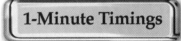

Timing 16.1

.81 85 823 8466 8877 7868 58 45 238 845 866 8143 8 8123
5671 82345 3458 8612348 3467 1238 886 81387 5834278
58743218 11386518 2251386 87 88 8811318 8 5481 8375
18 2368 8 7628 81 61842 8811318 18 8788 5792 6139 144

Figure 54.1 Memo Business Report Content for Document 54.1—Continued

The first message seems deliberately difficult to understand and is unclear due to lack of dates and use of acronyms that may not be understood. The second message is clearer, more concrete, more informative, and frankly, less annoying.

If you need a response by a certain date or time, include that information as well as how your reader should respond (via email or phone). Allow ∧ enough time for a careful response. *the recipient*

If you are making several points, put them in a logical order (most important first, or chronological order, for example). You may also want to list your ideas numerically or as a bullet list.

We are excited to have you join our staff, Elizabeth, and look forward to your contributions. *Send copies to Don Harriss and Mary Schlumpf.*

Document 54.2 Request for Proposal

1 Read all instructions for this document activity, navigate to the Document 54.2 launch page in the Online Lab, and then click the Launch Activity button. The Online Lab will open **Doc054.02** in the activity window. The timer will start as soon as you begin keying the document.

2 Implement the following formatting to the document:

   a Change the line spacing to single with no additional space between paragraphs.

   b Set a hanging indent at the default indent setting (0.5 inch).

   c Turn off the automatic list numbering feature if it is turned on.

3 Key the text in Figure 54.2. This document is part of a longer RFP. Consider the following as you key the text:

   a Key the section title in all caps, bold, and centered. After keying the section title, turn off bold, and press Enter twice.

   b Change alignment from center back to left.

   c Key the first paragraph and press the Enter key two times.

   d Select the paragraph that you just keyed and remove the hanging indent. ***Hint: Set the indentation setting to* (none)**.

   e Move the insertion point to the end of the document, turn on bold formatting, key **4.1**, press Tab, key **Food and Supplies**, turn off bold formatting, and then press the Enter key two times.

   f Click the Increase Indent button before keying **4.1.1**. Do not underline the period at the end of the heading. Key the 4.1.1 paragraph and at the end of that paragraph, press the Enter key two times.

steps continue

Timing 16.2

91 95 923 8466 9977 7898 69 45 239 945 966 9143 9 9123
5671 92345 3458 9612349 3467 12392 996 81389 5934278
59743219 11386519 2251396 973 99 9911319 9 5491 9375
19 2368 9 7629 947 61942 99111319 19 979 7426 5187 239

Timing 16.3

27 821 59361 40352 89734 92035 64019 9356 693 958 3177
501 6512 96 8742 56034 56832 85923 780 847 91 6409 7483
9467 3520 5945 2635 5705 8932 6485 1956 23670 81251800
165 208125635 69312 9871 6017340 2 716941 8320193 5163
8613 5113818 8542001 88490 6 2361 15432 11621618 11234
19051 3399 668 45441 4091 25937 68465 21893 492 591 783

If you are learning to key numbers before letters and thus have not completed Sessions 1–13, do not complete Timings 16.4 through 16.6. *Note: Do not complete these timings if you have not first completed Sessions 1–13.*

Goals: 30 WAM and two or fewer error

1-Minute Timings

Timing 16.4

Zeb went to the zoo to see the 179 new animals. He went especially to see the 18 species of lizards. He wants to be a zoologist when he gets older. He knows many things about animals, and his parents are really amazed.

Timing 16.5

A cookout on the beach could include 6 kinds of cheese, carrots, 3 types of meat sandwiches, and 14 cans of cold juice. If the chill of the ocean is too much, hot chocolate and hot coffee can chase the cold chills. The decent lunch and a chat with friends can enrich affection.

Timing 16.6

An office clerk who lacks basic ethics could become the subject of scorn. Those who gossip about or verbally abuse new workers can cause problems. It is smart to follow the 13 rules that are printed on the bulletin board about getting along with fellow workers. Do the right thing and be sincere.

Ergonomic Tip

The human body is made to move. When you stay in one position too long, you will end up stiff, sore, and stressed. After sitting at your workstation for 45-60 minutes, stand up and stretch your arms and legs.

Ending the Session

The Online Lab automatically saves the work you completed for this session. You can continue with the next session or exit the Online Lab and continue later.

Figure 54.1 Memo Business Report Content for Document 54.1—Continued

Use both lower and uppercase letters. Using all uppercase is like shouting and is more difficult to read, as is all lower case.

Use an easy-to-read font, such as Calibri, Times New Roman, or Arial in black on a white background. is expected.

To avoid confusion, write out dates rather than using numbers (March 5 instead of 3/5).

In educational and professional correspondence, avoid using email acronyms such as TTYL (talk to you later) and emoticons (smiley faces or other graphic symbols).

Proofread carefully for spelling, grammar, and punctuation; errors detract from the importance of what you have to say. Your writing should represent you and our company in the best possible way.

Create an Outlook signature including your name, title, department, mailing address, email address, and telephone number. Include this signature in all outgoing email you send.

Consider the Content of Your Email Message: Be considerate of your reader's time—keep your message as brief and to-the-point as possible. Write clearly and plainly. Shorter sentences are better when possible, but do write in complete sentences and fully formed paragraphs.

Offer only as much background information as necessary. make your main point the primary piece of information.

Compare the following messages:

1. To better facilitate our exchange this afternoon, please be ready to produce all documents related to EPPC's last meeting.

2. Please bring your notes from last Thursday's Employee Picnic Planning Committee meeting to our meeting at 2 p.m. on Tuesday, April 30.

continues

Session 17

Number Patterns, Columns of Numbers, and Number Style Guidelines

Session Objectives

- Explore and use number patterns
- Learn to use preset tabs to key columns of numbers
- Investigate style guidelines for expressing numbers

Timing Goals

- 1 minute: 30 WAM and two or fewer errors

Getting Started and Warming Up

Exercise 17.1 If you are continuing immediately from Session 16, you may skip the Exercise 17.1 warm-up drill. However, if you exited the Online Lab at the end of Session 16, warm up by completing Exercise 17.1.

In addition to being a warm-up exercise, Exercise 17.1 provides an opportunity for further practice syllabizing numbers. Syllabizing helps you keep track of where you are in combinations of five or more numbers.

Exercises 17.2–17.4 Continue developing your number keyboarding skills by completing Exercises 17.2 through 17.4. Exercise 17.2 is a series of number drill lines and Exercises 17.3 and 17.4 are text-based speed and accuracy drills, which you should skip if you have not already completed Sessions 1–13. When keying drill lines for these exercises, follow the instruction prompts provided in the Online Lab.

⟳ Reinforcing Your Skills

After working through the previous exercises, complete Exercises 17.5 through 17.13 in the Online Lab. Reference the drill lines from the textbook as you key and keep your eyes on the textbook pages, not on your fingers. Complete each exercise at least once, but repeat exercises if you want to improve your WAM rate or accuracy.

Exercise 17.5 **Numbers Drill**

Key the following line for speed. The goal is at least 25 WAM. Your WAM rate will appear at the end of the line.

Key the line again. This time, focus on control. The goals are to key at least 25 WAM and to make two or fewer errors. Your WAM rate will appear at the end of each line. Any errors will be highlighted. If either goal is not met, key the line again.

1 11 22 33 44 55 66 77 88 99 00

d Key the reference initials **jmm** and the file name to the bottom of the memo.

e Before keying the copy notation, set a left tab at 0.25 inch so you can tab after it and before each recipient's name.

3 Proofread the document and correct any errors.

4 Save the document.

5 Click the Check button to stop the timer and upload the document for checking. The Online Lab will report the WAM rate and number of errors for the activity.

6 If errors are reported, view the results document, correct the errors in the submitted document, save the document, and then click the Check button.

Figure 54.1 Memo Business Report Content for Document 54.1

TO:	Elizabeth Ryan
FROM:	Esther Ramell, Human Resources
DATE:	October 23, 2014
SUBJECT:	Email Style

Welcome to HG Small Investments, LLC. Following are a few ~~simple~~ guidelines *that* will help you communicate more effectively and get better responses when ~~communicating~~ *interacting* via email.

Before You Write: Consider your reader and the content of your message. Send only what will be valuable to the person receiving your email. You don't want your name to be associated with an immediate urge to hit the Delete key!

Write only what you would be willing to say in person. Write as if someone other than ~~its~~ *your* intended recipient could read your message.

Remember that without facial expressions and tone of voice, humor or irony may be more difficult to identify and easily could be misunderstood.

Email Form and Mechanics: Create a clear, meaningful topic for the subject line.

Use your reader's name in a salutation at the beginning of your message, followed by a comma or a colon. If you are sending to more than one recipient, a group greeting such as "Hello:" or "Good morning," ~~or "Dear Book Club Members:"~~ is fine.

continues

Exercise 17.6   Most Common Numbers Drill

The most frequently used number is 0, followed by 5. To build your skills with these numbers, key to 500 by tens, and then key to 200 by fives. Space once between numbers. Your WAM rate will appear after the last number, and any errors will be highlighted. Concentrate on keying without error while maintaining your WAM rate.

1   10 20 30 40 50 60 …

2   5 10 15 20 25 30 35 40 45 50 …

Exercise 17.7   Numbers by Threes Drill

To reinforce your ability to think while keying numbers, start at 100 and key to 1 by threes.

1   100 97 94 91 88 85 82 79 …

Repeat these drills whenever you can. They will help you key numbers accurately.

Exercise 17.8   Reading Number Groups Drill

As a reminder, when numbers are grouped naturally by commas, spaces, and decimals, read the number by those groups. For example, read 1,676,352.17 as *one, comma, six seventy-six, comma, three fifty-two, decimal, seventeen.*

Key lines 1–2 one time for speed. Concentrate on reading numbers in groups. The goal is to key at least 25 WAM. Your WAM rate will appear at the end of each line.

1   1,676,352.17 3,131 2.24 436,342 101.31 166,891 89

2   236,731 831,643 534.67 4,091,867 3,587.13 501,316

Key line 3 one time and concentrate on control. The goal is to key without error. Any errors will be highlighted.

3   61,301.04 .36 89,341.76 31,700.73 151,317 416,319

Exercise 17.9   Columns of Numbers Drill

Using the tabs preset at every 0.5 inch, create the following columns of numbers by keying the first four-digit number, and then pressing the Tab key to move to the next columns. Press the Enter key at the end of each line.

Key the columns of numbers for control. The goal is to key without errors. Any errors will be highlighted.

1 4901	8702	3303	3904	7205
2 6106	8307	9408	2709	3710
3 1511	5712	2613	9114	1515
4 5716	9117	5618	6619	3820
5 2621	3122	4523	2324	3125
6 6726	3528	8528	3529	4130
7 7731	6932	8533	7434	9935
8 8836	2337	6138	1639	5840

Ergonomic Tip

Keep your phone within easy reach and on the most convenient side of your desk. If you are right handed, place your telephone on the left side of the desk and hold it with your left hand. Your right hand will be free for taking notes. Left handed? Just reverse the process.

Checking Production Progress: Business Reports

Sessions 49–53 discussed the procedures for preparing and formatting different types of business reports. In this session, you will be assessed on how quickly and accurately you can key these types of documents. In the following document activities, each completed document is to be useable or "mailable," which means that it contains no errors. A document that requires additional corrections before being distributed is not considered mailable.

Your goals are to key each document in mailable form and at a rate of at least 25 WAM. If your rate is less than 25 WAM, or if your document contains uncorrected errors, your instructor may ask you to repeat documents.

To help you succeed, carefully review the instructions and content for each document before keying. To minimize formatting errors identified by the document checker, be sure to follow the directions carefully.

Success Tip

Before you begin the following documents, review all of the instruction steps and the content to be keyed prior to actually launching the document. If you are unsure how to complete a specific formatting or software task, review the content of Sessions 49 to 53.

Document **Memo Business Report**

54.1

1 Read all instructions for this document activity, navigate to the Document 54.1 launch page in the Online Lab, and then click the Launch Activity button. The Online Lab will open **Doc054.01** in the activity window. The timer will start as soon as you begin keying the document.

2 Key the text in Figure 54.1 as a plain-paper memo business report, implementing the proofreading marks shown in the figure. As you key the memo, consider the following directions:

a When keying the bold headings within the memo, format the colons following the headings in bold. Remember to turn off bold formatting after keying the colon but before spacing or tabbing to ensure that your document is scored correctly by the Online Lab.

b Allow Word to automatically format the numbered sentences in the memo. However, decrease the indent so the numbers begin at the left margin. Insert an extra blank line between the numbered items. *Hint: Press Shift + Enter at the end of the first numbered item.*

c Key a vertical-style header for pages except the first page. The header margin should begin 1.0 inch from the top of the page.

steps continue

Exercise 17.10 Numbers Drill

Key lines 1–2 one time for speed. Remember to read the numbers in 2-3-2 combinations. The goal is to key at least 25 WAM. Your WAM rate will appear at the end of each line.

1 7371130 91368840 1534986003 51673455189 963310931

2 21468159 515113 6873931 438761 223026501 89340013

Key line 3 one time and concentrate on control. Try to key without error. Any errors will be highlighted.

3 6135910 619822385 3676 1090101 3948131 1788434341

Exercise 17.11 Reinforcement Drill

Key lines 1–2 one time for speed. Remember to read the numbers in 2-3-2 combinations. The goal is to key at least 25 WAM. Your WAM rate will appear at the end of each line.

1 2 34141 38886190 1 5133459 789 386005138 45134157

2 9,586,713 39,913,867 55,565,577 231,464 2,361,731

Key line 3 one time and concentrate on control. The goal is to key without error. Any errors will be highlighted.

3 4,131 59.39 13,667 63,485 .98 78,431 40.83 76,924

Follow the previous speed instructions for lines 4–5 and 7–8. Follow the previous control instructions for lines 6 and 9.

4 47 681107 741 23 15281 59,602,388 2.95 96175 284 4

5 56451089 904 82 67,832,523.15 571.28 903 84.22 99

6 15 510 67414451 281,401,282.00 61700 29.15 106 80

7 4559 71.26 8674005 21 4.86 489,753 4605141 50 224

8 531 78911 556 9,454.89 49724301 5,410 8.26 667101

9 2,466 61780 434215 5436 33216 4457004 96.48 82 46

Complete two 5-minute timings on the timing text below. Timings 54.3 and 54.4 use the same paragraphs.

Goals: 35 WAM and five or fewer errors
SI: 1.51 syllables per word

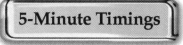

5-Minute Timings

Timings 54.3–54.4

A site that allows you to share contacts and build a network of "friends" is a social networking site. Using social media technology, people can blog, network, post wikis, and share media such as photos, video, and music.

A blog is an online journal that may be focused on a topic or simply be a random collection of thoughts. Blogs can contain text, images and videos, and links to other online content. Those who read blogs can post comments. Blogs and comments are listed in reverse date order, with the most recent posting at the top. You may create your own blog on a blog hosting site, or you may post to a blog that is part of a social networking site. Firms often host blogs on their websites, and blogs have taken on a new role in sharing news stories. Sites such as Twitter, which use brief comments, are called microblogging sites.

Social networking sites include a blogging feature and are able to share media, but what makes them different from other such sites is that they can share contacts and build a network of friends. Many websites include features such as profiles, friends' lists, and media sharing. Trends for these types of sites include greater use by older people and the quick use of social media. The social web is also giving some great chances for businesses that have their own pages on sites such as Facebook where they can interact with their clients. The term mocial means using a networking engine such as Facebook, Twitter, FourSquare or Google Places through any mobile device.

Social bookmarking helps users make new content as well as recommend content to each other. This approach uses a fairly new item known as metadata, which is more or less data about data. Bookmarking sites save users' bookmarks as tags since you can sort and make bookmark tags, it is easy for you to search and catalogue data.

Wikis are a new way to share knowledge about just about any topic. These take the form of online sources of knowledge, and are similar to libraries. Wikis let people post and edit content in a way that creates a network of knowledge that anyone can read and edit.

Exercise 17.12   Guidelines for Expressing Numbers Drill

Note: If you are learning to key numbers before letters and therefore have not completed Sessions 1–13, skip this exercise.

Authorities do not always agree on when to spell out numbers and when to use numerals. However, the following guidelines are widely accepted. For each guideline, key the examples. To help you impress a mental image of the examples for each guideline, after keying each line reread what you have keyed.

1   Spell out numbers one through ten. Use numerals for numbers 11 and above.

1 The computer science class includes six women.
2 At least 40 men are enrolled in beginning keyboarding.

2   If any of the numbers in a series is greater than ten, use numerals for all the numbers.

3 We have 16 Compaq computers, 14 Dell computers, and 8 Gateway computers.

3   When a sentence begins with a number, spell it out (or rewrite the sentence).

4 Three hundred students are majoring in business.
5 Business majors number 300.

4   If the day of the month precedes the month, express it in words.

6 We will meet on the sixth of December.

5   If the day of the month follows the month, express it in numerals.

7 We will meet on December 6 at the restaurant.

6   If the date is in the form of month, day, and year, express the day and year in numerals. Always follow the year with a comma unless it appears at the end of a sentence.

8 We will meet on December 6, 2014, at the restaurant.

7   Use numerals for measurements, percentages, and other mathematical expressions.

9 We need new carpet for a room that is 11 feet x 12 feet.
10 The package weighs about 7 pounds.
11 I will ask for a 6 percent raise.

8   In general, use numerals to express fractions and mixed numbers in technical writing or in physical measurements. If a fraction appears alone or does not express a direct physical measurement, spell out the fraction.

12 They used 3.5 feet of coaxial cable.
13 He makes only half of what she makes.

drill continues

Session 54 — Production Progress Check: Business Reports Part I

Session Objectives

- Format a memo report
- Format a Request for Proposal
- Create an outline

Timing Goals

- 1 minute: 45 WAM and one or no errors
- 5 minutes: 35 WAM and five or fewer errors

Getting Started and Warming Up

Exercise 54.1 If you are continuing immediately from Session 53, you may skip the Exercise 54.1 warm-up drill. However, if you exited the Online Lab at the end of Session 53, warm up by completing Exercise 54.1.

Exercise 54.2 Begin your session work by completing Exercise 54.2, a timed short drill, in the Online Lab.

Assessing Your Speed and Accuracy

Complete Timings 54.1 through 54.4 in the Online Lab. At the end of each timing, the Online Lab will display your WAM rate and any errors. Results will be saved in your Timings Performance report. If you have been surpassing the speed and accuracy goals, set slightly more challenging personal goals and strive to exceed them.

Complete two 1-minute timings on the timing text below. Timings 54.1 and 54.2 use the same paragraph.

Goals: 45 WAM and one or no errors
SI: 1.44 syllables per word

1-Minute Timings

Timings 54.1–54.2

There are many well-known websites and fine journals on the Internet that contain articles written by professional people. However, anyone with access to a computer and who has some basic skills can post text online. Inaccurate items may be found next to very reliable content. It is possible to find information that has no solid research behind its content and no data to support its findings. Worse yet, it is possible for someone to make up data, which has happened in the print world as well. When researching online, it is up to the reader to question the content and to be certain it is correct. You need to be careful not to be fooled by blogs and posts--most of these are not well thought-out.

9 Use numerals to express decimals.

¹⁴ He is 6.5 feet tall.

10 For ages, follow the general guidelines for numbers.

¹⁵ He is 20 years old.
¹⁶ She is nine months old.

11 Use numerals to express clock time.

¹⁷ Pack your bags right away so we can make the 5:20 p.m. flight.

12 Key house numbers in numerals.

¹⁸ His address is 13038 N. Westgate Drive.

13 Spell out street names that contain numbers ten or below. If the numbers are above ten, express the names in numerals.

¹⁹ The store is located on First Avenue.
²⁰ My address is 17815 N. 13th Avenue.

Exercise 17.13 **Sentences Drill**

Note: If you are learning to key numbers before letters and therefore have not completed Sessions 1–13, skip this exercise.

Key lines 1–10 one time for speed. The goal is to key at least 30 WAM. Your WAM rate will appear at the end of each line.

Key lines 1–10 again. This time, focus on control. The goals are to key at least 30 WAM and to make two or fewer errors. Your WAM rate will appear at the end of each line, and any errors will be highlighted.

1 Did Van ever deliver the varnish and the 150 shelves?
2 Vinnie lives in their villa; he enjoys the vast veranda.
3 It is evident; the vital lever reverses the vexing vent.

4 Ron delivered the 18 leather chairs late this evening.
5 Marvel served 286 vanilla shakes at two gala events.
6 The driver developed a fever; give him 13 vitamins.

7 That starving animal evaded 103 vigilant observers.
8 She does not fool them; she is not an honest senator.
9 Opal ordered the onions and olives from the market.
10 Did the florist remove all the thorns from the roses?

Figure 53.4 RFP Section 3 Content for Document 53.1—Continued

severity of problem, steps for resolving problem escalation when a solution is not forthcoming or an implemented solution is unsatisfactory.

3.1.7.5 Indicate your response time goals and statistics regarding meeting that goal.

Figure 53.5 RFP Sections 4 and 5 Content for Document 53.1

SECTION 4. CONTRACT  center text

The City anticipates a two-year contract. Renewal of the contract will require City Council reauthorization. All fees should be set for a two-year term and clearly stated in the proposal. The City expects all submitting firms to consent to the City Scope of Work and Specifications. Exception desired must be noted in the proposal submittal. The City reserves the right to revise the stated contract terms and conditions prior to contract signature.

SECTION 5. TERMINATION OF CONTRACT

The contract may be terminated by mutual agreement in writing or it may be terminated at any time by either party by delivery of a sixty (90) day written notice to the other party.

document, save the document, and then click the Check button.

Ending the Session

The Online Lab automatically saves the work you completed for this session. You may continue with the next session or exit the Online Lab and continue later.

Assessing Your Speed and Accuracy

Complete Timing 17.1 through 17.4. Timing 17.1 will assess your number keying skills learned in Sessions 14–17, whereas Timings 17.2 through 17.4 will assess your general keying skills. Refer to the following numerical text or paragraphs as you key. The timings will start as soon as you begin keying. For each timing, if you complete keying all lines before time expires, press Enter and start keying the first line again.

When time expires, the Online Lab will give you a WAM rate and will highlight any errors you made. The results will be stored in your Timings Performance report.

Hint: For the number timing, Timing 17.1, press Enter at the end of each line.

Goals: 25 WAM and two or fewer errors

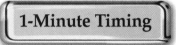

Timing 17.1

```
10 10 5,854 22.30 853375 55102 4,209.55 76,238,974 500.54
55,000 212,887 79,237 99,723.54 2,200 7978 33,344 897 2366
1133 477 98,545 28544 90,255.54 850 198,355 67,284 334542
1p14 2013 3030 2019 71523 36274 18054 55,112,445 459,100
1 4 8 0 38 87 61 90 47k2 874 982 380 5843 8787 45,88,10,21,34
```

For Timings 17.2 through 17.4 refer to the following paragraphs as you key. Remember to press Tab at the beginning of a paragraph. If you complete keying the paragraph before time expires, press Enter and start keying the paragraph again.

Goals: 30 WAM and two or fewer errors

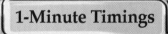

Timing 17.2

The United States Agency for International Development sponsors a speakers program that provides citizens with an opportunity to learn about the culture of other countries. Educators, business men and women, and school administrators with a need to have firsthand information are eligible. More than 125 countries participate in this program.

Timing 17.3

A career in science involves selecting a path among several options. One could choose to become a doctor in a clinic or a teacher in a medical school. An active search through more than 190 college catalogs will indicate which courses to select. Contact campus finance officers to check cost factors.

Timing 17.4

Mack, a black Scottie, is a champion canine. A constant companion is the yellow cat called Chicco. Crowds laugh and applaud as Mack and Chicco do their tricks to music. Mack can count 15 objects and walk on his hind legs. Chicco jumps over Mack, adding a certain clownish touch to the act.

Figure 53.4 RFP Section 3 Content for Document 53.1—Continued

3.1.4   Provide name, title, and contact information of three (3) references of clients for whom you have provided, or currently provide, similar services. Provide information referencing the actual services provided, customer size (number of users), and the length of time you have provided services to each client.

3.1.5   Answer the following questions regarding support services to be provided:

    3.1.5.1   Is help desk support available?

    3.1.5.2   When is support available? Indicate a.m. to p.m. times and days of the week.

    3.1.5.3   How are charges for support structures documented? *and tracked*

    ~~3.1.5.4   How are charges for support structures tracked?~~

3.1.5.6   As a municipal government, City departments include those of Police and Fire. Explain your familiarity and experience in the support of the specialized technology requirements of these departments. With the understanding that these departments operate on a 24/7, 365 days/year schedule, what would your availability be in the event of any technology issues requiring immediate attention during any non-routine business hours?

3.1.7   Cost of services, to include:

3.1.7.1   Fee schedule indicating hourly ~~fees~~ *rates* for proposed services.

3.1.7.2   Description of service pricing and any specific pricing you are able to provide.

3.1.7.3   Description of any additional charges (e.g., travel expense).

3.1.7.4   Description of problem escalation process, including initial problem identification, determination of priority and

continues

Ergonomic Tip

You should not have to reach for your keyboard. Move the keyboard so that you can keep your elbows at your side as you position your fingers over the home row keys.

Ending the Session

The Online Lab automatically saves the work you completed for this session. You can continue with the next session or exit the Online Lab and continue later.

Figure 53.4 RFP Section 3 Content for Document 53.1

SECTION 3. SUBMITTAL REQUIREMENTS

3.1   Required information to be included in the RFP submittal is detailed below.

     3.1.1   Letter of transmittal, to include:

         3.1.1.1   Company name, address, and telephone number of the firm submitting the proposal.

                    3.1.1.2 Employer identification number.

         3.1.1.~~2~~ *3*   Brief statement of understanding of the services to be performed along with a positive commitment to provide the services specified.

         3.1.1.~~3~~ *4*   A statement including the language "proposal and cost schedule shall be valid and binding for ninety (90) days following proposal due date and will become part of the contract that is negotiated with the City."

     3.1.2   General Vendor Information, to include:

         3.1.2.1   Length of time in business.

         3.1.2.~~1~~ *2*   Total number of clients and total number of public sector clients.

         3.1.2.3   Number of full-time personnel in consulting, installation and training, sales, marketing, and administrative support. Summarize the experience and technical expertise of key personnel who will actually provide the information technology services.

         3.1.2.4   Location of office that would service our account. The local availability of the staff providing these services will be an important consideration.

     3.1.3   Describe ~~the~~ *your* approach to providing these services and your methodology for providing ongoing support.

continues

Unit 3
Punctuation and Symbol Keys

Figure 53.3 RFP Section 2 Content for Document 53.1—Continued

2.1.3 <u>Server Administration Services</u>. Manage ~~our~~ computer network and ~~related~~ *associated* hardware, software, communications, and operating system necessary for the quality, security, performance, availability, recoverability, and reliability of the system. Monitor server performance and capacity management services. Ensure scheduled preventive maintenance for equipment is promptly performed; develop back-up plans and procedural documentation. Confidentiality of information is ~~important.~~ *vital* The selected vendor and their employees will be required to sign and adhere to a confidentiality clause that information in the system must remain confidential under penalty of law. Following initial assessment and upon mutual agreement between vendor and the City, it may be determined that City staff may assist vendor in daily tasks such as new user set-up and maintenance, management of user logins and security, and monitoring of server performance.

2.1.4 <u>Network Administration Services</u>. Scope of activity includes all City network equipment including switches, firewalls, routers, and ~~any~~ other security devices. The scope may also include primary installation and maintenance of printers, network copiers/scanners, etc. as deemed necessary. Monitor network performance and capacity management services.

Do not underline period.

2.1.5 <u>Security</u>. Maintenance of virus/malware detection and spam reduction programs on City servers, email, and all other City computers, laptops, and tablets. Perform security audits as requested and notify City personnel immediately of suspected breaches of security.

2.1.6 <u>Strategic Planning</u>. Provide technical leadership for server technology issues. Make recommendations for future purchasing and technology needs. Install new servers, software and hardware, and transfer data when acquired.

Session 18

Hyphen, Underline

Session Objectives

- Use the hyphen and underline keys
- Explore hyphenating words and using dashes
- Utilize rules for division of words and compound words

Timing Goals

- 1 minute: 30 WAM and two or fewer errors
- 3 minutes: 25 WAM and six or fewer errors

Getting Started and Warming Up

Exercise 18.1 If you are continuing immediately from Session 17, you may skip the Exercise 18.1 warm-up drill. However, if you exited the Online Lab at the end of Session 17, warm up by completing Exercise 18.1.

Introducing the Hyphen and Underline Keys

Videos 18.1–18.2 The hyphen (-) and underline (_) symbols are made by using the same key, and the location of that key is shown in the following diagram. Strike the hyphen key two times to key a dash (--). Press the left Shift key when pressing the hyphen key to type an underline. The underline symbol is also called the underscore symbol. Watch Videos 18.1 and 18.2 and practice these key reaches.

Exercises 18.2–18.4 Complete Exercises 18.2 and 18.3 to learn these new keys. When keying the drill lines, follow the instruction prompts provided in the Online Lab. Work on improving your general speed and accuracy by completing Exercise 18.4.

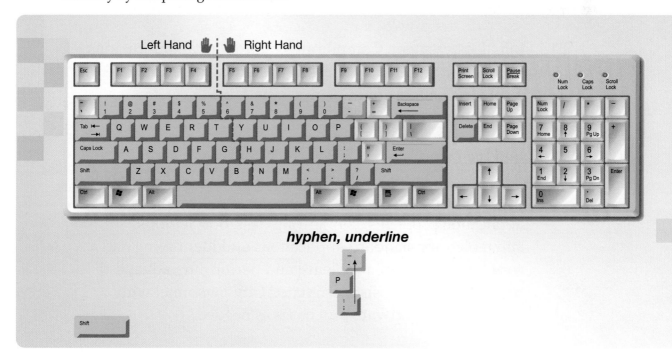

hyphen, underline

Figure 53.2 RFP Section 1 Content for Document 53.1

SECTION 1. INTRODUCTION

1.1　OVERVIEW

The City of Milton is soliciting proposals from qualified professional vendors for Information Technology (IT) support services. The qualified vendor will enable the City to significantly improve information technology effectiveness, enhance its quality of services, minimize downtime and support costs, ensure security of data, and maximize return on investment in IT.

1.2　BACKGROUND

The City of Milton currently runs a Windows 2008 server with workstations running Windows 7 Professional. The City has approximately 50 employees, including police, fire, and public works departments. All workstations, with the exception of laptops used in police vehicles, are connected to the server.

Figure 53.3 RFP Section 2 Content for Document 53.1

SECTION 2. SERVICES REQUIRED

2.1　Services to be provided to the City of Milton in the area of information services are detailed below.

2.1.1　Initial Assessment. With the assistance of City staff, compile an inventory of all information technology related assets, assess system assets, and make recommendations for improved citywide IT system performance.

2.1.2　End User Applications Support. Perform basic support functions including installation of desktops, laptops, tablets, printers, and software; diagnosing and connecting desktop application problems; configuring desktops, laptops, and tablets for standard applications and identifying and correcting hardware problems; and performing advanced troubleshooting. Assist designated City personnel with hardware and software purchases as needed.

continues

Correctly Using Hyphens in Text

The hyphen is a versatile punctuation mark that has several applications. The hyphen indicates where a word is divided over a line break. The hyphen also connects words, such as compound adjectives and the words in spelled-out fractions. Finally, a hyphen can be used to indicate subtraction as in 100 - 25 = 75.

General Guidelines for Word Division

As noted earlier, most word processing programs use word wrap, so the keyboardist does not define each line break by pressing the Enter key. Instead, the Enter key is pressed only at the end of a paragraph. When using word wrap, typically the software will start a new line with the start of a new word, but word processing programs also allow words to hyphenate or break at the end of lines. Although hyphenating words can make them more difficult to read, hyphenation can allow a page of text to have a more visually consistent right margin. Most word processing programs offer an automatic hyphenation feature, and the software sometimes asks the user to make hyphenation decisions during the hyphenating process.

The following guidelines include the essential rules for determining where to break words, but note that some of these rules have exceptions. If in doubt, consult a dictionary for the appropriate place to break a particular word.

1   Leave three or more letters of a word at the end of a line and carry over three or more letters to the next line. This rule is commonly modified since software programs leave or carry over only two letters of a word when automatic hyphenation is used.

2   Do not divide the last word of a paragraph or a page.

3   Do not key more than two consecutive lines that end with hyphens. This rule is commonly modified to allow three lines with automatic hyphenation.

4   Divide words using the following rules:

	Example	Correct Division
Between syllables according to pronunciation	provoke	pro-voke
Between two consonants unless a root word would be destroyed	napkin billing	nap-kin bill-ing (not bil-ling)
Between two vowels that are pronounced separately	continuation	continu-ation
After a one-syllable vowel	benefactor	bene-factor
Between two parts of a compound word	salesperson	sales-person

5   The following are examples of words or phrases that should not be divided.

	Example	Incorrect Division
Words of one syllable	storm	sto-rm
Words with a one-letter prefix	along enough	a-long e-nough
A syllable with a silent vowel sound	yelled strained	yel-led strain-ed
Proper nouns, abbreviations, contractions, or number combinations	Barbara FBI couldn't 31 Oak Lane March 14	Bar-bara F-BI could-n't 3-1 Oak Lane March 1-4

    h Press the Increase Indent button in the Paragraph group.

    i Key **3.1.1.1**, press Tab, key the sentence that begins *Company name, address, and telephone*, and then press the Enter key two times.

    j Key the text for sections 3.1.1.2 through 3.1.1.4 as shown in Figure 53.4. At the end of section 3.1.1.4, press the Enter key two times.

    k Press the Decrease Indent button in the Paragraph group.

    l Key the text for sections 3.1.2 through 3.1.7 as shown in Figure 53.4 following the same pattern. Press the Enter key two times at the end of 3.1.7.5.

    m Save the document.

8 Complete the following steps to key the text shown in Figure 53.5, implementing the proofreader's marks as you key:

    a Press the Decrease Indent button two times to move the insertion point to the left margin.

    b Press Ctrl + E, press Ctrl + B, key **SECTION 4. CONTRACT**, and then press Ctrl + B.

    c Press Enter two times.

    d Press Ctrl + L to move the insertion point to the left margin.

    e Format the insertion point so that the paragraph you will key will not have a hanging indent. ***Hint: Set the indentation setting to (none).***

    f Key the paragraph that begins *The City anticipates a* as shown in Figure 53.5. At the end of the paragraph, press the Enter key two times. ***Note: If this paragraph displays with a hanging indent, select the paragraph and press Ctrl + Shift + T to remove the hanging indent.***

    g Key the last section of the document (*SECTION 5. TERMINATION OF CONTRACT*) shown in Figure 53.5. Do not press the Enter key at the end of the paragraph.

    h Save the document.

9 Insert a plain page number at the right margin of the header on all pages of the document except the first page.

10 Save the document.

11 Proofread the document and correct any errors.

12 Hide nonprinting characters by clicking the Show/Hide ¶ button in the Paragraph group on the Home tab. Double check the document.

13 Save the document.

14 Click the Check button to stop the timer and upload the document for checking. The Online Lab will report the WAM rate and number of errors for the activity.

15 If errors are reported, view the results document, correct the errors in the submitted

Complete Exercises 18.5 and 18.6 to practice applying these word division rules. Follow the instruction prompts provided in the Online Lab.

General Guidelines for Compound Words and Numbers

The following guidelines will explain when to use hyphens in a compound word, such as compound adjectives and the words in spelled-out fractions. Do not press the space bar before or after the hyphen.

1　Use a hyphen to combine compound adjectives that describe a noun.

> a 15-story building
>
> the still-active volcano
>
> a hard-working person

2　If the word combination is used as a unit after a noun, do not use a hyphen.

> a building 15 stories high
>
> the volcano that is still active
>
> a person who is hard working

3　Do not use a hyphen when the first word in a compound adjective is an adverb ending in ly.

> a highly rated movie
>
> a quickly moving car

4　Words beginning with ex, self, and vice are usually hyphenated.

> ex-roommate
>
> self-taught
>
> vice-principal

5　Hyphenate spelled-out fractions and spelled out numbers between 21 and 99 if they stand alone or if they are used with numbers beyond 100. Do not hyphenate numerals.

> one and one-third
>
> sixty-six
>
> one hundred sixty-six

Complete Exercises 18.7 and 18.8 to practice applying these rules for using hyphens in compound words and numbers. Follow the instruction prompts provided in the Online Lab.

Correctly Using Dashes in Text

A dash is also called an em dash, because its length is roughly equivalent to the length of the capital M in a given font. Create a dash by typing two hyphens. Typically word processing programs will automatically replace two hyphens with a dash symbol when a space is keyed after a word following the hyphens. Do not press the space bar before, between, or after the double hyphens. Do not key a space before or after a dash.

The dash is commonly used in one of four instances.

1　In place of quotation marks to set off dialog.

2　To avoid the confusion of too many commas in a sentence.

> All books—fiction, poetry, and drama—are on sale.

3　For special emphasis.

> I cooked the meal—but they got the credit for it.
>
> There is a flaw in the plan—a fatal one.

a Press Ctrl + E, press Ctrl + B, key **SECTION 1. INTRODUCTION**, and then press Ctrl + B.

b Press Enter two times.

c Press Ctrl + L to move the insertion point to the left margin.

d Set the paragraph indentation to a hanging 0.5 inch indent.

e Key **1.1**, press Tab, key **OVERVIEW**, and then press Shift + Enter two times.

f Key the paragraph that begins *The City of Milton is soliciting* in the *OVERVIEW* section in Figure 53.2 and at the end of the paragraph, press the Enter key two times.

g Key **1.2**, press Tab, key **BACKGROUND**, and then press Shift + Enter two times.

h Key the paragraph that begins *The City of Milton currently runs* in the *BACKGROUND* section in Figure 53.2 and at the end of the paragraph, press the Enter key two times.

i Save the file.

6 Complete the following steps to key the text shown in Figure 53.3, implementing the proofreading marks as you key:

a Press Ctrl + E, press Ctrl + B, key **SECTION 2. SERVICES REQUIRED**, and then press Ctrl + B.

b Press Enter two times.

c Press Ctrl + L to move the insertion point to the left margin.

d Key **2.1**, press Tab, key the sentence in Figure 53.3 that begins *Services to be provided to*, and then press the Enter key two times.

e Click the Increase Indent button in the Paragraph group on the Home tab.

f Key **2.1.1**, press Tab, and then key the text for the entry shown in Figure 53.3. Format the subheading in section 2.1.1 as underlined text, but do not underline the period following the heading. Press Enter two times at the end of the section.

g Key the text for sections 2.1.2 through 2.1.6 as shown in Figure 53.3, following the instructions provided in step 6f for section 2.1.1. At the end of section 2.1.6, press the Enter key two times.

h Save the document.

7 Complete the following steps to key the text shown in Figure 53.4, implementing the proofreader's marks as you key:

a Press the Decrease Indent button in the Paragraph group to return the insertion point to the left margin. *Note: If you skip this step, the heading you key in the next step will be centered between the hanging indent position and the right margin, not between the left and right margins.*

b Press Ctrl + E, press Ctrl + B, key **SECTION 3. SUBMITTAL REQUIREMENTS**, and then press Ctrl + B.

c Press Enter two times.

d Press Ctrl + L to move the insertion point to the left margin.

e Key **3.1**, press Tab, key the sentence in Figure 53.4 that begins *Required information to*, and then press the Enter key two times.

f Press the Increase Indent button in the Paragraph group.

g Key **3.1.1**, press Tab, key the sentence in Figure 53.4 that begins *Letter of transmittal,* and then press the Enter key two times.

steps continue

4   To indicate a side comment, instead of using parenthesis.

> I said once—when we were in the garden—I disagree.

Exercise 18.9   Complete Exercise 18.9 to practice applying these rules for using dashes. Follow the instruction prompts provided in the Online Lab.

⟳ Reinforcing Your Skills

Complete Exercises 18.10 and 18.11 in the Online Lab. Reference the drill lines from the textbook as you key and keep your eyes on the textbook pages, not on your fingers. Complete each exercise at least once, but repeat exercises if you want to improve your WAM rate or accuracy.

Exercise 18.10 ## Underline Drill

To practice using the underline key, key lines 1–2 for speed. Key lines 1–2 again for control. Press the space bar before the underline. Press the underline key ten times. If you hold down the underline key, you will get a continuous line until you release the Shift key and the underline key. *Note: The answer lines in this and subsequent drills are to be keyed with ten underline strokes.*

1   The number of persons who will attend: _____.

2   Enter the street address here: _____.

Exercise 18.11 ## Reinforcement Drill

Key the following lines one time. Press the Enter key after each line.

1   ;-; ;-; ;-; ;-; ;-; ;- ;- -;-; ;-; ;-; ;- ;- ;-

2   ex-roommate, self-taught, vice-principal, one and one-third

3   sixty-six, a self-employed person, a last-minute effort

4   one hundred fifty-six, eight-cylinder engine, twenty-six

5   ;--; ;--; --;--; --;--; ;--; -- -- ;--; --;--; --

6   There is a flaw in the plan--a fatal one.

7   All books--fiction, poetry, and drama--are on sale.

8   I said once--and I will say it again--I disagree.

9   I cooked the meal--but they got the credit for it.

10   ;-;_ ;- _;_ _;_ -- -- ;__; ;-_; ;-_; ___ ;- ;_;_;_ ;-;_

11   The pin number is _____

12   Enter your name here _____

Assessing Your Speed and Accuracy

Complete Timings 18.1 through 18.3 in the Online Lab. Refer to the following paragraphs from the textbook as you key.

The timing will start as soon as you begin keying the paragraph. Remember to press the Tab key at the start of the paragraph. If you finish keying the paragraph before time expires, press Enter and start keying the paragraph again.

To manually set a hanging indent, complete the following steps:

1   Click the Paragraph dialog box launcher in the Paragraph group on the Home tab.

2   Click the Indents and Spacing tab if it is not selected.

3   In the *Indentation* section, click the arrow next to the *Special* text box and then select *Hanging* from the drop-down list.

4   Word will automatically change the number in the *By* measurement box to *0.5"*. This setting can be adjusted by clicking the up or down arrows. For the document activities in this session, use the default setting.

5   Click OK to accept the settings and to close the dialog box.

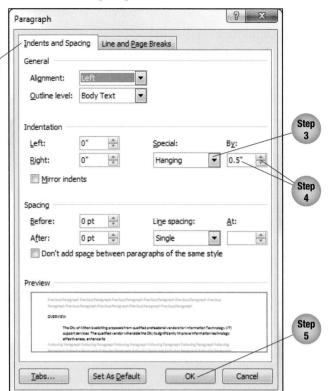

Success Tip

The keyboard shortcut for setting or increasing a hanging indent using the default settings is Ctrl + T. The keyboard shortcut Ctrl + Shift + T decreases or removes a hanging indent.

Document   Request for Proposal

53.1

1   Read all instructions for this document activity, navigate to the Document 53.1 launch page in the Online Lab, and then click the Launch Activity button. The Online Lab will open **Doc053.01** in the activity window. The timer will start as soon as you begin keying the document.

2   Before keying any text, check that the automatic list numbering feature is turned off. If necessary, review the instructions for turning off the automatic list numbering feature in Session 50.

3   Change the format of the document to single spacing with no additional spacing after paragraphs.

4   Show nonprinting characters by clicking the Show/Hide ¶ button in the Paragraph group on the Home tab.

5   Complete the following steps to key the text shown in Figure 53.2, implementing the proofreading marks as you key:

steps continue

When time expires, the Online Lab will give you a WAM rate and error report for the timing. The results of the timings will be stored in your Timings Performance report.

Goals: 30 WAM and two or fewer errors

1-Minute Timings

Timing 18.1
You can have a friend, representative, or someone else help you. There are groups that can help you find a representative or give you free legal services if you qualify. There are also representatives who do not charge unless you win your appeal. Your local Social Security office has a list of groups that can help you with your appeal.

Timing 18.2
The school will leave the campus, scattered throughout 6.5 acres in the area's academic and commercial center, for a new 23-story facility in Salem. The proposal includes open space, saving of many existing buildings, housing for varying income levels, and parking for the community. The cost is expected to be $1 billion.

This 3-minute timing will help prepare you for keying longer documents such as reports. Speed generally decreases and errors generally increase when the duration of the timing is extended.

Goals: 25 WAM and six or fewer errors

3-Minute Timing

Timing 18.3
Nails date back to 3000 B.C. They have been found in diggings and sunken ships that sailed in the years around 500 A.D. The Romans hand-forged nails and began the new trend toward complete use in building with wood. Most nails were first made in small shops; demand for nails grew so fast that the small, but well-made supply of handmade nails was not quite enough for the demand. Today, most companies that make nails can trace their own beginnings back to those early times.

Ergonomic Tip
Try using a document stand to hold your source materials. Position the stand so that the distance from your eyes to the copy is the same distance as your eyes to the screen.

Ending the Session

The Online Lab automatically saves the work you completed for this session. You can continue with the next session or exit the Online Lab and continue later.

bid on a needed product or service such as paving a parking lot, catering luncheons, or writing computer programs in an Online Lab to support a textbook. A unique numbering format is used in an RFP so that the vendor or service provider can respond to each section when submitting a proposal. RFPs vary in length depending on the complexity of the proposed product or service.

Review the excerpt of an RFP shown in Figure 53.1. Typical formatting for a RFP includes:

- 1-inch side, top, and bottom margins
- Section titles that are horizontally centered in bold font using all capital letters
- Text formatted as indented paragraphs under subheadings
- No page number on the first page and a plain page number set aligned to the right margin of the header on pages following the first page

In addition to including a page number, the header or footer may also contain information about the subject of the RFP or the name of the company preparing the document. The document prepared for this session will not include this additional information.

As shown in Figure 53.1, paragraphs in an RFP contain hanging indents. In a **hanging indent**, the second and subsequent lines of text are indented from the left margin and are aligned. A hanging indent is generally used in numbered and bulleted lists and is produced automatically in Word.

Figure 53.1 Page 2 from an RFP Document

2

SECTION 3. SPECIFICATIONS

3.1   **General Requirements**

The following general characteristics of the proposed system are required.

3.1.1   Support concurrent batch and interactive processing.

3.1.2   Support a minimum of 16 concurrent active workstations. It is projected that there will be a need for six workstations initially, with growth to approximately 55 within five years.

3.1.3   Support a broad range of intelligent workstations, including:

    3.1.3.1   Upper/lower-case characters (ASCII character set)

    3.1.3.2   Data storage capabilities

    3.1.3.3   Graphics capabilities

    3.1.3.4   Communication capabilities from remote locations

3.2   **Hardware**

The following specifications are intended to be general in nature, and are not designed to exclude any specific architecture or configuration. The vendor should propose that system from

Session 19

Apostrophe, Quotation Mark

Session Objectives

- Use the apostrophe and quotation mark keys
- Apply guidelines for use of the apostrophe and quotation marks

Timing Goals

- 1 minute: 30 WAM and two or fewer errors
- 3 minutes: 25 WAM and six or fewer errors

Getting Started and Warming Up

Exercise 19.1 If you are continuing immediately from Session 18, you may skip the Exercise 19.1 warm-up drill. However, if you exited the Online Lab at the end of Session 18, warm up by completing Exercise 19.1.

Introducing the Apostrophe and Quotation Keys

Videos 19.1–19.2 The apostrophe (') and the quotation mark (") symbols are made by using the same key, and the location of that key is shown in the following diagram. Press the left Shift key when pressing the apostrophe key to type a quotation mark. Watch Videos 19.1 and 19.2 and practice these key reaches.

Exercises 19.2–19.4 Complete Exercises 19.2 and 19.3 to learn these new keys. When keying the drill lines, follow the instruction prompts provided in the Online Lab. Work on improving your general speed and accuracy by completing Exercise 19.4.

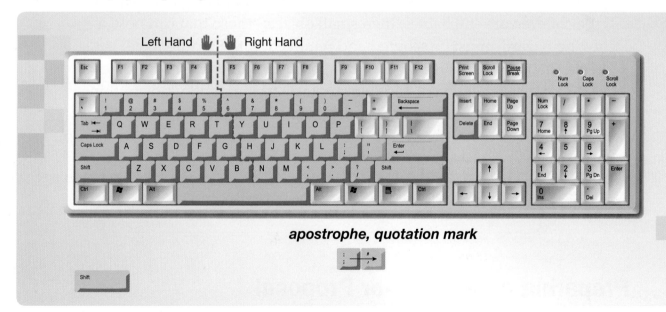

apostrophe, quotation mark

Complete two 5-minute timings on the timing text below. Timings 53.3 and 53.4 use the same paragraphs. Note that with this session, the WAM goal for 5-minute timings has been increased from 30 to 35 WAM.

Goals: 35 WAM and five or fewer errors
SI: 1.64 syllables per word

5-Minute Timings

Timings 53.3–53.4

When guests visit our homes, most of us enjoy the experience. The preparation period preceding a visit may not be so enjoyable, however. Usually, a thorough cleaning, organizing, and polishing is in order, along with planning special meals for the guests. The entire family may be enlisted to prepare their home for the expected visitors. Excitement mounts as the time for their arrival draws nearer. After the guests have arrived, there is usually an excited hustle and bustle during the initial welcome and as the unpacking chores are completed. Everyone can then settle down for a friendly chat and perhaps refreshments while catching up on all the news at a more leisurely pace.

A welcome guest is one who tries not to intrude in established family routines. Guests might assist, whenever possible, with the burden of routine chores such as cooking, cleaning, or other duties. If a visit is lengthy, it is traditional to send a gift or a small token of appreciation to the host family after the visit concludes. Regardless of the length of the visit, a personal note should be sent promptly thanking the host family for their hospitality.

When guests arrive with small children, special planning is required. If the children are still babies, then small objects--those that can pose a choking hazard--must be scouted and removed. If the toddlers will be guests, then anything breakable or dangerous within three or four feet of the floor must be removed. Toddlers are fast, curious, and grab anything that looks interesting. Everyone must be vigilant if toddlers are visiting.

Ergonomic Tip
Unhappy with the touch or layout of the keyboard on your laptop? Consider a wireless keyboard with a more "traditional" feel.

Preparing a Request for Proposal

In addition to the memo business report and the formal business report discussed in the previous sessions, a variety of specialized report formats are used in business. One example of a specialized report is a Request for Proposal (RFP). RFPs are used to invite vendors and service providers to

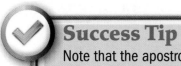

Success Tip
Note that the apostrophe and the quotation mark are on the same key.

Correctly Using Apostrophes in Text

The apostrophe has several applications in text. The typical uses of this symbol are listed below.

1   An apostrophe is used in formation of a contraction. A contraction is a word in which one or more letters are omitted. To create a contraction, insert an apostrophe where the letters are omitted.

cannot   can't
could not   couldn't

Some people have trouble determining if a word is a personal pronoun or a contraction.

their   they're   its   it's

The apostrophe indicates a missing letter. Therefore, *they're* indicates *they are*, and *it's* stands for *it is*. Here are additional examples:

They're taking their own sleeping bags.
not
They're taking they're (they are) own sleeping bags.

It's a treat to give the dog its bone.
not
It's a treat to give the dog it's (it is) bone.

2   When followed by the letter *s*, an apostrophe can show possession.

a hat belonging to John   John's hat
the voices of the people   people's voices
the guess of anybody   anybody's guess

For plural nouns that end in s, add the apostrophe only.

the carts of the golfers   golfers' carts
the clothes of the girls   girls' clothes

3   An apostrophe can be used as a symbol for feet.

100 feet   100'
255 feet   255'

Exercise 19.5   Complete Exercise 19.5 to practice applying these rules for using apostrophes. Follow the instruction prompts provided in the Online Lab.

Correctly Using Quotation Marks in Text

The three most common uses for quotation marks are to indicate spoken words in written materials, to identify titles of specific types of work, and to indicate emphasis.

Session 53

Creating a Request for Proposal

Session Objectives

- Prepare a Request for Proposal
- Use Hanging Indents
- Insert Page Numbers

Timing Goals

- 1 minute: 45 WAM and one or no errors
- 5 minutes: 35 WAM and five or fewer errors

Getting Started and Warming Up

Exercise 53.1 If you are continuing immediately from Session 52, you may skip the Exercise 53.1 warm-up drill. However, if you exited the Online Lab at the end of Session 52, warm up by completing Exercise 53.1.

Exercise 53.2 Begin your session work by completing Exercise 53.2, a timed short drill, in the Online Lab.

Assessing Your Speed and Accuracy

Complete Timings 53.1 through 53.4 in the Online Lab. At the end of each timing, the Online Lab will display your WAM rate and any errors. Results will be saved in your Timings Performance report. If you have been surpassing the speed and accuracy goals, set slightly more challenging personal goals and strive to exceed them.

Complete two 1-minute timings on the timing text below. Timings 53.1 and 53.2 use the same paragraph. Note that with this session, the 1-minute WAM goal has been increased from 40 to 45 WAM.

Goals: 45 WAM and one or no errors
SI: 1.41 syllables per word

1-Minute Timings

Timings 53.1–53.2

How fast should you exercise? It may surprise you to know that experts say that exercising slow and easy may be better for you than exercising fast and hard. This is true especially if you are significantly out of shape. The human body burns two different types of fuel: glycogen (high-grade) and fat (low-grade). It stands to reason that if you are driving your body as if it were a high-caliber race car, you are going to consume high-grade fuel. However, if you are rolling smoothly along, your body will consume more of the low-grade stuff, which is body fat.

Quotation Marks in Written Conversation

Typically, when dialog is presented, each new speaker's words are started on a new line (or paragraph) and the text is indented. The quotation marks indicate the beginning and ending of what each individual speaker says. Study these examples:

"The weather is really nasty," said Nancy.
Relaxed, Jan yawned and said, "Oh, I really hadn't noticed."
"That's because you have been sleeping all morning," murmured Nancy with a slight sneer in her voice.

Titles Using Quotation Marks

Quotation marks are used to identify titles of works such as poems; short stories; chapters, essays, or articles in magazines, and other larger works; radio and television programs; and short musical works. The following sentences show examples of these uses.

"The Midnight Ride of Paul Revere" is a good poem.
The last episode of "Mad Men" was really interesting.
"Last Rays of Daylight" was a dull short story.
Did the band perform "Stardust" last evening?
I read the article "Thirty Ways to Avoid Work" in the magazine.

Quotation Marks to Indicate Emphasis

Quotation marks are also used within a sentence to emphasize one or more words. Examples include a technical word used in a nontechnical sentence, slang expressions, or humorous expressions. (It should be noted that emphasized words are commonly set in italics rather than placed in quotes.) Be careful not to overuse quotation marks in this manner. The following sentences provide a few examples of quotation marks being used for emphasis.

The "Aglaonema" is commonly called the Chinese evergreen.
Nathan loved the concert and thought it was "the bomb."
Their idea of "fast" service is serving one customer at a time.
If the last word of a paragraph appears on a line by itself, the word is an "orphan."

Quotation Marks with Other Punctuation Symbols

When keying quotation marks with other punctuation symbols, it is important to note the order to present the marks. The following is a list of some of the common rules to remember.

1   Place commas and periods inside the quotation marks. (See the previous examples.)

2   A question mark is placed either inside or outside the ending quotation mark, depending on the sentence logic. Place the question mark inside of the quotation if the quotation is a question.

The owner shouted, "Why don't you just leave?"
She asked, "Do you know if the train is late?"

If the sentence is a question, but the quotation is not, the question mark is set outside of the ending quotation mark, as shown in the following examples.

When did he say, "I shall not return"?
Did he say, "I saw ten paintings at the exhibit"?

3   When an end quotation mark is followed by a semicolon or colon, the punctuation symbol follows the quotation mark.

Last week she announced, "Recreation time will be lengthened"; however, we have not experienced it yet.
I will never forget the first line of "The Tragedy of Macbeth": "When shall we meet again? In thunder, lighting, or rain?"

Figure 52.5 Outline Content for Document 52.3—Continued

[Tab] [Tab] C. [Tab] Gaelic [Enter]

[Tab] [Tab] D. [Tab] Monospaced [Enter]

[Tab] [Tab] E. [Tab] Symbol [Enter]

[Enter]

[Tab] VI. [Tab] DISPLAY TYPE

Reinforcing Writing Skills

Practice composing and formatting an outline in the following document activity.

Document 52.4

Composing an Outline

1   Navigate to the Document 52.4 launch page in the Online Lab and then click the Launch Activity button. The Online Lab will open **Doc052.04** in the activity window.

2   Turn off the automatic formatting of numbered lists.

3   Using Figure 52.4 as a formatting sample, compose and format an outline that identifies how you spend your time in a typical week. One way to outline your activities is by using the days of the week as the main-level topics. Your second-level topics could be the activities done each day. A third level can be used for additional details.

4   Proofread the document and correct any errors.

5   Save the document.

6   Turn on the automatic formatting of numbered lists.

7   Click the Upload button to upload the document for instructor review.

Ending the Session

The Online Lab automatically saves the work you completed for this session. You may continue with the next session or exit the Online Lab and continue later.

↻ Reinforcing Your Skills

Complete Exercises 19.6 through 19.8 in the Online Lab. For Exercises 19.6 and 19.7, you will need to key the missing quotation marks as you key the drill lines. If quotation marks are missing or misplaced in the keyed text, the Online Lab will indicate the error. Exercise 19.8 is a reinforcement drill. Remember to keep your eyes on the textbook pages, not on your fingers, as you key these exercises. Complete each exercise at least once, but repeat exercises if you want to improve your WAM rate or accuracy.

Exercise 19.6 Quotation Marks for Conversations Drill

Key the following three sentences, inserting quotation marks where appropriate. Press the Enter key after each line.

1 The computer is old, stated Mr. Barlow, and must be replaced.

2 Why did the pilot say, We'll be 30 minutes late?

3 Catherine sleepily asked, Why don't you just be quiet?

Key the following three sentences of dialog, adding quotation marks as appropriate. Press the Tab key before each line of dialog and press the Enter key at the end of each line.

4 We will be landing 30 minutes late, announced the pilot.

5 Deanna muttered, I suppose that means we miss dinner.

6 The flight attendant smiled and said, Perhaps we'll be on time after all.

Key the following paragraph as conversation, adding quotation marks as appropriate.

7   The pilot announced, Due to fog, we will be forced to land in Omaha instead of Minneapolis. Deanna's fears were confirmed. Omaha? she blurted. Yes, it's a wonderful city. I vacation there often, replied the flight attendant. The pilot was heard again, We may not be able to leave Omaha for 36 hours. Be prepared to spend the night in the airport. An unexpected treat, said the smiling flight attendant.

Exercise 19.7 Quotation Marks with Titles and for Emphasis Drill

Key each of the following sentences, inserting quotation marks to enclose titles or special words of emphasis. Press the Enter key at the end of each line.

1 The story was a real corker.

2 The gemot was used largely in early English government.

3 With friends like you, who needs enemies?

4 A narrow path or ledge is sometimes called a berm.

drill continues

   b Click the Bold button in the Font group (or press Ctrl + B) to turn on bold formatting.

   c Key **ALL ABOUT FONTS**.

   d Click the Bold button in the Font group (or press Ctrl +B) to turn off bold formatting.

   e Press Enter.

   f Click the Align Text Left button (or press Ctrl + E) to turn off the centering formatting.

   g Press Enter two times.

6 Key the outline text shown in Figure 52.5.

7 Proofread the document and correct any errors. Check that the Roman numerals, letters, and Arabic numbers are properly aligned, and compare the layout to the document shown in Figure 52.4.

8 Save the document.

9 Reactivate the automatic number formatting feature in Word.

10 Click the Check button to stop the timer and upload the document for checking. The Online Lab will report the WAM rate and number of errors for the activity.

11 If errors are reported, view the results document, correct the errors in the submitted document, save the document, and then click the Check button.

Figure 52.5 Outline Content for Document 52.3

[Tab] I. [Tab] TERMINOLOGY [Enter]

[Enter]

[Tab] II. [Tab] HISTORY [Enter]

[Enter]

[Tab] III. [Tab] DIGITAL TYPE [Enter]

[Enter]

[Tab] IV. [Tab] TYPEFACE ANATOMY [Enter]

[Enter]

[Tab] [Tab] A. [Tab] Serif [Enter]

[Tab] [Tab] B. [Tab] Proportional [Enter]

[Enter]

[Tab] V. [Tab] TYPES OF TYPEFACES [Enter]

[Enter]

[Tab] [Tab] A. [Tab] Roman [Enter]

[Tab] [Tab] [Tab] 1. [Tab] Serif [Enter]

[Tab] [Tab] [Tab] 2. [Tab] Sans serif [Enter]

[Tab] [Tab] [Tab] 3. [Tab] Script [Enter]

[Tab] [Tab] [Tab] 4. [Tab] Ornamental [Enter]

[Tab] [Tab] B. [Tab] Blackletter [Enter]

continues

5 The poem entitled Barney's Revenge is not very long.

6 At midnight, Joan saw The Light of Laughter on television.

7 The author's last short story, Bars on the Doors, was a mystery.

8 Her favorite song is Thunder Serenade by Mario Zahn.

Exercise 19.8 Reinforcement Drill

Key the following drill lines one time. Press the Enter key after each line.

1 ;';' ;';.;' ;' ;' ;' ';'.;' ;' ;' ;'

2 can't couldn't John's hat, people's voice, anybody's guess

3 Donne's sonnets, girls' clothes, 100', 255', they're, it's

4 ;".;" ;' ;" ;".;" ;".;;" ;' ;" ;' ;".;".;".;" ;' ;' ;'

5 "The weather is really nasty," said Nancy.

6 When did you say, "I shall not return"?

7 She asked, "Do you know if the train is late?"

8 "The Midnight Ride of Paul Revere" is a good poem.

9 My grandfather said the concert was "far out" and enjoyable.

Assessing Your Speed and Accuracy

Complete Timings 19.1 through 19.4 in the Online Lab. Refer to the following paragraphs from the textbook as you key. Timings 19.3 and 19.4 use the same paragraph of text.

The timing will start as soon as you begin keying the paragraph. Remember to press the Tab key at the start of the paragraph. If you finish keying the paragraph before time expires, press Enter and start keying the paragraph again.

When time expires, the Online Lab will give you a WAM rate and error report for the timing. The results of the timings will be stored in your Timings Performance report.

Goals: 30 WAM and two or fewer errors

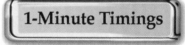

Timing 19.1

This new book on soccer has an excellent chapter on coaching soccer that offers 14 "awesome" tips to be used in working with young people new to the sport. There are some excellent suggestions on how to get positive support from the parents of the players. It's a great resource for coaches and their assistants.

Figure 52.4 Outline Format for Document 52.3

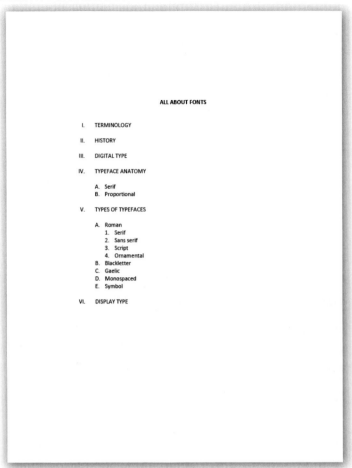

Document
52.3

Outline with Three Levels of Headings

1 Read all instructions for this document activity, navigate to the Document 52.3 launch page in the Online Lab, and then click the Launch Activity button. The Online Lab will open **Doc052.03** in the activity window. The timer will start as soon as you begin keying the document.

2 Before keying any text, check that the Word automatic list numbering feature is turned off. If necessary, review the directions for turning off the automatic list numbering feature in Session 50. Change the format of the document to single spacing with no additional spacing after paragraphs.

3 Set the following tabs in the document:

   a Set a right tab at 0.5 inch on the horizontal Ruler.

   b Set left tabs at 0.75 inch, 1.0 inch, and 1.25 inches. See Session 51, if necessary, to review directions for setting tabs.

4 With the vertical position from top of page measurement added to the Word Status bar, press Enter as needed to move the insertion point 2 inches from the top of the page. *Hint: The Status bar should read* **At: 2.1".**

5 Key the title of the outline by completing the following steps:

   a Click the Center button in the Paragraph group on the Home tab (or press Ctrl + E) to center the title.

steps continue

Success Tip

Try to increase your speed while maintaining accuracy.

Timing 19.2

A personal computer's components determine the limitations. For example, a computer without a video adapter and a video "codec" wouldn't be able to store the filming done via a camcorder. What can be done with the right components in today's microcomputers is amazing. It wouldn't take long to think of 101 things that could be done on a computer with the "right" components.

Goals: 25 WAM and two or fewer errors

3-Minute Timings

Timings 19.3–19.4

Fair time is near. Last year, our county had a great fair. Lots of people came to see the fine views and have a good time. Just imagine that 539,437 people attended, which was a record. We are hoping that by the next year we can have over 600,000 at the fair. The new rides were colorful and exciting. Both the young and old had a great time. We hope that the same old amusement company will come back and bring some of those new rides and fun shows that are bigger and better.

Ergonomic Tip

Clean your monitor regularly with an anti-static screen cleaner recommended by the manufacturer.

Ending the Session

The Online Lab automatically saves the work you completed for this session. You can continue with the next session or exit the Online Lab and continue later.

Preparing an Outline

A vital step in planning a long document such as a report, manuscript, or research paper is preparing an outline of the information. The outline should be prepared early in the document production process. By organizing the key points with their subtopics and placing them in a logical order, it is easier for you to know what points to cover and where in the document it should be discussed. Follow these guidelines when preparing outlines:

- Make sure that each major point is equal in importance to the others. If one does not seem as important, perhaps it could be included as a subpoint. Each major point should have a heading title, which is the name of that section of your report.

- Any outline entry that is subdivided into subentries must consist of more than one subentry. In other words, do not use a point A if you cannot include at least a point B. This is true at all levels regardless of whether the levels are specified with Roman numerals, letters, or Arabic numbers. Each subentry should have a subheading title, which is the name of that subsection of your report.

- Name each entry within a level using the same language structure. For example, if an entry heading title at one level begins with a noun, then all entry heading titles at that level should begin with a noun. This is called *parallel construction* or *parallelism*.

An outline is helpful to both the person creating it and the person reading it. Text is kept to a minimum so that both parties can concentrate on pertinent information. Keep the guidelines presented in the preceding paragraph in mind as you develop effective outlines.

Figure 52.4 shows a properly formatted outline that you will key. The outline title is bold and centered in all caps approximately 2 inches from the top of the page. The outline title is followed with two blank lines. The body of the outline is single-spaced with no additional space following paragraphs and one blank line before and after the first-level (main) entries. The outline in Figure 52.4 contains six main headings, designated with Roman numerals. Sections IV and V are divided into first-level subsections, designated with capital letters. Finally, subsection A of section V is, in turn, divided into second-level subsections, designated with Arabic numerals.

 Success Tip

In single-spaced text with no additional space following a paragraph, create two blank lines by pressing the Enter key three times and create one blank line by pressing the Enter key two times.

Note in the outline shown in Figure 52.4, the Roman numerals are right-aligned (the periods line up vertically; this alignment is also used when working with Arabic numbers). Word does not right-justify Roman numerals when formatting them in lists. However, you can right-align Roman numerals when creating an outline manually (without the use of automatic list numbering) by setting a right tab for the location of the period following the Roman numeral.

Using a left tab setting of 0.25 inch between the Roman numerals (and letters and Arabic numerals) and text following the numerals and letters creates a more visually appealing and easier-to-read outline than using the default 0.5 inch tab settings.

Session 20

Exclamation Point, Pound Sign, Dollar Sign, Ampersand

Session Objectives

- Use the !, #, $, and & keys
- Apply guidelines for use of the exclamation mark

Timing Goals

- 1 minute: 30 WAM and two or fewer errors
- 3 minutes: 25 WAM and six or fewer errors

Getting Started and Warming Up

Exercise 20.1

If you are continuing immediately from Session 19, you may skip the Exercise 20.1 warm-up drill. However, if you exited the Online Lab at the end of Session 19, warm up by completing Exercise 20.1.

Introducing the Exclamation Point, Pound Sign, Dollar Sign, and Ampersand Keys

Videos 20.1–20.4

The exclamation point (!), pound sign (#), dollar sign ($), and ampersand (&) are all located on the number key row. These symbols are produced by typing the appropriate key along with a Shift key. The locations and correct finger reaches for these keys are shown in the following diagram and in Videos 20.1 through 20.4. Watch these videos and practice keying these symbols.

Exercises 20.2–20.6

Complete Exercises 20.2 through 20.5 to learn these new keys. When keying the drill lines, follow the instruction prompts provided in the Online Lab. Work on improving your general speed and accuracy by completing Exercise 20.6.

Figure 52.3 Title Page Format for Document 52.1

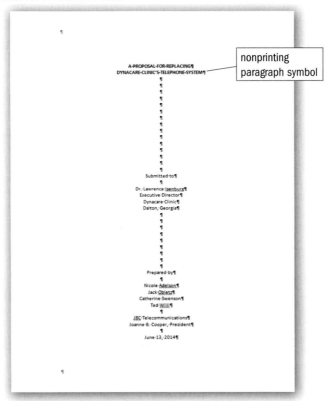

Customizing the Word Status Bar

For documents that contain a title or other information that begins 2 inches from the top of the page, it is very helpful to verify the cursor position before beginning to key. By default, the Word Status bar does not contain the vertical page position of the insertion point, but this can be easily added. When added to the Status bar, the vertical page position will appear after the word *At*, followed by a number in inches. This number indicates the location of the insertion point *from the top of the page*. **Note: The numerical value on the Status bar is not the distance from the top margin. In contrast, the vertical Ruler indicates the vertical location of the insertion point relative to the top text margin.** To add the Vertical Page Position information to the Word Status bar, complete the following steps:

1 Right-click the Status bar at the bottom edge of the document window.

2 In the Customize Status Bar menu, click the *Vertical Page Position* option to insert a check mark.

3 Verify that the insertion point position appears in the Status bar.

4 Click anywhere in the document to close the Customize Status Bar menu.

Correctly Using the Exclamation Point

The exclamation point is used to express a high degree of emotion or strong feeling. As with other end-of-sentence punctuation, you should key only one space after an exclamation point when it ends a sentence (unless it is at the end of a paragraph). Review the following examples before completing Exercise 20.7.

What! You mean the fight has been delayed for six hours?
How frightening! The fire broke out only 10 minutes after we left.
The date of the meeting—mark it on your calendar!—is November 10.
So there you are, rascal!
My brother yelled, "Run for your life!"
I simply do not believe the fiscal report that states, "The absentee rate was increasing by 500 percent"!

 Exercise 20.7 **Exclamation Point Drill**

Key the missing exclamation point as you key the following drill lines. If the exclamation point is missing or misplaced in the keyed text, the Online Lab will indicate the error. Press the Enter key at the end of each line.

1 Congratulations You won the first prize

2 Jan shouted What a mess

3 I emphatically restate my position: I will not fire those workers

4 Help Help I'm locked in this room

5 Oh, how ridiculous He's never even seen the inside of a bank

Correctly Using the Pound and Dollar Signs

The pound sign is also commonly referred to as the number sign. When the symbol appears before a number, it is read as "number." For example, "item #10" would be read as "item number ten." When the symbol follows a number, it is read as "pound." For example, "buy 3#" would be read as "buy three pounds." In either instance, do not insert a space between the number and the symbol.

Correctly Using the Ampersand

The ampersand symbol is equivalent to the word "and." When an ampersand is used within a line of text, key one space before and one space after it.

⟳ Reinforcing Your Skills

Complete Exercises 20.8 through 20.12 in the Online Lab. Reference the drill lines from the textbook as you key and keep your eyes on the textbook pages, not on your fingers. Complete each exercise at least once, but repeat exercises if you want to improve your WAM rate or accuracy.

3 Key the information shown in Figure 52.2. When keying the two-line title, turn on bold formatting before keying the title and then turn off bold formatting before pressing Enter at the end of the second line of the title. Follow the directions for the number of times to press the Enter key as shown in the figure. Press Enter one time at the end of each line unless otherwise directed.

4 Change the vertical page alignment to center. If necessary, review the directions for changing page alignment in Session 38.

5 Proofread the document and correct any errors.

    a Turn on Show/Hide ¶ to verify that there are no Enters before the title or after the date and that there are no spaces at the end of the lines of text in the document.

    b Use Figure 52.3 as a reference to make sure the spacing in the file is correct.

6 Save the document.

7 Click the Check button to stop the timer and upload the document for checking. The Online Lab will report the WAM rate and number of errors for the activity.

8 If errors are reported, view the results document, correct the errors in the submitted document, save the document, and then click the Check button.

Figure 52.2 Title Page Content for Document 52.2

A PROPOSAL FOR REPLACING
DYNACARE CLINIC'S TELEPHONE SYSTEM [16 Enters]
Submitted to [2 Enters]
Dr. Lawrence Isenburg
Executive Director
Dynacare Clinic
Dalton, Georgia [10 Enters]
Prepared by [2 Enters]
Nicole Adelson
Jack Obletz
Catherine Swenson
Ted Willi [2 Enters]
JBC Telecommunications
Joanne B. Cooper, President [2 Enters]
June 13, 2014

Exercise 20.8 Exclamation Point Drill

Key the following drill lines one time. Space once after the exclamation point (except at the end of the line).

1 Help! Stop! No! Yes! Go! Wait! Begin! Halt! None!
2 Walter, stop right now! You had all better stop!
3 No, you cannot go right now! Listen to them now!

Exercise 20.9 Pound and Number Sign Drill

Key the following drill lines one time. Concentrate on control.

1 #33 33# 39 9# #168 168# #106 106# #3 3#3 21# #122
2 Items #10, #7, #3, #6, #4, #12, and #19 are mine.
3 Get #61 weighing 10# and #2299 weighing 189,756#.

Exercise 20.10 Dollar Sign Drill

Key the following drill lines one time. Concentrate on control.

1 $1 $2 $3 $4 $5 $6 $7 $8 $9 $10 $11 $120 $16.00 f$
2 Add $1.16, $28.96, $17.44, $18.00, $21.13, $4.26.
3 The gifts cost $1.10, $6.90, $19.89, and $101.13.

Exercise 20.11 Ampersand Drill

Key the following drill lines one time. Concentrate on control.

1 17 & 60 & 9 & 16 & 14 & 71 & 77 & 45 & 61 & 9891
2 Buy gifts from the J & K store and the R & Sons.
3 Contact Hart & Sons for the products you need.

Exercise 20.12 Reinforcement Drill

Key the following drill lines one time. Concentrate on control. Press Enter after each line.

1 fff f4f ff ff f4f4 $$$ f$ f$ f4 f$ f$ f4 f4
2 $40.00 4$ $4.00 $$44 $4.00 $$44 44 $4 $4 f$f$ 444
3 $143,789.00 $1,640.68 $689.33 $17.31 $26.80 $1.44

4 d#d d3d# d#d# d#d# d3d3 ### d# d# d3 d# d# d3 d3
5 d#d d3#d #3 3# ##33 3# #3 ##33 33 #3 #3 3#3# 333
6 Buy 14#, 23#, 71#, 3#, 8#, 41#, 13#, 21#, and 6#.

drill continues

To change the line spacing of a document to single spacing with no additional space after paragraphs, complete the following steps immediately upon opening the new document:

1 Click the Paragraph dialog box launcher in the bottom right corner of the Paragraph group on the Home tab.

2 Click the Indents and Spacing tab if it is not already selected.

3 In the *Spacing* section of the Paragraph dialog box, click the down arrow of the *After* measurement box until *0 pt* appears.

4 Click the arrow next to the *Line spacing* text box and then click *Single* from the option menu.

5 Click the OK button to apply the changes to the document.

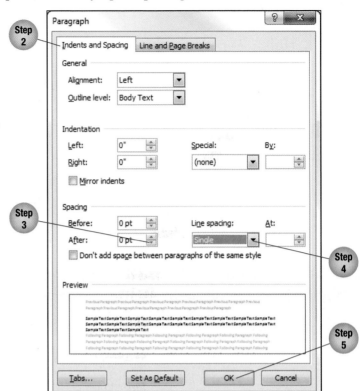

To change the line spacing in a document that has already been keyed, select the text (press Ctrl + A to select all of the text in a document) and then follow the steps outlined above.

Success Tip

A quick method of changing to single spacing with no additional space after paragraphs is to click the *No Spacing* style in the Styles group on the Home tab.

Document 52.2 Title Page of a Report

1 Read all instructions for this document activity, navigate to the Document 52.2 launch page in the Online Lab, and then click the Launch Activity button. The Online Lab will open **Doc052.02** in the activity window. The timer will start as soon as you begin keying the document.

2 Before keying, change the formatting of the document as follows:

   a Change the line spacing to single spacing.

   b Change the spacing after paragraphs to 0 points.

   c Change the left margin to 1.5 inches.

   d Change the text alignment to center.

steps continue

7 j7j j7j& j&j& j&j& j7j7 &&& j& j& j7 j& j& j7j7

8 &j& j7j& j&j& && j7j& j7& &&77 77 &7 &7 7&7& 777

9 Patricia and Ron went to Samuelsons & Bigsby today.

10 a!a! a!a a!a a!a! a! a! a!a! a!a a!a a!a a! a! a!

11 What! How frightening! Mark your calendar!

12 My brother yelled, "Run for your life!" Wow!

Assessing Your Speed and Accuracy

Complete Timings 20.1 through 20.4 in the Online Lab. Refer to the following paragraphs as you key. Timings 20.3 and 20.4 will use the same paragraph of text.

The timing will start as soon as you begin keying the paragraph. Remember to press the Tab key at the start of the paragraph. If you finish keying the paragraph before the timing expires, press Enter and start keying the paragraph again.

When the time expires, the Online Lab will give you a WAM rate and error report for the timing. The results of the timings will be stored in your Timings Performance report.

Goals: 30 WAM and two or fewer errors

1-Minute Timings

Timing 20.1
State, county, and regional fairs provide wholesome entertainment for more than 150 million Americans each year. The Texas State Fair has an annual $160-million-dollar impact on the Dallas-Fort Worth area with more than 3.1 million attendees. From animals to high-tech displays, there's something for everyone, and the price is right!

Timing 20.2
When ordering team jerseys, be sure to include #223-852 in the category box on the order form. JB & K provides an additional 15-percent discount for orders in excess of 25 jerseys. There is a significant savings on two-color jerseys compared to those with three or more colors. Prices are listed on the attached sheet.

Success Tip
Try to increase your speed while maintaining accuracy.

Figure 52.1 Letter Text for Document 52.1—Continued

This proposal contains two alternatives for consideration as a replacement of the current telephone system. The basis for the choices is whether Dynacare wants to lease or purchase equipment. The addendum to this report details the advantages of each alternative. Implementing either system provides numerous features to improve the quality of health care for Dynacare patients, including a feature called *Automatic Call Distribution* to prevent long waiting periods when patients call any medical unit within the clinic. ¶ Please review the proposal and addendum. I will call you next Monday between 10 a.m. and noon to set up an appointment to discuss any questions you may have regarding the proposal. With your approval, we can prepare the Request for Proposal to submit to potential bidders so that Dynacare will once again have a state-of-the-art voice communication system. ¶ Sincerely, ¶ Joanne B. Cooper ¶ President

Creating a Title Page for a Report

The title page for a business report consists of three sections:

1   The top third of the page displays the report title. One of the critical elements of the title is that it clearly identifies the topic of the report. The title is keyed in bold and all caps and should be centered vertically and horizontally within the top third of the page. If the title is long, key it on two or more lines, dividing it into meaningful phrases.

2   The middle third of the page includes the name(s) of the individual(s) who will receive the report, their company name, city, and state. This information is also centered vertically and horizontally.

3   The bottom third of the page indicates the name(s) of the individual(s) who prepared the report, their company affiliation, and the date of the report. Again, the text is centered vertically and horizontally.

If the report is to be bound, and if the side binding requires additional space, set the left margin of the title page at 1.5 inches. As you horizontally center the information on the title page, the Word centering feature adjusts to accommodate the wider left margin.

When beginning a title page, leave approximately 2 inches of space between the top and middle groups of text and between the middle and bottom groups of text. After you have keyed the required information for the title page, vertically center the text on the page using the vertical alignment option on the Layout tab of the Page Setup dialog box. If necessary, adjust the space between the groups of text for better balance on the page. For the Document 52.2 activity, specific placement directions will be provided in order to ensure accurate document checking by the Online Lab.

Changing Line Spacing

The Word default line spacing is 1.15 lines with 10 points of space after each paragraph. Documents such as title pages and outlines are easier to format using single spacing with no additional space after each paragraph. In a document with single spacing and no additional spacing after the paragraphs, press the Enter key two times to leave one blank line space, such as between paragraphs.

3-Minute Timings

**Timings
20.3–20.4**

Why should seat belts be fastened when a car is moving? Seat belts will reduce injuries and deaths. Many tests and studies have been done to prove this point. Half of all the traffic deaths happen within 25 miles from home. Traffic deaths can occur when an auto is moving just 40 miles an hour or less. If a car is moving at 30 miles per hour, the impact is like hitting the ground after hurtling from the top of a building that is three stories high.

Ergonomic Tip

If you are experiencing eye pain, flashes of light, floaters, blind spots, or blurred vision, make an appointment immediately with a qualified professional.

Ending the Session

The Online Lab automatically saves the work you completed for this session. You can continue with the next session or exit the Online Lab and continue later.

Preparing a Letter of Transmittal

Typically, a letter of transmittal accompanies a formal report and is addressed to the person(s) who requested the report. The letter usually includes the following information:

- A brief description of what is being transmitted
- A brief background on the subject of the report and who prepared the report
- Specific examples of the most significant findings contained in the report
- Suggested actions to be taken by the recipient (or, in some instances, the subject of the report)

In some cases the letter of transmittal is bound with the report inside the front cover. The left margin of both the report and letter of transmittal is generally 1.5 inches. However, if the binding process does not require additional space at the left margin, the default 1-inch left margin is used.

An alternative to binding the letter of transmittal is to send the letter as a separate sheet with the report as an enclosure. Company policy and procedure manuals should identify the preferred method.

Document 52.1 **Transmittal Letter**

1 Read all instructions for this document activity, navigate to the Document 52.1 launch page in the Online Lab, and then click the Launch Activity button. The Online Lab will open **Doc052.01** in the activity window. The timer will start as soon as you begin keying the document.

2 Because this letter will be bound with the report, it should use the same left margin as the report document. Change the left margin to 1.5 inches.

3 Key June 16, 2014, as the current date of the letter.

4 Key the text shown in Figure 52.1 using the block style letter formatting. If necessary, review Session 39 for formatting information.

5 After the title line, key the reference initials **fpo** and the file name. Also include a reference to the attachment.

6 Proofread the document and correct any errors.

7 Save the document.

8 Click the Check button to stop the timer and upload the document for checking. The Online Lab will report the WAM rate and number of errors for the activity.

9 If errors are reported, view the results document, correct the errors in the submitted document, save the document, and then click the Check button.

Figure 52.1 Letter Content for Document 52.1

Dr. Lawrence Isenburg
Executive Director
Dynacare Clinic
214 College Drive
Dalton, GA 30721-9883

Dear Dr. Isenburg: ¶ JBC Telecommunications is pleased to submit this proposal containing recommendations for replacing Dynacare's current telephone system. Under separate cover we are sending an addendum to this report that includes the justifications and benefits of the recommendations. ¶

continues

Session 21

Percent Sign, Asterisk, Parentheses, Brackets

Session Objectives

- Use the %, *, ( ), and [ ] keys

Timing Goals

- 1 minute: 30 WAM and two or fewer errors
- 3 minutes: 25 WAM and six or fewer errors

Getting Started and Warming Up

Exercise 21.1 If you are continuing immediately from Session 20, you may skip the Exercise 21.1 warm-up drill. However, if you exited the Online Lab at the end of Session 20, warm up by completing Exercise 21.1.

Introducing the Percent Sign, the Asterisk, Parentheses, and Bracket Symbols

Videos 21.1–21.6 The location of the keys to type the percent sign (%) and asterisk (*), left and right parentheses, and left and right brackets are shown in the following diagram and the reaches are demonstrated in Videos 21.1 through 21.6. All of the keys except the left and right bracket keys require the use of the Shift key. Practice the key reaches and Shift key combinations while watching the videos.

Exercises 21.2–21.9 Complete Exercises 21.2 through 21.7 to learn these new keys. When keying the drill lines, follow the instruction prompts provided in the Online Lab. Work on improving your general speed and accuracy by completing Exercise 21.8. Finally, check your understanding of symbols by completing the Thinking Drill, Exercise 21.9.

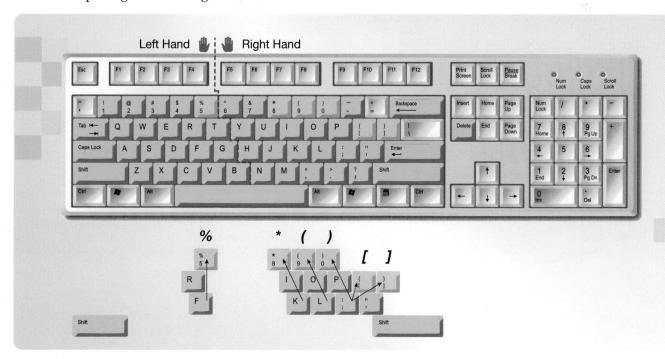

Complete two 3-minute timings on the timing text below. Timings 52.3 and 52.4 use the same paragraphs. Push for speed or accuracy, depending on results of your recent timings.

Goals: 35 WAM and three or fewer errors
SI: 1.45 syllables per word

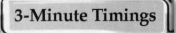
3-Minute Timings

Timings 52.3–52.4

Are you planning a vacation and wondering how to get there? There are several factors to consider when making that decision. Are you going alone, with a group of friends, or with a spouse and kids?

If you are thinking of driving, how many travelers will be able to share the driving? Will there be motel costs or will you drive throughout the night? How much time do you want to spend traveling to and from your destination? Will you enjoy the scenery along the way? The price of gasoline (to, from, and while at your destination) must also be considered.

If flying is an option, remember to include the cost of checked baggage in addition to the airfare. Airport parking fees will add to your overall expenses, too. You will likely reach your destination more quickly if you travel by air, but will you want or need to rent a vehicle to get to your hotel and/or for the duration of the vacation?

You might want to investigate taking either a bus or train. Bus fares can be an incredible value, while trains can provide more room to move around. It can be very relaxing to enjoy the scenery along the way.

Whatever mode of travel you choose, spending time planning up front will help keep your finances in line and reduce the stress of what is supposed to be an enjoyable experience.

Ergonomic Tip
To relieve pressure on your mouse hand and fingers, alternate between using the mouse and the keyboard to move the insertion point. Some moves can be made more easily with the mouse and some are easier with the arrow keys.

↻ Reinforcing Your Skills

Complete Exercises 21.10 through 21.16 in the Online Lab. Reference the drill lines from the textbook as you key and keep your eyes on the textbook pages, not on your fingers. Complete each exercise at least once, but repeat exercises if you want to improve your WAM rate or accuracy.

Exercise 21.10 **Percent Sign Drill**

Be sure to press the right Shift key. Place both hands on the home row and practice the move from the F key to the percent sign key. Be sure to anchor your left little finger to the A key.

Key lines 1–4 for speed. Key lines 1–4 a second time while focusing on control.

1 f5f f5f f5f f5f f5f f%f F%F f5f F%F5 f%f5 f%f f%f

2 55% 555% 5% 5%5% 555% 55% 5% 5% 55% 555% 5%, 555%

3 A 6% discount and a 10% reduction will equal 16%.

4 They made 55% of their shots and 8% of the fouls.

Exercise 21.11 **Asterisk Drill**

In addition to signaling a footnote or indicating spacing, the asterisk serves as a multiplication sign in some programming languages. Anchor a finger on the J key to make the reach to the asterisk key.

Key lines 1–4 for speed. Key lines 1–4 a second time while focusing on control. Remember to press the left Shift key.

1 k8k k8k k8k ki8k ki8k ki8*k k*k K*K k*k k*k *ki*k

2 8*8 8*8 8*8 k8*k ki8*k k*k 8*8*8 *** 8*8 ki8* k*k

3 The check was for $***4.65 and it should be $.46.

4 The * symbol is used in programming: A - B * 38.

Exercise 21.12 **Left Parenthesis Drill**

Key lines 1 and 2 for speed. Key lines 1 and 2 a second time while focusing on control. Remember to press the left Shift key. Anchor your finger on the J key. *Note: Be sure to use the lowercase letter L and not the number 1 in this drill.*

1 l9l l9l l9l l9l lo9l lo9l lo9(l l(l l(l lo(l lo9(

2 l(l l(l l9l l9l l9(l lo9(l lo(l lo9(l l9Ll l(l l9

Exercise 21.13 **Right Parenthesis Drill**

Key lines 1–4 for speed. Key lines 1–4 a second time while focusing on control. Remember to press the left Shift key. Anchor your finger on the J key.

1 ;0; ;0; ;0; ;0; ;p0; ;p0; ;p0; ;p0; ;p); ;p); ;0;

2 ;); ;); ;); ;); ;); ;0); ;); ;0); ;p0); ;p0); ;);

3 The price ($5.95) was more ($2 more) than I paid.

4 Most of the teams (at least 6) won all six games.

Session 52

Enhancing Formal Business Reports

Session Objectives

- Prepare a letter of transmittal
- Create a title page for a report
- Change line spacing
- Customize the Word Status bar
- Format an outline
- Draft an outline

Timing Goals

- 1 minute: 40 WAM and or one or no errors
- 3 minutes: 35 WAM and three or fewer errors

Getting Started and Warming Up

Exercise 52.1 If you are continuing immediately from Session 51, you may skip the Exercise 52.1 warm-up drill. However, if you exited the Online Lab at the end of Session 51, warm up by completing Exercise 52.1.

Exercise 52.2 Begin your session work by completing Exercise 52.2, a timed short drill, in the Online Lab.

Assessing Your Speed and Accuracy

Complete Timings 52.1 through 52.4 in the Online Lab. At the end of each timing, the Online Lab will display your WAM rate and any errors. Results will be saved in your Timings Performance report. If you have been surpassing the speed and accuracy goals, set slightly more challenging personal goals and strive to exceed them.

Complete two 1-minute timings on the timing text below. Timings 52.1 and 52.2 use the same paragraph. If your keying speed is less than 40 WAM, push for speed. If your keying rate is at least 40 WAM but you make more than one error, concentrate on accuracy. If you are meeting both the speed (WAM) and accuracy goals, push for speed.

Goals: 40 WAM and one or no errors
SI: 1.52 syllables per word

1-Minute Timings

Timings 52.1–52.2
A user interface is what you see when you look at your computer screen. Most operating systems provide a graphical user interface. This means that icons and pictures take the place of the text-based operating systems of the past. On the desktop, you can move icons and folders, pin programs to the taskbar at the bottom of the screen, and display a variety of background images. For background images, some people chose photos of their friends and family, others display scenic pictures from family trips, and others show pictures of cats and dogs.

Exercise **Left Bracket Drill**
21.14

Key lines 1 and 2 for speed. Key lines 1 and 2 a second time while focusing on control. Do not use the Shift key. Anchor your finger on the J key.

1 ;[; ;[; ;[; ;[; ;[; ;[; ;[;[;[;[;[; ;[;[;[;[;

2 ;[;[;[;[; ;[;[;[;[;[;[;[;[;[;[; ;[;[;

 Exercise **Left and Right Brackets Drill**
21.15

Key lines 1 and 2 and then key the two lines again. Focus on control.

1 ;[; ;]; ;[; ;]; ;[; ;]; ;]; ;[; ;]; ;[; ;]; ;]];

2 ;[ ]; ;[; ;]; ;[; [;] [;] [;] [;] [;] [;] [;] [;]

 Exercise **Reinforcement Drill**
21.16

Key the following drill lines one time. Press Enter after each line.

1 k* K*K k*k k8*k k8k*k k*k*k k8*k k8*k k*k K*K k*k

2 The * symbol is used in formulas: A1*B2-C2*49.

3 f%f f5%f f%f f5%5 f5%f f5%f f5%f f%5f 5%5 5%5 555

4 Did you know that 5% of 5,000 equals 250% of 100?

5 ;[;[;[;[;[;[;[;[;[; ;[; ;[; ;[; ;[;; ;[; ;[;

6 ;]]; ;]; ;]; ;]; ;];]; ;];];];];]; ;]; ;]; ;]];

7 [;] [;] [;] [;] [;] [;] [;] [;] ;[; ;[; ;]; ;]; ;[;]

8 ;[; ;]; ;[; ;[; ;[; ;]; ;]; ;[; ;]; ;[; ;]; ;[;

9 l9 l(l 19L1 19(l l(l 19(l 19(l 19l 19l l(l l(l

10 ;); ;0); ;0); ;0); ;); ;0); ;); ;); ;); ;); ;);(0)

11 The amount ($6.96) was more ($2 more) than I paid.

12 Most of the table (see Table 3.2) was accurate.

As an exercise in choosing which information in a report is better formatted graphically, in a line chart, a bar chart, or a pie chart, complete the Document 51.3 activity.

Document 51.3   Composing a Memo that Discusses Graphical Data Presentation

1   Navigate to the Document 51.3 launch page in the Online Lab and then click the Launch Activity button. The Online Lab will open **Doc051.03** in the activity window.

2   Complete the top of the memo template as follows:

   a   Turn on Show/Hide ¶ so you can position the insertion point just before the paragraph mark in the *TO* line and then key your instructor's name.

   b   Use your name in the *FROM* line.

   c   Use the current date in the *DATE* line.

   d   Key **Graphing Report Data** in the *SUBJECT* line.

3   Review the content of the report completed in the Document 51.2 activity. Select areas of information that could be represented in a graph of some kind. In the body of the **Doc051.03** memo, explain what information you would graph, the kind of graph you would use, and why this information should be charted. If you can think of other visuals or displays that would help explain the report data, mention those as well.

4   Check that your memo is written in complete, clear sentences and that you have used correct punctuation, sentence structure, word choices, and capitalization. Correct any errors.

5   Save the document.

6   Click the Upload button to upload the document for instructor review.

Ending the Session

The Online Lab automatically saves the work you completed for this session. You may continue with the next session or exit the Online Lab and continue later.

Assessing Your Speed and Accuracy

Complete Timings 21.1 through 21.4 in the Online Lab. Refer to the following paragraphs as you key. Timings 21.3 and 21.4 will use the same paragraph of text.

The timing will start as soon as you begin keying the paragraph. Remember to press the Tab key at the start of the paragraph. If you finish keying the paragraph before the timing expires, press Enter and start keying the paragraph again.

When time expires, the Online Lab will give you a WAM rate and error report for the timing. The results of the timings will be stored in your Timings Performance report.

Goals: 30 WAM and two or fewer errors

1-Minute Timings

Timing 21.1

The stock market gets a lot of people's attention. When Standard & Poor's index increases, many people will hold on to their stocks in anticipation of further gains. A 4% drop in durable goods orders would most likely increase short-term interest rates; this has an impact on the Federal Reserve Board's next move.

Timing 21.2

While walking on the 200 block of West Division Street on the afternoon of July 31, 2012, a 26-year-old man was approached by an unknown man believed to be in his fifties who asked if he was disabled. The man answered that he was, and the stranger told him to hand over five dollars. The man then took out his wallet, which contained $17 in cash, and the offender snatched it from him. A foot chase ensured, and the two fought in a parking lot until the offender agreed to give the wallet and money back.

Goals: 25 WAM and two or fewer errors

3-Minute Timings

Timings 21.3–21.4

The fifty-three story building features 248 spacious and elegant one-, two-, and three-bedroom apartments that offer nine floor plans with dramatic views of the cityscape. The apartments offer everything you need to feel comfortable, relaxed, and positive about life. Though they come standard with a range of high-end amenities and thoughtful details, custom amenities and features are available to reflect your personal sense of style. All apartments have full state-of-the-art kitchens, washers and dryers, and floor-to-ceiling windows with panoramic views. Fast elevator service connects residents to several floors and well-appointed, warm, and inviting common areas. These levels include a spa, fitness center, and pool. On the fifty-third floor is a gathering spot with awesome views of the city and lake. Floor plans are available for viewing now and will go on sale April 2012.

Figure 51.6 Line Chart

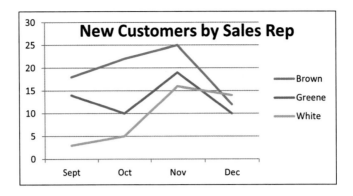

A **bar chart** also shows relationships between sets of data. Instead of a line connecting plotted data points, bars are drawn either vertically or horizontally. An example of a bar graph that illustrates the occupancy rate for a hotel during its first six months of operation is shown in Figure 51.7.

A **pie chart** represents simple data such as percentages of a total amount. A budget, for example, is commonly depicted as a pie chart. The total pie represents 100 percent. Expense categories are shown as slices of the pie. The largest piece of the pie is the largest expense item. In the example shown in Figure 51.8 the biggest expense category for this family is housing costs.

Figure 51.7 Bar Chart

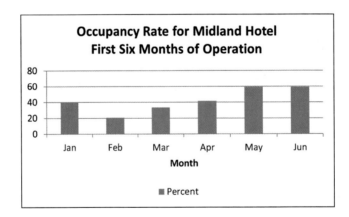

Figure 51.8 Pie Chart

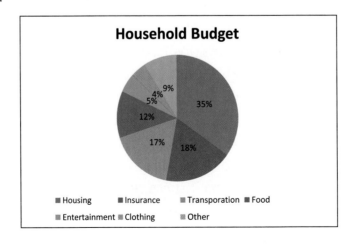

Ergonomic Tip

Rest your forearms on the edge of a table. Grasp the fingers of one hand and gently bend your wrist back for five seconds to relax your hand and fingers.

Ending the Session

The Online Lab automatically saves the work you completed for this session. You can continue with the next session or exit the Online Lab and continue later.

Figure 51.5 Report Format for Document 51.2

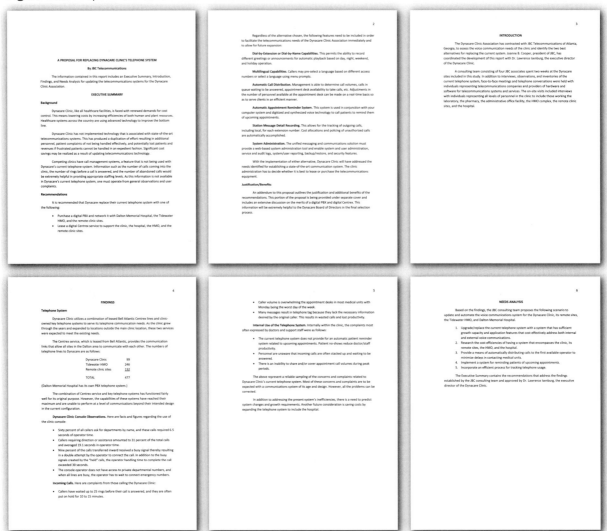

Reinforcing Writing Skills

There are a variety of ways to help individuals better understand and retain written information. Charts and graphs, for example, are an excellent choice because they display numerical data and illustrate numerical relationships almost instantly.

The three most common types of charts or graphs are line, bar, and pie. A **line chart** shows the relationship between two types of data (sets of information). One set of data is plotted horizontally; the other set is plotted vertically. A line connects the points formed by plotting the two sets of data. As an example, a line chart is shown in Figure 51.6 and indicates the number of new customers signed by three different account representatives for the months of September through December. It is easy to see that November had the largest number of new customers.

Session 22

At, Equals, and Plus Signs

Session Objectives

- Use the @, =, and + keys

Timing Goals

- 1 minute: 30 WAM and two or fewer errors
- 3 minutes: 25 WAM and six or fewer errors

Getting Started and Warming Up

Exercise 22.1
If you are continuing immediately from Session 21, you may skip the Exercise 22.1 warm-up drill. However, if you exited the Online Lab at the end of Session 21, warm up by completing Exercise 22.1.

Introducing the At, Equals, and Plus Sign Keys

Videos 22.1–22.3
The location of the keys to type the at sign (@), equals sign (=), and plus sign (+) are shown in the following diagram and the reaches are demonstrated in Videos 22.1 through 22.3. The at sign and the plus sign require the use of the Shift key. Practice the key reaches and Shift key combinations while watching the videos.

Exercises 22.2–22.6
Complete Exercises 22.2 through 22.4 to learn these new keys. When keying the drill lines, follow the instruction prompts provided in the Online Lab. Work on improving your general speed and accuracy by completing Exercise 22.5. Finally, check your understanding of symbols by completing the Thinking Drill, Exercise 22.6.

Figure 51.4 Report Content for Document 51.2—Continued

The above represent a reliable sampling of the concerns and complaints related to Dynacare Clinic's current telephone system. Most of these concerns and complaints are to be expected with a communications system of its age and design. However, all the problems can be corrected.

In addition to addressing the present system's inefficiencies, there is a need to predict system changes and growth requirements. Another future consideration is saving costs by expanding the telephone system to include the hospital. *insert page break*

NEEDS ANALYSIS

Based on the findings, the JBC Consulting Team proposes the following scenario to update and automate the voice communications system for the Dynacare Clinic, its remote sites, the Tidewater HMO, and Dalton Memorial Hospital.

1. Upgrade/replace the current telephone system with a system that has sufficient growth capacity and application features that address cost-effectively both internal and external voice communications.
2. Research the cost efficiencies of having a system that encompasses the Clinic, its remote sites, the HMO, and the Hospital.
3. Provide a means of automatically distributing calls to the first available operator to minimize delays in contacting medical units.
4. Implement a system for reminding patients of upcoming appointments.
5. Incorporate an efficient process for tracking telephone usage.

The executive summary contains the recommendations that address the findings established by the JBC Consulting Team and approved by Dr. Lawrence Isenburg, the Executive Director of the Dynacare Clinic.

↻ Reinforcing Your Skills

Complete Exercises 22.7 through 22.10 in the Online Lab. Reference the drill lines from the textbook as you key and keep your eyes on the textbook pages, not on your fingers. Complete each exercise at least once, but repeat exercises if you want to improve your WAM rate or accuracy.

> **✓ Success Tip**
> In the next four sets of drills, watch your finger make the reach from the home row to the symbol key the first three times you press it. Then concentrate on keeping your eyes on the copy to gain speed.

Exercise
22.7

At Sign Drill

Key lines 1–5 one time and then key the four lines again. Concentrate on control. Be sure to press the right Shift key and anchor the F finger when keying the at sign (@).

1 .s2s s2s s2s s2s s2s s2s s2s s@s s@s s2@s s2@s

2 14 @ $2.50, 16 @ $55.80, 1 @ $17.59, 13 @ $124.66

3 It is better to buy 99 @ 18 rather than 180 @ 10.

4 jjones@emcp.net; Xavier@emcp.net; vang@emcp.net

5 @chicagotheatre.info @auditoriumtheatre.com @cnet @facebook

Exercise
22.8

Equals Sign Drill

Key lines 1–4 one time and then key the four lines again. Concentrate on control. Anchor the J finger when keying the equals sign (=).

1 .;=; ;=; ;=; ;=; ;=; ;=; ;=; ;=; =;= =;= =;= =;= ;=

2 a = b c = d e = f g = g j = j k = k l = l ;=; ;=;;

3 A = D C = D J = J K = K L = L A = B C = D E = R =;

4 The = sign is generally used in math problems now.

Exercise
22.9

Plus Sign Drill

Key lines 1–4 one time and then key the four lines again. Concentrate on control. Remember to press the left Shift key for the plus sign (+). Anchor the J finger when making this reach.

1 ;=; ;+; ;+; ;=+; ;+:+:+=; ;=; ;+; ;=; ;+; ;=; :+;

2 The equations were: A = D + F + G and E = E + RT.

3 The equations were: A = B + C + E and H = A + BC.

4 The computer program stated A = (B + C + D) * AK.

Figure 51.4 Report Content for Document 51.2—Continued

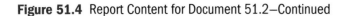

- Sixty percent of all callers ask for departments by name and these calls required 6.5 seconds of operator time.
- Callers requiring direction or assistance amounted to 31 percent of the total calls and averaged 19.1 seconds in operator time.
- Nine percent of the calls transferred inward received a busy signal thereby resulting in a double attempt by the operator to connect the call. In addition to the busy signals created by the "held" calls, the operator handling time to complete the call exceeded 30 seconds.
- The console operator does not have access to private departmental numbers, and when all lines are busy, the operator has to wait to connect emergency numbers.

Incoming Calls. Here are complaints from those calling the Dynacare Clinic: *bf*

- Callers have waited up to 25 rings before their call is answered, and they are often put on hold for 10 to 15 minutes.
- Caller volume is overwhelming the appointment desks in most medical units with Monday being the worst day of the week.
- Many messages result in telephone tag because they lack the necessary information desired by the original caller. This results in wasted calls and lost productivity.

bf / lc / lc Internal Use Of The Telephone System. Internally within the Clinic, *lc* the complaints most often expressed by doctors and support staff were as follows:

- The current telephone system ~~doesn't~~ *does not* provide for an automatic patient reminder system related to upcoming appointments. Patient no-shows reduces doctor/staff productivity.
- Personnel are unaware that incoming calls are often stacked up and waiting to be answered.
- There is an inability to share and/or cover appointed *ment* call volumes during peak periods.

continues

22.10 Key lines 1–9 one time while concentrating on control. Press the Enter key after each line.

1   s2@s s@2s s2s s@s S@S S@S S@S s@s s@s s2s s@s

2   23 @ $2.31, 172 @ $8.91; 17 @ 57, 98 @ 34, 8,934 @ 90, 2 @ 4

3   dsmith@emcp.net; phantom@emcp.net; tmodl@emcp.net

4   =; =;= =;= =;= ;=; ;=; =;= =;= ;=; ;=; = =

5   a=b c=d e=f G=J H=I K=L m=n o=p q=r

6   The = sign is used in formulas when working in spreadsheets.

7   ;+; ;=; ;+; ;=; ;+; ;=; ;+:+:=; ;=+; :=+: :+=:

8   The formula A = C + BA is the same as A = (C+BA).

9   The spreadsheet formula stated D1 = (B2 + C3 + A1) * F4.

Assessing Your Speed and Accuracy

Complete Timings 22.1 through 22.4 in the Online Lab. Reference the paragraphs from the textbook as you key. Timings 22.3 and 22.4 will use the same paragraph of text.

The timing will start as soon as you begin keying the paragraph. Remember to press the Tab key at the start of the paragraph. If you finish keying the paragraph before the timing expires, press Enter and start keying the paragraph again.

When time expires, the Online Lab will give you a WAM rate and error report for the timing. The results of the timings will be stored in your Timings Performance report.

Goals: 30 WAM and two or fewer errors

1-Minute Timings

Timing 22.1   Symbols are used frequently in computer programming languages. Of course, the plus (+), minus (-), and equals (=) keys are used. The asterisk (*) is used as a multiplication sign, and the diagonal (introduced in the next session) is used for division. It is important that we key symbols just as quickly as we key numbers and letters.

Timing 22.2   Silicon Valley's technology frenzy burst onto the stock market Thursday as XYZ Corp.'s shares more than doubled in their first day of trading, setting the stage for debuts from other Internet companies in the next six months. The outsize demand for the stock of an Internet company that is growing rapidly but had a profit of $12.5 million last year is the largest sign of the surge (some say bubble) in web valuations even as the broader US economy tries to rebound.

Figure 51.4 Report Content for Document 51.2—Continued

representing telecommunications companies and providers of hardware and software for telecommunications systems and services. The on-site visits included interviews with individuals representing all levels of personnel in the Clinic to include those working in the laboratory, the pharmacy, the administrative office facility, the HMO complex, the remote Clinic sites, and the Hospital. *insert page break*

FINDINGS

Telephone System

Dynacare Clinic utilizes a combination of leased Bell Atlantic Centrex lines and Clinic-owned key telephone systems to serve its telephone communication needs. As the Clinic grew through the years and expanded to locations outside the main Clinic location, these two services were expected to meet the existing needs.

The Centrex service, which is leased from Bell Atlantic provides the communication links that allow all sites in the Dalton area to communicate with each other. The number of telephone lines to Dynacare are as follows:

Dynacare Clinic	99
Tidewater HMO	246
Remote Clinic sites	132
TOTAL	499

check total

(Dalton Memorial Hospital has its own PBX telephone system.)

The combination of Centrex service and key telephone systems has functioned fairly well for its original purpose. However, the capabilities of these systems have reached their maximum and are unable to perform at a level of communications beyond their intended design in the current configuration.

Dynacare Clinic Console Observations. Here are facts and figures regarding the use of the Clinic Console:

continues

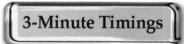

Timings
22.3–22.4

There is a new way to lay out a great garden that uses grids of neat 1-foot by 1-foot squares. Then, you plant the seeds and plants with certain spacings. The system is a simple one that allows persons to make the most of a garden space and at the same time conserve water and labor. Talented experts feel that 1-foot by 1-foot garden schemes let you grow the same amount of food as a regular garden does in less than one-fifth of the space.

Ergonomic Tip

Use a desk lamp (task lighting) instead of overhead lights to eliminate screen glare.

Ending the Session

The Online Lab automatically saves the work you completed for this session. You can continue with the next session or exit the Online Lab and continue later.

Figure 51.4 Report Content for Document 51.2—Continued

Automatic Appointment Reminder System. This system is used in conjunction with your computer system and digitized and synthesized voice technology to call patients to remind them of upcoming appoints. [ment]

Station Message Detail Recording. This allows for the tracking of outgoing calls, including local, for each extension number. Cost allocations and policing of unauthorized calls is automatically accomplished. [are]

System Administration. The unified messaging and communications solution must provide a web-based system administration tool and enable system and user administration, service and audit logs, system/user reporting, backup/restore, and security features.

With the implementation of either alternative, Dynacare Clinic will have addressed the needs identified for establishing a state-of-the-art communication system. The Clinic administration has to decide whether [lc] it is best to lease or purchase the telecommunications equipment.

Justification/Benefits

An addendum to this proposal outlines the justification and additional benefits of the recommendations. This portion of the proposal is being provided under separate cover and includes an extensive discussion on the merits of a digital PBX and digital Centrex. This information will be extremely helpful to the Dynacare Board of Directors in the final selection process. [start new page]

INTRODUCTION

The Dynacare Clinic Association has contracted with JBC Telecommunications of Atlanta, Georgia, to assess the voice communication needs of the Clinic and identify the two best alternatives for replacing the [lc] current system. Joanne B. Cooper, president of JBC, has coordinated the development of this report with Dr. Lawrence Isenburg, the Executive [lc] Director of the Dynacare Clinic. [lc]

A consulting team consisting of four JBC associates spent two weeks at the Dynacare sites included in this study. In addition to interviews, observations, and inventories of the current telephone system, face-to-face meetings and telephone conversations were held with individuals

continues

Circumflex Accent, Less Than, Greater Than, Diagonal, Backlash

Session Objectives

- Use the ^, <, >, /, and \ keys

Timing Goals

- 1 minute: 30 WAM and two or fewer errors
- 3 minutes: 25 WAM and six or fewer errors

Getting Started and Warming Up

Exercise 23.1
If you are continuing immediately from Session 22, you may skip the Exercise 23.1 warm-up drill. However, if you exited the Online Lab at the end of Session 22, warm up by completing Exercise 23.1.

Introducing the Circumflex Accent, Less Than, Greater Than, Diagonal, and Backslash Symbol Keys

Videos 23.1–23.5
The location of the keys to type the circumflex accent (^), less than (<), greater than (>), diagonal (/), and backslash (\) symbols are shown in the following diagram and the reaches are demonstrated in Videos 23.1 through 23.5. The circumflex accent, less than, and greater than symbols require the use of the appropriate Shift key. Practice the key reaches and Shift key combinations while watching the videos.

Exercises 23.2–23.9
Complete Exercises 23.2 through 23.6 to learn these new keys. When keying drill lines, follow the instruction prompts provided in the Online Lab. Work on improving your general speed and accuracy by completing Exercises 23.7 and 23.8. Finally, check your understanding of symbols by completing the Thinking Drill, Exercise 23.9.

Figure 51.4 Report Content for Document 51.2—Continued

of effort resulting in additional personnel, patient complaints of not being handled effectively, and potentially lost patients and revenues if frustrated patients cannot be handled in an expedient fashion. Significant cost savings may be realized as a result of updating telecommunications technology.

Competing clinics have call management systems, ~~which~~ *a feature that* is not being used with Dynacare's current telephone system. Information such as the number of calls coming into the Clinic, the number of rings before a call ⓛⓒ is answered, and the number of abandoned calls would be extremely helpful in providing appropriate staffing levels. As this information is not available in Dynacare's current telephone system, one must operate from general observations and user complaints.

Recommendations

It is recommended that Dynacare replace their current telephone system with one of the following:

- Purchase a digital PBX and network it with ~~the~~ *Dalton Memorial* hospital, the Tidewater HMO, and the remote Clinic sites. ⓛⓒ
- Lease a digital Centrex service to support the Clinic, the hospital, the ⓛⓒ HMO, and the remote Clinic sites. ⓛⓒ

Regardless of the alternative chosen, the following features need to be included in order to facilitate the telecommunications needs of the Dynacare Clinic Association immediately and to allow for future expansion:

Dial-by-Extension or Dial-by-Name Capabilities. This ~~allows~~ *permits* the ability to record different greetings or announcements for automatic payback based on day, night, weekend, and holiday operation.

Multi-lingual Capabilities. Callers may pre-select a language based on different access numbers or select a language using menu prompts.

Automatic Call Distribution. Management is able to determine call volumes, calls in queue waiting to be answered, appointment desk availability to take calls, etc. Adjustments in the number of personnel available at the appointment desk can be made on a real-time basis so as to serve clients in an efficient manner.

continues

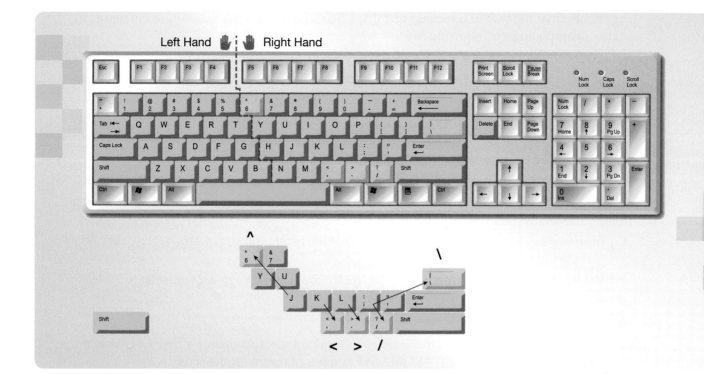

⟳ Reinforcing Your Skills

Complete Exercises 23.10 through 23.15 in the Online Lab. Reference the drill lines from the textbook as you key and keep your eyes on the textbook pages, not on your fingers. Complete each exercise at least once, but repeat exercises if you want to improve your WAM rate or accuracy.

Exercise 23.10 Circumflex Accent Drill

Key lines 1–3 once and then key the lines again. Concentrate on control. Anchor the semicolon (;) finger when making this reach.

1 j6j j6j j6j j^j j^j j^j j^j J^J J^J J^J J^J J^J J^

2 The ^ sign is used to raise an integer to a power.

3 For example, 2^2 is the square of the numeral two.

Exercise 23.11 Less Than Drill

The less than symbol (<) can be keyed with a space before and after it or with no space. Whichever you select, be consistent. Remember to use the left Shift key and anchor the J or the semicolon (;) finger for this reach.

Key lines 1–3 once and then key the lines again. Concentrate on control.

1 2<7 3<8 4<9 5<6 8<9 1<2 5<7 6<8 k<l k<l 5<6 1<8<9

2 12 < 43 16 < 58 17 < 89 15 < 28 123 < 456 17 < 77

3 2 < 4, j < k, 1 < m, K < L; S < Z; K < L; JK < LM

c   Format the tabbed columnar text displayed in the *FINDINGS* section of the report by completing the following steps:

1) Press Tab, key **Dynacare Clinic**, press Tab, key **99**, and then press Shift + Enter.

2) Press Tab, key **Tidewater HMO**, press Tab, key **246**, and then press Shift + Enter.

3) Press Tab, key **Remote clinic sites**, press Tab, press Ctrl + U, key **132**, press Ctrl + U, and then press Enter.

4) Press Tab, key **TOTAL**, press Tab, key the corrected total, and then press Enter.

5) Key **(Dalton Memorial Hospital has its own PBX telephone system.)**

6) Select the text from *Dynacare Clinic* through the total amount.

7) Set a left tab at 2.0 inch and a right tab at 4.0 inch using either the Ruler or the Tabs dialog box.

6   Insert a plain page number in the right side of the header on pages 2 through 6. Do not include the page number on page 1.

7   Review the format of your typed document by comparing it against Figure 51.5.

8   Proofread the document and correct any errors.

9   Save the document.

10   Click the Check button to stop the timer and upload the document for checking. The Online Lab will report the WAM rate and number of errors for the activity.

11   If errors are reported, view the results document, correct the errors in the submitted document, save the document, and then click the Check button.

Figure 51.4 Report Content for Document 51.2

A PROPOSAL FOR REPLACING DYNACARE CLINIC'S TELEPHONE SYSTEM

By JBC Telecommunications

The information ~~included~~ contained in this report includes an Executive Summary, Introduction, Findings, and Needs Analysis for updating the telecommunications systems for the Dynacare Clinic Association.

EXECUTIVE SUMMARY

Background

Dynacare Clinic, as all ~~other~~ like healthcare facilities, is faced with renewed demands for cost control. This means lowering costs by increasing efficiencies of both human and plant resources. Health care systems across the country are using advanced technology to improve the bottom line.

Dynacare Clinic has not implemented technology that is associated with state-of-the-art telecommunications systems. This has ~~resulted in~~ produced a duplication

continues

Exercise 23.12 Greater Than and Less Than Drill

As with the less than symbol (<), the greater than symbol (>) can be keyed with a space before and after it or with no space. Whichever you select, be consistent.

Key lines 1–3 once and then key the lines again. Concentrate on control. Anchor the J finger for this reach and use the left Shift key.

Note: The first drill line contains lowercase Ls and the third line contains number 1s.

1 l<l l<l ;<; ;<; 6>4 6>2 5>1 9>7 l>l ;>>;;

2 L>M L>R ;>; 56 > 43 126 > 78 198 > 48 66 > 55 6>>

3 6 > 2 < 6; 6 > 1.2; 78 > 8; 1234 > 678; 56 < 234;

Exercise 23.13 Diagonal Drill

The diagonal symbol (/) is used as a division sign in computer programming languages and in Web addresses such as http://www.emcp.com. It is also used to divide characters such as month, day, and year in a date (for example, 04/14/97).

Key lines 1–3 once and then key the lines again. Concentrate on control. Anchor the J finger when making this reach.

1 ;/; ;/; ;/; l;/ ;/; ;/; l;/ ;/; l;/ ;/ ;/ ;/;/ ;/

2 a = b/c d = f/g h=j/l t=k/j r = j / k fgh = rty/j

3 The equation: miles/hours will equal speed rate.

Exercise 23.14 Backslash Drill

Key lines 1–3 once and then key the lines again. Concentrate on control. Anchor the J finger when making this reach.

1 The \ sign is used to designate a given file path.

2 For example, c:\windows will take you to windows in C drive.

3 c:\user\pat\documents\guestlist c:\braymore\lrp\minutes

Exercise 23.15 Reinforcement Drill

Key each line one time.

1 Two-thirds of the three-fourths are very gifted.

2 John said: Data Structures is a great textbook.

3 Jerome's cat ran to Mary's house and said meow!!

4 "Hello," said Jim. "How are you this fine day?"

5 "Help!" yells the old man as the bees followed.

6 If the dress is $35.95, why is the coat $125.75?

drill continues

Figure 51.3 Formatting Sample   *Note: Do not key this document.*

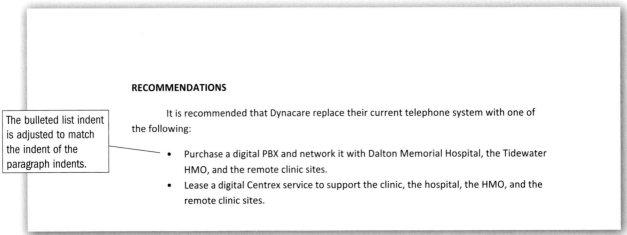

RECOMMENDATIONS

It is recommended that Dynacare replace their current telephone system with one of the following:

The bulleted list indent is adjusted to match the indent of the paragraph indents.

- Purchase a digital PBX and network it with Dalton Memorial Hospital, the Tidewater HMO, and the remote clinic sites.
- Lease a digital Centrex service to support the clinic, the hospital, the HMO, and the remote clinic sites.

Changing Indents in Bulleted and Numbered Lists

When regular paragraphs in a document begin with a tab, any bulleted or numbered lists in the same document should begin at the same distance from the left margin as the paragraphs, typically 0.5 inch. The Word default indent for a bulleted or numbered list is 0.25 inch, but you can increase the indent. After keying such a list, select the entire list, and click the Increase Indent button in the Paragraph group on the Home tab until the bullet or number begins at 0.5 inch. If you indent too far, use the Decrease Indent button to move the text to the left and reduce the amount of indent. Figure 51.3 shows correctly indented text and bullets.

Document 51.2 · **Bound Business Report with Tabbed Columnar Text and Bulleted Items**

1 Read all instructions for this document activity, navigate to the Document 51.2 launch page in the Online Lab, and then click the Launch Activity button. The Online Lab will open **Doc051.02** in the activity window. The timer will start as soon as you begin keying the document.

2 Read the multiple-page business report manuscript shown in Figure 51.4. The figure contains proofreading marks that identify corrections that will need to be made as you key the document. Refer to Appendix B if you are not sure what some of the proofreading marks mean.

3 Format the document so that the left margin is 1.5 inches, which is the margin needed for a bound business report.

4 Press Enter three times to move the insertion point 2 inches from the top of the first page.

5 Key the document shown in Figure 51.4, but note the following formatting instructions:

a Center align and set both the title and subtitle in bold. Set the title in all uppercase letters and key the title on one line.

b Allow Word to automatically format the bulleted and numbered paragraphs in the report. However, increase the indent so that the bullets align with the paragraph indent of 0.5 inch. Set the headings in bold as shown in the figure. Bold the period following the headings but not the space following the period.

steps continue

7 Take #33 and move it to #66. Move #66 to #1234.

8 Farber & Daughters is the name of my law firm.

9 The check was made out for at least $*******.99.

10 You scored 89% on the exam and 78% on the drill.

11 Now is the time (11:45) for you (Ginny) to move.

12 I make $9 per hour, but I would like to make $16.

13 Sixteen @ $1.23 and 57 @ $23.45 is far too much.

14 If hours = 40 and rate = $5.00 then gross = $200.

15 The equation was A = B + C + F + D + G + H + I + J.

16 Jerry thought that A < B and F < G and JK < JKL.

17 However, Tom knew that A > B and F > G and I > IK.

18 If you raise 2^2 the answer will be squared now.

19 Enter your last name on the line that follows: _____.

20 LET X = A + B + C / D * H * (HH - K) + (HH + JJ).

21 Go to http://www.uwec.edu for information on course availability.

22 IF GH < AN AND TH > HJ OR TY < TU MOVE TRY TO A.

23 There will be a reaction--perhaps not good--if you do that.

24 PRINT TAB[17] "PLAYER" TAB[34] "FG PERCENT"; FG

25 The #12 category weighs 18#; the #7 category weighs 6#.

Success Tip

If you hesitated while keying or are unsure of the reaches required for symbols in Exercise 23.15, repeat the appropriate exercises in the sessions in Unit 3.

Assessing Your Speed and Accuracy

Complete Timings 23.1 through 23.5 in the Online Lab. Refer to the following paragraphs as you key. Timings 23.4 and 23.5 will use the same paragraph of text.

The timing will start as soon as you begin keying the paragraph. Remember to press the Tab key at the start of the paragraph. If you finish keying the paragraph before the timing expires, press Enter and start keying the paragraph again.

When the time expires, the Online Lab will give you a WAM rate and error report for the timing. The results of the timings will be stored in your Timings Performance report.

3 In the Tabs dialog box, key the location (in inches) of the tab stop in the *Tab stop position* box.

4 Set the type of tab in the *Alignment* section of the Tabs dialog box.

5 Click the Set button to set the tab.

6 Repeat steps 3 through 5 for each tab that needs to be set.

7 Click OK when all of the needed tabs are set and to apply the new tab stops to the document.

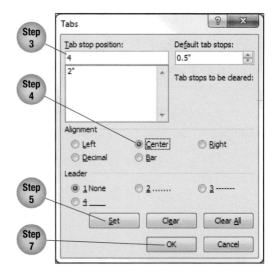

Deleting Tabs

Just as with setting tabs, deleting tabs may be done on the Ruler or at the Tabs dialog box.

To delete a tab from the Ruler, click on the tab symbol and hold down the mouse button, drag it downward and off the Ruler, and then release the mouse button. *Note: If you set another tab by mistake, use Undo.*

To delete a tab using the Tabs dialog box, complete the following steps:

1 Display the Tabs dialog box.

2 Select the tab to be deleted in the *Tab stop position* list box.

3 Click the Clear button (or click Clear All if you want to remove all of the tabs).

4 Click OK to close the Tabs dialog box.

Document Document with Text Formatted with Tabs

51.1

1 Read all instructions for this document activity, navigate to the Document 51.1 launch page in the Online Lab, and then click the Launch Activity button. The Online Lab will open **Doc051.01** in the activity window.

2 Select all of the text in the document (press Ctrl + A).

3 Remove the decimal tab from the 3.5-inch mark on the Ruler. The decimal tab aligns the Points column.

4 Place a right tab at the 3-inch mark on the Ruler.

5 Move the center tab from the 5-inch mark to the 4-inch mark on the Ruler.

6 Move the insertion point to the end of the document (press Ctrl + end) and then press Enter two times.

7 Open the Tabs dialog box and clear all of the tabs at the insertion point by clicking the Clear All button.

8 Using the Tabs dialog box, set a left tab at the 1-inch tab stop position and then close the dialog box.

9 With the insertion point at the end of the document, press Tab and then key **Bonuses are distributed in January.**

10 Proofread the document and correct any errors.

11 Click the Check button to upload the document for checking. The Online Lab will report the number of errors for the activity.

12 If errors are reported, view the results document, correct the errors in the submitted document, save the document, and then click the Check button.

1-Minute Timings

Timing 23.1

Barlow, a shrewd fellow, winked as he waited in the shadows. A whistle warned him of the slow walk of his fellow worker. As he wallowed in the warmth of that workshop, Will worked in the wild, blowing wind. Barlow was worthless.

Timing 23.2

Malaysia is in the process of shifting from an agricultural to an industrial economy. Their government has a plan entitled Vision 2020 that will make them fully industrialized by that year. Many government and business people feel that the ethnic balance of Malay, Chinese, and Indian races must remain intact. Banks are offering low-interest loans for Malay-owned businesses.

Timing 23.3

A lazy bicycle ride in the country is surely a healthy and worthy activity. A sunny sky and a dry day is surely an omen to any type of cyclist. Be wary of cloudy and windy days. A daily remedy for a healthy and spry body is a ride on a cycle. Energy is enjoyed by young and not so young.

Goals: 25 WAM and six or fewer errors

3-Minute Timings

Timings 23.4–23.5

The Transportation Security Authority (TSA) has announced it will be trial testing a new prescreening program that could offer some airline passengers expedited screening through US security checkpoints. Travel Fast Airlines is pleased to announce our partnership with the TSA in testing this new concept at our hubs in Dallas/Fort Worth and Miami. You may be eligible to participate and potentially be cleared through the TSA pre-vetting process, resulting in some screening benefits at the checkpoint. During the first phase of testing, certain frequent flyers and members of Customs and Border Protection's Global Entry, NEXUS, and SENTRI programs, who are United States citizens, will be eligible to participate in this pilot program which could qualify them for expedited screening. The TSA will determine who participates in the trial on a per-flight segment basis.

Setting Tabs Using the Ruler

If you do not see a horizontal Ruler that appears along the top of your document just below the ribbon, click the View tab and then click the *Ruler* check box in the Show group to insert a check mark. A quicker method is to click the View Ruler button at the top of the vertical scroll bar on the right side of your screen (see Figure 51.2). If the Ruler is displayed, clicking this button will hide the Ruler and remove the check mark from the *Ruler* check box in the Show group on the View tab.

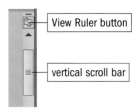

Figure 51.2 View Ruler Button

View Ruler button

vertical scroll bar

The numbers on the horizontal Ruler represent inches from the left margin of the document.

Set a tab by completing the following steps:

1 Click the Alignment button at the left end of the Ruler until it displays the type of tab that you want selected. Refer to Table 51.1 for Alignment button images and descriptions of what each type of tab does.

2 Click the Ruler where you want to set the tab stop. The tab symbol will appear on that location on the Ruler.

When setting tabs, consider the following:

• If your tab does not appear exactly where you want it on the Ruler, or if you did not get the tab type desired, use Undo (Ctrl + Z) and start again.

• Word will automatically remove (clear) tabs to the left of the first tab set.

• The Word tab default of every 0.5 inch will continue to the right of the last tab set.

Setting Tabs Using the Tabs Dialog Box

You can also use the Tabs dialog box to set tabs at a precise measurement, to clear one or all tabs, or to set character leaders to appear before the text keyed at a tab.

To display the Tabs dialog box, complete the following steps:

1 Click the Paragraph group dialog box launcher on the Home tab.

2 At the Paragraph dialog box, with either the Indents and Spacing tab or Line and Page Breaks tab selected, click the Tabs button located in the bottom left corner.

steps continue

Step 1

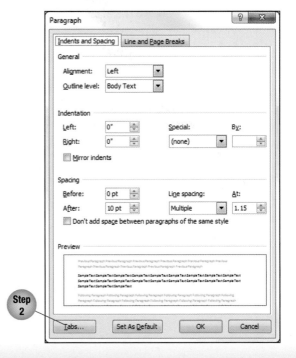

Step 2

Ergonomic Tip
Use your entire hand to press hard-to-reach keys rather than forcing your hands into awkward positions. Make sure you bring your fingers back to the home-row keys.

Ending the Session

The Online Lab automatically saves the work you completed for this session. You can continue with the next session or exit the Online Lab and continue later.

5 Click the *Different First Page* check box in the Options group to insert a check mark.

6 Click the Close Header and Footer button in the Close group or double-click in the body of the document to make the body of the document active.

Manipulating Tabs

In a new blank document, Word provides a tab stop every 0.5 inch beginning at the left margin, although these default tabs are *not* shown on the Ruler. In some situations, these default tab stops are appropriate; in other situations, you may want to create your own tab stops. There are two methods of setting tabs: on the Ruler or at the Tabs dialog box. Both methods will be presented, but first we will review fundamental features of tabs in Word.

Word features five types of tab alignment (and two indents). The five tab stops that may be set are described in Table 51.1. Figure 51.1 shows how text is aligned when each tab is used.

You can set tabs before keying text or key text using the default tab stops and then set tabs. When tabs are set before keying the text, the tab formatting is inserted in the paragraph mark at the end of the line. Each time you press the Enter key, the paragraph mark is copied down to the next line and the tab stops remain in place for keying the next line.

If you key text before setting tabs, press the Tab key before keying each column entry, including the first one. After the text is keyed, select the lines of text to be formatted with the new tabs and then set the tabs.

If necessary, the tab settings may be changed easily after keying the text. Select the tabbed text and then change the tabs either using the Ruler or the Tabs dialog box.

Table 51.1 Types of Tab Alignment

⌊	A **Left Tab** stop sets the start position of text that will then run to the right as you key.
⊥	A **Center Tab** stop sets the position of the middle of the text. The text centers on this position as you key.
⌋	A **Right Tab** stop sets the right end of the text. As you key, the text moves to the left.
⊥	A **Decimal Tab** stop aligns numbers around a decimal point. Independent of the number of digits, the decimal point will be in the same position. (You can align numbers around a decimal character only; you cannot use the decimal tab to align numbers around a different character, such as a hyphen or an ampersand symbol.)
⎮	A **Bar Tab** stop does not position text. Rather, it inserts a vertical bar at the tab position.

Figure 51.1 Tab Alignment Examples

Left Tab	Center Tab	Right Tab	Decimal Tab	Bar Tab
Valencia	Washington	Olympia	22.908	
Yang	Oregon	Salem	1,655.05555	
Nicholson	California	Sacramento	623.5	

Unit 4

Numeric Keypad Keys

Inserting a Page Break

Sometimes you will want to begin a new page before reaching the bottom of the previous page. Other changes to a document might be made later, so do not continue to press Enter until a new page appears. Rather, insert a page break.

Insert a page break in the document by completing the following steps:

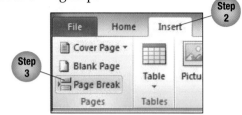

1. Position the insertion point where you want a page to end (such as after the period in the last sentence on a page).
2. Click the Insert tab.
3. Click the Page Break button in the Pages group.

> ✓ **Success Tip**
> The keyboard shortcut for inserting a page break is Ctrl + Enter.

Inserting Page Numbers

RFP documents include page numbers, aligned with the right margin, on the headers of pages following the first page. In previous sessions, page numbers were inserted as part of a header along with other information.

When inserting headers or footers on pages following the first page of a document, it is less complicated to key the first page and at least part of the second page of the document before inserting the header and footer information. To insert only a page number on pages following the first page, follow these steps after keying the first page and part of the second page of text:

1. With the insertion point anywhere on the second page, click the Insert tab.
2. Click the Page Number button in the Header & Footer group.
3. Point to *Top of Page* from the drop-down list.
4. Click *Plain Number 3* in the *Simple* section to insert the page number and to open the Header & Footer Tools Design tab.

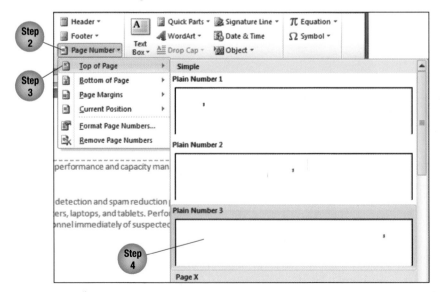

steps continue

Session Objectives

- **Explore the typical numeric keypad configuration**
- **Investigate the numeric keypads home row (4, 5, 6) and 0 keys**
- **Learn to key numbers in rows**

Timing Goals

- **1 minute (numeric keypad): 25 WAM and no errors**
- **1 minute (alphabetic): 30 WAM and two or fewer errors**

Getting Started and Warming Up

Exercise 24.1 If you are continuing immediately from Session 23, you may skip the Exercise 24.1 warm-up drill. However, if you exited the Online Lab at the end of Session 23, warm up by completing Exercise 24.1.

Introducing the Numeric Keypad

Computer keyboards typically have a numeric keypad located to the right of the alphabetic keys. The numeric keypad allows you to enter numeric data with one hand. You can use this keypad instead of the numeric row above the alphabetic keys. A common use of the numeric keypad includes entering numbers in cells and rows of spreadsheets. With a minimum amount of practice, you can enter numeric data at speeds significantly greater than 100 digits per minute. By industry standards, a rate of 250 digits per minute is considered average (equivalent to 50 WAM).

Typical Numeric Keypad Configuration

The following illustration shows the general arrangement of most numeric keypads. The top row contains the 7, 8, and 9 keys. The middle row is the home row and contains the 4, 5, and 6 keys. The bottom row contains the 1, 2, and 3 keys. The 0 (zero) and decimal point (.) keys are at the bottom of the numeric keypad.

In addition to the numbers 0 through 9, several symbol keys are included on the numeric keypad. These symbol keys include plus (+), minus (–), diagonal or forward slash (/), and asterisk (*) keys. Using the symbol keys next to the numeric keypad often saves time when working extensively with numbers.

To use the numeric keypad on a computer, the Num Lock key must be on. A light usually displays by Num Lock when it is on. Num Lock is a toggle key. If Num Lock is not on, press the *Num Lock* key to turn it on. Press the key again to turn it off. *Note: The Num Lock key may be labeled as Num Loc, Num Lk, or NL.*

When working with spreadsheets or tables, use the Tab key (keyed with the A finger) to move across the screen from cell to cell. Use the Enter key to move vertically down a column from one row to the next. The Enter key is located to the right of the 3 key.

Changing Page Margins

Set custom page margins in a document by completing the following steps:

1. Click the Page Layout tab.

2. Click the Margins button in the Page Setup group. This action displays a list of preset margin options.

3. Click *Custom Margins* to open the Page Setup dialog box with the Margins tab selected.

4. Adjust the settings in the *Margins* section of the dialog box. By default, margin settings are shown in inches. Click in the measurement box for the margin to be changed and key the new margin desired or use the up or down arrows to change the value in the measurement box.

5. Note that the image in the *Preview* section will display how the settings will alter the look of the document.

6. Click OK to apply the changes and to close the Page Setup dialog box.

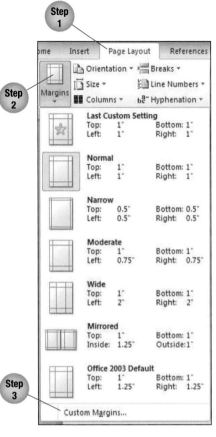

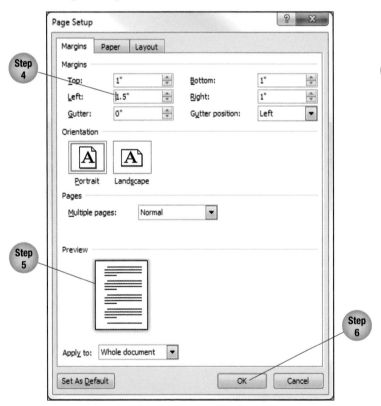

Success Tip

Double-click on the Ruler *outside* of the current margin settings to quickly access the Page Setup dialog box.

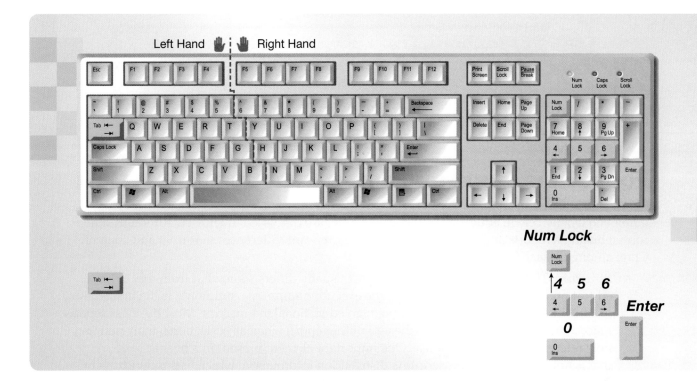

Num Lock

Videos
24.1–24.4
Video 24.1 presents the hand position for the home-row keys on the numeric keypad, Video 24.2 provides reinforcement on the use of the Tab key to the left of the alphabetic keys. Video 24.3 presents the 0 key reach on the numeric keypad. Finally, Video 24.4 presents the Num Lock key reach.

Exercises
24.2–24.5
Complete Exercises 24.2 through 24.3 to learn these new keys. Exercises 24.4 through 24.5 provide practice keying using the alphabetic keys. When keying the drill lines, follow the instruction prompts provided in the Online Lab.

Alternate Numeric Keypad Configurations

Many laptop computers do not have a separate numeric keypad. Instead, they have an embedded numeric keypad, which includes the symbol keys +, –, /, and *. The embedded numeric keyboard can be activated when the function key is used with some of the right-hand alphabetic keys.

To use the embedded numeric keyboard on a laptop computer, look for the Num Lock on a function key. Use the appropriate command—probably holding down the function key (FN or Fn) near the space bar while tapping the appropriate function key on the top row—to turn Num Lock on or off. When Num Lock is on, place your JKL; (semicolon) fingers on the UIO keys (or the keys designated for 4, 5, 6) as the numeric keypad home row. You can now use the alphabetic keyboard as a numeric keyboard.

The function key is usually located above the number row on a laptop. When keying numeric text, use the semicolon (;) finger for the Enter key.

↻ Reinforcing Your Skills

Complete Exercises 24.6 through 24.8 in the Online Lab. Reference the drill lines from the textbook as you key and keep your eyes on the textbook pages, not on your fingers. Complete each exercise at least once, but repeat exercises if you want to improve your WAM rate or accuracy.

Ergonomic Tip

Computer settings, such as the size of print, contrast (especially, the lack of), color, speed, and the size of the pointer, can all be customized to make looking at the screen easier.

Formatting Formal Business Reports

Formal business reports are similar in some ways to manuscripts. Manuscripts, which are employed extensively in education and in publishing, are discussed in Unit 11. Although similar, formal business reports and manuscripts do have significant differences in format and content. Chief among these difference are:

- **Structure:** The sequence of a business report usually differs somewhat from that of an educational manuscript. For example, the executive summary commonly is the first section of a business report but the last section of an educational manuscript. Most business reports place all reference information at the end of the report, whereas educational manuscripts note references at the point of use. One important element present in a business report that is not included in manuscripts is distribution information, which lists individuals or institutions who received copies of the report. Distribution information occurs on either the title page or at the end of the formal business report.

- **Format:** Business reports are similar to letters and memos in that they use the Word 2010 defaults of 1.15-line spacing and 10 points of space after each paragraph. The space between paragraphs is created by a single hard return or by pressing the Enter key. Business reports may also be single spaced with a double space between paragraphs (which requires pressing the Enter key two times between paragraphs). Manuscripts are double spaced, which allows room for handwritten reviewer comments, and are formatted with indented paragraphs.

- **Displays or Exhibits:** Business reports commonly contain graphic elements such as photographs, boxed tables, charts, graphs, drawings, illustrations, and so on. Manuscripts typically include tables, graphs, and illustrations as the most common method of displaying information. The keyboarder can create most, if not all, of the visual displays needed for both types of reports. In all documents and report types, always place a display *after* it has been referred to in the text. When graphic elements are too long or too large to illustrate within a business report, they are usually placed at the back and identified as exhibits.

- **Packaging or Binding:** Business reports are generally placed in some type of booklet with attractive cover designs and with the various sections tabbed throughout to help the reader quickly find areas of particular interest. To allow room for a binding such as punched holes, increase the left margin by 0.5 inch (for a total of 1.5 inches). Manuscripts, on the other hand, are more conservative in appearance and adhere to formal guidelines in terms of how they are to be bound. An unbound manuscript will have a 1-inch default left margin. A bound manuscript will have a 1.5-inch left margin.

As might be expected, business reports can be prepared with a wide variety of possible formats. If you are asked to format a business report, always attempt to ascertain if there are preferred formats at your company. Consult your company style manual if one has been developed. You might also check the files for copies of similar reports created previously and use that format.

As you key these drill lines on the numeric keypad, press the Tab key between number groups and press the Enter key when you reach the end of each row. The Tab key is located to the left of the alphabetic keys and the Enter key is on the numeric keypad. Think of numbers as combinations to help you key more easily. Review the instructions in Session 14, if needed.

Exercise 24.6 **Keypad Home Row Drill**

Key rows 1–5 one time and push for speed. Key rows 1–5 again and concentrate on accuracy. Place your right hand on home row (4, 5, 6). Tab between number groups (that is, after the "6" in 456). Press Enter after each row.

1	456	456	456	654	654	654	546	546	546	564	564	645	65
2	444	445	455	454	555	564	565	566	645	654	644	554	46
3	555	556	554	445	446	444	666	654	655	645	564	546	54
4	666	655	654	645	555	546	564	566	544	546	466	455	64
5	464	465	646	454	455	556	564	565	566	654	666	546	55

Exercise 24.7 **Keypad 0 Drill**

Key rows 1–5 one time and push for speed. Key rows 1–5 again and concentrate on accuracy. Use your right thumb for the 0 key. Tab between number groups. Press Enter after each row.

1	0	00	000	000	000	000	50	50	50	50	50
2	400	400	400	500	500	500	500	600	600	500	400
3	405	504	506	605	440	400	550	660	660	550	440
4	440	500	450	450	560	4560	4560	4650	6540	6540	56000
5	550	600	540	540	650	6540	6440	4560	6405	6054	56005

Success Tip
Building your skill with the numeric keypad allows you to enter numerical data quickly and accurately.

Timings 51.1–51.2

Firms take time and money to train new employees. Every effort is made to involve workers in decision making and to allow them to be creative. Employers who prepare workers are more profitable than employers who do not.

Many studies have shown that one of the best roads to high profits and worker output is to treat employees as resources to be developed rather than expenses to be cut. Successes to a firm's operation are high when needed changes are made by providing ongoing training programs that are easy for employees to use on the job. Workers must be given time to absorb any changes and to start applying those changes. Employees must also be given a chance to make decisions that will affect their work.

Complete two 3-minute timings on the timing text below. Timings 51.3 and 51.4 use the same paragraphs.

Goals: 35 WAM and three or fewer errors
SI: 1.47 syllables per word

3-Minute Timings

Timings 51.3–51.4

Growing annual plants in containers has become very popular. Creative gardeners will move containers from one place to another to highlight the most beautiful plants in bloom. A movable or mobile green garden allows for the maximum use of color.

Plants that have been started can be purchased at all local nursery or garden shops in the spring. Usually, these flowers are in full bloom at the period when they are offered for sale; the gardener can then select the colors and kinds of plants that will look best in the specific garden sites and areas. After the flower garden bed has been prepared, the gardener can simply place the fine blooming plants in the earth and soon there will be a bright garden.

Planning flower displays is a time-consuming but rewarding task. A mass of brilliant colors and textures could brighten a dark corner or highlight darker foliage and shrubs. Some annuals are better suited for border planting or edging. Others that grow quite tall can be used for unique backgrounds or for screening. There are many annuals that make gorgeous bouquets of cut flowers. The gardener can enjoy the fruits of his or her labor with vases of beautiful blossoms placed all around the house.

Exercise 24.8 Keypad Reinforcement Drill

Key rows 1–9 one time. Concentrate on keying as accurately as possible. Tab between number groups. Press Enter after each row.

1	654	654	456	456	456	456	456	655	556	556	664	664	56
2	456	546	546	546	645	456	546	566	566	664	665	444	44
3	544	544	566	544	644	644	554	555	444	655	444	555	44
4	64	456	456	654	456	666	444	555	654	654	456	456	456
5	45	666	555	444	654	654	465	55	44	45	65	64	56
6	500	600	400	545	545	6545	4505	5460	5440	5540	50404	54	446
7	644	654	4560	4560	4560	4560	6540	6540	6540	450	406	654	604
8	556	654	6540	5460	5046	0564	0546	5040	5000	605	404	4055	64
9	600	500	4000	4005	5004	6005	5004	6005	0665	044	606	505	606

Assessing Your Speed and Accuracy

Complete Timings 24.1 through 24.5 in the Online Lab. Refer to the following numerical timing text as you key. The timing will start as soon as you begin keying. If you finish keying before time expires, press Enter and start keying the timing text again. When time expires, the Online Lab will give you a WAM rate and error report for the timing. The results of the timings will be stored in your Timings Performance report.

For the following numeric keypad timings, remember to press Tab between number groups and Enter at the end of each row. Timings 24.2 and 24.3 use the same timing text.

Goals: 25 WAM and no errors

1-Minute Timings

Timing 24.1

654	654	654	456	456	666	444	555	546	546	546	456	46
555	666	444	555	654	555	456	456	654	645	645	645	45
654	654	456	456	456	456	456	655	556	556	664	664	56
456	546	546	546	645	456	546	566	566	644	665	444	44
544	544	566	544	644	644	554	555	444	655	444	555	44

Timings 24.2–24.3

550	600	540	540	650	6540	6440	4560	6540	6054	56605
500	600	400	545	545	6545	4505	5460	5440	5540	50404
644	654	4560	4560	4560	4560	6540	6540	6540	450	406
556	654	6540	5460	5046	0564	0546	5040	5000	605	404
600	500	4000	4005	5004	6005	5004	6005	0665	044	606

Session 51 — Producing Formal Business Reports

Session Objectives

- Format a formal business report
- Change page margins
- Insert page breaks
- Change text alignment
- Manipulate tabs
- Change indents in bulleted and numbered lists
- Choose graphic formats

Timing Goals

- 1 minute: 40 WAM and one or no errors
- 3 minutes: 35 WAM and three or fewer errors

Getting Started and Warming Up

Exercise 51.1 If you are continuing immediately from Session 50, you may skip the Exercise 51.1 warm-up drill. However, if you exited the Online Lab at the end of Session 50, warm up by completing Exercise 51.1.

Exercise 51.2 Begin your session work by completing Exercise 51.2, a timed short drill, in the Online Lab.

Assessing Your Speed and Accuracy

Complete Timings 51.1 through 51.4 in the Online Lab. At the end of each timing, the Online Lab will display your WAM rate and any errors. Results will be saved in your Timings Performance report. If you have been surpassing the speed and accuracy goals, set slightly more challenging personal goals and strive to exceed them.

Note that beginning with this session, accuracy goals for timings are now set at a maximum of one error *per minute*. Thus, the accuracy goal for 1-minute timings is one or no errors, the goal for 3-minute timings is three or fewer errors, and the goal for 5-minute timings is five or fewer errors.

Complete two 1-minute timings on the following timing text. Timings 51.1 and 51.2 use the same paragraphs.

For the following alphabetic timings, remember to press Tab at the start of the paragraph.

Goals: 30 WAM and two or fewer errors

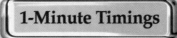

Timing 24.4

The way you shut down your computer is important because the proper procedure avoids losing unsaved data and properly saves systems settings. Use features with names such as Sleep or Hibernate to save computer power but still be able to return to your desktop and any running programs quickly without having to reboot.

Timing 24.5

Spreadsheet software is an electronic version of the ruled worksheets accountants used in the past. Spreadsheet software provides a means of organizing, calculating, and presenting financial, statistical, and other numerical information. For example, an instructor may use a spreadsheet to calculate student grades.

Ergonomic Tip
Keep your neck and shoulders relaxed as you key.

Ending the Session

The Online Lab automatically saves the work you completed for this session. You can continue with the next session or exit the Online Lab and continue later.

3   Use the Word Find and Replace feature to change all instances of *Program Director* to *Program Manager*. Insert a check mark in the Match case check box (if necessary).

4   Proofread the document to make sure spacing errors were not implemented because of the replacements.

5   Save the document.

6   Click the Check button to upload the document for checking. The Online Lab will report the number of errors for the activity.

7   If errors are reported, view the results document, correct the errors in the submitted document, save the document, and then click the Check button.

Reinforcing Writing Skills

Communicating with printed documents or email messages offers distinct advantages when compared with communicating by telephone or in person, including:

- A written (printed) message provides a permanent record.
- A written message usually implies greater authority.
- The reader can reread and study printed documents, whereas orally conveyed information is presented only once. This is important when the information is complicated.
- The act of preparing a written or printed document allows the author the opportunity to carefully craft a statement, so that the information is precise and the tone is as desired.

Document 50.3   Composing a Memo Business Report

1   Navigate to the Document 50.3 launch page in the Online Lab and then click the Launch Activity button. The Online Lab will open **Doc050.03** in the activity window.

2   In the active document, begin a memo business report with the following information at the top of the document:

a   Key your instructor's name in the *TO* line at the top of the memo.

b   Indicate that the memo is from you.

c   Use the current date for the memo.

d   Include the subject line *A Summary of the Language Arts Guidelines in Sessions 38 to 43 and 49 to 53.*

3   In the body of the memo, compose a report that contains at least one-and-a-half pages on the subject indicated at the top of the memo. Include subheadings to help direct the reader's attention.

4   On the second page of the memo, format a vertical continuation header.

5   At the end of the memo, include the file name.

6   Edit the memo for complete, well-written sentences and correct grammar, punctuation, and capitalization.

7   Save the document.

8   Click the Upload button to upload the document for instructor review.

Ending the Session

The Online Lab automatically saves the work you completed for this session. You may continue with the next session or exit the Online Lab and continue later.

7, 8, 9, Decimal Point

Session Objectives

- Investigate the 7, 8, 9, and decimal point keys on the numeric keypad
- Explore keying numbers in rows

Timing Goals

- 1 minute (numeric keypad): 25 WAM and no errors
- 1 minute (alphabetic): 30 WAM and two or fewer errors

Getting Started and Warming Up

Exercise 25.1 If you are continuing immediately from Session 24, you may skip the Exercise 25.1 warm-up drill. However, if you exited the Online Lab at the end of Session 24, warm up by completing Exercise 25.1.

Introducing the 7, 8, 9, and Decimal Point Keys on the Numeric Keypad

Videos 25.1–25.4 The location of the 7, 8, 9, and decimal point (.) keys on the numeric keypad are shown in the following diagram and the reaches are demonstrated in Videos 25.1 through 25.4.

Exercises 25.2–25.7 Complete Exercises 25.2 through 25.7 to learn these new keys. When keying the drill lines, follow the instruction prompts provided in the Online Lab.

decimal point

Figure 50.6 Find and Replace Dialog Box with the Replace Tab Selected and Search Options Displayed

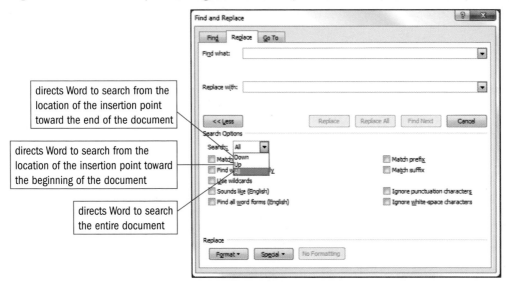

directs Word to search from the location of the insertion point toward the end of the document

directs Word to search from the location of the insertion point toward the beginning of the document

directs Word to search the entire document

Select options in the *Search Options* section by inserting a check mark in the check boxes to limit the search and replace actions. In the next document activity, you will practice using the *Match case* search option.

Success Tip

To ensure that you have searched the entire document, move the insertion point to the beginning of the document (press Ctrl + Home) before implementing a Find or a Find and Replace action. When you open a document, the insertion point is always at the beginning of a document.

Document 50.2 Memo Business Report Edited Using Find and Replace

1   Navigate to the Document 50.2 launch page in the Online Lab and then click the Launch Activity button. The Online Lab will open **Doc050.02** in the activity window.

2   Use the Word Find and Replace feature to change all instances of *program director* to *program manager* by completing the following steps:

a   Click the Replace button in the Editing group on the Home tab.

b   Click in the *Find what* text box and key **program director**. *Note: If existing text appears in the Find what text box, select the text before keying.*

c   Click in the *Replace with* text box and key **program manager**.

d   If the *Search Options* section of the Find and Replace dialog box is not displayed, click the More button.

e   Insert a check mark in the *Match case* check box and confirm that no other options in the *Search Options* section are selected. *Note: "Case" refers to uppercase or lowercase letters.*

f   Click the Replace All button to replace three instances in the document.

steps continue

↻ Reinforcing Your Skills

Complete Exercises 25.8 through 25.12 in the Online Lab. Reference the drill lines from the textbook as you key and keep your eyes on the textbook pages, not on your fingers. Complete each exercise at least once, but repeat exercises if you want to improve your WAM rate or accuracy.

As you key these drill lines on the numeric keypad, press the Tab key on the alphabetic keyboard between numbers and press the Enter key on the numeric keypad at the end of each row. Think of numbers as combinations to help you key more easily.

Exercise 25.8 **Keypad 7 Drill**

Key rows 1–4 one time and push for speed. Key rows 1–4 again and concentrate on accuracy.

1	44	47	47	47	55	57	57	57	66	67	67	67
2	76	74	74	567	567	765	765	4567	4567	7	456	457
3	65	45	67	4567	6	777	765	7567	5560	57670	5666	056
4	70	45670	45670	567	5560	5456	6747	44760	547	645	747	757

Exercise 25.9 **Keypad Decimal Point Drill**

Key rows 1–4 one time and push for speed. Key rows 1–4 again and concentrate on accuracy.

1	45.7	74.5	56.5	65.4	67.4	74.7	75.0
2	5.00	6.75	6.50	7.50	7.45	5.50	6.50
3	1.5	5.1	6.47	7.50	5.5	4.4	7.6
4	.75	.50	4.00	6.75	56.70	7.75	.755

Exercise 25.10 **Keypad 8 Drill**

Key rows 1–4 one time and push for speed. Key rows 1–4 again and concentrate on accuracy.

1	888	585	588	855	858	787	568
2	850	857	758	457	458	758	848
3	800	888	886	855	758	846	468
4	007	780	786	807	876	558	855

Success Tip

Keep your wrist straight and off the keyboard while using the numeric keypad.

Figure 50.4 Business Memo Report Content for Document 50.1—Continued

program size with regard to supply and demand of graduates. This has the potential to address program candidate quality and faculty load.

3. Encourage the Program Director and the GWK Advisory Board to identify accreditation opportunities specific to the GWK program. Work with the Vice President of Academic Affairs to secure funding for such an accreditation, if needed.

4. Work with the Vice President of Academic Affairs, the Program Director, and the GWK Advisory Board to study the feasibility and resources needed to implement a local professional student chapter affiliated with a state or national-level professional networking organization.

The PRC recommends continuation of this program through the next scheduled review in 2020-21. Additionally, the committee wishes that the recommendations outlined in this report be implemented.

Jack, I think the recommendations that the PRC team has developed provide the impetus needed to make our GWK program a state-of-the-art model for other colleges. Let's plan to meet next week after you have had a chance to digest the recommendations.

Using Find and Replace Options

The Word Find and Replace feature, introduced in Session 41, is used to replace one or more words with one or more other words. There are options within the Find and Replace dialog box that allow the user to choose specific conditions for finding text. To access these options, click the More button in the Find and Replace dialog box (see Figure 50.5) to expand it to reveal the *Search Options* section. (When the Find and Replace dialog box is expanded, the More button changes to the Less button. Click the Less button to hide the *Search Options* section of the dialog box.)

In the *Search Options* section, the options in the *Search* list box will direct how the Find and Replace feature will search in the document (see Figure 50.6). When *All* is selected, Word will search the entire document. When *Up* is selected, Word will search from the location of the insertion point toward the beginning of the document. When *Down* is selected, Word will search from the insertion point toward the end of the document.

Figure 50.5 Find and Replace Dialog Box with the Replace Tab Selected

Exercise 25.11 — Keypad 9 Drill

Key rows 1–4 one time and push for speed. Key rows 1–4 again and concentrate on accuracy.

1 66	69	69	99	96	96	66	90	90
2 90	98	97	797	894	869	759	6599	9589
3 695	696	697	698	699	789	798	788	799
4 6979	69879	69879	69857	96857	9678	9687	898	999

Exercise 25.12 — Keypad Reinforcement Drill

Key the following rows one time. Concentrate on keying as accurately as possible.

1 876	568	678	468	780	786	807	876	558	558	778	788
2 45678	87654	80765	876	8888	7787	7877	6778	5678	458	775	499
3 900	909	969	969	696	898	797	690	578	589	987	95
4 96.78	96.87	89.85	96.78	967.45	456.78	567.89	987.65	976.54	4.56	6.65	6.5
5 05058	60060	54904	85358	79964	84946	89757	48965	80086	478	489	450

Assessing Your Speed and Accuracy

Complete Timings 25.1 through 25.5 in the Online Lab. Refer to the following numerical timing text as you key. The timing will start as soon as you begin keying. If you finish keying before time expires, press Enter and start keying the timing text again. When time expires, the Online Lab will give you a WAM rate and error report for the timing. The results of the timings will be stored in your Timings Performance report.

For the following numeric keypad timings, remember to press Tab between number groups and Enter at the end of each row. Timings 25.2 and 25.3 use the same timing text.

Goals: 25 WAM and no errors

1-Minute Timings

Timing 25.1

99	89	89	79	79	66	69	69	59	59	49	49
789	789	456	456	475	678	789	908	970	970	987	09
900	909	909	969	696	898	797	690	578	589	987	95
9678	9687	8985	6978	96745	45678	56789	98765	98765	7584	7605	4557
9889	8899	9999	7999	69969	69969	94569	49566	59469	8940	4875	4658

Timings 25.2–25.3

9889	8899	9999	7999	69969	69969	94569	49566	59469	7059	6587	6789
900	909	909	969	969	696	898	797	690	578	589	987
9678	9687	8985	6978	96745	45678	56789	98765	98765	9876	446	5579
789	789	456	456	475	678	789	908	970	970	987	09
.99	.89	.89	.79	.79	.66	.69	.69	.59	.59	.49	.49

Figure 50.4 Business Memo Report Content for Document 50.1—Continued

4. Excellent industry-based intern placements with strong evidence of program students and employers supporting the value of the intern experience.

Several significant **concerns** were identified. The source of each concern is shown in parentheses.

1. GWK Program Director indicated that the range of required courses are taught by a few faculty with significant course outsourcing to another department thereby challenging the process of refining curriculum based on course evaluations. (Program Director comment, Student Survey)
2. Lack of GWK faculty designated to the program to support its growing student demand. The program is operating with one full-time faculty and one full-time academic staff. (Program Director Self-Study, Advisory Board Survey, and Faculty Survey)
3. Program has no accreditation. (Student Survey, Advisory Board Survey)
4. Program student involvement in professional networking is a need and an improvement opportunity. (Advisory Board Survey)

Recommendations for the Chair of the Department of Tourism and Entertainment have been developed to correspond with the concerns identified.

1. Support GWK faculty with the resources needed to analyze key learning assessments across program courses in alignment with the program's goals. Encourage and support GWK faculty to implement cross-discipline workgroups to identify artifacts that assure minimum GWK program outcomes according to the approved program goals.
2. Work with the Vice President of Academic Affairs to support the Program Director with the resources to address the GWK program need for at least one additional faculty position to meet the needs of the program.
   a. Work with the Vice President of Academic Affairs and Program Director to secure a faculty position with expertise in both classroom teaching and online teaching to support a sustainable re-engagement of the online GWK program.
   b. Work with the Vice President of Academic Affairs, the Program Director, and the GWK Advisory Board to identify the optimum

continues

For the following alphabetic timings, remember to press Tab at the start of the paragraph.

Goals: 30 WAM and two or fewer errors

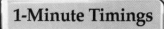

Timing 25.4

Traveling in this vast land is a great experience. The endless rivers, vast prairies that stretch as far as the eye can see, and mountains that reach for the sky are all impressive. Rural villages reveal something of the past in terms of how they are laid out. These vivid scenes revive the mind and lift the spirits.

Timing 25.5

During your working life, you will meet and work with people of many different cultures. Although each of us is a member of a racial or ethnic group, our work groups make up one large community. The beliefs we share give us a common base and a list of topics to discuss.

Ergonomic Tip
To relax your fingers, lightly clench your hand and then release, fanning out fingers. Repeat five times.

Ending the Session

The Online Lab automatically saves the work you completed for this session. You can continue with the next session or exit the Online Lab and continue later.

9 If errors are reported, view the results document, correct the errors in the submitted document, save the document, and then click the Check button.

Figure 50.3 Format Sample for Document 50.1

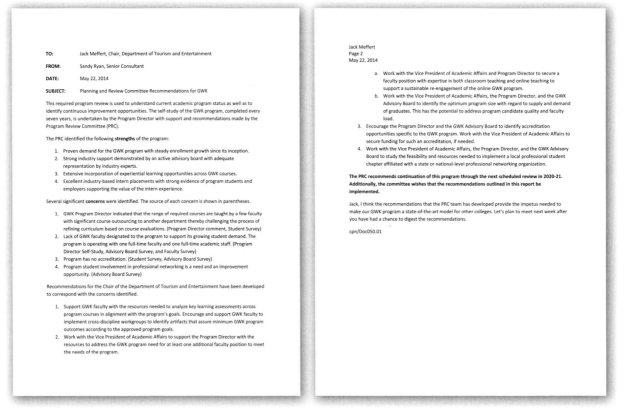

Figure 50.4 Business Memo Report Content for Document 50.1

This required program review is used to understand current academic program status as well as to identify continuous improvement opportunities. The self-study of the GWK program, completed every seven years, is undertaken by the Program Director with support and recommendations made by the Program Review Committee (PRC).

The PRC identified the following **strengths** of the program:

1. Proven demand for the GWK program with steady enrollment growth since its inception.
2. Strong industry support demonstrated by an active advisory board with adequate representation by industry experts.
3. Extensive incorporation of experiential learning opportunities across GWK courses.

continues

1, 2, 3

Session Objectives

- Investigate the 1, 2, and 3 keys on the numeric keypad
- Investigate keying numbers in columns

Timing Goals

- 1 minute (numeric keypad): 25 WAM and no errors
- 1 minute (alphabetic): 30 WAM and two or fewer errors

Getting Started and Warming Up

Exercise 26.1 If you are continuing immediately from Session 25, you may skip the Exercise 26.1 warm-up drill. However, if you exited the Online Lab at the end of Session 25, warm up by completing Exercise 26.1.

Introducing the 1, 2, and 3 Keys on the Numeric Keypad

Videos 26.1–26.3 The location of the 1, 2, and 3 keys on the numeric keypad are shown in the following diagram and the reaches are demonstrated in Videos 26.1 through 26.3.

Exercises 26.2–26.7 Complete Exercises 26.2 through 26.4 to learn these new keys. Exercises 26.5 through 26.7 are speed and accuracy drills for the alphabetic keys. When keying the drill lines, follow the instruction prompts provided in the Online Lab.

Figure 50.2 Quick Access Toolbar

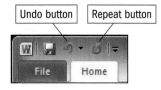
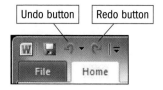

Using Undo and Redo

The Quick Access Toolbar (see Figure 50.2) contains frequently used commands. Although this toolbar can be customized, by default it includes the Save, Undo, and Repeat or Redo buttons. Click the Undo button to undo or reverse the last action, which can be keyed text or another action, such as tab, indent, and return. To undo several actions at the same time, click the down arrow next to the Undo button and select the actions in the list that you want to undo.

Once an action is undone, the Repeat button will become the Redo button. To redo one or more actions that you undid, click the Redo button on the Quick Access Toolbar. The Undo and Redo actions will be helpful, especially as you work with new formats and something unexpected happens as you key.

> ✓ **Success Tip**
> Learning to use the keyboard shortcuts for Undo (Ctrl + Z) and Redo (Ctrl + Y) will keep your hands on the keyboard and save time.

Document 50.1

Memo Business Report with Numbered Lists and Lettered Sublists

1   Read all instructions for this document activity, navigate to the Document 50.1 launch page in the Online Lab, and then click the Launch Activity button. The Online Lab will open **Doc050.01** in the activity window. The timer will start as soon as you begin keying the document.

2   Referring to the format shown in Figure 50.3, key a memo report with the following guide words and information:

TO:	Jack Meffert, Chair, Department of Tourism and Entertainment
FROM:	Sandy Ryan, Senior Consultant
DATE:	May 22, 2014
SUBJECT:	Planning and Review Committee Recommendations for GWK

3   Key the body of the memo shown in Figure 50.4.

   a   Allow Word to automatically format the numbered paragraphs and lettered sublist paragraphs. *Hint: Press the Increase Indent button to demote the lettered sublist.*

   b   Set the words in bold as shown in Figure 50.4.

4   Insert a vertical continuation header to appear 1 inch from the top of the page.

5   Key the reference initials **cpn** and the file name at the end of the report.

6   Proofread the document and correct any errors.

7   Save the document.

8   Click the Check button to stop the timer and upload the document for checking. The Online Lab will report the WAM rate and number of errors for the activity.

steps continue

⟳ Reinforcing Your Skills

Complete Exercises 26.8 through 26.11 in the Online Lab. Refer to the following columns of drill line numbers as you key and keep your eyes on the textbook pages, not on your fingers. Complete each exercise at least once, but repeat exercises if you want to improve your WAM rate or accuracy.

As you key these columnar drill lines on the numeric keypad, press the Enter key on the numeric keypad after each number. Think of numbers as combinations to help you key more easily.

Exercise 26.8 **Keypad 1 Drill**

Key columns 1–5 one time and push for speed. Key columns 1–5 again and concentrate on accuracy. Think of the numbers in groups as you key them. Press Enter after each number.

1	2	3	4	5
41	61	16.8	145	1474
14	61	18.7	156	4010
41	61	18.7	195	4561
41	51	18.6	157	4561
41	71	17.5	145	4710
14	81	17.7	198	46678
14	91	10.9	966	15851
14	17	18.6	919	979711
451	171	10.1	818	5987
415	171	18.6	717	
514	187	18.6	616	
614	187	196.58	515	
614	191		41	
716	151			
41	19			

5 Click the AutoFormat As You Type tab in the AutoCorrect dialog box.

6 In the *Apply as you type* section, click the *Automatic bulleted lists* and *Automatic numbered lists* options to insert check marks in the check boxes if the options are not selected. (They are selected if the check boxes contain check marks.)

7 Click OK to save the changes and close the AutoCorrect dialog box.

8 Click OK to close the Word Options dialog box (see diagram on previous page) and to return to the document.

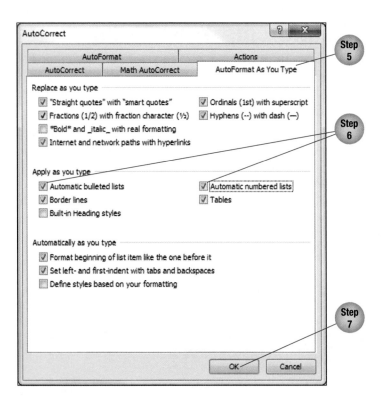

Formatting Numbered Lists and Lettered Sublists

Session 42 introduced how to format numbered paragraphs. As discussed in that session, the Word default setting automatically formats a numbered list when a line begins with *1.* and is followed by a space. Word indents the number and replaces the space with a nonprinting Tab symbol. If the numbered paragraph continues to a second line, word wrap will begin the second line as a hanging indent. In other words, the run-over line will align with the text that follows the nonprinting Tab symbol, not with the number. To stop the numbering of paragraphs, press the Enter key twice.

To format a lettered list, follow the same procedure for creating a numbered list, but key **a.** followed by a space.

In addition to formatting numbered and lettered lists, Word automatically formats lettered paragraphs within numbered lists. To demote an entry in a numbered list to a lettered sublist, click the Increase Indent button in the Paragraph group while the insertion point is located within the numbered paragraph. To promote a lettered sublist paragraph to a numbered paragraph, click the Decrease Indent button in the Paragraph group while the insertion point is located within the lettered paragraph (see Figure 50.1).

Figure 50.1 Decrease Indent and Increase Indent Buttons in the Paragraph Group

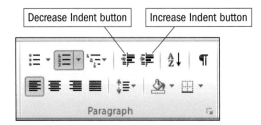

Exercise 26.9 Keypad 2 Drill

Key columns 1–5 one time and push for speed. Key columns 1–5 again and concentrate on accuracy. Think of the numbers in groups as you key them. Press Enter after each number.

1	2	3	4	5
52	25	242	222	24.56
52	62	252	224	27.89
52	72	252	225	20.10
52	82	262	226	24.56
52	92	852	227	26.78
52	02	258	228	25.25
25	42	158	228	245.67
25	52	148	822	278.90
25	27	284	922	124.56
25	85	282	202	1.27
25	58	272	202	
24	85	958	212	
24	95	594	2169	
42	96			
62	90			
72	88			
82	56			
52	24			

Setting Automatic Formatting Options

The Word AutoCorrect feature provides options to automatically format text as you are preparing your document. For example, if you key a word immediately followed by two hyphens (--) and another word, the two hyphens will automatically be formatted as a type of dash (—) called an *em dash*.

The memo report in this session uses a numbered list to organize its content. Word will automate the creation of a numbered list if you key a number followed by a period or a hyphen, then a space or tab, and then start keying. This option is set within the Word AutoCorrect options. Follow these steps to check the AutoCorrect settings on your computer:

1 Click the File tab.

2 Click the Options button to open the Word Options dialog box.

3 On the left side panel of the Word Options dialog box, click *Proofing*.

4 Click the AutoCorrect Options button to open the AutoCorrect dialog box.

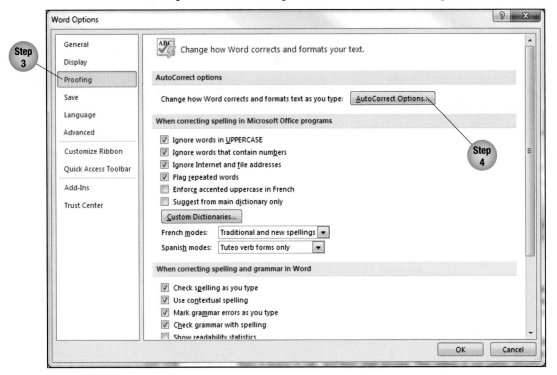

steps continue

Keypad 3 Drill

Key columns 1–5 one time and push for speed. Key columns 1–5 again and concentrate on accuracy. Think of the numbers in groups as you key them. Press Enter after each number.

1	2	3	4	5
63	36	45.6	464	2343
63	73	38.3	585	2334
63	73	83.8	484	4873
63	93	93.8	737	4848
63	83	73.6	363	3929
36	23	37.3	922	26282
36	13	36.9	291	4844
36	30	93.6	302	6673
36	54	96.3	30	8733
36	65	3.3	4435	5663
93	63	56.8	4344	55
39	36	93.6	3345	
39	83	94.7	3443	
39	49	37.3		
69	34			
69	234			
63	354			
34	345			
35				

Complete two 3-minute timings on the timing text below. Timings 50.3 and 50.4 use the same paragraphs. For Timing 50.4, try to increase your speed while maintaining your accuracy.

Goals: 35 WAM and six or fewer errors
SI: 1.47 syllables per word

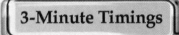
3-Minute Timings

Timings
50.3–50.4

During every moment of the day or night, all kinds of storms are in the process of raging over land and sea. More than 1,800 thunderstorms or blizzards pelt the earth with rain or snow. Somewhere over a high sea, a hurricane with an awesome wind may be forming. In some areas, people may be looking at a cloudless sky, but not more than a few hundred miles away others are sheltering themselves from a wild and furious snowstorm or a pelting rain.

A storm is a disturbance of the upper atmosphere and contains an added element of strong winds. During many storms, destructive winds have been known to cause great damage. During a blizzard on the wide-open prairie, snowdrifts pile high and block roads. Ice storms cause widespread damage to telephone and power lines and make driving extremely dangerous.

Distinctive forms of clouds and precipitation, as well as winds, are common to storms. Precipitation is the weather bureau's name for all forms of water falling from the sky. Clouds are the first signal of an incoming storm. Signals of a hurricane, for example, move in with little or no noise. An alert weather person is well aware of the danger signals. Wispy, veil-like cirrus clouds appearing to dance on the horizon is an early signal of a storm.

Ergonomic Tip
Keep the angle between your trunk and thigh greater than 90 degrees when seated. If you lean forward when sitting, it puts pressure on your back muscles and vertebrae.

Exploring Formatting Options for Memo Reports

Word provides several ways to format numbered and lettered paragraphs. In this session, you will work with the Word automatic numbering feature to create a multiple-page memo report containing such paragraphs.

Exercise 26.11 Keypad Reinforcemment Drill

Key columns 1–9 one time. Concentrate on keying with control so your results will be as accurate as possible. Press Enter after each number.

1	2	3	4	5
.41	100	4111	24	456
.41	104	1444	56	789
.51	145	4568	25	125
.61	414	1787	58	125
.71	151	1679	47	128
.81	149	88981	71	124
.91	109	98871	89	126
.11	011	019091	80	129
1.41	084	001001	20	125
1.41	171		20	128
1.41	155		20	982
1.41	109		50	982
1.45	18		50	12
1.46			20	
1.4			70	
			45	
			86	

6	7	8	9
2222	345	5.68	4844
2525	636	9.36	6673
2582	663	9.47	8733
2582	663	3.73	5663
9792	663	4.64	5543
2728	336	5.85	3323
26267	393	4.84	6788
88771	393	7.37	6733
07862	993	3.63	2343
72	993	9.22	23343
	339	2.91	2657
	936	3.02	
	93	3.0	

Formatting Memo Business Reports

Session Objectives

- Format memo reports with numbered paragraphs and lettered sublists
- Use AutoFormat options
- Use Undo and Redo buttons
- Use find and replace options
- Compose a memo report

Timing Goals

- 1 minute: 40 WAM and two or fewer errors
- 3 minutes: 35 WAM and six or fewer errors

Getting Started and Warming Up

Exercise 50.1 If you are continuing immediately from Session 49, you may skip the Exercise 50.1 warm-up drill. However, if you exited the Online Lab at the end of Session 49, warm up by completing Exercise 50.1.

Exercise 50.2 Begin your session work by completing Exercise 50.2, a timed short drill, in the Online Lab.

Assessing Your Speed and Accuracy

Complete Timings 50.1 through 50.4 in the Online Lab. At the end of each timing, the Online Lab will display your WAM rate and any errors. Results will be saved in your Timings Performance report. If you have been surpassing the speed and accuracy goals, set slightly more challenging personal goals and strive to exceed them.

Complete two 1-minute timings on the timing text below. Timings 50.1 and 50.2 use the same paragraph.

Goals: 40 WAM and two or fewer errors
SI: 1.48 syllables per word

1-Minute Timings

Timings 50.1–50.2   A good keyboarder soon learns how to proofread. Glaring errors will blemish the neatness and quality of a good report. Find all the mistakes before printing the final copy. Learn to watch for correct spelling and grammar. Compare the rough draft with your printed copy. You will want to be diligent and examine your document two or three times to make quite certain it is without mistakes. In the long run, you will be pleased that you have carefully prepared an excellent printed copy that needs no revisions. The person who reads your output will have much respect for your ability to prepare accurate documents.

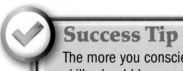

Success Tip

The more you conscientiously practice, the better your keyboarding skills should become.

Assessing Your Speed and Accuracy

Complete Timings 26.1 through 26.5 in the Online Lab. Refer to the following numerical timing text as you key. The timing will start as soon as you begin keying. If you finish keying before time expires, press Enter and start keying the timing text again. When time expires, the Online Lab will give you a WAM rate and error report for the timing. The results of the timings will be stored in your Timings Performance report.

For the following numeric keypad timings that employ columns of numbers, remember to press Enter after each number. Timings 26.2 and 26.3 use the same timing text.

Goals: 25 WAM and no errors

1-Minute Timings

Timing 26.1

1	2	3	4	5
34	345	568	37.48	4844
35	636	936	38.33	6673
36	663	947	93.74	8733
73	663	373	05.85	5663
93	663	464	03.92	5543
83	336	585	04.58	3323
23	393	484	03.82	6788
13	393	737	04.83	6733
30	993	363	32.30	2343
54	93	922	30.339	23343
65	339	291		
63	936	302		

Who was leaving next week, the assistant or his boss? The sentence construction leaves the writer's meaning ambiguous. To correct the problem, rewrite the sentence so that the modifying clause *who was leaving next week* is placed as closely as possible to the word it describes.

The assistant, who was leaving next week, took his boss to lunch.

Document 49.3 **Fixing Misplaced Modifiers in a Fax**

1 Navigate to the Document 49.3 launch page in the Online Lab and then click the Launch Activity button. The Online Lab will open **Doc049.03** in the activity window.

2 Some of the sentences in the memo to Megan contain misplaced modifiers that make the meaning unclear. Usually, you would know all the background information to clarify the meaning. In this case, you only have the document. Edit the fax cover sheet and make any corrections you feel clarify the message.

3 Save the document.

4 Click the Upload button to upload the document for instructor review.

Ending the Session

The Online Lab automatically saves the work you completed for this session. You may continue with the next session or exit the Online Lab and continue later.

¹	²	³	⁴	⁵
4.844	3748	568	345	34
6.673	3833	936	636	35
8.733	9374	947	663	36
5.663	0585	373	663	73
5.543	0392	464	663	93
3.323	0458	585	336	83
6.788	0382	484	393	23
6.733	0483	737	393	13
2.343	3230	363	993	30
2.3343	30339	922	993	54
		291	339	65
		302	936	63

For the following alphabetic timings, remember to press Tab at the start of the paragraph.

Goals: 30 WAM and two or fewer errors

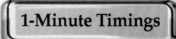

1-Minute Timings

Timing 26.4

   Students in school today must be prepared to live and compete in a global economy. They must develop a respect for life and work in a society of diverse cultures. Being exposed to the cultures of other countries can open doors to future job opportunities.

Timing 26.5

   The vessel sank in 510 feet of water in Lake Superior during a raging storm. An adept team of divers salvaged 149,683 parts. Seven local residents were among those who assisted in this job. The additional divers were welcome. The salvage company made a profit on their investment.

Ergonomic Tip
Adjust the screen position to eliminate glare from windows and ceiling lights.

Ending the Session
The Online Lab automatically saves the work you completed for this session. You can continue with the next session or exit the Online Lab and continue later.

6   Proofread the document and correct any errors.

7   Save the document.

8   Click the Check button to stop the timer and upload the document for checking. The Online Lab will report the WAM rate and number of errors for the activity.

9   If errors are reported, view the results document, correct the errors in the submitted document, save the document, and then click the Check button.

Figure 49.5 Message Content for Document 49.2

Christine, thank you for meeting with me last weak to discuss you're needs for the new keyboarding course at South Community College. Here's a brief description of some of the features of the *Paradigm Keyboarding Online Lab*, which is an integral part of the keyboarding courseware developed by Paradigm Publishing, Inc.

• Diagnostic software identifies keys that students struggle with and assigns remedial drill work to provide additional practice

• Live-in-the-application word processing using Microsoft Word

• Work is saved on the Web and students can save their work and pick up where they left off in their practice, from any location with Internet access

• Integrated grade book for assigning, grading, and tracking student progress

I hope you will consider adopting this product for the spring semester. Please do not hesitate to contact me if you have any questions about the courseware.

Reinforcing Writing Skills

One of the most common causes of unclear communication is the *misplaced modifier*. Words, phrases, and clauses can serve as modifiers. If these modifiers are not placed as closely as possible to the sentence elements they describe, the meaning of the sentence becomes unclear. The following sentences, for example, are unclear because of the location of the modifiers:

Managing the office last week, the problems piled up for him.

Did the problems manage the office? The position of the phrase *managing the office last week* makes it modify *the problems,* but we know that the writer meant the phrase to describe the person. Either of the following revised sentences could clarify the meaning of the sentence.

Managing the office last week, he saw the problems pile up.
The problems piled up for him when he managed the office last week.

Here is another ambiguous (unclear) sentence:

The assistant took his boss to lunch, who was leaving next week.

Session 27

Skills Reinforcement and Proficiency Exercises: Sessions 1–26

Session Objectives

- Review and practice keys and reaches for Sessions 1–26

Timing Goals

- 1 minute (numeric keypad): 25 WAM and no errors
- 1 minute (alphabetic): 30 WAM and two or fewer errors

Getting Started and Warming Up

Exercise 27.1
If you are continuing immediately from Session 26, you may skip the Exercise 27.1 warm-up drill. However, if you exited the Online Lab at the end of Session 26, warm up by completing Exercise 27.1.

↻ Reinforcing Your Skills

Exercises 27.2–27.8
The exercises in this session are designed to reinforce your keyboarding skills of the alphabetic, number, and numeric keypad keys. Begin this session work by completing Exercises 27.2 through 27.8 in the Online Lab. When keying the drill lines, follow the instruction prompts provided in the Online Lab. Complete each exercise at least once, but repeat exercises if you want to improve your WAM rate and accuracy.

Next, complete Exercises 27.9 through 27.11 in the Online Lab. For these exercises, reference the drill lines from the textbook as you key and keep your eyes on the textbook pages, not on your fingers. Complete each exercise at least once, but repeat exercises if you want to improve your WAM rate and accuracy.

Exercise 27.9 Sentences Drill

Key lines 1–3 one time and push for speed. Key lines 1–3 again and concentrate on control.

1 It seems that I missed the road; it makes me angry.

2 Those wrecked cars were in the ditch at the curve.

3 Endure the thousand, routine, unexpected problems.

Exercise 27.10 Number Row Drill

Key lines 1–9 one time and push for speed. Key lines 1–9 again and concentrate on control.

1 Find 5,000 medium weight legal size file folders.

2 The Merkel 9000 offers 23 channels with .6 watts.

3 Please trace orders 1169, 2978, 67890, and 14989.

drill continues

Figure 49.4 Fax Template

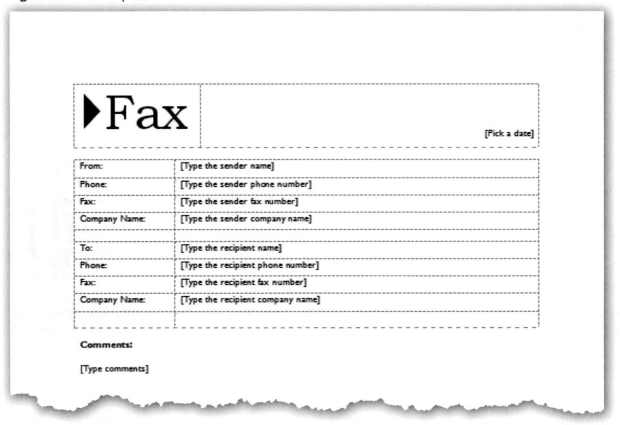

Document Fax Cover Sheet

49.2

1 Read all instructions for this document activity, navigate to the Document 49.2 launch page in the Online Lab, and then click the Launch Activity button. The Online Lab will open **Doc049.02** in the activity window. The timer will start as soon as you begin keying the document.

2 Fill in the fax cover sheet with the following information:

Date: 9/10/2014

Sender phone: (651) 555-1907

Sender fax: (651) 555-1000

Recipient: Christine McLellan

Recipient phone: (801) 555-6824

Recipient fax: (801) 555-6825

Recipient company name: South Community College

3 Edit the copy for the body of the message shown in Figure 49.5. *Hint: There are errors in the figure that have not been corrected with proofreading marks. Implement the necessary corrections.*

4 Because this memo is short, it will fit on the fax cover sheet. Click the *[Type comments]* field in the document and key the edited message shown in Figure 49.5. Include the italic formatting as shown in the figure. *Hint: Do not format the punctuation following the italicized text.* For the bulleted list, use the default bulleted list format.

5 Key the initials **wby** and the file name at the bottom of the memo.

steps continue

4 Return the 420 reams of 16 lb. paper now, please.

5 She is purchasing a Group 857 biometrics system.

6 I would like to use 9 shades and 16 gray scales.

7 Send me 13 of Item 4 and 7 of Item 9 immediately.

8 West Arn 20 lb. paper has 99 percent rag content.

9 I have: 360 folders, 75 pencils, and 99 punches.

Success Tip

Your persistence with keeping your eyes on the source—rather than on your fingers, the keyboard, or the screen—will pay off in terms of speed and accuracy.

Exercise 27.11

Keypad Reinforcement Drill

In this drill, you will enter data vertically down a column by pressing Enter after each number. Key the following nine columns using the numeric keypad. Press Enter after each number. Concentrate on control and remember to think of numbers in groups as you key them.

1	2	3	4	5
654	687	78	08	19105
54	577	81	080	05084
76	575	8687	797	88
56	876	782	580	384
46	754	8422	680	18
767	796	789	4986	682
46	697	987	7984	9764
654	757	432	47782	7976
6054	885	8282	78853	8828
567	855	6732	88795	55130
7655	644	321	85	56
6054	54	989		
456	66			

drill continues

Figure 49.3 Memo Business Report Content for Document 49.1—Continued

name, report it in writing to the school where the loan was opened. If someone is using your driver's license number for identification on bad checks, call the Department of Motor Vehicles (DVM) in your state to see if another driver's license was issued in your name. You might have to get a new license number.

Do not pay any bill that is a result of fraud. It might later be considered an admission of guilt. Do not cover checks that were written fraudulently. Do not file for bankruptcy.

If debt collectors try to collet on the fraudulent accounts, tell them that you are a victim of fraud and are not responsible for the debts. Ask for the name of the person contacting you, the name of the collection company, the phone number, and the address. Also get the name, phone number, and address of the creditor, as well as the amount of the debt and dates of the purchases. Share this information with law enforcement authorities.

rpq/Doc049.01

Creating Fax Cover Sheets

In addition to email messages, another means of communicating text and graphics is with a standalone fax (short for facsimile) machine. The fax machine can transmit handwritten messages, printed text, architectural drawings, pictures, memos, letters, reports, etc.

Fax technology is now frequently replaced by Internet-based technology. However, fax machines have some advantages, particularly when sending sensitive material that may be vulnerable to interception. In many companies, standalone fax machines have been replaced by computerized systems capable of receiving and storing incoming faxes, and then routing them to users either on paper or by secured email attachments.

Generally, when sending something by way of a fax machine, a cover sheet is sent with the document. Figure 49.4 shows a Word template (a predesigned format for creating new documents with a similar format) for a fax cover sheet. For short faxes, the memo information may be keyed on the cover sheet itself. In the Document 49.2 activity, you will start with a Word document that has been created from a template of a fax cover sheet.

To insert text into a template such as the one shown in Figure 49.4, click in the fields, such as *[Type the sender name]*, and then key the appropriate information. Besides clicking, you can navigate to the fields by pressing the Tab key. For the *[Pick a date]* field, click the field and then click the down arrow and navigate to the appropriate date on the calendar, or click the Today button for the current date.

6		7		8		9	
66938		10.18		7.8		4.8	
88282		7.85		67.8		21.6	
775		8.94		67.21		41.72	
993		15.63		478.231		687.452	
5549		40.38		123.456		4.872	
7970		.89		1.456		48.729	
2810		95.93		14.567		72.94	
82		24.56		89.90		729.45	
879		67.36		.65		65.8	
8322087		3.69					

Assessing Your Speed and Accuracy

Complete Timings 27.1 through 27.5 in the Online Lab. Refer to the following numerical timing text as you key. The timing will start as soon as you begin keying. If you finish keying before time expires, press Enter and start keying the timing text again. When time expires, the Online Lab will give you a WAM rate and error report for the timing. The results of the timings will be stored in your Timings Performance report.

For the following numeric keypad timings that employ columns of numbers, remember to press Enter after each number. Timings 27.2 and 27.3 use the same timing text.

Goals: 25 WAM and no errors

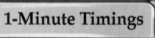

Timing 27.1

1		2		3		4		5	
12		98		76		54		32	
34		76		89		12		54	
56		54		32		12		78	
78		32		12		34		56	
90		10		01		28		58	
123		321		789		897		978	
456		654		564		546		645	
789		897		987		978		789	
987		978		654		123		101	
654		456		545		466		654	
321		123		231		132		213	
4321		1234		2413		1432		2431	

Figure 49.3 Memo Business Report Content for Document 49.1—Continued

nationwide credit bureaus to correct your file. If the investigation does not resolve your dispute, your statement about the inaccuracy must be included in your file.

bf Reporting Fraud and Identity Theft: If it seems clear that you have become a victim of credit fraud or identity theft, report the crime immediately and take action to prevent further damage to your finances and your reputation. Keep a record of all converations, dates, names, and phone numbers. Record the time and cost of all the work you do to clear your name. Take the following actions for your protection.

bf Notify the Authorities: Contact at least one of the three national credit bureaus (Equifax, Experian, or TransUnion). Tell them that you belive you are an identity theft victim. (When you notify one bureau, it will nhotify the other two.) Ask that a *fraud alert* be placed on your credit file. Also ask for a *security freeze*. A security freeze locks access to your credit report and credit score until you instruct the credit bureau to unfreeze your report. To see if your state allows a security freeze, check the Consumers Union Guide to Security Freeze Protection at http://fin.emcp.net/freeze.

Of course you should also report the crime to your local police or sheriff. Report the crime to the Federal Trade Commission (FTC) as well.

bf Notify Your Creditors: If your credit report lists new accounts in your name—accounts that you did not open—notify those creditors immediately by phone and in writing. If your current credit, debit, or ATM cards were stolen or used fraudulently, immediately report this crime by phone and in writing to the card company. You should request new cards with new account numbers. If your checks were stolen or if bank accounts were set up fraudulently in your name, you should tell your bank to report it to Chex Systems. Chex Systems is a network of financial institutions that report on mishandled checking and savings accounts.

bf Other Precautions: If you suspect that someone changed your address with the U.S. Postal Service, notify the local postal inspector. If you suspect that an imposter has opened a cell phone account in your name, contact the company immediately. If someone has obtained a student loan in your

continues

Timings 27.2–27.3

1	2	3	4	5
130	8	427	72	18724
12.9	67.8	32.56	687.45	9.678
14.87	67.21	978.12	4.872	96.78
123.4	478.23	3.462	48.729	8.69
1.456	2.789	34.620	72.94	687.89
14.56	27.879	62.08	729.45	2
56.21	87.90	620.81	25.2	672.3
156.02	879.08	84.8	52.5	598
47	56.49	61	98.12	390.26

For the following alphabetic timings, remember to press Tab at the start of the paragraph.

Goals: 30 WAM and two or fewer errors.

1-Minute Timings

Timing 27.4

The population of the United States has become more varied culturally. It is extremely important that individuals be made aware of the need to communicate with other cultures in ways that are satisfying to both parties. As people interact on a daily basis, meanings are discovered that form a bond for common understanding.

Timing 27.5

Basically, employers like a loyal employee. Honesty and courtesy always pay off in any job or assignment. Apathy and sloppy work are always very costly to a company. On the other hand, any employee who consistently does good work will be properly rewarded and can expect to receive a salary increase.

Ergonomic Tip

To help you relax, occasionally lift your shoulders slowly while inhaling and then slowly drop them while exhaling. Repeat several times.

Ending the Session

The Online Lab automatically saves the work you completed for this session. You can continue with the next session or exit the Online Lab and continue later.

5 Proofread the document and correct any errors.

6 Save the document.

7 Click the Check button to stop the timer and upload the document for checking. The Online Lab will report the WAM rate and number of errors for the activity.

8 If errors are reported, view the results document, correct the errors in the submitted document, save the document, and then click the Check button.

Figure 49.3 Memo Business Report Content for Document 49.1

bf

TO: All GEMS Employees

FROM: Jack McKinnon, CFO

DATE: September 17, 2014

SUBJECT: Fraud and Identity Theft

In light of the recent newspaper areticle about the number of identity theft cases in Waterloo during the past month, this memo outlines what you should do if you find yourself in a similar position.

bf

Monitoring Your Credit History: One way you can protect yourself against identity theft is to obtain your credit report and monitor your credit history. The only authorized online source for free credit reports under federal law is AnnualCreditReport.com http://fin.emcp.net/annualcreditreport.com. You can also get one by calling the Annual Credit Report Request Service at their toll-free number.

Once you get your report, review it carefully. Look for inquiries from companies you did not contact, accounts you did not open, and debts on your accounts that you cannot explain. Check to be sure all your personal information is correct—including including your name, Social Security number, address, and employers' names.

If you find fraudulent or inaccurate information, get it removed as soon as possible. Under the Fair Credit reporting Act (FCRA), both you and the business that sent incorrect information to the credit bureau (such as a bank or credit card company) are responsible for the accuracy of your report.

ital

You must contact both the credit bureau and the information provider in writing. The information provider is required by law to investiage *investigate* your complaint and report its findings to the credit bureau. If your credit information was indeed inaccurate, the provider must notify all

continues

Unit 5

Thinking and Composing at the Keyboard

Access the Word Widow/Orphan control setting by completing the following steps:

1. Select all document text by pressing Ctrl + A. This step is not necessary if text has not been keyed in the document.

2. Click the dialog box launcher in the Paragraph group on the Home tab.

3. Click the Line and Page Breaks tab.

4. If there is no check mark next to the *Widow/Orphan control* option, click the check box to insert a check mark.

5. Click OK to return to the document.

Document Memo Business Report

49.1

1. Read all instructions for this document activity, navigate to the Document 49.1 launch page in the Online Lab, and then click the Launch Activity button. The Online Lab will open **Doc049.01** in the activity window. The timer will start as soon as you begin keying the document.

2. Read the proofread memo report shown in Figure 49.3. If necessary, refer to Appendix B for a list of proofreading marks and their meanings. Mark additional editing corrections before keying the memo report.

3. Activate the Widow/Orphan control setting in the document.

4. Key the memo report, making the necessary revisions marked by the proofreader as you key.

    a. Format the memo report using the style shown in Figure 49.1.

    b. Allow Word to automatically format the website addresses in the body of the report as hyperlinks.

    c. Create a vertical continuation header that is set 1 inch from the top margin on the second page of the report. The header should include the name that is displayed in the *TO* line, the page number (key **Page**, press the space bar, and then insert an automatic page number field), and the date of the letter. *Note: There should be a blank line under the date in the running head.*

steps continue

Session 28 | Composing Words at the Keyboard

Session Objectives

- **Think and compose at the keyboard**
- **Compose responses at the word level**

Timing Goals

- **1 minute: 35 WAM and two or fewer errors**
- **3 minutes: 30 WAM and six or fewer errors**
- **5 minutes: 25 WAM and ten or fewer errors**

Getting Started and Warming Up

Exercise 28.1 If you are continuing immediately from Session 27, you may skip the Exercise 28.1 warm-up drill. However, if you exited the Online Lab at the end of Session 27, warm up by completing Exercise 28.1.

↺ Reinforcing Your Skills

Exercises 28.2–28.4 Begin your session work by completing Exercises 28.2 and 28.3 in the Online Lab. These drills will give you the opportunity to further reinforce your keyboarding skills by providing practice using the numeric keypad and keying sentences.

Exercise 28.4 is a timed short drill. In this drill, you (1) indicate if your goal is to work to improve speed or accuracy; (2) set the drill duration at 15 seconds, 30 seconds, or 60 seconds; and (3) identify your personal WAM goal for the timing. Complete each exercise at least once, but repeat exercises if you want to improve your WAM rate or accuracy. It is important that you select appropriate goals each time and that you focus intently on meeting those goals.

Timed short drills, which you will encounter in many of the remaining sessions in this book, are very effective in developing speed and accuracy. They are particularly useful for students whose skills have plateaued. That is, if your WAM rate has not improved during the last several sessions, you can select a short duration time and a WAM rate slightly greater than what you have recently achieved. Repeat the drill until you attain your new WAM goal. Likewise, you can improve accuracy by selecting an error goal that is superior (that is, a lower value) to what you have recently achieved. Repeat the drill until you attain your new error goal.

Composing at the Keyboard

In this session, you will learn to think and compose at the keyboard, which will assist you in using a computer efficiently. The four stages in building composition skills are:

1. Developing skill at the **word-response** level.
2. Developing skill at the **phrase-response** level.
3. Developing skill at the **sentence-response** level.
4. Developing skill at the **paragraph-response** level.

Figure 49.1 Sample Memo Business Report—Continued

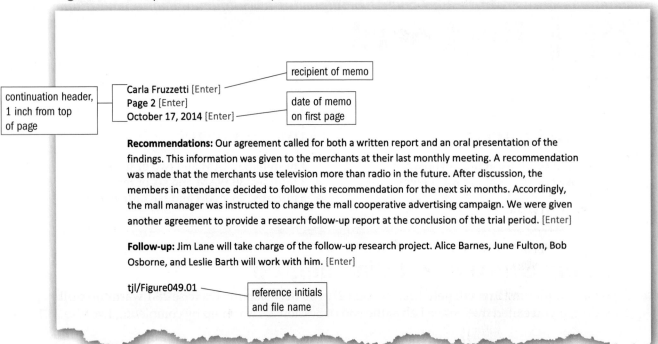

recipient of memo

continuation header, 1 inch from top of page

Carla Fruzzetti [Enter]
Page 2 [Enter]
October 17, 2014 [Enter]

date of memo on first page

Recommendations: Our agreement called for both a written report and an oral presentation of the findings. This information was given to the merchants at their last monthly meeting. A recommendation was made that the merchants use television more than radio in the future. After discussion, the members in attendance decided to follow this recommendation for the next six months. Accordingly, the mall manager was instructed to change the mall cooperative advertising campaign. We were given another agreement to provide a research follow-up report at the conclusion of the trial period. [Enter]

Follow-up: Jim Lane will take charge of the follow-up research project. Alice Barnes, June Fulton, Bob Osborne, and Leslie Barth will work with him. [Enter]

tjl/Figure049.01

reference initials and file name

recipient of the memo (the addressee), the page number, and the date and should appear on all pages after the first page. Memo reports will set the header 1-inch from the top of the page rather than the Word default of 0.5 inch. The second page of the memo shown in Figure 49.1 contains a vertical continuation header.

When creating a header for a memo, you will change the space from the header to the top of the page. If necessary, review the directions in Session 42 for inserting a header. To create the continuation header, make sure the *Different First Page* option is selected in the Options group on the Header & Footer Tools Design tab. To change the position of the header, select the number in the *Header from Top* measurement box in the Position group on the Header & Footer Tools Design tab and then key 1 (see Figure 49.2).

Using Widow/Orphan Control

Sometimes a paragraph in a document such as a memo report does not entirely fit at the bottom of a page. Just as the Word Wrap feature flows text from one line to the next, the bottom margin setting determines when text flows to a new page.

For ease of reading, a single line of a paragraph should *not* be left alone either at the bottom of a page or at the top of the next. Such single lines are referred to as **orphans** (when left at the bottom of a page) or **widows** (when carried to the top of the next page). Word has a feature called **Widow/Orphan control** that will prevent single lines from being stranded.

Figure 49.2 Settings for a Continuation Header

position of header

You will work on developing your keyboarding skill at the word-response level in Exercises 28.5 through 28.7 in the Online Lab. Carefully read the drill instructions that accompany each exercise in the textbook. Do not watch your fingers as you key.

Exercise 28.5 Word Response Drill: Yes or No

For the first question in each group, type the question number followed by a period, press the Tab key (indicated with a → in the drill line), key **a.**, press the space bar once, and then type the question. Following the question, press the space bar once, type your answer (**yes**, **no**, or **not sure**), and then press Enter. For the next question, press the Tab key, type the question letter followed by a period, type the question, type your answer, and then press Enter. Think about the question as you key the question text, and try to key your answer as quickly as possible after striking the question mark and space bar at the end of the question.

1.→ a. Do you like the weather today?
→ b. Do you use Facebook?
→ c. Are you hungry?
→ d. Do you read the newspaper?
→ e. Would you like to go into politics?
→ f. Do you participate in any sport?
→ g. Do you like animals?
→ h. Do you text message?
→ i. Do you read the newspaper online?
→ j. Do you watch television every day?

2.→ a. Are you tired?
→ b. Do you have any brothers?
→ c. Do you have any sisters?
→ d. Do you have a job?
→ e. Are you a "good" speller?
→ f. Are you going on vacation soon?
→ g. Do you like English?
→ h. Do you like coffee?
→ i. Would you like to travel overseas?
→ j. Do you like to cook?

Figure 49.1 Sample Memo Business Report *Note: Do not key this document.*

bold guide words

TO: [2 Tabs]   Carla Fruzzetti [Enter]

FROM: [2 Tabs] Thomas King [Enter]

DATE: [2 Tabs] October 17, 2014 [Enter]

SUBJECT: [Tab] Memo Report Preparation [Enter]

Reports in business are frequently prepared in different forms from those in education. You are looking at a very popular example, the memo report. [Enter]

Rather than prepare both a report and an accompanying letter or memo, the two are combined. This method is usually used for short reports that are fewer than five pages. The headings of the memo report include the date, receiver, sender, and subject or title. [Enter]

Many times you will find that the report content lends itself to the use of subheadings as shown in the samples that follow. [Enter]

bold subheadings

Summary: The findings of the survey of advertising at Old London Square Mall are similar to the national trends. All the mall stores use some type of outside media in addition to local cooperative advertising. The choice of outside media compares quite closely with national trends, since newspapers are rated most effective and are used most frequently, followed by radio, television, direct mailing, and magazines. [Enter]

Background: Our organization entered into an agreement three months ago with the merchants of the Old London Square Mall to investigate avenues of approach to effective advertising. We assigned methods currently in use throughout the nation, and especially those methods used by businesses in some type of physical location arrangement (shopping centers, malls, and so on). After gathering the evidence used throughout the country, a questionnaire was prepared and administered to all the merchants located in the Old London Square Mall. The results of both the nationwide survey and the mall survey were then compared. [Enter]

Findings: National merchants agree that individual firms must do more advertising than the cooperative efforts the mall association makes. Cooperative efforts seem to be quite effective when the entire mall conducts some type of sale (usually seasonal), but for the remainder of the time it is the individual firm that must generate sales by individual advertising efforts. The Old London Square Mall merchants agree with this 100 percent. Nationally, the use and popularity of various types of advertising media differ somewhat from what the Old London Square Mall merchants now use. [Enter]

Conclusion: The use of advertising media by merchants at the Old London Square Mall closely follows what is being done on a national scale. The only difference occurs in the ranking of television and radio. Television is second in popularity nationwide, and radio is third. At the Old London Square Mall, radio is second in popularity and television is third. [Enter]

continues

Exercise 28.6 Word Response Drill: Which One?

Key the questions in this drill and at the end of each line, type your one-word answers. Follow the same procedure of pressing the Tab key, space bar, and Enter key as you did for Exercise 28.5. Try not to hesitate when keying your answer to each question.

1. → a. Would you rather ski or swim?
   → b. Would you rather drive or ride?
   → c. Would you rather eat or cook?
   → d. Would you rather walk or talk?
   → e. Would you rather hike or bike?

2. → a. Are you a female or a male?
   → b. Are you right- or left-handed?
   → c. Is the instructor of this class male or female?
   → d. Would you rather drink milk or tea?
   → e. Would you rather dance or read?

3. → a. Would you rather dance or sing?
   → b. Would you rather eat fish or steak?
   → c. Would you rather write or read?
   → d. Would you rather study or play?
   → e. Would you rather own a dog or a cat?

4. → a. Do you like summer or winter best?
   → b. Would you rather be short or tall?
   → c. Would you rather be dirty or clean?
   → d. Would you rather win or lose?
   → e. Would you rather run or walk?

A *report* should not be confused with a *manuscript*; the latter is a form of printed communication used primarily in the academic and publishing fields. A report creates an organizational loop whereby the information within a report moves upward in an organization. Management uses the information within reports to develop plans and directives to be followed, which flow downward in the organization.

There are three categories of business reports: memo business reports, formal business reports, and specialized business reports.

Memo Business Reports

Before email, communication within a business was done using printed memos. Today, emails that contain information of a temporary nature usually take the place of short memos. Longer reports may become permanent records for the organization and are commonly sent as email attachments along with the body of the email introducing the report. A memo business report (commonly referred to as a *memo report*) is typically one to five pages in length. Regardless if a memo report is printed for distribution or sent as an email attachment, the format of the report is the same.

Figure 49.1 (shown on the next two pages) shows a sample plain-paper memo report that uses bold guide words and bold subheadings, which help to organize the content. The document also includes a continuation header on the second page, which will be discussed later in this session.

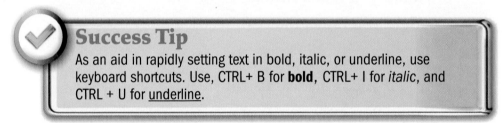

Success Tip

As an aid in rapidly setting text in bold, italic, or underline, use keyboard shortcuts. Use, CTRL+ B for **bold**, CTRL+ I for *italic*, and CTRL + U for underline.

Formal Business Reports

Formal reports are typically longer than five pages for the body and include a cover or title page, a table of contents, and graphics (tables, charts, etc.) in the body of the report.

Specialized Business Reports

There are a variety of specialized reports. One example is a Request for Proposal (RFP). A RFP is used by a business to encourage vendors (other companies or individuals) to bid their products and/or services.

Formatting Memo Business Reports

The memo format was described in Session 36. A memo includes the date, recipient, sender, and subject at the top of the first page. Those four elements are also used in the longer memo report, but they may appear in a different order and are formatted differently. There is no uniform format for memo reports. For this reason, the memos keyed in this unit will have a slightly different format from the memos keyed in previous sessions. Some businesses use a plain-paper format, some design their own memo format, and some customize one of the templates provided by Word.

Changing the Header Margin

When a document, such as a memo report, is longer than one page, it generally has a continuation header. The purpose of the continuation header is to identify the document if the printed pages become separated from the first page. The continuation header of a memo report includes the

Word Response Drill: Opposites

In this drill, rather than keying the word shown, you will key the antonym of the word, or a word with the opposite meaning. Press the Tab key before each letter and press the Enter key immediately after each antonym.

1. → a. day
   → b. salt
   → c. mother
   → d. uncle
   → e. grandmother
   → f. rich
   → g. war
   → h. young
   → i. love
   → j. hot

2. → a. clean
   → b. male
   → c. minus
   → d. seldom
   → e. floor
   → f. stop
   → g. no
   → h. winter
   → i. sick
   → j. true

Assessing Your Speed and Accuracy

Beginning with this session, syllabic intensity, which is a measure of keying difficulty, is listed for all 1-, 3-, and 5-minute timings. **Syllabic intensity (SI)** is the average number of syllables per word. An SI value will give an approximate indication of how difficult a particular block of text will be to key. A block of text with a low SI value will contain words with relatively few syllables and the material will be relatively easy to key. A block of text with a high SI value will contain longer words with more syllables, and thus will be more difficult to key.

When you take the timings, you will want to decide if your personal goal is to improve either your speed or your accuracy. It is important to concentrate on only one goal at a time. Your goal will probably change daily—or even during a particular class period. Timings throughout this text will provide WAM and accuracy goals for you to work toward. Note that with this session, the WAM goals for both the 1-minute and 3-minute timings, have been increased by 5 WAM.

Complete two 3-minute timings on the timing text below. Timings 49.3 and 49.4 use the same paragraphs. For Timing 49.4, try to increase your speed while maintaining your accuracy.

Goals: 35 WAM and six or fewer errors
SI: 1.49 syllables per word

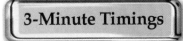

**Timings
49.3–49.4**

In the autumn, when the days get cooler and the leaves begin to change color, many people turn their attention to the upcoming sports season. High on the list for sports fans is football. Whatever level team you follow--high school, college, or professional--there is a variety of exciting games to listen to, watch, or attend every weekend. Fans love the runs, fun passes, hard tackles, and even punts, since the punt return can produce a fumble or a quick score. As the season progresses, much excitement is evident; the excitement culminates in the last big game of the year. For the Canadian pro teams, it's the Grey Cup; in the United States, it's the Super Bowl. The winning team in each country is declared to be "the" football league champion.

Other winter sports games draw the attention of many folks. Ice hockey has grown considerably in popularity. The whizzing skaters, the skills of the players, and the element of competition will add to a winter spectator's enjoyment. Fans love the fast action on ice. The hard checks also draw loud cheers from the home fans.

Basketball draws its share of attention during the long winters. The game of basketball is played at a steady pace and usually is very exciting. As in other professional sports, the teams travel all over the nation, giving the spectators one thrilling game after another.

Ergonomic Tip
Keep your neck straight or bent slightly forward to minimize straining your neck muscles.

Exploring Business Reports

A business report is a document that presents data or other types of information. Commonly, the report summarizes information, has an intended audience, and is used by that audience to make decisions. Reports are the most expensive type of printed communication used in business, government, and education. They are more costly to produce than memos, emails, and letters because of the time and effort necessary to gather and compile the content and write the final product. Reports commonly represent the work of more than one person. Although software with collaborative features is available and can streamline the process, obtaining and mastering such software adds to the preparation costs of these documents. Many reports are typically more than one page in length, which also adds to their cost.

Both WAM goals are 5 WAM greater than what was suggested in previous sessions. The 5-minute timing goal is 25 WAM. Continue striving to make two or fewer errors per minute in all of the timings.

As has been the case in all previous timings, the timing will begin as soon as you begin keying the paragraph in the Online Lab. Remember to press the Tab key at the beginning of a paragraph. If you finish keying the passage before time expires, press Enter and start keying the paragraph again.

When time expires, the Online Lab will give you a WAM rate and error report for the timing and will highlight any errors you made. The results will be stored in your Timings Performance Report.

Timings 28.1 and 28.2 use the same paragraphs of text.

Goals: 35 WAM and two or fewer errors
SI: 1.28 syllables per word

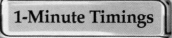

1-Minute Timings

Timings 28.1–28.2

Long ago, pilgrims loved to indulge in blunt folklore. Tales, sometimes false, were told with glee daily. One old tale included a blazing clash of sailors in balky sailboats on a bottomless lake. The last sailor alive was a lad that was blind. As he lay clinging to a slim balsa log in filth and slimy silt, the leader's falcon led help to him. Balmy days followed as the lad's leg healed slowly and the salves applied to his eyes let the light in.

Timings 28.3 and 28.4 use the same paragraphs of text.

Goals: 30 WAM and six or fewer errors
SI: 1.32 syllables per word

3-Minute Timings

Timings 28.3–28.4

To change a US unit of measure to a metric unit of measure takes some practice and knowledge. To change back and forth, a table of metric measures and US units of measures is great to have at hand. For instance, 1 mile is equal to a metric measurement of 1.6 kilometers (or km for short). One yard is about the same as a metric measure of 0.9 meters. One can change a large metric unit to a small one by moving the decimal point one place to the right.

Creating Memo Business Reports and Fax Cover Sheets

Session Objectives

- **Format memo business reports**
- **Change the header margin**
- **Use Widow/Orphan control**
- **Use a template to create fax cover sheets**
- **Correct misplaced modifiers**

Timing Goals

- **1 minute: 40 WAM and two or fewer errors**
- **3 minutes: 35 WAM and six or fewer errors**

Getting Started and Warming Up

Exercise 49.1 If you are continuing immediately from Session 48, you may skip the Exercise 49.1 warm-up drill. However, if you exited the Online Lab at the end of Session 48, warm up by completing Exercise 49.1.

Exercise 49.2 Begin your session work by completing Exercise 49.2, a timed short drill, in the Online Lab.

Assessing Your Speed and Accuracy

Complete Timings 49.1 through 49.4 in the Online Lab. At the end of each timing, the Online Lab will display your WAM rate and any errors. Results will be saved in your Timings Performance report. If you have been surpassing the speed and accuracy goals, set slightly more challenging personal goals and strive to exceed them.

Complete two 1-minute timings on the timing text below. Timings 49.1 and 49.2 use the same paragraph.

Goals: 40 WAM and two or fewer errors
SI: 1.50 syllables per word

1-Minute Timings

Timings 49.1–49.2 Outdoor recreation is one way to enjoy the winter months, and snowshoeing is popular for all ages. There are benefits for those who spend time snowshoeing. The few basic beginning instructions are simple to master. If you can walk, you can snowshoe. Easy to learn, snowshoeing is a fun and active way to spend time outdoors. This is a sport you can enjoy the first time out. It is a fun social activity for a group. The excitement of going into forests, around lakes, and into places not accessible by skis cannot be beat. It provides great cardiovascular exercise for kids and adults, too. Try it!

Timing 28.5 is the first 5-minute timing. It is intended to help you build endurance for keying longer documents.

Goals: 25 WAM and ten or fewer errors
SI: 1.32 syllables per word

5-Minute Timing

Timing 28.5

The most important piece of furniture in an office is the chair. Workers will spend most of their day doing their work while seated. If people are uncomfortable, they will not be as productive as they could be with the right chair. It has been stated that a person's productivity will increase 15 to 20 percent when using a chair that fits his or her body.

There are several features to look for in selecting a chair to be used in an office setting. First, make sure it has a five-star base so that it won't tip over. Next, make sure that the seat adjusts upward and downward to fit the person using it. The back rest must be adjustable up and down so that it supports the worker's back. The front of the chair must have a "water fall," or downward-curved cushion, so that there is no pressure behind the knees while the worker is seated.

Any adjustments to be made to chair height, back support, or tilt must be easy to do. There are chairs on the market that adjust as the person sits down; no manual adjustments need to be made. Another important part of a chair is the covering. Some coverings are warm (because they don't breathe). Chairs can be purchased with arms that drop so that the chair can be moved closer to the desk.

Ergonomic Tip
Take small breaks as short as 10 seconds every 30 minutes to stretch. Short breaks like this will help you relax and relieve tension.

Ending the Session

The Online Lab automatically saves the work you completed for this session. You can continue with the next session or exit the Online Lab and continue later.

Unit 10

Business Reports Part I

Session 29 Composing Phrases and Sentences at the Keyboard

Session Objectives

- **Think and compose at the keyboard**
- **Compose responses at the phrase and sentence level**

Timing Goals

- **1 minute: 35 WAM and two or fewer errors**
- **3 minutes: 30 WAM and six or fewer errors**
- **5 minutes: 25 WAM and ten or fewer errors**

Getting Started and Warming Up

Exercise 29.1 If you are continuing immediately from Session 28, you may skip the Exercise 29.1 warm-up drill. However, if you exited the Online Lab at the end of Session 28, warm up by completing Exercise 29.1.

↻ Reinforcing Your Skills

Exercises 29.2–29.4 Begin your session work by completing Exercises 29.2 and 29.3 in the Online Lab. These drills will give you the opportunity to further reinforce your keyboarding skills by providing practice using the numeric keypad and keying sentences. Exercise 29.4 is a timed short drill. As described in Session 28, in this drill you (1) indicate your goal of working to improve speed or accuracy; (2) set the drill duration at 15 seconds, 30 seconds, or 60 seconds; and (3) identify your personal WAM goal for the timing. Complete each exercise at least once, but repeat exercises if you want to improve your WAM rate and accuracy.

Composing Phrases at the Keyboard

In Session 28, you worked on single word-responses. In this session, you will focus on developing your phrase-response and sentence-response level keyboarding skills.

Exercise 29.5 **Short Phrases Drill**

For the first question in each group, type the question number followed by a period, press the Tab key (indicated with a → in the drill line), key a., press the space bar once, and then type the question. Following the question, press the space bar once, type your answer in the format of a short answer or phrase and then press Enter. For the next question, press the Tab key, type the question letter followed by a period, type the question, type your answer, and then press Enter. Think about the question as you key the question text, and try to key your answer as quickly as possible after striking the question mark and space bar at the end of the question.

3   Add formatting to the table as follows:
  a   Apply the style *Light List - Accent 1*.
  b   Apply the Standard Yellow shading to row 2.
  c   Change the line style of the outside borders of the entire table to a triple line , ½ pt, Black.
  d   Change the line style of the inside borders of rows 3–6 to a double wavy line , ¾ pt.
4   Proofread the table and correct any errors.
5   Save the document.
6   Click the Check button to stop the timer and upload the document for checking. The Online Lab will report the WAM rate and number of errors for the activity.
7   If errors are reported, view the results document, correct the errors in the submitted document, save the document, and then click the Check button.

Figure 48.3 Table Content for Document 48.3

FIND A LAPTOP			
PRICE	*BRAND*	*SCREEN SIZE (in inches)*	*LAPTOP TYPE*
Less than $400	Dell	18 and larger	Budget
$400 to $500	HP	16 to 17	Mid-size
$500 to $600	Gateway	13 to 15	Gaming
$600 to $700	Apple	10 to 12	Thin and light

Ending the Session

The Online Lab automatically saves the work you completed for this session. You may continue with the next session or exit the Online Lab and continue later.

1.→ a. What is the name of a town and state or province that you would
        like to visit?
  → b. What are your instructor's first and last names?
  → c. What is the president's or prime minister's last name?
  → d. What is the name of this book?
  → e. What is the name of this course?

2.→ a. What are your first and last names?
  → b. What is your street address?
  → c. What is the title of your favorite song?
  → d. What is the name of the last movie you saw?
  → e. What is the name of the last television show you saw?

3.→ a. Where were you born?
  → b. Where did you attend elementary school?
  → c. Where did you go on your last vacation?
  → d. Where are you going after class today?
  → e. Where will you be tomorrow at this time?

4.→ a. What are your favorite sports?
  → b. What are your favorite colors?
  → c. What will you be doing five years from now?
  → d. What is the name of your favorite class?
  → e. What is the name of your best friend?

Exercise Longer Phrases Drill
29.6
Key the incomplete statements listed for this drill and complete each sentence by keying the
appropriate phrase in replace of the blank line. Type the number, a period, and press the Tab key
at the beginning of each sentence. Press the Enter key at the end of each sentence.

1.→ Because the clock was wrong, I _____.
2.→ Because the road was icy, I _____.
3.→ Because the team won, I _____.
4.→ Because I was late, I _____.
5.→ Because I cannot drive, I _____.

drill continues

4 Insert a new third column and key the heading **Cost**.

5 Insert a new row between the *Apple MacBook* and the *Dell Inspiron* rows and key the following:

Vendor: **Asus Eee**

Screen Size: **12.1**

Cost: **$437**

6 Insert a new row between the *Dell Inspiron* and the *HP Pavilion* rows and key the following:

Vendor: **Gateway**

Screen Size: **14**

Cost: **$849**

7 Add a new row at the bottom of the table and key the following:

Vendor: **Sony VAIO**

Screen Size: **15.5**

Cost: **$549**

8 Key the cost information shown in Figure 48.2.

9 Proofread the table and correct any errors.

10 Save the document.

11 Click the Check button to stop the timer and upload the document for checking. The Online Lab will report the WAM rate and number of errors for the activity.

12 If errors are reported, view the results document, correct the errors in the submitted document, save the document, and then click the Check button.

Figure 48.2 Table Content for Document 48.2

Vendor	Screen Size (in inches)	Cost
Apple MacBook	13.3	$999
Asus Eee	12.1	$437
Dell Inspiron	15.6	$499
Gateway	14	$849
HP Pavilion	14	$480
Sony VAIO	15.5	$549

Document 48.3 Merging Cells and Applying Shading, Borders, and a Table Style

1 Read all instructions for this document activity, navigate to the Document 48.3 launch page in the Online Lab, and then click the Launch Activity button. The Online Lab will open **Doc048.03** in the activity window. The timer will start as soon as you begin keying the document.

2 Key the table shown in Figure 48.3 using the following information to assist you:

a Create a table that contains four columns by six rows and then merge the cells in the first row.

b Format the text in the second row in italic and insert a line break, using Shift + Enter, after *SCREEN SIZE* in the third column heading.

steps continue

6.→ If I pass this test, I _____.

7.→ If I finish early, I _____.

8.→ If I get the job, I _____.

9.→ If the price is right, I _____.

10.→ If the beach is crowded, I _____.

11.→ I do not like to use Twitter because _____.

12.→ I do not study at the library because _____.

13.→ I do obey the speed limit because _____.

14.→ I do like math because _____.

15.→ I do play sports because _____.

16.→ A hammer is used to _____.

17.→ A lawn mower is used to _____.

18.→ Scissors are used to _____.

19.→ A blog is used to_____.

20.→ An eraser is used to _____.

Exercise 29.7 Sentences Drill

Read each sentence and compose a full sentence that answers each question. Before each sentence answer, type the question number, a period, and press the Tab key. For example, in response to the first question, you might key the following:

1.→A police officer enforces the laws.

In the previous example, the → represents pressing the Tab key. Try not to hesitate and to key your sentence answer as quickly as possible after reading the question.

1 What does a police officer do? A police officer enforces the laws.

2 What does a plumber do?

3 What does a firefighter do?

4 What does a lawyer do?

5 What does a teacher do?

6 What does an auto mechanic do?

7 What does YouTube have to offer the public?

8 What does a dentist do?

9 What does an accountant do?

10 What does a chef do?

Checking Production Progress: Tables

Sessions 45–47 discussed the procedures for preparing and formatting tables. In this session, you will be assessed on how quickly and accurately you can key these types of documents. In the following document activities, each completed document is to be "mailable," which means that it contains no errors. A document that requires additional corrections is not considered mailable.

Your goals are to key each document in mailable form and at a rate of at least 20 WAM. If your rate is less than 20 WAM or if the document includes uncorrected errors, your instructor may ask you to repeat documents. To help you succeed, carefully review the document instructions and the document before launching the document activity. *Note: If necessary, review the content of Sessions 45–47 if you are unsure how to complete a specific task.*

Document 48.1 Creating a Table and Entering Data

1 Read all instructions for this document activity, navigate to the Document 48.1 launch page in the Online Lab, and then click the Launch Activity button. The Online Lab will open **Doc048.01** in the activity window. The timer will start as soon as you begin keying the document.

2 Create and key the table shown in Figure 48.1.

   a When keying the last column heading, press Shift + Enter after *Screen Size* to insert the line break.

   b Format the column headings in bold.

   c Make sure that the model number for the HP Pavilion laptop is not capitalized.

3 Proofread the table and correct any errors.

4 Save the document.

5 Click the Check button to stop the timer and upload the document for checking. The Online Lab will report the WAM rate and number of errors for the activity.

6 If errors are reported, view the results document, correct the errors in the submitted document, save the document, and then click the Check button.

Figure 48.1 Table Content for Document 48.1

Vendor	Model	Screen Size (in inches)
Dell Inspiron	N5010	15.6
Compaq Presario	CQ56-110US	15.6
HP Pavilion	g4t	14
Apple	MacBook	13.3

Document 48.2 Inserting and Deleting Rows and Columns

1 Read all instructions for this document activity, navigate to the Document 48.2 launch page in the Online Lab, and then click the Launch Activity button. The Online Lab will open **Doc048.02** in the activity window. The timer will start as soon as you begin keying the document.

2 Delete the *Compaq Presario* row.

3 Delete the *Model* column and key the model name **MacBook** after *Apple* in cell A2.

steps continue

Assessing Your Speed and Accuracy

Complete Timings 29.1 through 29.5 in the Online Lab. Refer to the following paragraphs as you key.

The timing will start as soon as you begin keying in the Online Lab. If you finish keying the passage before time expires, press Enter and start keying the timing text again. Remember to press the Tab key at the start of each paragraph.

When time expires, the Online Lab will give you a WAM rate and error report for the timing and will highlight any errors you made. The results will be stored in your Timings Performance Report.

Goals: 35 WAM and two or fewer errors
SI: 1.34 syllables per word

1-Minute Timings

Timings 29.1–29.2

The news on the network newscast might spawn a winning wealth of followers. If the newscaster can draw a wider range of viewers, the rewards are power and wealth. Watchers and followers of a witty newscaster are won when the daily news is written well. It is not a waste to rewrite the worst of interviews when witless words can wreck a well planned show or review. They who dawdle in the newsroom will not work or write very long. Their reward will be awful reviews.

Goals: 30 WAM and six or fewer errors
SI: 1.38 syllables per word

3-Minute Timings

Timings 29.3–29.4

Taking photos with a good camera can be fun. A cheap brand does not work well. Though most cell phones now take good photos with ease, a real camera gives you more control. Most photo equipment has some method of setting a variety of focal lengths. A focal length setting of 35 mm gives a wider picture angle, and it can be used for group portraits or photos of landscapes. Most folks like good pictures of pretty green hills with blue lakes. A focal length setting of 70 mm has a narrow angle for making a portrait or taking a good photo of a good scene or object that is far away. Using the zoom lens requires some practice before a picture can be a work of art.

Complete two 3-minute timings on the timing text below. Timings 48.3 and 48.4 use the same paragraphs. For Timing 48.4, try to increase your speed while keeping the error count at no more than two errors per minute, or no more than six total errors.

Goals: 35 WAM and six or fewer errors
SI: 1.51 syllables per word

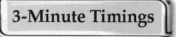

Timings 48.3–48.4

Sport is for enjoyment—but hey, what would life be without competition? And that is why kitesurfing, too, has its events and tournaments to determine the best out there. There is an international KTA circuit that attracts the best kiters in the world, as well as a South African circuit.

While many people follow the sport and their favorite kiters, one of the downsides of spectating top class kiteboarding events is that when the kiting is great, it is normally miserable on the beach. While this is perhaps a deterrent to followers, it is nonetheless a spectacular sport to watch for those who brave the conditions.

It was American playwright Tennessee Williams who suggested: "Security is a kind of death." Meandering your way through life, safe and sound, is often just a meek way of surrendering to a slow, purposeless wasting away. Rather, kitesurfers enjoy life to the fullest and embrace its combination of beauty and danger.

Kitesurfing offers one of the most exhilarating experiences as it combines the art of surfing and the thrill of harnessing the wind, similar to windsurfing. Whether it is jumping and tricks that you are into, or carving away on the waves, the sport of kitesurfing has got you covered.

Fun, adventure, and some fabulous wave riding and entertainment are what kitesurfing can guarantee. There is certainly no place for boredom when one is hauled along at speed, at one with nature, across the expanse of the ocean. Can there be a more spectacular setting, a more pleasurable environment? South Africa's coastline and its weather conditions provide the kitesurfer with many places to revel in his or her beloved sport.

Ergonomic Tip

Instead of using a mouse, try a touch pad. Individuals working with laptop computers and netbooks generally have this option.

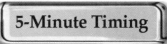

Timing
29.5

Education has become a lifelong process. No longer can we say that a person's formal schooling will last for a lifetime. Business spends almost as much for training programs as is spent for our public school system. The average age of students in schools offering programs above the high school level is on the rise.

Adult learners enter school programs with needs and wants that differ from the requirements of traditional students. They are goal-oriented. They are looking for skills and knowledge that will help them keep a job, prepare for a new job, or advance to a higher-level job. Adults don't want to waste time in reaching new skills; they want to spend their time on those things that relate to their goals.

Teachers and trainers of adult learners are faced with a tough task. In most cases, they must narrow the focus of their programs to meet the needs of the learners. Courses must be designed that draw upon the learners' skills and knowledge. To design a good program, you must assess what the learners know and what their goals are.

The next step in the process is to design a performance outcome that shows that the person can demonstrate a mastery of what was presented in the course. Once the outcome has been set, the instructor can choose teaching methods, course length, texts needed, and program content. Problem-solving, learn by doing, and case studies are methods of teaching that help adult students.

Ergonomic Tip

Sit up straight, drop your shoulders back, and let your arms and hands hang loosely. This takes the strain off your back and allows your lungs and other organs to function correctly.

Ending the Session

The Online Lab automatically saves the work you completed for this session. You can continue with the next session or exit the Online Lab and continue later.

Production Progress Check: Tables Part I

Session 48

Session Objectives

- Review and practice word processing features presented in Sessions 45–47
- Produce documents at a rate of 20 WAM and in mailable form

Timing Goals

- 1 minute: 40 WAM and two or fewer errors
- 3 minutes: 35 WAM and six or fewer errors

Getting Started and Warming Up

Exercise 48.1 If you are continuing immediately from Session 47, you may skip the Exercise 48.1 warm-up drill. However, if you exited the Online Lab at the end of Session 47, warm up by completing Exercise 48.1.

Exercise 48.2 Begin your session work by completing Exercise 48.2, a timed short drill, in the Online Lab.

Assessing Your Speed and Accuracy

Complete Timings 48.1 through 48.4 in the Online Lab. At the end of each timing, the Online Lab will display your WAM rate and any errors. Results will be saved in your Timings Performance report. If you have been surpassing the speed and accuracy goals, set slightly more challenging personal goals and strive to exceed them.

Complete two 1-minute timings on the timing text below. Timings 48.1 and 48.2 use the same paragraph.

Goals: 40 WAM and two or fewer errors
SI: 1.44 syllables per word

1-Minute Timings

Timings 48.1–48.2

The nature of our jobs means we're all too often stuck with our current computer screen--and, unfortunately, the eyestrain that comes with it. Eyestrain is apparently the most common form of repetitive strain injury, which if left uncorrected, can lead to general fatigue and a decrease in overall efficiency. Although the jury is still out on whether computers can cause permanent damage on our eyes, that is hardly any compensation for those who have learned to live with a range of symptoms that can vary from blurred vision and headaches to dry, gritty eyes. What isn't in question is the fact that our eyes are made up of more than one million parts, working in perfect harmony. And we definitely want to keep them that way.

Session 30

Composing Sentences and Paragraphs at the Keyboard

Session Objectives

- **Think and compose at the keyboard**
- **Choose the correct word form and use in varying circumstances**
- **Compose responses at the phrase, sentence, and paragraph level**

Timing Goals

- **1 minute: 35 WAM and two or fewer errors**
- **3 minutes: 30 WAM and six or fewer errors**
- **5 minutes: 25 WAM and ten or fewer errors**

Getting Started and Warming Up

Exercise 30.1 If you are continuing immediately from Session 29, you may skip the Exercise 30.1 warm-up drill. However, if you exited the Online Lab at the end of Session 29, warm up by completing Exercise 30.1.

⟳ Reinforcing Your Skills

Exercises 30.2–30.3 Begin your session work by completing Exercises 30.2 in the Online Lab. This drill will give you the opportunity to further reinforce your keyboarding skills by providing practice using the numeric keypad and keying sentences. Then complete Exercise 30.3, a timed short drill.

Composing at the Keyboard

In Session 29, you worked on keying responses that were word phrases and sentences. In this session, you will focus on developing your composition skills at the sentence-response and paragraph-response levels.

General Guidelines for Correct Word Use

A common problem a writer faces is choosing the correct word to convey a certain thought or idea to the reader. Writing must be precise. Vague words or misuse of words may produce a meaning other than the author's intended meaning. The following are guidelines to help you choose the correct word.

1 Use nouns and descriptive adjectives, adverbs, and phrases that have a precise meaning. Be specific when you write. Do not use vague or abstract words such as nice, good, bad, thing, and work because they do not give the reader much information. Read each of the following examples and notice the differences.

Vague:	The lecture was good, and I learned a lot.
Better:	The lecture solved two problems for me. I learned how to balance a checkbook and how to calculate interest.
Vague:	a nice color
Better:	an emerald green, a vivid scarlet, a deep black

Figure 47.8 Table Content for Document 47.3

TEAM	LEAGUE	WINS	LOSSES
Chicago Cubs	National	45	46
Minnesota Twins	American	54	38
Atlanta Braves	National	47	46
Colorado Rockies	National	63	28
Texas Rangers	American	38	57

Reinforcing Writing Skills

In business or academic reports or letters, tables are commonly used to provide details that reinforce or support discussion in the text of a document. Tables are also especially effective at illustrating or comparing a series of related items, such as students in a course, the functions of departments in a company, and the cost of supplies and labor for a manufacturing plant.

Document 47.4 — **Creating a Table in a Memo for Company Distribution**

1   Navigate to the Document 47.4 launch page in the Online Lab and then click the Launch Activity button. The Online Lab will open **Doc047.04** in the activity window.

2   Assume you are a Vice President of a company who has had recent success. Choose any type of company and create names where necessary. As a result of that success, you have been able to hire five new employees over the last six months. Compose a memo to be distributed to all company employees to introduce the new employees and provide their contact information.

   a   In the first paragraph, discuss the recent success of your company and some of the reasons for the success. You decide those reasons.

   b   In the second paragraph, explain that six new employees have been hired and introduce the following table.

   c   Following the second paragraph, insert a table with column headings that includes the names of the employees and their start dates, department names, and telephone extensions (use only three digits).

   d   In the last paragraph, mention how pleased you are that these five individuals are now working for the company.

3   Format the table so that the overall appearance is pleasing and the information is easy to read and interpret.

4   Proofread the document and correct any errors in the document.

5   Save the document.

6   Click the Upload button to upload the document for instructor review.

Ending the Session

The Online Lab automatically saves the work you completed for this session. You may continue with the next session or exit the Online Lab and continue later.

Vague:	he said
Better:	he shouted defiantly, he muttered, he demanded, he whispered

2 Use the correct phrase. The following are commonly misused phrases.

Correct	*Incorrect*	*Correct*	*Incorrect*
acquitted of	acquitted from	in search of	in search for
aim to prove	aim at proving	kind of (+ noun)	kind of a (+ noun)
can't help feeling	can't help but feel	different from	different than
comply with	comply to	try to	try and
independent of	independent from		

3 Use the correct word. The following are commonly misused words.

accept *to take or receive*	except *to leave out; aside from*
advice *a recommendation*	advise *to recommend*
biannual *twice a year*	biennial *once every two years*
council *a governing body*	counsel *to give advice*
fewer *(use with nouns that can be counted: fewer apples)*	less *(use with nouns that cannot be counted: less noise)*
good *modifies a noun or pronoun*	well *modifies a verb or adverb*
angry at *(things and animals)*	angry with *(people)* angry about *(occasions or situations)*

Exercise 30.4 Descriptive Sentences Drill

Drawing from your experience and observations, think of descriptive words or phrases to make the following five sentences more interesting. Now key the sentence number and a period, press the Tab key, and then key your revised sentence. If your sentence extends beyond the right margin, let word wrap work automatically. At the end of each sentence, press the Enter key and continue with the next sentence.

> 1.→ The last book I read was good.
>
> 2.→ Today is a nice day.
>
> 3.→ My favorite sport is fun.
>
> 4.→ My favorite color is a nice color.
>
> 5.→ My best friend is nice.

Exercise 30.5 Correct Word Choice Drill

Select the correct phrase in the following sentences and key each sentence using the correct words.

> 1.→ (Try to, Try and) key the data without any errors.
>
> 2.→ Juan went (in search for, in search of) a new printer.
>
> 3.→ My book is (different from, different than) Harriet's book.

drill continues

To apply the selected line style, weight, and color, choose a border option. Click the Borders button arrow in the Table Styles group to display a list of border format options to apply to the selected cells in a table (see Figure 47.7). Select the border style from the drop-down list to apply that border style to the selected cells.

Document 47.3 Formatting Borders in a Table

1   Read all instructions for this document activity, navigate to the Document 47.3 launch page in the Online Lab, and then click the Launch Activity button. The Online Lab will open **Doc047.03** in the activity window. The timer will start as soon as you begin keying the document.

2   Create the table and key the text shown in Figure 47.8.

3   Apply the triple line style to the outside borders of the first row of the table by completing the following steps:

   a   Select the first row of the table.

   b   Click the Table Tools Design tab.

   c   Click the Line Style button in the Draw Borders group.

   d   At the drop-down menu, click the first triple row style option (three lines of equal weight).

   e   In the Table Styles group, click the Borders button arrow and then click *Outside Borders*.

4   Apply the Orange shading (in the *Standard Colors* section) to the first row of the table.

5   Apply a single red 1 ½ pt line to the outside borders of rows 2 through 6 by completing the following steps:

   a   Select rows 2 through 6.

   b   Click the Table Tools Design tab.

   c   Click the Line Style button in the Draw Borders group and at the drop-down list, click the single line style option.

   d   Click the Line Weight button and then click *1 ½ pt* from the drop-down list.

   e   Click the Pen Color button and then click *Red* in the *Standard Colors* section.

   f   In the Table Styles group, click the Borders button arrow and then click *Outside Borders*.

6   Apply a single wavy blue line style to the inside borders of rows 2 through 6 by completing the following steps:

   a   With rows 2 through 6 still selected, click the Line Style button in the Draw Borders group and then click the single wavy line style option.

   b   Click the Line Weight button and then click *¾ pt*.

   c   Click the Pen Color button and then click *Blue* in the *Standard Colors* section.

   d   In the Table Styles group, click the Borders button arrow and then click *Inside Borders*.

7   Proofread the table and correct any errors in the file.

8   Save the document.

9   Click the Check button to stop the timer and upload the document for checking. The Online Lab will report the WAM rate and number of errors for the activity.

10   If errors are reported, view the results document, correct the errors in the submitted document, save the document, and then click the Check button.

4. → I will try to (comply with, comply to) your wishes.

5. → This (kind of a, kind of) paper is easier to store.

6. → (Accept, Except) for Henry, the entire class went on the trip.

7. → Our teacher strongly (adviced, advised) us to study for the exam.

8. → There have been (fewer, less) absences this winter than last winter.

9. → We have (fewer, less) flour than we need.

10. → He is a (good, well) student.

11. → Heather doesn't feel (good, well) today.

12. → Sean plays the violin (good, well).

13. → I am angry (at, about, with) my best friend.

14. → I am angry (at, about, with) the rising cost of school.

15. → I am angry (at, about, with) Whiskers, my cat.

Exercise 30.6 · Sentence Composition Drill

Compose a complete sentence about each of the following items. Before keying your response, key the sentence number and a period, and then press Tab. If your sentence extends beyond the right margin, let word wrap work automatically. At the end of each sentence, press Enter and proceed with the next sentence. Be sure to correct any errors.

1. → hybrid car

2. → ice cream

3. → gas station

4. → bank

5. → elevator

6. → fire

7. → Facebook

8. → dance

9. → apple

10. → water

11. → mirror

12. → television

drill continues

4   Select the cells A2 through A6 and apply the *Aqua, Accent 5, Lighter 80%* color in the *Theme Colors* section.

5   Apply the same aqua color to cells D2 through D6.

6   Proofread the table and correct any errors.

7   Save the document.

8   Click the Check button to stop the timer and upload the document for checking. The Online Lab will report the WAM rate and number of errors for the activity.

9   If errors are reported, view the results document, correct the errors in the submitted document, save the document, and then click the Check button.

Figure 47.5 Table Content for Document 47.2

Name	Sales	Points	Bonus
Cameron	$92,902	8	$3,720
Emerson	$53,950	9	$1,691
Myers	$32,200	7	$1,366
Preston	$29,000	4	$1,203
Gunn	$24,000	3	$1,087

Formatting Table Borders

Word also provides tools that allow you to change the way the borders of cells in a table display. Select the cells in the table you want to apply a border design to and then click the Line Style button in the Draw Borders group on the Table Tools Design tab. Select the line style from the drop-down list (see Figure 47.6) to apply that line style. Similarly, choose the line weight by clicking an option from the Line Weight button drop-down list and choose the color of the line by clicking the Pen Color button arrow.

Figure 47.6 Line Style Button Drop-Down Menu

Figure 47.7 Borders Button Arrow Drop-Down Menu

13.→ dollar bill	
14.→ door	
15.→ chair	

16.→ text messaging	
17.→ shoe	
18.→ building	

19.→ sunset	
20.→ clock	

General Guidelines for Writing Paragraphs

As noted in Session 28, the fourth stage in building keyboarding composition skills is to compose at the keyboard at the paragraph-response level. A **paragraph** is a group of related sentences—an organized and meaningful unit in a piece of writing. A paragraph contains a topic sentence and several supporting sentences. In a well-written paragraph, the sentences are organized in a logical manner and flow from one to the next. Transitional words are used to connect one sentence to another sentence, and transitional phrases are used to connect one paragraph to another paragraph.

A **topic sentence** expresses the main idea of a paragraph and the supporting sentences describe, explain, or further develop the topic sentence. Because most readers like to know the subject of a paragraph before reading about it, the topic sentence is usually the first sentence of a paragraph. The following is an example of a paragraph with a topic sentence as the first sentence and supporting sentences following it.

A receptionist who works in a small office has a wide variety of duties. Answering the telephone and receiving callers are primary responsibilities of any receptionist. Sometimes an employer asks a receptionist to take an important client to lunch or to contact a business customer. The correspondence in a small office varies from simple letters, memos, and emails to complicated reports, and so the receptionist handles many types of communication.

Practice composing a paragraph at the keyboard by completing Exercise 30.7 in the Online Lab.

Exercise 30.7 **Paragraph Composition Drill**

Compose a paragraph about how you will use your keyboarding skills. Your paragraph should include a topic sentence and at least three supporting sentences. Start the paragraph by pressing the Tab key, allow text in the paragraph to wrap, and correct any errors.

Assessing Your Speed and Accuracy

Complete Timings 30.1 through 30.5 in the Online Lab. Refer to the following paragraphs as you key.

The timing will start as soon as you begin keying in the Online Lab. If you finish keying the passage before the timing expires, press Enter and start keying the timing text again. Remember to press the Tab key at the start of each paragraph.

Figure 47.3 Shading Button Color Palette

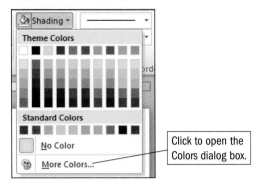

Click to open the Colors dialog box.

Figure 47.4 Colors Dialog Box

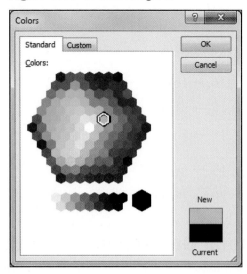

Applying Shading

In addition to applying styles, you can create your own shading for use in a table. To apply shading, select the portion of the table you want to shade and then click the Shading button arrow in the Table Styles group on the Table Tools Design tab to display the palette of color options that are available (see Figure 47.3). The color options are separated into a *Theme Colors* section and a *Standard Colors* section. Each color has a name, which will display when the mouse pointer points to the color and the shading will display in the selected portion of the table. Click a color to apply it.

If you find that the color choices are too limited on the color palette, click the *More Colors* option to open the Colors dialog box (see Figure 47.4). The Colors dialog box contains a Standard tab and a Custom tab. Click a color on the Standard tab and then click OK, or click Close to close the dialog box. Once you select a color from the Colors dialog box, the color option will appear in the *Recent Colors* section of the Shading button palette.

Once you apply a shade to a table, the paint bucket portion of the Shading button will indicate that color choice. Click the bucket portion of the button to apply the same color to other selected cells in the table. To change the color of the paint button bucket, click the Shading button arrow to display the color palette and then click a different color option.

Document 47.2 — Applying Shading to a Table

1   Read all instructions for this document activity, navigate to the Document 47.2 launch page in the Online Lab, and then click the Launch Activity button. The Online Lab will open **Doc047.02** in the activity window. The timer will start as soon as you begin keying the document.

2   Create the table and key the text shown in Figure 47.5.

3   Apply yellow shading to the first row of the table by completing the following steps:

   a   Place the mouse pointer over the left edge of any cell in the first row until the mouse pointer becomes an arrow pointing up and to the right and then double-click.

   b   Click the Table Tools Design tab.

   c   Click the Shading button arrow in the Table Styles group.

   d   Click *Yellow* in the *Standard Colors* section.

steps continue

When time expires, the Online Lab will give you a WAM rate and error report for the timing and will highlight any errors you made. The results will be stored in your Timings Performance report.

Goals: 35 WAM and two or fewer errors
SI: 1.38 syllables per word

1-Minute Timings

Timings 30.1–30.2

At sunset, it is nice to enjoy dining out on a bank of a pond. Unless uninvited insects and swarms of ants invade the picnic, you will certainly unwind. As those soft night sounds enfold you, frenzied inward nerves and the decisions that haunt you drain from your mind. You may enjoy napping on a nearby bench. Next, swing into action after your rest and inhale much air into your lungs. Unpack the nice lunch and munch away. Don't deny yourself this experience.

Goals: 30 WAM and six or fewer errors
SI: 1.46 syllables per word

3-Minute Timings

Timings 30.3–30.4

Simple salt and pepper shakers are very easy and quite simple to collect today. Lots of "fun" and very colorful pairs are available, either new or pre-owned. The bargains can be found at those family or group sales. Most folks try to see how many kinds they can find and buy. Some collect a mass of shakers that number over 500. The person or persons who are really collectors have shakers that number from 2,000 to 3,000 pairs. If anyone would like to begin the hobby of collecting, just look around and start a collection.

Figure 47.1 Table Tools Design Tab

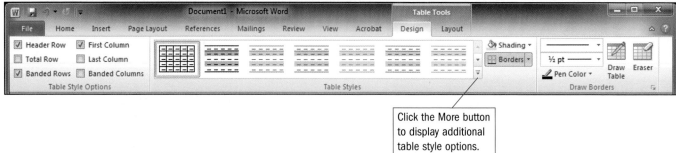

Click the More button to display additional table style options.

Using Table Styles

There are 98 style options available in the Table Styles group. Once a table is created, you can apply one of these styles to it. Click the More button to open the style gallery. When the mouse pointer moves over a style option, a screen tip with the style name will appear and the active table in your document will display with that style. The ability to preview the table when a particular style is applied to it (called *Live Preview*) will help you choose a style most suitable for your table. Click a style to apply it to the table.

Document 47.1 Applying a Table Style

1   Read all instructions for this document activity, navigate to the Document 47.1 launch page in the Online Lab, and then click the Launch Activity button. The Online Lab will open **Doc047.01** in the activity window. The timer will start as soon as you begin keying the document.

2   Create a table that contains five columns and six rows and then key the text in the cells shown in Figure 47.2.

3   Apply the *Light Shading* table style to the table by completing the following steps:

   a   Click the Table Tools Design tab.

   b   Click the More button in the Table Styles group.

   c   Click the *Light Shading* option, the first style in the *Built-In* group.

4   Proofread the table and correct any errors.

5   Save the document.

6   Click the Check button to stop the timer and upload the document for checking. The Online Lab will report the WAM rate and number of errors for the activity.

7   If errors are reported, view the results document, correct the errors in the submitted document, save the document, and then click the Check button.

Figure 47.2 Table Content for Document 47.1

Manufacturer	Model	Sticker Price	Engine	Drive
Chevrolet	Traverse	$42,342	V6	AWD
Ford	Explorer	$43,852	V6	FWD
Buick	Enclave	$46,799	V6	RWD
GMC	Acadia	$39,455	V6	FWD
Dodge	Durango	$41,618	V8	AWD

Timing
30.5

Most of the major events in communications grew out of a series of discoveries that took place over many years. Present-day systems can be traced to many great men and women who brought together the tools of their day to meet the needs of people on the job and in the home. The basis of this technology had its start in the 1830s. In the 1830s, if you wanted to tell people things, you either had to do it in person, or write a letter and send it by means of the Post Office. The Post Office used men on horses to transport letters from one place to big cities and small towns.

One of the first events occurred in Germany when their government built a telegraph network that spanned 8,000 feet. By the next decade, the use of this device had spread to the United States. Congress funded a line that ran from Washington to Baltimore. During the same time frame, Samuel F. B. Morse finished a new telegraph device and code that came to be known as the Morse Code. The Morse Code was used for more than 100 years. It was vital for both the North and South in the Civil War.

In the next few years, more developments took place. European telegraph wires and underwater cables became widely used. While the telegraph would continue to be used for many more years, other types of technology were taking shape. Bell developed the telephone in 1875, and he and Gray filed for a patent the next year. Bell later offered to sell his patents to Western Union, but they turned him down.

The evolution of the telephone is constantly on the move. Computer telephony has entered the scene. With a web cam you can see the person you are talking to, and she/he can see you. There are no handsets. You are talking to a microphone on your computer. A small camera attached to your monitor is taking a moving picture of you that is being transmitted to the person you are talking to.

Ergonomic Tip
You can make many adjustments in your own environment at little or no cost to you or your employer.

Ending the Session

The Online Lab automatically saves the work you completed for this session. You can continue with the next session or exit the Online Lab and continue later.

Complete two 3-minute timings on the timing text below. Timings 47.3 and 47.4 use the same paragraphs. Note that with this session, the WAM goal for 3-minute timings has been increased by 5 WAM.

Goals: 35 WAM and six or fewer errors
SI: 1.37 syllables per word

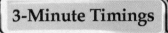

Timings 47.3–47.4

A wood chisel may be used to remove extra wood when another tool will not do the job efficiently. The wood chisel can also be used to make precision wood joint cuts.

Never use a steel hammer to strike a chisel. Use either a solid rubber or wooden mallet. You can also use the palm of your hand, of course, depending on the particular project. A mallet can work in cases where the edge to be cut is across the grain. If, however, the cutting edge is with the grain, a mallet could easily split the wood. Remember to angle the chisel slightly when starting a cut. The angle makes smooth or pared cuts easier to do. Cutting on the angle leaves the piece of wood much smoother when cutting either with or against the grain.

To make a vertical cut against the grain, tilt the chisel off to one side to initiate a sliding action to the flat cutting edge. A surface that is wider than the chisel is easier to cut if the chisel is pressed against the cut-out portion. The procedure will provide a guide for that portion of the chisel when cutting out the new portion or edge. Always remember to cut with the grain so that any excess or extra wood will split away in a straight line and not cause a further problem to the woodcutter.

Ergonomic Tip
To relax, squeeze a tennis ball or another solid object in your fist for 10 seconds. Release your grip on the object, then repeat several times.

Using the Table Tools Design Tab

Whereas Session 46 focused on features available on the Table Tools Layout tab, this session will focus on the Table Tools Design tab. This tab, shown in Figure 47.1, contains three groups: the Table Style Options group, the Table Styles group, and the Draw Borders group. In this session, you will work with the tools in the Table Styles and Draw Borders groups.

Unit 6 Alphabet Reinforcement

Formatting the Design of Tables

Session Objectives

- Use table styles
- Apply shading to tables
- Format table borders
- Create a table in a memo for distribution

Timing Goals

- 1 minute: 40 WAM and two or fewer errors
- 3 minutes: 35 WAM and six or fewer errors

Getting Started and Warming Up

Exercise 47.1 If you are continuing immediately from Session 46, you may skip the Exercise 47.1 warm-up drill. However, if you exited the Online Lab at the end of Session 46, warm up by completing Exercise 47.1.

Exercise 47.2 Begin your session work by completing Exercise 47.2, a timed short drill, in the Online Lab.

Assessing Your Speed and Accuracy

Complete Timings 47.1 through 47.4 in the Online Lab. At the end of each timing, the Online Lab will display your WAM rate and any errors. Results will be saved in your Timings Performance report. If you have been surpassing the speed and accuracy goals, set slightly more challenging personal goals and strive to exceed them.

Complete two 1-minute timings on the timing text below. Timings 47.1 and 47.2 use the same paragraph.

Goals: 40 WAM and two or fewer errors
SI: 1.45 syllables per word

1-Minute Timings

Timings 47.1–47.2   When considering the purchase of any article of clothing, do not let any salesperson convince you to take a garment that does not fit well. If you decide to buy something that does not fit, be sure that the store from which you buy the clothing has an excellent alteration department. Make sure that they understand that the clothing must be altered to fit before you make the final arrangements to purchase the item. To be completely assured and satisfied, take a friend along to give you another opinion on how you look.

Skillbuilding: Letters A–I

Session Objectives

- Review proper finger placement for letters A–I, numbers, and punctuation keys
- Improve keying speed and accuracy

Timing Goals

- 1 minute: 30 WAM and two or fewer errors

Getting Started and Warming Up

Exercise 31.1 If you are continuing immediately from Session 30, you can skip the Exercise 31.1 warm-up drill. However, if you exited the Online Lab at the end of Session 30, warm up by completing Exercise 31.1.

Reinforcing Your Skills

All timings and exercises for this session focus on a different letter of the alphabet. For each letter, first begin by taking a 1-minute timing. If you attain a rate of 30 WAM with two or fewer errors, push for speed in the next activities. If you commit more than two errors in the timing, focus on accuracy. Second, complete the exercise that focuses on that letter. Finally, take the timing for a second time. Evaluate your results. If, for a particular letter, you are not keying at least 30 WAM with two or fewer errors, return to the Online Lab session for that letter and repeat the appropriate drills. All timing results are stored in your Timing Performance report.

A Key Timings and Practice

Exercise 31.2 Complete Timing 31.1 by keying the following timing text. Continue to reinforce your proficiency with the A key by completing the drill lines in Exercise 31.2 in the Online Lab. Finally, complete Timing 31.2 using the same paragraph of text used in Timing 31.1.

> **1-Minute Timings**

Timings 31.1–31.2

That happy play has an amazing climax. It affects all 27 watchers. The absorbing last act is majestic with an array of blazing ideas. Many apt actors who speak well may apply and qualify for a part. The author is apt and adept; he is ascending toward a lavish share of awards. He is aware and now aims to avoid mistakes in reaching goals ahead. He had to fire an agent who made absurd demands and squandered all the cash on large purchases. He was a fraud and a hoax.

Figure 46.5 Scenario for Document 46.6

> You work for a company, Keith Banks & Associates. The company provides consulting services on employee success, called Employee Empowerment, to clients in many locations in the Midwest. Clients in St. Louis, Memphis, Cincinnati, and Indianapolis are having problems implementing the Employee Empowerment program and you feel that it is important that you visit these clients. You decide to write a memo to your company president, Mr. Keith Banks. In the memo, you will state the reason for the trip, outline the details of the trip itinerary, and indicate what you hope to accomplish on the trip.

Reinforcing Writing Skills

Tables are ideal for presenting numerical data or related items in a compact, easy-to-comprehend way. In the following document activity you will write a memo describing a trip you are about to embark on and include some details in a table.

Document 46.6

Creating a Table in a Memo

1 Navigate to the Document 46.6 launch page in the Online Lab and then click the Launch Activity button. The Online Lab will open **Doc046.06** in the activity window.

2 Review the scenario outlined in Figure 46.5. Using the information provided in the scenario, compose a three-paragraph memo consisting of the following information:

   a In the first paragraph, explain the reason for the trip.

   b In the second paragraph, outline the itinerary, which is two days in St. Louis, one day in Memphis, three days in Cincinnati, and one day in Indianapolis.

   c Following the second paragraph, insert a table that includes the names of the companies you will visit, the city in which they are located, the number of days you will be on-site, the number of employees at each company (choose numbers between 10 and 90), and the annual fee your company receives from each client (create numbers between $10,000 and $50,000). (Invent simple names for the client companies.)

   d In the third paragraph, indicate what you hope to accomplish on the trip.

3 Format the table so that the overall appearance is pleasing and the information is easy to read and interpret.

4 Proofread and correct any errors in the document.

5 Save the document.

6 Click the Upload button to upload the document for instructor review.

Ending the Session

The Online Lab automatically saves the work you completed for this session. You may continue with the next session or exit the Online Lab and continue later.

B Key Timings and Practice

Exercise 31.3 Complete Timing 31.3 by keying the following timing text. Continue to reinforce your proficiency with the B key by completing the drill lines in Exercise 31.3 in the Online Lab. Finally, complete Timing 31.4 using the same paragraph of text used in Timing 31.3.

Timings 31.3–31.4   While the 15 boys scrambled about, Barb baked a big batch of bars. The bleak cabin needed a good scrubbing. She had been able to buy a bulb for the amber lamp. The bright and probing beam chased the gloom away. A cheery robin sitting on a limb called to other birds. The tasty leg of lamb and herb dressing would soon be ready. The slight haze of that day made the family feel an abounding sense of peace. Soon they would climb aboard the boat and return to urban life. Barb prepared a blog about her experiences to share with her friends.

C Key Timings and Practice

Exercise 31.4 Complete Timing 31.5 by keying the following timing text. Continue to reinforce your proficiency with the C key by completing the drill lines in Exercise 31.4 in the Online Lab. Finally, complete Timing 31.6 using the same paragraph of text used in Timing 31.5.

Timings 31.5–31.6   The chief and the 14 crew members did concur. That ocean cruiser could be launched at once. It was a fact: The cursed, cruel pirates had discovered their recent acquisition of sacks of gold coins. As the panic arose, the excited crew scanned a curving cedar grove along the coast. Those ancient cypress boards crackled as the excess load caused the boat to crawl and cease almost all movement. The acute crisis excluded a quick chance at a complete escape.

D Key Timings and Practice

Exercise 31.5 Complete Timing 31.7 by keying the following timing text. Continue to reinforce your proficiency with the D key by completing the drill lines in Exercise 31.5 in the Online Lab. Finally, complete Timing 31.8 using the same paragraph of text used in Timing 31.7.

Timings 31.7–31.8   Even the steadfast must agree that some birthdays are dandy with abundant kindness and others seem to be dark and dull. Adults have undue qualms when adjusting to becoming 40 and older; a child stampedes through the days with wild abandonment. No doubt a small child full of daring and dynamic energy deals with life in a candid way. All the bedlam and wild dashing dispel any dim attitudes of dour adults. To avoid adverse thoughts on birthdays, spend them with children.

Document **Using AutoFit and Setting the Row Height in a Table**

46.4

1   Navigate to the Document 46.4 launch page in the Online Lab and then click the Launch Activity button. The Online Lab will open **Doc046.04** in the activity window.

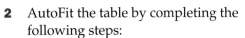

2   AutoFit the table by completing the following steps:

   a   With the insertion point in cell A1, click the Table Tools Layout tab.

   b   Click the AutoFit button in the Cell Size group.

   c   Click *AutoFit Contents*.

3   Change the height of the first row in the table to 0.4 inch by clicking the up arrow beside the *Table Row Height* measurement box in the Cell Size group until it displays as *0.4* inch.

4   Save the document.

5   Click the Check button to upload the document for checking. The Online Lab will report the number of errors for the activity.

6   If errors are reported, view the results document, correct the errors in the submitted document, save the document, and then click the Check button.

Document **Adjusting and Distributing Column Widths in a Table**

46.5

1   Navigate to the Document 46.5 launch page in the Online Lab and then click the Launch Activity button. The Online Lab will open **Doc046.05** in the activity window.

2   AutoFit the last column of the table by placing the mouse pointer over the right column border of column C and double-clicking.

3   Distribute the widths of the *City* and *State* columns evenly between the two columns by completing the following steps:

   a   Select the *City* and *State* columns.

   b   Click the Table Tools Layout tab.

   c   Click the Distribute Columns button in the Cell Size group.

4   Save the document.

5   Click the Check button to upload the document for checking. The Online Lab will report the number of errors for the activity.

6   If errors are reported, view the results document, correct the errors in the submitted document, save the document, and then click the Check button.

E Key Timings and Practice

Exercise 31.6 Complete Timing 31.9 by keying the following timing text. Continue to reinforce your proficiency with the E key by completing the drill lines in Exercise 31.6 in the Online Lab. Finally, complete Timing 31.10 using the same paragraph of text used in Timing 31.9.

Timings 31.9–31.10

That eccentric thief scares me. He swears that he did not steal the wealthy lady's 11 rings. He is either embarking on an evil route of crime, or else he is a cheap cheat. At best, he knows how to affect an illegal entry. Each of his creeping moves suggests a false value. He prizes money and exerts extra effort to obtain it. In any event, it appears that he has the stolen jewelry. He is edgy and tired. His tale may change soon.

F Key Timings and Practice

Exercise 31.7 Complete Timing 31.11 by keying the following timing text. Continue to reinforce your proficiency with the F key by completing the drill lines in Exercise 31.7 in the Online Lab. Finally, complete Timing 31.12 using the same paragraph of text used in Timing 31.11.

Timings 31.11–31.12

Often, before we face all the facts, our own fears may begin to defeat us. Life seems filled with deep strife and failures. We become inflamed at ourselves and fuss in 50 futile ways. This is the time to stop fretting and inflate our egos with a firm, fresh start. One thing you might do is to start a Facebook page to find new friends. Swiftly, our spirits are lifted. We have a fine feeling of being free from cares or defeat.

G Key Timings and Practice

Exercise 31.8 Complete Timing 31.13 by keying the following timing text. Continue to reinforce your proficiency with the G key by completing the drill lines in Exercise 31.8 in the Online Lab. Finally, complete Timing 31.14 using the same paragraph of text used in Timing 31.13.

Timings 31.13–31.14

The boy is going to grab a bag of hamburgers after the game. That last game was grim. The team's energy ought to be higher, for the rough, gripping coughs are gone. The last germs have given way to good health through better hygiene. It is our guess that the girls will get 15 goals. Those grounds are genuinely great. The eight dingy lights, which were illegal, glow brighter. When the gala bash is in full swing, the manager will give the guests a grand gift.

    f   Click in a cell in the *Hawaii* row.

    g   Click the Select button in the Table group.

    h   Click the *Select Row* option.

    i   Press Ctrl + V.

3   Cut the *State* column and paste it between the *Capital* and the *State Abbreviation* columns by completing the following steps:

    a   Select the *State* column.

    b   Press Ctrl + X.

    c   Select the *State Abbreviation* column.

    d   Press Ctrl + V.

4   Cut the contents of the New Mexico ZIP code and paste it into the ZIP code cell for South Dakota.

5   Key 87501 in the ZIP code cell for New Mexico.

6   Save the document.

7   Click the Check button to upload the document for checking. The Online Lab will report the number of errors for the activity.

8   If errors are reported, view the results document, correct the errors in the submitted document, save the document, and then click the Check button.

Changing Column Width and Row Height

When you create a table using the Table button in the Tables group on the Insert tab, all columns are of equal width (they are equally distributed) and all rows are likewise of equal height. The Cell Size group on the Table Tools Layout tab provides several tools for adjusting the height or width of a row or column in a table (see Figure 46.4).

Figure 46.4 Cell Size Group on the Table Tools Layout Tab

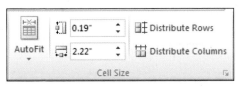

After keying text into the inserted table, place the insertion point in one of the cells in the table, click the AutoFit button in the Cell Size group on the Table Tools Layout tab, and then click the *AutoFit Contents* option. This action will automatically adjust the column widths based on the size of the contents of each column. You can also apply AutoFit to the width of an individual column by moving the mouse pointer over the right gridline of a column until it turns into a left and right arrow with a vertical double line between and then double-clicking.

To return the table to fill the space or window available on the page, click the AutoFit button and then click *AutoFit Window*.

If you want to distribute space evenly between more than one row or one column, select the rows or columns and then click either the Distribute Rows button or the Distribute Columns button in the Cell Size group.

To set a specific row height or column width, use the *Table Row Height* and *Table Column Width* measurement boxes in the Cell Size group on the Table Tools Layout tab. With the insertion point in the desired row or column, adjust the number in the measurement box by clicking the up or down arrows or select the number and key the desired measurement.

Practice using these features by following the steps outlined for Documents 46.4 and 46.5.

H Key Timings and Practice

Exercise 31.9 Complete Timing 31.15 by keying the following timing text. Continue to reinforce your proficiency with the H key by completing the drill lines in Exercise 31.9 in the Online Lab. Finally, complete Timing 31.16 using the same paragraph of text used in Timing 31.15.

Timings 31.15–31.16 Those happy chaps hope to hike to the south shore. It is 72 miles from their homes. If harsh weather hinders them, each has a small, tight tent. When they are en route, the head chef can prepare wholesome meals. Breakfast might be ham and eggs or hotcakes. A hearty lunch of milk, fresh fruit, and sandwiches will be eaten in haste. The plans for night meals include hash, mashed chickpeas, and other delights. They are healthy and hearty. The whole group may catch fresh fish.

I Key Timings and Practice

Exercise 31.10 Complete Timing 31.17 by keying the following timing text. Continue to reinforce your proficiency with the I key by completing the drill lines in Exercise 31.10 in the Online Lab. Finally, complete Timing 31.18 using the same paragraph of text used in Timing 31.17.

Timings 31.17–31.18 That stadium by the river isn't immune to crime. Last night a thief seized 18 expensive DVD videos from a taxi driver, who was picking up a rider. The thief ditched the videos in the river. A diver fished them out quickly. The weird irony is that the thief is out of jail on bail. It's likely that he bribed an ignorant civil aide. In spite of this, he has been identified. His alibi is nullified. Irate voices are being raised to swiftly close the issue.

Ergonomic Tip
Use wrist pads to help keep your wrists in a neutral position and support your forearms on the desk when using a mouse.

Ending the Session

The Online Lab automatically saves the work you completed for this session. You can continue with the next session or exit the Online Lab and continue later.

Selecting Cells, Columns, and Rows

To select a cell, a column, a row, or an entire table, use the Select button in the Table group on the Table Tools Layout tab. If you want to select a row, place the insertion point in any cell in that row, click the Select button in the Table group, and then click *Select Row*. If you want to select a column in the table, place the insertion point in any cell in that column, click the Select button, and then click *Select Column*. The selections are cumulative, so if you click *Select Column* without first deselecting a table row, you will end up selecting the entire table.

You can also use the mouse pointer to select columns, cells, and rows in a table. To select a column, position the mouse pointer at the top of the column you want to select until the pointer becomes a down-pointing arrow and then click. Select adjacent columns by pointing at the top of the first column, holding down the mouse button, dragging the mouse pointer over the last column, and then releasing the mouse button. To select nonadjacent columns, hold down the Ctrl key while selecting columns.

To select a cell, place the mouse pointer along the left edge of the cell until the mouse pointer becomes an arrow pointing up and to the right and then click. To select nonadjacent cells, hold down the Ctrl key while selecting the cells. Select adjacent cells by positioning the mouse pointer in the first cell to be selected, holding down the mouse button, dragging the mouse pointer over the last cell to be selected, and then releasing the mouse button.

To select a row using the mouse pointer, place the mouse pointer along the left edge of any cell in the row until the mouse pointer becomes an arrow pointing up and to the right and then double-click.

Cutting and Pasting Row, Column, and Cell Contents

After selecting a row or column, it is possible to cut or copy and paste selected content using keyboard shortcuts. For example, you can move a row to another position in a table by selecting it, cutting it using the keyboard shortcut Ctrl + X, selecting the row directly below where you want the cut row to be pasted, and then pressing Ctrl + V. The cut row will appear above the selected row. Similarly, after selecting and cutting a column from a table, select the column directly to the right of where you want the cut column to be pasted and then press Ctrl + V. The cut column will appear to the left of the selected column.

Selecting a cell in a table will select the cell contents, not the cell itself. You can select and cut the contents of one cell and paste it into another cell. When you cut the contents of a cell and paste it into another cell, the source cell will be empty and the pasted contents will replace the contents in the destination cell.

Document 46.3 Cutting and Pasting in a Table

1 Navigate to the Document 46.3 launch page in the Online Lab and then click the Launch Activity button. The Online Lab will open **Doc046.03** in the activity window.

2 Cut the *New Mexico* row and paste it between the *California* row and the *Hawaii* row by completing the following steps:

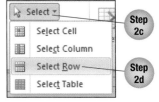

   a   Click in a cell in the *New Mexico* row.

   b   Click the Table Tools Layout tab.

   c   Click the Select button in the Table group.

   d   Click the *Select Row* option.

   e   Press Ctrl + X.

steps continue

Skillbuilding: Letters J–R

Session Objectives

- Review proper finger placement for letters J–R, numbers, and punctuation keys
- Improve keying speed and accuracy

Timing Goals

- 1 minute: 30 WAM and two or fewer errors

Getting Started and Warming Up

Exercise 32.1 If you are continuing immediately from Session 31, you can skip the Exercise 32.1 warm-up drill. However, if you exited the Online Lab at the end of Session 31, warm up by completing Exercise 32.1.

Reinforcing Your Skills

All timings and exercises for this session focus on a different letter of the alphabet. For each letter, first begin by taking a 1-minute timing. If you attain a rate of 30 WAM with two or fewer errors, push for speed in the next activities. If you commit more than two errors in the timing, focus on accuracy. Second, complete the exercise that focuses on that letter. Finally, take the timing for a second time. Evaluate your results. If, for a particular letter, you are not keying at least 30 WAM with two or fewer errors, return to the Online Lab session for that letter and repeat the appropriate drills. All timing results are stored in your Timing Performance report.

J Key Timings and Practice

Exercise 32.2 Complete Timing 32.1 by keying the following timing text. Continue to reinforce your proficiency with the J key by completing the drill lines in Exercise 32.2 in the Online Lab. Finally, complete Timing 32.2 using the same paragraph of text used in Timing 32.1.

1-Minute Timings

Timings 32.1–32.2

The object of the jury is to judge that subject and to be just. The adjacent jail adjoins the courtroom. A jaunt to the jail is not enjoyable. The judge's job is to remain judicious when the final judgment must be made. All 12 jurors must be adults; juveniles are not allowed on the jury. The jokers who jeer and jest will be ejected. Adjournment will take place after the judicial question has been resolved.

Document

Deleting a Table and Deleting Rows and Columns in a Table

46.2

1   Read all instructions for this document activity, navigate to the Document 46.2 launch page in the Online Lab, and then click the Launch Activity button. The Online Lab will open **Doc046.02** in the activity window. The timer will start as soon as you begin keying the document.

2   Delete the second table in the document by completing the following steps:

   a   Click in any cell in the second table.

   b   Click the Table Tools Layout tab.

   c   Click the Delete button in the Rows & Columns group.

   d   Click the *Delete Table* option.

3   Key the text shown in Figure 46.3 in the table. The last row has already been keyed.

4   Proofread and correct any errors in the table.

5   Delete the last row of the table by completing the following steps:

   a   Click in any cell in the last row of the table.

   b   Click the Table Tools Layout tab.

   c   Click the Delete button in the Rows & Columns group.

   d   Click the *Delete Rows* option.

6   Delete the second column of the table by completing the following steps:

   a   Click in any cell in the second column of the table, column B.

   b   Click the Table Tools Layout tab.

   c   Click the Delete button in the Rows & Columns group.

   d   Click the *Delete Columns* option.

7   Save the document.

8   Click the Check button to stop the timer and upload the document for checking. The Online Lab will report the WAM rate and number of errors for the activity.

9   If errors are reported, view the results document, correct the errors in the submitted document, save the document, and then click the Check button.

Figure 46.3 Table Content for Document 46.2

Age	$100,000	$250,000	$500,000	$1,000,000
30	$7	$9	$13	$20
35	$7	$9	$13	$21
40	$8	$11	$17	$28
45	$10	$16	$27	$45
50	$13	$21	$37	$67
55	$18	$31	$56	$102
60	$24	$43	$80	$153

K Key Timings and Practice

Exercise 32.3 Complete Timing 32.3 by keying the following timing text. Continue to reinforce your proficiency with the K key by completing the drill lines in Exercise 32.3 in the Online Lab. Finally, complete Timing 32.4 using the same paragraph of text used in Timing 32.3.

Timings 32.3–32.4 That old worker knows his work is risky. His kind of weakness is in his knees. He checks the skyline stockpiles from an airplane cockpit. It is awkward to go backwards or clockwise and keep a keen eye out for cracking walls. When he has checked the skyline, he has breakfast. His business is on the edge of bankruptcy. He needs a workable new plan for a husky bankroll. He hopes he will hit a $100,000 jackpot soon.

L Key Timings and Practice

Exercise 32.4 Complete Timing 32.5 by keying the following timing text. Continue to reinforce your proficiency with the L key by completing the drill lines in Exercise 32.4 in the Online Lab. Finally, complete Timing 32.8 using the same paragraph of text used in Timing 32.5.

Timings 32.5–32.6 Long ago, pilgrims loved to indulge in blunt folklore. Tales, sometimes false, were told with glee daily. One old tale included a blazing clash of 94 sailors in balky sailboats on a bottomless lake. The last sailor alive was a lad who was blind. As he lay clinging to a slim balsa log in filth and slimy silt, the leader's falcon led help to him. Balmy days followed as the lad's leg healed slowly and the salves applied to his eyes let the light in.

M Key Timings and Practice

Exercise 32.5 Complete Timing 32.7 by keying the following timing text. Continue to reinforce your proficiency with the M key by completing the drill lines in Exercise 32.5 in the Online Lab. Finally, complete Timing 32.8 using the same paragraph of text used in Timing 32.7.

Timings 32.7–32.8 The merger of an academy and the campus may take place in the autumn. It might bring mixed emotions from the 2,000 men and women. The stormy economic issue might make an anatomy class impossible at the academy. Some who must commute for months are not amused; many think that the merger is clumsy and dumb. There is not much warmth among the enemies. The teamwork is not smooth. The amount of stormy mass meetings must be diminished. An amendment must be made.

    c   Key Minnesota, St. Paul, Montana, and Helena in the proper cells of the two new rows. (The states will be in alphabetical order.)

5   Click in the cell that contains *New Mexico* and insert two new rows below the last row. Type **South Dakota, Pierre, Washington,** and **Olympia** in the proper cells of the two new rows.

6   Insert a new column in the table by completing the following steps:

    a   Click in any cell in the second column, column B.

    b   Click the Insert Right button in the Rows & Columns group.

    c   Key the following text in the cells, starting with cell C1: 85001, 94203, 96813, 66603, 55101, 59601, 87501, 57501, and 98501. *Hint: Use the Down Arrow instead of the Tab key to move to the next cell.*

7   Insert a new third column in the table by completing the following steps:

    a   Click in any cell in the third column, column C.

    b   Click the Insert Left button in the Rows & Columns group.

    c   Key the following text in the cells, starting with cell C1: **AZ, CA, HI, KS, MN, MT, NM, SD,** and **WA** in the proper cells of the new column.

8   Insert a new first row by completing the following steps:

    a   Click in any cell in the first row.

    b   Click the Insert Above button in the Rows & Columns group.

    c   With the cells in the new first row selected, click the Merge Cells button in the Merge group.

    d   Type **STATE CAPITALS** in the merged cell. *Note: Key the words in all capital letters.*

9   Proofread and correct any errors in the table.

10   Save the document.

11   Click the Check button to stop the timer and upload the document for checking. The Online Lab will report the WAM rate and number of errors for the activity.

12   If errors are reported, view the results document, correct the errors in the submitted document, save the document, and then click the Check button.

Figure 46.2 Table Content for Document 46.1

Arizona	Phoenix
Hawaii	Honolulu
Kansas	Topeka
New Mexico	Santa Fe

N Key Timings and Practice

Exercise 32.6
Complete Timing 32.9 by keying the following timing text. Continue to reinforce your proficiency with the N key by completing the drill lines in Exercise 32.6 in the Online Lab. Finally, complete Timing 32.10 using the same paragraph of text used in Timing 32.9.

Timings 32.9–32.10
At sunset, around 8:30 p.m., it is nice to enjoy dining out on the bank of a pond. Unless uninvited insects and swarms of ants invade the picnic, you will certainly unwind. As those soft night sounds enfold you, frenzied inward nerves and the decisions that haunt you drain from your mind. You may enjoy napping on a nearby bench. Next, swing into action after your rest and inhale much air into your lungs. Unpack the nice lunch and munch away. Don't deny yourself this experience.

O Key Timings and Practice

Exercise 32.7
Complete Timing 32.11 by keying the following timing text. Continue to reinforce your proficiency with the O key by completing the drill lines in Exercise 32.7 in the Online Lab. Finally, complete Timing 32.12 using the same paragraph of text used in Timing 32.11.

Timings 32.11–32.12
An old-time cowboy often chose a lonely life out on the open range. Hoards of prowling foxes snooped among the 25 old cows and their young ones. Owls often hooted as an obscure and occasional sound annoyed them. The food was often cold and soggy. Cooking his food and boiling his coffee over an orange-hot fire offered some enjoyment, however. Through a long night his mournful songs poured out. He was a proven, loyal worker who overcame obstacles or coped with problems.

P Key Timings and Practice

Exercise 32.8
Complete Timing 32.13 by keying the following timing text. Continue to reinforce your proficiency with the P key by completing the drill lines in Exercise 32.8 in the Online Lab. Finally, complete Timing 32.14 using the same paragraph of text used in Timing 32.13.

Timings 32.13–32.14
If the plan for upgrading the park in the spring would be accepted, the plot could be plowed now. Adept employees can plant the 225 maple and pine trees by the pond with the new equipment. Those sprigs of spindly aspens should be pulled up or snipped off. Most spaces for pleasant picnics should be paved, as well as the paths to the ponds. The chipmunks and other park pets won't be upset and peevish if the plans are to plant all spots with pleasant posies.

Ergonomic Tip

Maintain the natural "S" curve of your spine when you are seated. Sit up straight so that the back rest of your chair fits the small of your back. This posture helps minimize backaches.

Using the Table Tools Layout Tab

When the insertion point is in any cell in a table, the Table Tools Design and Table Tools Layout tabs are available. These contextual tabs include additional formatting features that help you design and lay out your tables. In this session, you will learn to use features in the Table, Rows & Columns, Merge, and Cell Size groups on the Table Tools Layout tab (see Figure 46.1).

Figure 46.1 Table Tools Layout Tab

Changing the Layout of a Table

Insert or delete rows or columns in a table by clicking the Table Tools Layout tab and then clicking the appropriate button in the Rows & Columns group. Before clicking one of these buttons, make sure the insertion point is in the correct position in the table. Click the Delete button to display options to delete a cell, a column, or a row in a table, or to delete the entire table.

To merge two or more adjacent cells, select the cells and then click the Merge Cells button in the Merge group. To split a cell, place the insertion point in the cell that you want to split and then click the Split Cells button in the Merge group to open the Split Cells dialog box. At this dialog box, indicate how many columns or rows you want the cell to be split into and then click OK.

Document 46.1

Inserting Rows and Columns and Merging Cells in a Table

1 Read all instructions for this document activity, navigate to the Document 46.1 launch page in the Online Lab, and then click the Launch Activity button. The Online Lab will open **Doc046.01** in the activity window. The timer will start as soon as you begin keying the document.

2 Create a two-column by four-row table and then key the text as shown in Figure 46.2. *Note: Do not resize the column widths*.

3 Add a new row above *Hawaii* by completing the following steps:

   a Click in the cell containing *Hawaii*.

   b Click the Table Tools Layout tab.

   c Click the Insert Above button in the Rows & Columns group.

   d Key **California** in the new A2 cell and key **Sacramento** in the new B2 cell.

4 Add two new rows above the last row of the table by completing the following steps:

   a Click in a cell in the last row of the table.

   b Click the Insert Above button in the Rows & Columns group two times.

steps continue

Q Key Timings and Practice

Exercise 32.9
Complete Timing 32.15 by keying the following timing text. Continue to reinforce your proficiency with the Q key by completing the drill lines in Exercise 32.9 in the Online Lab. Finally, complete Timing 32.16 using the same paragraph of text used in Timing 32.15.

Timings 32.15–32.16
At the request of an old acquaintance from the equator city, quotations for equipment will be sent quickly. Those earthquakes ruined her unique antique aquariums. The 13 techniques of restoring them require liquid lacquer and the equipment in question. Answer her inquiry and quote a good price to her. Ask her to reply quickly as to the quantity. The question of her delinquent account must be settled when the equipment is ordered.

R Key Timings and Practice

Exercise 32.10
Complete Timing 32.17 by keying the following timing text. Continue to reinforce your proficiency with the R key by completing the drill lines in Exercise 32.10 in the Online Lab. Finally, complete Timing 32.18 using the same paragraph of text used in Timing 32.17.

Timings 32.17–32.18
A rapid rise in industrial prices is normally absorbed by the consumers. Large firms that need raw materials work hard to realize a profit. It is a marvel that the poor and weary customer can afford to purchase services or products that have increased 15 percent. The grim race to raise prices must be curbed early. Scores of workers who earn small salaries find no mirth in fierce, sharp rises in the market. The rows and rows of bright and sparkling products are a farce to all concerned consumers.

Ergonomic Tip
Place your monitor at a right angle (perpendicular) to a window to reduce glare on your monitor and sun in your eyes.

Ending the Session

The Online Lab automatically saves the work you completed for this session. You can continue with the next session or exit the Online Lab and continue later.

Complete two 5-minute timings on the timing text below. Timings 46.3 and 46.4 use the same paragraphs.

Goals: 30 WAM and ten or fewer errors
SI: 1.44 syllables per word

Timings 46.3–46.4

Wise managers of money seem to have the ability or the foresight to make their money stretch a long way. Others spend haphazardly and always seem to be short of money long before the next salary check is due. What factors do the wise managers follow?

Food buying takes a large part of the salary check. In the area of buying groceries, one can save a large amount of money by wise and careful buying. There are many fine guides that a shopper can follow to economize and save money.

Probably the one best rule to attempt, at the outset, is to plan ahead. Plan all your meals in detail for a certain period, for example, a week or a month, but never day by day. After making the complete plan for your groceries, you are then ready to prepare your shopping list. Be sure that you have included all of the items required for cooking the meals to come. Many people forget to include the small items such as salt, pepper, and needed condiments. Once you have made a list, additional guides are very useful and helpful.

After making the major shopping list, you should compare prices. You should look at all the local advertisements in newspapers. Quite often, you will save considerable amounts of your money by comparison shopping. However, do not waste time or money for gas by driving your car from store to store. If you do this, you are defeating your purpose. After deciding where to do your shopping, your next step is that of doing the actual shopping.

An unhealthy and potentially expensive time to shop for food is when your stomach is growling. If you are hungry, there is a greater chance that you will purchase foods that you don't really need. Or you may acquire foods that are not in your financial plan. For example, when you are hungry, you might purchase premade chicken or seafood salads. These are expensive and loaded with saturated fats and cholesterol. Another reason not to shop while you are hungry is that your growling stomach may convince you to shorten the time in the store and to skip some foods that you need. If you don't have these foods available at home, you may end up taking the family out to dinner.

Skillbuilding: Letters S–Z

Session Objectives

- Review proper finger placement for letters S–Z, numeric keys, and punctuation keys
- Improve keying speed and accuracy

Timing Goals

- 1 minute: 30 WAM and two or fewer errors

Getting Started and Warming Up

Exercise 33.1 If you are continuing immediately from Session 32, you can skip the Exercise 33.1 warm-up drill. However, if you exited the Online Lab at the end of Session 32, warm up by completing Exercise 33.1.

↻ Reinforcing Your Skills

All timings and exercises for this session focus on a different letter of the alphabet. For each letter, first begin by taking a 1-minute timing. If you attain a rate of 30 WAM with two or fewer errors, push for speed in the next activities. If you commit more than two errors in the timing, focus on accuracy. Second, complete the exercise that focuses on that letter. Finally, take the timing for a second time. Evaluate your results. If, for a particular letter, you are not keying at least 30 WAM with two or fewer errors, return to the Online Lab session for that letter and repeat the appropriate drills. All timing results are stored in your Timing Performance report.

S Key Timings and Practice

Exercise 33.2 Complete Timing 33.1 by keying the following timing text. Continue to reinforce your proficiency with the S key by completing the drill lines in Exercise 33.2 in the Online Lab. Finally, complete Timing 33.2 using the same paragraph of text used in Timing 33.1.

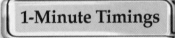

1-Minute Timings

Timings 33.1–33.2

The 14 sulky, sad losers are scorned by most of us. A dismal loss or misfortune doesn't have to end in disgrace. Surely most folks in such spots show disgust at a loss. But those persons briskly squelch those feelings and smile because life goes on. There is always a lesson to be learned from every mistake or loss. Stay in the driver's seat and see all the good things that come along. Solving basic problems easily is necessary to reduce tensions.

Modifying the Layout of Tables

Session Objectives

- Insert and delete table rows and columns
- Delete a table
- Merge and split cells
- Select cells, rows, columns, and tables
- Cut and paste row, column, and cell contents
- Change column width and height
- Format a table for improved readability
- Include a table in a memo

Timing Goals

- 1 minute: 40 WAM and two or fewer errors
- 5 minutes: 30 WAM and ten or fewer errors

Getting Started and Warming Up

Exercise 46.1 If you are continuing immediately from Session 45, you may skip the Exercise 46.1 warm-up drill. However, if you exited the Online Lab at the end of Session 45, warm up by completing Exercise 46.1.

Exercise 46.2 Begin your session work by completing Exercise 46.2, a timed short drill, in the Online Lab.

Assessing Your Speed and Accuracy

Complete Timings 46.1 through 46.4 in the Online Lab. At the end of each timing, the Online Lab will display your WAM rate and any errors. Results will be saved in your Timings Performance report. If you have been surpassing the speed and accuracy goals, set slightly more challenging personal goals and strive to exceed them.

Complete two 1-minute timings on the timing text below. Timings 46.1 and 46.2 use the same paragraph.

Goals: 40 WAM and two or fewer errors
SI: 1.51 syllables per word

> **1-Minute Timings**

Timings 46.1–46.2 To honor a deserving person in the community is a fine thing. A most interesting factor becomes apparent many times in the ugly form of jealousy for another's accomplishments. Most people can accept a high honor quite well (that is, if they were the ones to win). Those people who did not win may begin to hold a grudge against anyone who was a winner. Honors and awards must be given and accepted with a generous, happy spirit.

T Key Timings and Practice

Exercise 33.3 Complete Timing 33.3 by keying the following timing text. Continue to reinforce your proficiency with the T key by completing the drill lines in Exercise 33.3 in the Online Lab. Finally, complete Timing 33.4 using the same paragraph of text used in Timing 33.3.

Timings 33.3–33.4
Tenseness while keying causes costly mistakes. Take a gentle tip or two and practice them as you key. Watch out for fatigue: A tired receptionist tends to clutch at the 8 home row keys and doesn't tap them with a gentle touch. Twirling or twisting in your seat is a typical trick at the computer. Talking a lot as you key is first on the list of bad techniques. Do not try too hard, as this often turns those keys into something frustrating. Also, don't overlook Twitter as a potential supporter of your needs. Don't let the keyboarding mistakes continue.

U Key Timings and Practice

Exercise 33.4 Complete Timing 33.5 by keying the following timing text. Continue to reinforce your proficiency with the U key by completing the drill lines in Exercise 33.3 in the Online Lab. Finally, complete Timing 33.6 using the same paragraph of text used in Timing 33.5.

Timings 33.5–33.6
The impulse to judge individuals quickly causes faulty results. It is unwise and unfair to jump to conclusions in a hurry. Actually, a useful guide to a sound understanding of humans is to quietly assess the situation. A subtle and thorough query can subdue doubts and evaluate behavior. An ugly and cruel deduction about another's values could cause undue suffering. You are urged to utilize more time (even if it's only 15 to 20 minutes) if you are puzzled and used to useless, quick guesses.

V Key Timings and Practice

Exercise 33.5 Complete Timing 33.7 by keying the following timing text. Continue to reinforce your proficiency with the V key by completing the drill lines in Exercise 33.5 in the Online Lab. Finally, complete Timing 33.8 using the same paragraph of text used in Timing 33.7.

Timings 33.7–33.8
A visit to a village in a quiet valley gives vitality, vim, and vigor to the 46 tired individuals. The global positioning system proved to be very helpful. Nothing rivals the vacation voyage to revive the spirits. Heavy problems seem to vanish and vexing tribulations evaporate. Vivid visions of a diverse way of living evoke valuable impressive vistas of rest. Save those fevered nerves and prevent grievous or adverse tribulations. Endeavor to take advantage of events that elevate the spirits; you deserve the very best.

Reinforcing Writing Skills

Line, bar, and pie graphs provide a visual image of relationships that exist between sets of data. Graphs provide the reader with a picture of what is taking place. Tables, on the other hand, provide details that are not always evident in graphs because the reader sees the actual alphabetic or numeric values. A table can be used effectively where a series of items are compared. For example, assume that a group of individuals were being compared by age, sex, height, weight, and shoe size. A table can effectively display the information for each individual.

A table can be used to reinforce information that appears in text where conclusions have been made. The table, which is preceded by some type of introduction, can be followed with text that contains the conclusions drawn. The reader can refer to the table to verify the conclusion.

Document 45.4

Composing a Document with a Table

1 Navigate to the Document 45.4 launch page in the Online Lab and then click the Launch Activity button. The Online Lab will open **Doc045.04** in the activity window.

2 In the document, create a table that lists three jobs you might like. In the table, include information about location, salary, education requirements, skills, and responsibilities for each of the jobs. (If you don't know the actual details, make a realistic guess.)

3 Below the table, include a statement or conclusion about the data shown in the table.

4 Proofread and correct any errors in the document.

5 Save the document.

6 Click the Upload button to upload the document for instructor review.

Ending the Session

The Online Lab automatically saves the work you completed for this session. You may continue with the next session or exit the Online Lab and continue later.

W Key Timings and Practice

Exercise 33.6 Complete Timing 33.9 by keying the following timing text. Continue to reinforce your proficiency with the W key by completing the drill lines in Exercise 33.6 in the Online Lab. Finally, complete Timing 33.10 using the same paragraph of text used in Timing 33.9.

Timings 33.9–33.10

The news on the network newscast might spawn a winning wealth of followers. If the newscaster can draw a wider range of viewers, the rewards are power and wealth. Watchers and followers of a witty new reporter are won when the daily news is written well. It is not a waste to rewrite the worst of interviews when 18 witless words can wreck a well-planned show or review. Workers who dawdle in the newsroom will not work or write very long. Their award will be awful reviews.

X Key Timings and Practice

Exercise 33.7 Complete Timing 33.11 by keying the following timing text. Continue to reinforce your proficiency with the X key by completing the drill lines in Exercise 33.7 in the Online Lab. Finally, complete Timing 33.12 using the same paragraph of text used in Timing 33.11.

Timings 33.11–33.12

An example of a tedious exercise is the flexing of lax muscles daily. Excess anxieties are exhausting to all who are under extreme pressure. A program of extensive, complex exercises is a vexation. Most experts agree that exertion to exhaustion is wrong. A flexible, yet exuberant exercise involves exhaling noxious air and inhaling oxygen. Explore the exotic experience of a brisk 30-minute daily walk. One way to pass the time is to text message friends and business associates. That expended energy will excite you and extend your life.

Y Key Timings and Practice

Exercise 33.8 Complete Timing 33.13 by keying the following timing text. Continue to reinforce your proficiency with the Y key by completing the drill lines in Exercise 33.8 in the Online Lab. Finally, complete Timing 33.14 using the same paragraph of text used in Timing 33.13.

Timings 33.13–33.14

A hobby is healthy for nearly everyone. A typical and unhealthy symptom of an extremely busy employer is anxiety. You may enjoy skydiving or flying as an activity. Yet, you might fill joyful and happy days by playing the rhythm of a song on a piano keyboard with its 88 keys. Analyze your daydreams and style your life to trying entirely new ways of living. I usually have enjoyed a foray into the dynamic joy of geology as a hobby. In addition, you may find a variety of interesting information on YouTube. Prying through mystical layers of dirt is always fun.

6 Proofread and correct any errors in the document.

7 Save the document.

8 Click the Check button to stop the timer and upload the document for checking. The Online Lab will report the WAM rate and number of errors for the activity.

9 If errors are reported, view the results document, correct the errors in the submitted document, save the document, and then click the Check button.

Figure 45.5 Table Content for Document 45.2

Josephine Coughlin	894617	Product Planning
William Gaylord	894552	Financial Services
Rosaline Colorossi	863791	Human Resources
Brittany Davies-Penland	943882	Human Resources
Evan Schneider	999341	Financial Services
Alicia Robinette	760384	Human Resources

Document 45.3

Creating a Table Using a Quick Tables Template

1 Read all instructions for this document activity, navigate to the Document 45.3 launch page in the Online Lab, and then click the Launch Activity button. The Online Lab will open **Doc045.03** in the activity window. The timer will start as soon as you begin keying the document.

2 Insert a two-column list table using the *Quick Tables* option from the Table button drop-down menu by completing the following steps:

  a Click the Insert tab.

  b Click the Table button in the Tables group.

  c Point to *Quick Tables* to display the drop-down menu, scroll down the menu, and then click *Tabular List*.

3 Replace the text in the inserted table with the text shown in Figure 45.6 by completing the following steps:

  a Double-click the text in cell A2, *Books*, to select the text and then key **Cantaloupes**. When you begin to key, the selected text is deleted automatically.

  b Press the Tab key to select the number *1* in cell B2 and then key **3**.

  c Continue pressing the Tab key to move to the next cell select existing text in that cell and then key the new text.

4 Proofread and correct any errors in the document.

5 Save the document.

6 Click the Check button to stop the timer and upload the document for checking. The Online Lab will report the WAM rate and number of errors for the activity.

7 If errors are reported, view the results document, correct the errors in the submitted document, save the document, and then click the Check button.

Figure 45.6 Table Content for Document 45.3

ITEM	NEEDED
Cantaloupes	3
Tangerines	2
Pineapples	4
Grapes	2
Plums	6
Peaches	4
Watermelon	1
Nectarines	4

Z Key Timings and Practice

Exercise 33.9 Complete Timing 33.15 by keying the following timing text. Continue to reinforce your proficiency with the Z key by completing the drill lines in Exercise 33.9 in the Online Lab. Finally, complete Timing 33.16 using the same paragraph of text used in Timing 33.15.

Timings 33.15–33.16

That wizard of zoology amazes zillions of zoo visitors daily. The dazzling display of the 55 puzzling zebras dazes people of all sizes. Lazy lizards zigzag into a dizzy speed on an oozing pond. Monkeys puzzle many folks by their crazy antics on the hazardous horizontal bars. The graceful gazelles in brown graze in the park plazas. After a day at the zoo, it is fun to stop at a bazaar and have a zesty pizza.

Ergonomic Tip
Have a complete eye exam by a qualified professional at least every two years.

Ending the Session

The Online Lab automatically saves the work you completed for this session. You can continue with the next session or exit the Online Lab and continue later.

3 Insert a table that contains three columns and five rows by completing the following steps:

    a Click the Insert tab.

    b Click the Table button in the Tables group.

    c Move the mouse pointer down and to the right until the number above the grid displays as *3×5* and then click the mouse button.

4 Key the text shown in Figure 45.4 in the cells of the table. Do not make any formatting changes to the table cells.

5 Place the insertion point below the table, press Enter, and then key **These company leaders are available to answer your questions.**

6 Proofread and correct any errors in the document.

7 Save the document.

8 Click the Check button to stop the timer and upload the document for checking. The Online Lab will report the WAM rate and number of errors for the activity.

9 If errors are reported, view the results document, correct the errors in the submitted document, save the document, and then click the Check button.

Figure 45.4 Table Content for Document 45.1

Clifford Tumlinson	Chief Executive Officer	(801) 555-7905
Janet Whitford	President	(801) 555-7918
Claire Kazama	Vice President	(801) 555-7985
Keith Voight	Director of Finance	(801) 555-7944
Theresa Cruz	Director of Purchasing	(801) 555-7931

Document 45.2 · **Creating a Table Using the Insert Table Dialog Box**

1 Read all instructions for this document activity, navigate to the Document 45.2 launch page in the Online Lab, and then click the Launch Activity button. The Online Lab will open **Doc045.02** in the activity window. The timer will start as soon as you begin keying the document.

2 Key **New Employees** and then press Enter.

3 Insert a table that is made up of three columns and six rows by completing the following steps:

    a Click the Insert tab.

    b Click the Table button in the Tables group.

    c Click the *Insert Table* option.

    d At the Insert Table dialog box, with the number selected in the *Number of columns* measurement box, key 3.

    e Select the number in the *Number of rows* measurement box and then key 6.

    f Click OK.

4 Key the text shown in Figure 45.5 in the cells of the table. Do not make any formatting changes to the table cells.

5 Place the insertion point below the table, press Enter, and then key **These employees joined the company in June.**

steps continue

Unit 7

Email and Memos Part I

Figure 45.2 Table Button Drop-Down Menu   **Figure 45.3** Insert Table Dialog Box

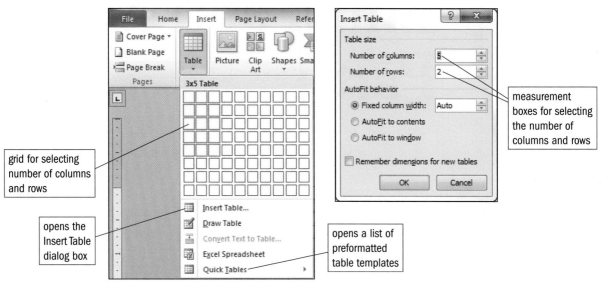

grid for selecting number of columns and rows

opens the Insert Table dialog box

opens a list of preformatted table templates

measurement boxes for selecting the number of columns and rows

Entering Text in a Table Cell

To key text or numbers within a cell, position the insertion point in that cell and then key the desired data. When you create a table, the insertion point displays in cell A1. Move the insertion point to other cells with the mouse by clicking in the desired cell or by using the arrow keys to move from cell to cell. You can also press the Tab key to move to the next cell or press Shift + Tab to move to the previous cell.

If the text you key in a cell does not fit on one line, the text will wrap to the next line within the same cell. If you press the Enter key within a cell, the insertion point moves to the next line within the same cell. The height of the cell increases to accommodate the new line of text, and the height of all of the cells in that row also increases.

To edit text within a cell, double-click to select a single word or triple-click to select the entire cell content if the cell contains more than one word.

When all information has been entered in the table cells, move the insertion point below the table by clicking the left mouse button in the blank line below the table or by pressing the Down Arrow key until the insertion point appears below the table.

Adding a Row to an Existing Table

Once a table is created, you can adjust the number of columns or rows in that table. If you place the insertion point to the immediate right of the last row of a table and press Enter, a new row will be inserted at the end of the table. You can undo this action by pressing Ctrl + Z or clicking the Undo button on the Quick Access toolbar. In Session 46 you will investigate other ways to change the number of columns or rows in a table.

 Document 45.1

Creating a Table Using the Table Button Grid

1 Read all instructions for this document activity, navigate to the Document 45.1 launch page in the Online Lab, and then click the Launch Activity button. The Online Lab will open **Doc045.01** in the activity window. The timer will start as soon as you begin keying the document.

2 Key the main heading **COMPANY LEADERS** and then press Enter. *Note: Key the main heading in uppercase using the default font color (black not red), and do not make any formatting changes to the main heading.*

steps continue

Using Basic Word Processing and Proofreading Techniques

Session Objectives

- Set personal speed and accuracy goals
- Open Microsoft Word 2010
- Save and print a Word document
- Insert and delete text
- Move the insertion point
- Use the Show/Hide feature
- Split and join paragraphs
- Review proofreading marks and techniques
- Practice Word spelling and grammar functions

Timing Goals

- 1 minute: 35 WAM and two or fewer errors

Getting Started and Warming Up

Exercise 34.1 If you are continuing immediately from Session 33, you may skip the Exercise 34.1 warm-up drill. However, if you exited the Online Lab at the end of Session 33, warm up by completing Exercise 34.1.

Exercise 34.2 Begin your session work by completing Exercise 34.2 in the Online Lab. In this timed short drill, you (1) select the drill goal to key for either speed or accuracy, (2) set the desired drill duration at 15 seconds, 30 seconds, or 60 seconds, and (3) identify your personal WAM goal. It is important that you select appropriate goals each time and that you focus intently on meeting those goals. You can repeat this exercise as many times as you like before moving on to the timing assessments.

Assessing Your Speed and Accuracy

Complete Timings 34.1 and 34.2 in the Online Lab using the timing text shown on the next page. Both timings use the same paragraph.

The timing will start as soon as you begin keying. Remember to press the Tab key at the start of the paragraph. Do not press Enter at the end of each line; only at the end of the paragraph. If you finish keying the paragraph before the time expires, press Enter, Tab, and then start keying the paragraph again.

When time expires, the Online Lab will report your WAM score and will highlight any errors. The results of both timings will be stored in your Timings Performance report.

The goals are to key at least 35 WAM and to make two or fewer errors. Note that with this session the WAM goal has been increased by 5 WAM.

 Success Tip

The textbook provides WAM rate and error goals for each timing. If you have been surpassing these goals, set slightly more challenging personal goals and strive to exceed those.

Creating Tables

Tables are commonly used in business correspondence such as manuscripts and business reports that contain large amounts of numerical data. Because of the nature of numerical information, it is commonly difficult and impractical to present it in sentence and paragraph form. When data are presented in a table the reader has an opportunity to visualize and comprehend the total picture. Tables, of course, can also contain only alphabetic content or a combination of alphabetic and numerical information, depending on the circumstance.

Before creating a table, the content to be displayed should be analyzed to determine which information will be listed in columns and which information will be listed in rows. **Columns** are vertical and **rows** are horizontal. The number of columns and rows are ideally determined before producing a table. However, columns and rows can be added or deleted later if you decide that your original choices need to be adjusted.

Figure 45.1 shows a 3 × 5 table (three columns and five rows). The segments of a table that contain information are called **cells**. Cells in a table contain a cell designation. Columns in a table are lettered from left to right, beginning with A. The cell in the upper-left corner of the table is cell A1. The cell to the right of A1 is B1, the cell to the right of B1 is C1, and so on. Rows are numbered, beginning at the top of the table, with 1. The cells below A1 are A2, A3, A4, and so on. The lines that form the cells of the table are called **borders**.

Inserting a Table

Insert a table in a document by clicking the Insert tab and then clicking the Table button in the Tables group. Click the Table button to display a drop-down menu (see Figure 45.2). Use options in the Table button drop-down menu to create the table by selecting cells in the grid or by clicking the *Insert Table* option and selecting the number of columns and rows you want in the *Table size* section of the Insert Table dialog box (see Figure 45.3). You can also use the *Quick Tables* option from the Table button drop-down menu to create a table using a template that contains a preformatted table.

Figure 45.1 Table with Three Columns and Five Rows

cell A1	column B	
Mary Felkins	Northridge Corporation	(310) 555-5478
Russell Gates	Green Valley Electrical	(360) 555-0997
Christina Cline	Cline Corporation	(206) 555-4511
Timothy Sloan	Pacific Foundry	(218) 555-5590
Tina Roberts	Hart Construction	(312) 555-8473

row 3

cell borders

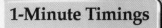

**Timings
34.1–34.2**

Never use a steel hammer to strike a chisel. Utilize either the solid rubber or wooden mallet. You can use the palm of your hand, of course, depending on the particular project. A mallet can be used in cases where the edge to be cut is across the grain. If, however, the cutting edge is with the grain, a mallet could easily split the wood. Remember to angle the chisel slightly when starting a cut. The angle makes smooth or pared cuts easier to do.

Ergonomic Tip
Keep your feet flat on the floor (or on a footrest) while you key.

Using the Online Lab to Complete Document Activities

Throughout this session and the remaining sessions of this textbook, you will be using Microsoft Word 2010 (hereafter referred to simply as Word) to create and edit a variety of types of documents. In order to track your coursework, you will complete document activities through the Online Lab, which will launch Word on your computer.

**Video
34.1**

After finishing Timing 34.2, watch Video 34.1 in the Online Lab. The video shows how to complete document activities in the Online Lab. After you have finished viewing the video, click Next to navigate to the Document 34.1 launch screen. Read the following textbook material on editing Word documents before clicking the Launch Activity button. The activity instructions for Document 34.1 on page 174 will instruct you when to click the Launch Activity button.

Editing Word Documents

In today's world, people very rarely create documents by hand. Instead, documents are prepared using word-processing programs such as Microsoft Word 2010. This session will introduce you to the Word interface for creating and editing Word documents.

Opening Microsoft Word and Creating, Saving, and Printing a Word Document

The steps to open Word may vary depending on your system setup. Generally, to open Word, click the Start button on the Taskbar at the Windows desktop, point to *All Programs*, click *Microsoft Office*, and then click *Microsoft Word 2010*.

When Word opens, a blank document displays, as shown in Figure 34.1. Figure 34.1 also shows some of the commonly used features in the Word 2010 interface. The Word interface features a **ribbon** that contains several tabs. Each **tab** provides a different set of formatting tools and buttons. Tabs are located immediately above the ribbon. The Home tab is indicated in Figure 34.1. The content of each tab is presented in different **groups**.

Complete two 5-minute timings on the timing text below. Timings 45.3 and 45.4 use the same paragraphs.

Goals: 30 WAM and ten or fewer errors
SI: 1.46 syllables per word

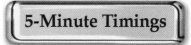
5-Minute Timings

Timings 45.3–45.4

As a direct result of the strides being made in telecommunications, the new systems that we have are hard to believe. The number of systems adds to the task we have of knowing how these systems function. It is next to impossible for one person to know about all the systems now being used in transmitting voice, data, and video, much less all of the products and services being developed.

One way to help understand telecom systems in use today is to study technical concepts used in sending and receiving all forms of information. While the number of systems is huge, the number of concepts is small by comparison. If one knows the basic concepts used in systems, then that person need not study in detail each device or system by itself. He or she can apply the concepts that relate to the system being reviewed to grasp how and why it works the way it does. This applies not only to current systems but to new ones being released each day.

The concepts of telecom can be divided into six parts. They are encoding, transmitting, receiving, storing, retrieving, and decoding. A person who wants to know how and why a system works can start by dividing the process into each of the six parts noted. This will make it easier to learn and compare since the parts will not be as complex as the whole.

One of the concepts used in telecom systems relates to transmitting. This is the part that moves the data from one point to another point. Often, a signal is sent right after the encoding step is done. This step takes many forms that we use daily, such as the wire that connects our phone to a local telephone office. Other means include radio waves that go between antennas that are found in many places such as towers, cars, homes, and buildings. Satellite networks and fiber optic networks provide another means to send data between and among two or more points.

Whatever system is used, it must move data from its origin to its destination as fast and efficiently as possible. Transmitting is done by putting the data in or through space or by sending it through a copper wire or optical fiber. By being able to break a system into parts, we can digest the concepts for each part.

Figure 34.1 Microsoft Word 2010 Home Tab

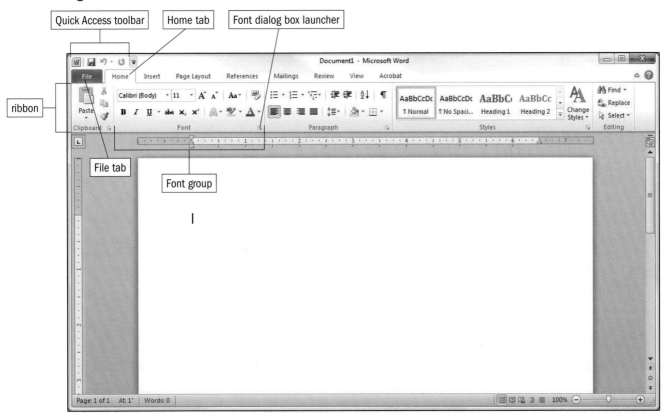

A group contains a set of options that allow you to control related aspects of document preparation and editing. For example, the Font group on the Home tab contains buttons that will change the way type appears in the document. You can use the buttons in this group to increase or decrease the size of the type, make it **bold** or *italic*, and change the color of the type. You can also use the Font dialog box launcher to open a dialog box, which allows you to make additional formatting changes to the way the text is presented in the document.

No matter which tab you select, the **Quick Access toolbar** is always available at the top of the screen. By default, this toolbar provides buttons to save, undo a change, and repeat a change. You can customize this toolbar by adding or removing buttons.

There are several ways to save a Word document. The most common are: press Ctrl + S; click the Save button on the Quick Access toolbar; or click the File tab followed by *Save As* in the Quick Commands area. Clicking *Save As* will open the Save As dialog box shown in Figure 34.2. Type the name of the file in the *File name* text box and use the Navigation pane to indicate where the file will be saved on your computer.

The image of the document on the screen is called a **soft copy**. To print a copy of a document, referred to as a **hard copy**, click the File tab and then click the Print tab to display the Print tab Backstage view, shown in Figure 34.3. You can also display the Print tab Backstage view by pressing Ctrl + P.

The Print tab Backstage view displays a preview of how the document will print, and the Navigation buttons allow you to advance through the document pages (for documents with more than one page). Before clicking the Print button, set the desired number of copies to print in the *Copies* option text box in the Print section. Use the gallery in the Printer section to select a printer. The galleries in the Settings section provide options for specifying how a document is printed including which pages are to be printed, the orientation, and the paper size.

Session 45

Creating Tables

Session Objectives

- Create a table
- Enter data into a table
- Use a table to compare data in a document
- Write a statement that discusses tabular data

Timing goals

- 1 minute: 40 WAM and two or fewer errors
- 5 minutes: 30 WAM and ten or fewer errors

Getting Started and Warming Up

Exercise 45.1 If you are continuing immediately from Session 44, you may skip the Exercise 45.1 warm-up drill. However, if you exited the Online Lab at the end of Session 44, warm up by completing Exercise 45.1.

Exercise 45.2 Begin your session work by completing Exercise 45.2, a timed short drill, in the Online Lab.

Assessing Your Speed and Accuracy

Complete Timings 45.1 through 45.4 in the Online Lab. At the end of each timing, the Online Lab will display your WAM rate and any errors. Results will be saved in your Timings Performance report. If you have been surpassing the speed and accuracy goals, set slightly more challenging personal goals and strive to exceed them.

Complete two 1-minute timings on the timing text below. Timings 45.1 and 45.2 use the same paragraph.

Goals: 40 WAM and two or fewer errors
SI: 1.32 syllables per word

1-Minute Timings

Timings 45.1–45.2

Snowshoes add two dimensions to the feet by increasing the surface area of the bottoms of feet. Snowshoes are big and add a lot of weight. To compensate for size, you must use your eyes, as well as your brain, to pick the way. Normally, in walking through the forests, most of us look ahead about ten feet. When walking with snowshoes, it is best to look ahead about 20 or 30 feet. The size of the shoes requires that a person turn bigger corners and also allow more room to maneuver. Most brush and bramble bushes are a big problem and should be avoided.

Figure 34.2 Save As Dialog Box

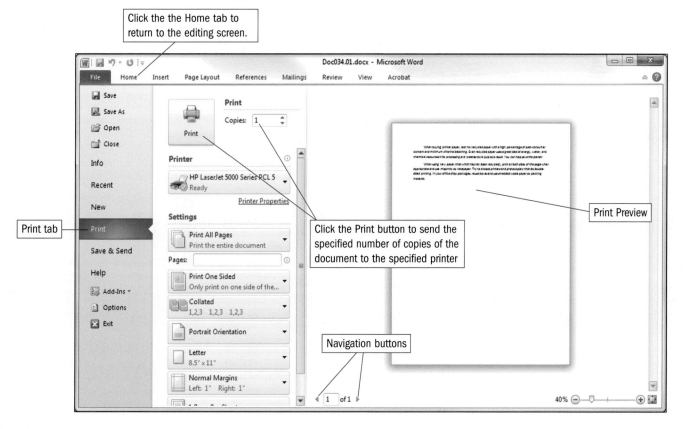

Figure 34.3 Print Tab Backstage View

Unit 9 Tables Part I

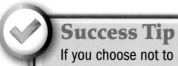

Success Tip
If you choose not to print a document after opening the Print tab Backstage view, click the Home tab to return to the editing screen.

Inserting Text

By default, when you open a document in Word, the program is in Insert mode and the insertion point, or cursor, is at the top of the document. In **Insert mode**, newly keyed content is added at the insertion point location and does not replace existing text. If you want to add text, simply click to position the insertion point—the active location on the screen—where you want to insert new text and then key the new text.

If, however, you want to replace old text with new text, turn on the Overtype mode by pressing the Insert key. The Insert key is located between the Backspace and Home keys on most keyboards. When the **Overtype mode** is activated, the text you key replaces previous text, letter by letter.

Overtype will stay in effect until you press the Insert key again or until you exit the program. *Caution: Accidentally keying over text you want to keep is easy, so be careful about remaining in Overtype mode.*

Deleting Text

In Word you can delete text in several ways. The keys used to delete text were introduced in Session 6. For example, you can delete text by pressing the Backspace key to delete characters to the left of the insertion point. The Delete key will delete characters to the right of the insertion point.

Moving the Insertion Point

The insertion point moves as you key text, press the Backspace key, or press the Delete key. You can move the insertion point to other locations in the document by using the mouse. However, it is also possible to move the insertion point using keys or key combinations. Table 34.1 lists some commonly used keyboard commands for moving the insertion point. The plus (+) symbol means that you use two keys at the same time. For example, to move the insertion point to the beginning of a document, press and hold a Ctrl key (on either side of the space bar) and then tap the Home key. You will want to practice using these keyboard shortcuts as you work with keyed documents. For more keyboard shortcuts, see Appendix A.

Table 34.1 Insertion Point Movement Key Commands

Pressing this key or key combination...	moves the insertion point...
Ctrl + ←	one word to the left
Ctrl + →	one word to the right
End	to the end of a line
Home	to the beginning of a line
Page Down	one screen down
Page Up	one screen up
Ctrl + Home	to the beginning of a document
Ctrl + End	to the end of a document

Figure 44.4 Proofread Letter for Document 44.4—Continued

to the Vice President of Marketing in under two years. That is very impressive.

- When your boss left the company, she invited you to stay with her as her assistant in her new company. At Stellar, Inc. you ~~organized~~ the (stet) office from the beginning and trained the staff as they were acquired. You helped many of the new staff attend classes at BTC and to get their degrees as they worked.
- You served on the Advisory Committee for the Administrative Assistant Program.
- Whenever we have called, you have been a speaker for our classes, always bringing a lively program to share.
- You allowed B(C)T students to shadow you at work and to learn what it is like to be an administrative ~~assistant.~~ *professional*
- You hired students as interns as the placements became available.
- The IAAP organization was able to benefit from your expertise also as you served them over the years in so many officer positions that I cannot recall them all.
- With the sale of Stellar, Inc. this year, you are heading on to another ~~spot~~ *position* where you will be able to help others while your former boss enjoys her retirement. This new hospital will be able to profit from your guidance and experience from the ground up. How wonderful for them!

Over the years, you have kept in touch with your former instructors and kept us up to date on the world of the administrative ~~assistant.~~ *professional* What a wonderful treat it has been to be introduced as your instructors on so many occasions.

Keep up the good work, Laura, and know that you have left your mark on the community, your work, and the people who have known you along the way!

Sincerely, (#)

Patricia McDugle / Instructor

c: Jacki King

Ending the Session

The Online Lab automatically saves the work you completed for this session. You may continue with the next session or exit the Online Lab and continue later.

Note that the left- and right-pointing arrows are typically located on the right side of the keyboard. However, on some keyboards they are integrated into the numeric keyboard. If this is the case on your keyboard, make sure to use the numbers lock feature (activated and deactivated by pressing the Num Lock key) before you use those keys.

Document **Keying a Word Document**

34.1

1   Read all instructions for this document activity presented in the following steps. *Hint: Video 34.1 demonstrates how to complete this document activity.*

2   Navigate to the Document 34.1 launch page in the Online Lab, and then click the Launch Activity button. The Online Lab will open Word and **Doc034.01** in the activity window. The timer will start as soon as you begin keying the document.

3   Key the two paragraphs of text shown in Figure 34.4. Remember to press the Tab key at the start of each paragraph and press the Enter key once at the end of the first paragraph. Your text will wrap differently than shown in the book, since you are using a different font. As you key the text, tap the Backspace key immediately to correct errors that you "feel," but do not take time to check your screen as you key. (As you gain more keying experience, you will sense many errors as you make them and can correct them immediately.) *Hint: Remember to click the space bar one time after sentence endings (not two times).*

4   Read your document on the screen to look for any errors you may have missed. If you see any red or green wavy lines under words, the Word spelling and grammar checker has flagged them for you to review. (The Word spelling and grammar checking features will be discussed more completely later in this session.) If you see an error, correct it.

5   Save the document by clicking the Save button on the Quick Access toolbar or use the keyboard shortcut Ctrl + S.

6   Click the Check button to stop the timer and upload **Doc034.01** for checking. When the evaluation is complete, the Online Lab will display a Submitted button and a Results button below the Check button. Your WAM rate and the number of errors made will display at the lower-right corner of the Online Lab screen.

7   If errors are reported, view your results document and correct the errors in the submitted document by completing the following steps:

   a   Click the Results button to view a document showing the words you keyed incorrectly. You can print this document if necessary (press Ctrl + P).

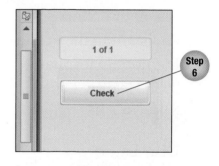

   b   Click the Submitted button to view the submitted document.

   c   Click the Show Both button to view both the submitted document and the results document within the same Word window.

   d   Edit the submitted document to correct any errors, save the document (press Ctrl + S), and then click the Check button.

   e   If the Online Lab still reports errors, repeat Steps 7a–7d. When you are finished, click Next.

1 Read all instructions for this document activity, navigate to the Document 44.4 launch page in the Online Lab, and then click the Launch Activity button. The Online Lab will open **Doc044.04** in the activity window. The timer will start as soon as you begin keying the document.

2 Key the letter shown in Figure 44.4 in the block-style letter format. Do not format an envelope for this letter.

    a Use February 6, 2014, as the date.

    b Be sure to make the changes noted by the proofreading marks.

    c Use the solid circle bullets for the bulleted paragraphs. Do not leave extra space between the paragraphs. Include an appropriate vertical style heading for page 2 of the letter.

    d Key the reference initials jpf and the file name.

3 Use the Find and Replace feature to find all instances of BTC and replace it with Butler Technical College. Note: The college name should not be in italic formatting in the final document. *Hint: Select the Match case search option in the Find and Replace dialog box.*

4 Proofread and correct any errors in the letter.

5 Save the document.

6 Click the Check button to stop the timer and upload the document for checking. The Online Lab will report the WAM rate and number of errors for the activity.

7 If errors are reported, view the results document, correct the errors in the submitted document, save the document, and then click the Content button.

Figure 44.4 Letter for Document 44.4

Ms. Laura Nimz

Assistant to the President

Memorial Hospital

7958 Healthy Lane

Mesa, AZ 85216-0896

Dear Laura:

Congratulations on you're new position! I know that you will do fine *well* as you have demonstrated in the past.

You have represented our program well as you have moved throughout your career.

- You helped to establish the first Business Students Club at BTC. Of course, that wasn't enough for you; you also helped the club by serving as parliamentarian, Secretary, and President as needed.
- After graduation, you worked for Lab Supply and Company. While there you managed to move from an entry-level position to Assistant

continues

Figure 34.4 Content for Document 34.1

When buying printer paper, look for recycled paper with a high percentage of post-consumer content and minimum chlorine bleaching. Even recycled paper uses a great deal of energy, water, and chemical resources in its processing and creates toxic pulp as a result. You can help save the planet!

When using new paper (that which has not been recycled), print on both sides of the page when appropriate and use misprints as notepaper. Try to choose printers and photocopiers that do double-sided printing. If your office ships packages, reuse boxes and use shredded waste paper as packing material.

Using the Show/Hide Feature

By default, when you work in Word, you are working with documents in Print Layout view, so what you see on screen is what will print. However, sometimes it is helpful to see nonprinting characters as you are keying or editing a file. Nonprinting characters include spaces, tabs, and paragraph symbols. The Show/Hide feature in Word will either show or hide these nonprinting characters. If nonprinting characters are hidden, click the Show/Hide ¶ button in the Paragraph group on the Home tab (see Figure 34.5). When the nonprinting characters are shown, a space appears as a dot between words, a tab appears as a right-pointing arrow, and a paragraph symbol (created by pressing the Enter key) appears as a ¶.

Splitting and Joining Paragraphs

Word 2010 uses a default line spacing of 1.15 lines and 10 points of spacing after a paragraph. This means that the default line spacing is slightly greater than single spacing (which is 1.0 lines). With this default spacing setting, you only need to press Enter *once* to create the extra distance between paragraphs. (In later sessions you will learn how to change line spacing to accommodate specific formats.)

To split a paragraph into two smaller paragraphs, position the insertion point immediately to the left of the letter that will be the first letter of the new paragraph and then press Enter. When you press Enter, the text is moved to the next line and additional white space is added above the text on the next line. If necessary, press Tab at the beginning of the new paragraph.

To join two paragraphs, delete the white space between them. There are two ways to do this. One method is to position the insertion point immediately before the first character of the second paragraph and press the Backspace key until the paragraphs combine into one. The second method is to position the insertion point one space *past* the period (or other punctuation mark) at the end of the first paragraph and tap Delete until the paragraphs join. When you join the two paragraphs, the line lengths of the new paragraph are automatically adjusted by the Word Wrap feature.

Figure 34.5 Paragraph Group on the Home Tab

44.3

1   Read all instructions for this document activity, navigate to the Document 44.3 launch page in the Online Lab, and then click the Launch Activity button. The Online Lab will open **Doc044.03** in the activity window. The timer will start as soon as you begin keying the document.

2   Key the letter shown in Figure 44.3 in the block-style letter format. Do not format an envelope for this letter.

  a   Use February 3, 2014, as the date.

  b   Do not format the email address within the body of the letter as a hyperlink.

  c   Key the reference initials **gwk** and the file name.

  d   Indicate that the letter will be copied to Bryan Byrne, Norm Fjelstad, and Wanda Holmes.

3   Justify the three paragraphs in the body of the letter.

4   Proofread and correct any errors in the letter.

5   Save the document.

6   Click the Check button to stop the timer and upload the document for checking. The Online Lab will report the WAM rate and number of errors for the activity.

7   If errors are reported, view the results document, correct the errors in the submitted document, save the document, and then click the Check button.

Figure 44.3 Letter Content for Document 44.3

Ms. Judy Heller
Marian Community College
261 Kenyon Road
Franklin, VA 23852-1141
Dear Ms. Heller: ¶ I talked with Bryan Byrne, one of CME's tech support representatives. He has received approval to bring in our software developer, Norm Fjelstad, to work with Wanda Holmes to resolve the installation problem she reported in one of the labs. ¶ Norm has already contacted Wanda via email for information regarding the issue. I'm confident that Norm can diagnose and repair the problem quickly. ¶ Be sure to email me (jbutcher@emcp.net) a copy of your Intro to 103-106 MS Office syllabus when it's finished. I will be happy to review and return it with my comments using Word's Track Changes feature. ¶ Sincerely yours, ¶ James Butcher ¶ CME National Consultant

Document **Moving the Insertion Point and Using the Show/Hide Feature to Edit**

34.2

1   Read all instructions for this document activity presented in the following steps.

2   If you have not already, navigate to the Document 34.2 launch page in the Online Lab and then click the Launch Activity button. The Online Lab will open **Doc034.02** in the activity window.

3   If it is not already on, turn on the display of nonprinting characters by clicking the Show/Hide ¶ button in the Paragraph group on the Home tab.

4   Delete the extra space between the words *look* and *for* in the first sentence of the first paragraph.

5   Delete the extra space between the second and third sentence in the first paragraph.

6   Join the two paragraphs. *Hint: Remember to remove the extra Tab using Show/Hide.*

7   Split the paragraph so that the second paragraph starts with the words *When using new paper*.

  a   Place the insertion point immediately to the left of the words *When using new paper* and then press the Backspace key one time. This will delete the space after the previous sentence.

  b   Press the Enter key to insert a paragraph break and then press the Tab key to indicate the start of the second paragraph.

8   Click the Show/Hide ¶ button in the Paragraph group to hide the nonprinting characters.

9   Press Ctrl + End to move to the end of the document and then key the missing period after the last sentence.

10 Save the document by clicking the Save button on the Quick Access toolbar or use the keyboard shortcut Ctrl + S.

11 Click the Check button to upload the document for checking. The Online Lab will report the number of errors for the activity.

12 If errors are reported, view your results document and correct the errors in the submitted document by completing the following steps:

  a   Click the Results button to view a document showing the errors.

  b   Click the Submitted button to view the submitted document. *Hint: Click the Show Both button to view the submitted and results documents within the same Word window.*

  c   Edit the submitted document to correct any errors, save the document (press Ctrl + S), and then click the Check button.

  d   If the Online Lab still reports errors, repeat Steps 12a–12c.

Proofreading Documents and Correcting Errors

Proofreading involves checking a document for errors. In some instances, this entails checking a newly produced document against an original document. The following section provides several tools and suggestions for proofreading.

1. Read all instructions for this document activity, navigate to the Document 44.2 launch page in the Online Lab, and then click the Launch Activity button. The Online Lab will open **Doc044.02** in the activity window. The timer will start as soon as you begin keying the document.

2. Key the letter shown in Figure 44.2 in the block-style letter format.

   a. Use March 14, 2014, as the letter's date.

   b. Key the reference initials **bct** and the file name.

   c. Include a reference to an enclosure.

3. Proofread and correct any errors in the letter. *Note: Make sure the period following the italic title is **not** formatted as italic*.

4. Format a Number 10 envelope for the letter. Do not include a return address. Rather than actually printing the envelope, add the envelope to the document.

5. Save the document.

6. Click the Check button to stop the timer and upload the document for checking. The Online Lab will report the WAM rate and number of errors for the activity.

7. If errors are reported, view the results document, correct the errors in the submitted document, save the document, and then click the Check button.

Figure 44.2 Letter Content for Document 44.2

Ms. Isabelle Martinez ¶ Consumer Representative Supervisor ¶ Glenn and Blumenfeld, Inc. ¶ P.O. Box 3168 ¶ Dallas, TX 76231-3168 ¶ Dear Ms. Martinez: ¶ Our seminar program speakers have already been contracted for this year's convention. A list of the speakers and their presentation titles is enclosed. Should any of them withdraw from the program, I will contact you as a possible alternative. ¶ By the way, have you considered renting an exhibit booth at the convention in Houston? This would give you an opportunity to display your products. Our Executive Board is currently making a decision regarding the revision of the *Business Etiquette Manual*. Should this manual be revised, you can be sure that your material will be included. ¶ You referred to the possibility of having your products listed in the "Weekly Division Newsletter." To my knowledge, there is no such publication; however, there is a monthly organizational report that is sent to all divisions. If you are interested, I can submit your material to the editor for possible inclusion in the report. Please let me know if you would like that. ¶ Sincerely, ¶ Dale McNary ¶ Editor

Table 34.2 Common Proofreading Marks

Proofreader Mark	Intended Action	Proofreading Mark in Use	Corrected Copy
∧ ∨	insert	Dale has a chance to win. *good*	Dale has a good chance to win.
୧ ୧	delete	Billey has the ~~exact~~ same book.	Billy has the same book.
‿	combine or close up	The mark up on that is 50 percent.	The markup on that is 50 percent.
⟋	move text	The dog bark. The cat (will) meowed.	The dog will bark. The cat meowed.

Using Proofreading Marks

Proofreading marks are an efficient way to indicate changes or edits that need to be made to an existing document. Table 34.2 shows examples of how these marks are used to indicate inserting, deleting, combining, and moving text. Appendix B provides a more complete list of commonly used proofreading marks.

Document 34.3

Editing from Proofreading Marks

1 Read all instructions for this document activity, navigate to the Document 34.3 launch page in the Online Lab, and then click the Launch Activity button. The Online Lab will open **Doc034.03** in the activity window. The timer will start as soon as you begin keying the document.

2 Make all of the changes indicated by the proofreading marks shown in Figure 34.6.

3 Save the document (Ctrl + S).

4 Click the Check button to stop the timer and upload the document for checking. The Online Lab will report the WAM rate and the number of errors for the activity.

5 If errors are reported, view the results document, correct the errors in the submitted document, save the document, and then click the Check button.

Figure 34.6 Proofreading Corrections for Document 34.3

When buying printer *or copier* ∧ paper, look for recycled paper with a high percentage of post-consumer content and minimum chlorine bleaching. Even recycled paper uses ~~a great deal of~~ *significant* energy, water, and chemical resources in its processing and creates toxic pulp as a result. (You can help save the planet!)

∨ When using new paper (that which has not been recycled), print on both sides of the page when ~~appropriate~~ *possible* and use mis prints as notepaper. Try to choose printers and ~~photo~~copiers that ~~do double-sided~~ *duplex* printing. If your office ships packages, reuse boxes and use shredded waste paper as packing material.

Checking Production Progress: Business Correspondence

Sessions 38–43 discussed the procedures for preparing and formatting business correspondence. In this session, you will be assessed on how quickly and accurately you can key these types of documents. In the following document activities, each completed letter is to be "mailable," which means that it contains no errors. A document that requires additional corrections is not considered mailable.

Your goals are to key each document in mailable form and at a rate of at least 25 WAM. If your rate is less than 25 WAM or if you are missing errors that should be corrected, your instructor may ask you to repeat documents. To help you succeed, carefully review the document instructions and the document before starting the document activity in the Online Lab. *Note: If necessary, review the content of Sessions 38–43 if you are unsure how to complete a specific task.*

Document 44.1 **Block-Style Letter**

1 Read all instructions for this document activity, navigate to the Document 44.1 launch page in the Online Lab, and then click the Launch Activity button. The Online Lab will open **Doc044.01** in the activity window. The timer will start as soon as you begin keying the document.

2 Key the letter shown in Figure 44.1 in the block-style letter format. Do not format an envelope for this letter.

   a Use March 6, 2014, as the date.

   b Key the reference initials **jam** and the file name.

3 Proofread and correct any errors in the letter.

4 Save the document.

5 Click the Check button to stop the timer and upload the document for checking. The Online Lab will report the WAM rate and number of errors for the activity.

6 If errors are reported, view the results document, correct the errors in the submitted document, save the document, and then click the Check button.

Figure 44.1 Letter Content for Document 44.1

Mr. James P. Forrest ¶ Creditors' Discount & Audit Co. ¶ 3209 Forrest Building ¶ Pontiac, IL 61764-1804 ¶ Dear Mr. Forrest: ¶ We are looking for a company to attempt to collect on unpaid bills. Your firm, Creditors' Discount & Audit Co., was recommended by John Knolls of St. James Hospital. ¶ We are a small clinic in the Pontiac-Chenoa area. We do a lot of work with the uninsured, and we understand that paying medical bills is not always a top priority—food and shelter come first. Mr. Knolls told me that you work with the clients to help them learn how to pay these bills to the best of their ability without intruding too much on their expenses. We like that approach much better than that of "hounding" them to pay us. ¶ Our goal is to help people; unfortunately, we must also recover our costs to stay in existence. Please contact me at your earliest convenience to discuss ways your company might be of service to our clinic. ¶ Sincerely, Jill Greene, M.D. ¶ Pontiac Clinic, Inc.

Success Tip

When moving words from one location of a document to another location, use the cut and paste keyboard shortcuts. Select the text that should be moved, press Ctrl + X, place the insertion point at the new position for the cut text, and then press Ctrl + V. To help remember these shortcuts, think of the X as a scissors for cutting and the V as a proofreader's insert mark.

Proofreading Techniques

Developing effective proofreading techniques is an essential skill whether you are writing your own documents or preparing documents for others. Proofreading involves reviewing the document you created to verify that it accurately reflects what you were supposed to key. The finished product represents you, or in a business environment, you and your employer.

When proofreading, place a ruler, an index card, or another guide below the line you are proofreading on the original or source document to help you keep your place. If you have printed your keyed version of the document, use a pen to move along the same place on your printed or hard copy as you are reading from the original. When you find differences, indicate changes to be made on the printed copy with proofreading marks.

If you are proofreading from a printed source document against a file displayed on the computer screen, place a ruler, an index card, or another guide below the line you are proofreading on the original or source document and place your cursor at the same location on the screen. When you find a difference, immediately make the change to the electronic document.

Table 34.3 lists some common types of errors to look for while proofreading.

Table 34.3 Common Types of Errors to Look for While Proofreading

Errors	Examples
wrong word	now/not, you/your, form/from, than/that, than/then
word endings	formed/former, point/pointing, typed/types
words or names that sound alike	Larson/Larsen, your/you're, knew/new
added words	may repeat multiple words as a result of losing place in text while keying
omitted words	may result when a word appears in the same place in two consecutive lines and the eye skips from one line to the next when keying
transpositions	characters or words that are reversed and make a new word not detected by spelling check
numbers	dates; times; addresses; phone numbers; items listed in a sequence such as 1, 2, 4, 5 or a, b, d, e
punctuation errors	missing or incorrectly placed punctuation, beginning quotation mark (") but no ending mark ("), missing serial comma
capitalization errors	inconsistent or incorrect capitalization
word use	principal (head of school, sum of money, main or primary) vs. principle (rule)
top, bottom, and sides of document	your eyes tend to focus on the middle of a document and tend to skip over material at the top, bottom, and sides

Complete two 5-minute timings on the timing text below. Timings 44.3 and 44.4 use the same paragraphs.

Goals: 30 WAM and ten or fewer errors
SI: 1.54 syllables per word

5-Minute Timings

Timings 44.3–44.4

Our present time is called the Information Age because computers, which can store and rapidly retrieve vast amounts of information, are central to today's business and government functions. In this Age, machines store vast amounts of data and perform routine calculations in no time at all.

A database is an organized collection of related data. (It should be noted that data is a plural word; the singular form of the word is datum.) Examples of what can be stored in a database include employee names and pay rates, the list of orders for a store, and facts about students. The software used for creating a database is called a relational database management system. Database software is used to manage data, answer questions about the data, create user-friendly forms for data entry, and produce printed reports about stored data.

A database is organized into a series of tables. Tables contain linked data, such as all of the data on orders, clients, or staff. In a table, fields store data. The database displays a table in a form that arranges fields into columns. Each field has a name. The name of each field can be simple or complex, but no two names can be the same.

A record is a set of data stored in the fields of a table. The records in a sheet are organized into rows, one record after another. In a database, information is stored in separate tables to reduce confusion. Sometimes, data duplication is avoided by combining fields. A case in point is when redundant data are removed when two sets of data, stored in two tables, are combined. This improves efficiency for those who enter and retrieve data.

Ergonomic Tip
Getting up and walking down the hall relaxes your hands, wrists, arms, back, neck, eyes, and mind—by moving, you increase productivity.

Once changes have been made and saved, review the changes on the screen. Check them again after printing the document to make sure you made all the changes and did not make any new errors.

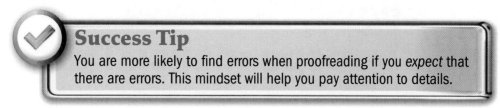

Success Tip

You are more likely to find errors when proofreading if you *expect* that there are errors. This mindset will help you pay attention to details.

In addition to comparing documents, it is also important to read the document you are proofreading slowly, word for word. For best results, proofread the document at least three times. The first time through the document, check for completeness. Confirm that all of the information from the original document is included and if you are proofreading corrections, confirm that the requested changes were made correctly. On the second time through the document, check the content. When checking for content, confirm that the general message and meaning of individual sentences and paragraphs are clear. On the third and final check of the document, check the punctuation, grammar usage, and numbers.

Checking Spelling and Grammar

The Word Spelling & Grammar feature provides spelling and grammar suggestions. While keying a document, Word will mark each word that is not in its dictionary with a red wavy underline. Note that some words that are spelled correctly will appear with a red wavy underline such as proper names. Potential grammar errors are indicated with green wavy underlines. All marked instances should be reviewed carefully.

You can also prompt Word to run a complete document spelling and grammar check. To do so, move the insertion point to the beginning of the document (press Ctrl + Home), click the Review tab, and then click the Spelling & Grammar button in the Proofing group (see Figure 34.7). During a spelling and grammar check, the Spelling and Grammar dialog box will display each flagged word and will provide suggestions for replacements. See Figure 34.8.

The Word AutoCorrect feature will even correct some common keyboarding errors for you while you type. One such example is replacing *teh* with *the*. You can access the settings for these features from the Backstage view. On the File tab, click Options, and then click Proofing to see how Word corrects and formats your text as shown in Figure 34.9. Options that are active have a check mark in the option check box. It is strongly suggested that you remove the check mark for the option *Ignore words in UPPERCASE* so Word will check items that are keyed with all capital letters.

Click the AutoCorrect Options button in this dialog box and then the individual tabs for the AutoCorrect and AutoFormat settings currently active for Word. Here you will see the types of items that AutoCorrect and AutoFormat can address. As you gain more experience with Word, you may want to make changes in these settings.

Remember that even with these powerful tools, it is still important to carefully proofread a document before considering it final.

Figure 34.7 Proofing Group on the Review Tab

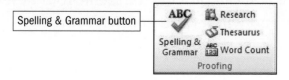

Session 44

Production Progress Check: Business Correspondence Part I

Session Objectives

- Review and practice word processing features presented in Sessions 38–43
- Produce documents at a rate of 25 WAM and in mailable form

Timing Goals

- 1 minute: 40 WAM and two or fewer errors
- 5 minutes: 30 WAM and ten or fewer errors

Getting Started and Warming Up

Exercise 44.1 If you are continuing immediately from Session 43, you may skip the Exercise 44.1 warm-up drill. However, if you exited the Online Lab at the end of Session 43, warm up by completing Exercise 44.1.

Exercise 44.2 Begin your session work by completing Exercise 44.2, a timed short drill, in the Online Lab.

Assessing Your Speed and Accuracy

Complete Timings 44.1 through 44.4 in the Online Lab. At the end of each timing, the Online Lab will display your WAM rate and any errors. Results will be saved in your Timings Performance report. If you have been surpassing the speed and accuracy goals, set slightly more challenging personal goals and strive to exceed them.

Complete two 1-minute timings on the timing text below. Timings 44.1 and 44.2 use the same paragraph.

Goals: 40 WAM with two or fewer errors
SI: 1.43 syllables per word

1-Minute Timings

Timings 44.1–44.2   If you enjoy observing the many species of birds, there are many ways of attracting them. A bird requires a shelter, food, and water. Provide fresh, clean drinking and bathing water each day. Place fresh seeds and fruit in accessible feeders that cannot be reached by squirrels. The bird shelters should be quite durable and waterproof. All baths, feeders, and shelters should be kept out of the reach of other animals. Those birds need all the security and safety that you can provide for them. Your new friends will appreciate your efforts and will reward you with singing.

Figure 34.8 Spelling and Grammar Dialog Box

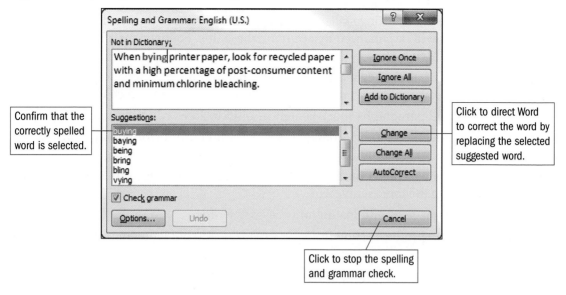

Confirm that the correctly spelled word is selected.

Click to direct Word to correct the word by replacing the selected suggested word.

Click to stop the spelling and grammar check.

Figure 34.9 Spelling and Grammar Settings

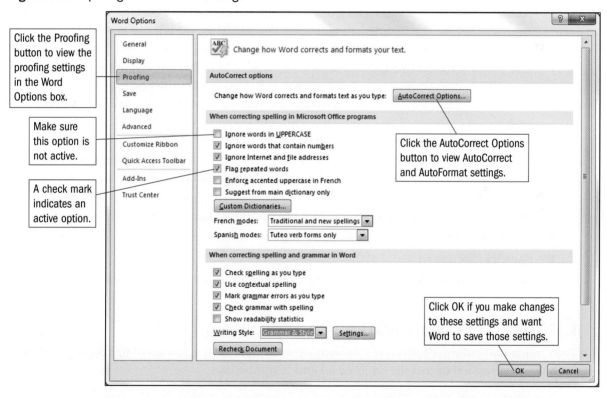

Click the Proofing button to view the proofing settings in the Word Options box.

Make sure this option is not active.

A check mark indicates an active option.

Click the AutoCorrect Options button to view AutoCorrect and AutoFormat settings.

Click OK if you make changes to these settings and want Word to save those settings.

Success Tip

If you right click on a word that is marked with a red wavy underline as spelled incorrectly, a pop-up menu will appear with alternative spellings. Click the correctly spelled word from the provided options and that spelling will be substituted in the document.

Reinforcing Writing Skills

Tips on how to improve your writing skills have appeared throughout the previous sessions. Your effectiveness as a writer will be enhanced by applying these tips. Following is a brief summary of the tips that have been discussed:

- Compose documents at the keyboard—it is faster than writing in longhand. Documents composed at the keyboard serve as your rough draft and can be edited and changed accordingly.
- Keep sentences and paragraphs short. Sentences of 15 to 25 words are recommended.
- Organize your letters so that they contain three parts: an introductory paragraph, one or more paragraphs that communicate the main content, and a closing paragraph.
- Make sure your paragraphs contain only one topic sentence and that other sentences in the paragraph relate to the topic sentence.
- Reduce excess verbiage by eliminating unnecessary words.
- Use your writing to produce action from your readers—do not let them procrastinate.
- Use positive words.

Apply these tips to the following writing activity.

Document 43.3   **Composing a Letter to Your Instructor**

1. Navigate to the Document 43.3 launch page in the Online Lab and then click the Launch Activity button. The Online Lab will open **Doc043.03** in the activity window.

2. Compose a letter to your instructor, and assume your instructor is considering hiring you for a position in a company where you would like to work. Begin the letter with a compelling paragraph that states why you are interested in the position. In the second paragraph, list at least three skills that make you qualified for the position. For each skill, provide an example of an experience that demonstrates your qualifications. In the last paragraph, include an action statement with your contact information.

3. Indicate your name for the signature line. Because you have written and keyed the letter, do not include your initials below the signature line. Include the file name.

4. Edit the letter to enhance its readability by focusing on the writing reinforcement techniques that have been presented in the previous sessions.

5. Proofread and correct any errors in the letter.

6. Save the document.

7. Click the Upload button to upload the document for instructor review.

Ending the Session

The Online Lab automatically saves the work you completed for this session. You may continue with the next session or exit the Online Lab and continue later.

Document 34.4 Using Proofreading Marks to Correct Sentences

1 Proofread the text shown in Figure 34.10 and using proofreading marks, indicate the necessary corrections on the textbook page. Watch for misspelled words or words that are incorrect based on the context of the sentence in which they are used.

2 Navigate to the Document 34.4 launch page in the Online Lab, and then click the Launch Activity button. The Online Lab will open **Doc034.04** in the activity window. The timer will start as soon as you begin keying the document.

3 Key the text shown in Figure 34.10, making the necessary corrections. Press Enter one time after each line.

4 Move the insertion point to the beginning of the document (Ctrl + Home), and run a spelling and grammar check by clicking the Spelling & Grammar button in the Proofing group on the Review tab. Make the necessary corrections.

5 Save the document (Ctrl + S).

6 Click the Check button to stop the timer and upload the document for checking. The Online Lab will report the WAM rate and number of errors for the activity.

7 If errors are reported, view the results document, correct the errors in the submitted document, save the document, and then click the Check button.

Figure 34.10 Content for Document 34.4

He paid me a great complement.

Please except our apology for the delay in shipping your order.

Many of our patience request literature on the subject.

The principle of the new loan was stated as $10,500.

Far to many errors are made as a result of not listening to directions.

The personal in the Marketing Department planned the annual picnic.

I strongly advice you to consult your attorney before signing the papers.

I do think that their are advantages to be gained from a variety of media.

Honesty is it's own reward.

The bookend is weighted with led to prevent it from sliding.

Document 34.5 Using Proofreading Marks to Correct Paragraphs

1 Proofread the text shown in Figure 34.11 and using proofreading marks, indicate the needed corrections on the textbook page. Watch for misspelled words or words that are incorrect based on the context of the sentence in which they are used.

2 Navigate to the Document 34.5 launch page in the Online Lab, and then click the Launch Activity button. The Online Lab will open **Doc034.05** in the activity window. The timer will start as soon as you begin keying the document.

3 Key the text shown in Figure 34.11, making the necessary corrections.

4 Move the insertion point to the beginning of the document (Ctrl + Home), and run a spelling and grammar check by clicking the Spelling & Grammar button in the Proofing group on the Review tab. Make the necessary corrections.

steps continue

Fold a letter to be enclosed and mailed in a Number 10 envelope with a mailing window by completing the following steps (see Figure 43.2):

1 Place the letter on the desk in the normal reading position.

2 Flip the letter over so that the back side of the letter is facing up and the letterhead (top of the page) is now on the bottom of the document; that is, closest to you.

3 Fold the top one-third of the letter down and crease.

4 Fold the bottom of the letter up so that the inside address is facing you.

5 Insert the letter into a window envelope with the address facing the front. Check to make sure the complete address shows in the window even if the letter shifts in the envelope.

Figure 43.2 Folding and Enclosing a Letter for a No. 10 Window Envelope

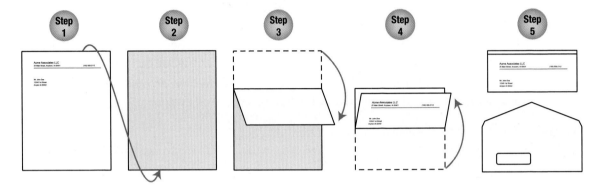

Fold a letter to be enclosed and mailed in a small 6¾ size envelope by completing the following steps (see Figure 43.3):

1 Place the letter on the desk in the normal reading position.

2 Fold from the bottom up to within ⅜ inch from the top.

3 Fold slightly less than the right one-third of the letter over to the left and crease.

4 Fold the left one-third over to within ⅜ inch of the fold you made in Step 3 and crease.

5 Insert the last folded edge into the envelope first.

Figure 43.3 Folding and Enclosing a Letter for a 6¾ Size Envelope

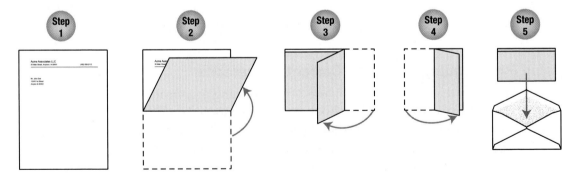

5 Save the document (Ctrl + S).

6 Click the Check button to stop the timer and upload the document for checking. The Online Lab will report the WAM rate and number of errors for the activity.

7 If errors are reported, view the results document, correct the errors in the submitted document, save the document, and then click the Check button.

Figure 34.11 Content for Document 34.5

You may not no this storey, but it is told by hunters talking about their hunting experiences.

Every hear during the deer hunting season, a certain farmer lost one or two cows to overzealous hunters. In their enthusism to bring back a prize buck or doe, some hunters would shoot at anything that moved or didn't mover.

It got so bad that the farmer and his family were afraid to come out of their house for fair of being shoot. At first, the farmer put up signs warning the hunters not to hunt on his propety. This was not very succesful becuz the hunders would shoot at the signs. All that mattered to the poor famer is that he new something had to be done or he could get kilt.

Proofreading Technical Material

Proofreading technical, statistical, or other difficult material poses special challenges, particularly if you are not familiar with the content. This type of material should be proofread very slowly. Check for content (words left out or use of the wrong word), numbers, initials, and technical terms. If you have questions, consult with the person who provided the document to you or with the document author.

If possible, proofread technical material with another person. The person who keyed the document reads from the original while the other person marks corrections on the printed document using proofreading marks. When reading from the original, the reader should spell out unusual words. Also indicate any corrections to paragraphs, format, capitalization, and decimal points. Read numbers digit by digit; for example, 4,230.62 should be read aloud as "four comma two three zero point six two."

Practice keying and making spelling and proofreading corrections in a document in the following document activity.

Document 34.6

Keying and Proofreading Technical Material

1 Navigate to the Document 34.6 launch page in the Online Lab and then click the Launch Activity button. The Online Lab will open **Doc034.06** in the activity window. The timer will start as soon as you begin keying the document.

2 Key the text as it is shown in Figure 34.12.

3 Proofread your keyed document. If possible, ask another student to read the paragraphs from the book while you proofread the text on screen. Make any needed corrections to your document.

steps continue

3 Rather than actually printing the envelope, click the Add to Document button at the bottom of the Envelopes tab of the Envelopes and Labels dialog box. Do not make the return address the default return address. It will be used for this file only.

4 Save the document.

5 Click the Check button to stop the timer and upload the document for checking. The Online Lab will report the WAM rate and number of errors for the activity.

6 If errors are reported, view the results document, correct the errors in the submitted document, save the document, and then click the Check button.

Folding and Enclosing Letters in Envelopes

Insert a letter into an envelope so that when it is removed and unfolded it is in a normal reading position. Below are directions for folding and enclosing letters into Number 10 envelopes (without and with a window) and 6¾ size envelopes.

Fold a letter to be enclosed and mailed in a Number 10 envelope by completing the following steps (see Figure 43.1):

1 Place the letter on the desk in the normal reading position.

2 Starting with the bottom edge of the letter, fold the paper up so that the bottom edge is positioned approximately two-thirds of the way up from the original bottom (or one-third of the way down from the top edge) and crease.

3 Fold the top of the letter down to within ⅜ inch of the first fold and crease.

4 Insert the last fold into the envelope first. The top of the sheet of paper is at the top of the envelope.

Figure 43.1 Folding and Enclosing a Letter for a No. 10 Envelope

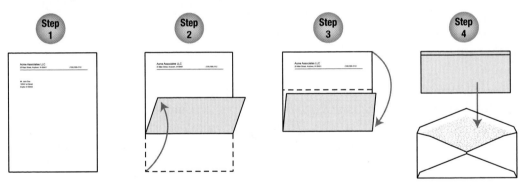

4 Save the document (Ctrl + S).

5 Click the Check button to stop the timer and upload the document for checking. The Online Lab will report the WAM rate and number of errors for the activity.

6 If errors are reported, view the results document, correct the errors in the submitted document, save the document, and then click the Check button.

Figure 34.12 Content for Document 34.6

Mr. Smythe suggested that our selling price on Item 16-780-32 was entirely too high. He recommends that we reduce the price by approximately 5 percent, from $14 to $13.

I believe he has a good idea, but I would like you to check it with Sandra Dennis in Accounting. Perhaps she has some additional recommendations that should be considered.

Please get back to me as soon as possible. The new catalogs will have to go to the printer by September 23. If something unexpected comes up, contact me at extension 1617.

Viewing the Document Performance Report for Completed Document Activities

The Online Lab provides a report showing the results of all of the document activities completed in the Online Lab. To view your Document Performance report, showing the document activity work you completed for Session 34, complete the following steps:

1 Click the Unit Contents tab to open the Online Lab Unit Contents page.

2 Click *Reports* in the navigation pane.

3 Click *Documents Performance* to open the report. The report displays in a table that shows the WAM rate and error results of the first check you did on each of your document activities.

4 Click *Attempts* to view your submitted documents and the corresponding results documents for all attempts you make on the document activities.

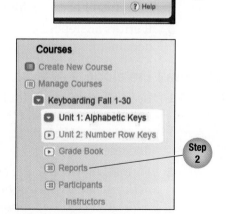

Ending the Session

The Online Lab automatically saves the work you completed for this session. You may continue with the next session or exit the Online Lab and continue later.

6 Click the Envelope Options tab if it is not selected.

7 Confirm that the correct envelope size is selected in the *Envelope size* list box. The default envelope size is Size 10. If the correct size is not shown, click the down arrow and then click the correct option from the list provided.

8 If necessary, adjust the font style of either the delivery address or the return address by clicking the appropriate Font button and making adjustments to the settings.

9 To close the Envelope Options dialog box and return to the Envelopes and Labels dialog box, click OK.

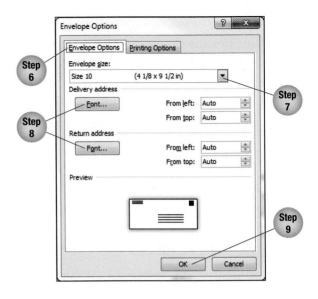

10 After proofreading the copy that will be printed on the envelope on the Envelopes tab of the Envelopes and Labels dialog box, place the envelope in the printer and then click the Print button.

Document Number 10 Envelope
43.1

1 Navigate to the Document 43.1 launch page in the Online Lab and then click the Launch Activity button. The Online Lab, will open **Doc043.01** in the activity window.

2 Format a Number 10 envelope for the letter in **Doc43.01**. Do not include a return address. *Hint: When you select the delivery address, select the nonprinting paragraph symbol at the end of the last line of the address.*

3 Rather than actually printing the envelope, click the Add to Document button at the bottom of the Envelopes tab of the Envelopes and Labels dialog box.

4 Save the document.

5 Click the Check button to upload the document for checking. The Online Lab will report the number of errors for the activity.

6 If errors are reported, view the results document, correct the errors in the submitted document, save the document, and then click the Check button.

Document Small Envelope
43.2

1 Read all instructions for this document activity, navigate to the Document 43.2 launch page in the Online Lab, and then click the Launch Activity button. The Online Lab will open **Doc043.02** in the activity window. The timer will start as soon as you begin keying the document.

2 Format a small, 6¾ size envelope for the letter in **Doc043.02**. *Hint: When you select the delivery address, select the nonprinting paragraph symbol at the end of the last line of the address.* Include an appropriate return address using the following information:

> Jill Greene, MD
> Pontiac Clinic, Inc.
> 715 N. Route 66
> Pontiac, IL 61764

steps continue

Session 35

Preparing Email Messages

Session Objectives

- Explore basic features of emails
- Use bold, italics, and underline functions while composing emails
- Practice composing emails

Timing Goals

- 1 minute: 35 WAM and two or fewer errors
- 3 minutes: 30 WAM and six or fewer errors

Getting Started and Warming Up

Exercise 35.1 If you are continuing immediately from Session 34, you may skip the Exercise 35.1 warm-up drill. However, if you exited the Online Lab at the end of Session 34, warm up by completing Exercise 35.1.

Exercise 35.2 Begin your session work by completing Exercise 35.2, a timed short drill, in the Online Lab.

Assessing Your Speed and Accuracy

Complete Timings 35.1 through 35.4 using the provided text. For all timings, once you are on an active timing screen, the timing will start as soon as you begin keying. Remember to press the Tab key at the beginning of each paragraph. Do not press Enter at the end of each line, but only at the end of the paragraph. If you finish keying a timing passage before time expires, press Enter, Tab, and then begin keying the passage again. When time expires, the Online Lab will report your WAM rate and will highlight any errors. The results of the timings will be stored in your Timings Performance report. If you have been surpassing the speed and accuracy goals, set slightly more challenging personal goals and strive to exceed them.

Complete two 1-minute timings on the timing text below. Timings 35.1 and 35.2 use the same paragraph.

Goals: 35 WAM and two or fewer errors
SI: 1.35 syllables per word

1-Minute Timings

Timings 35.1–35.2 Your ability to key at a very rapid rate will be a skill that you will never forget. It will be a skill that you will use almost all of the time if you work with computers. It will be an important skill if you end up using it only to access the Internet to do research, to send email messages, and to interact with others in real time.

Preparing Documents for Mailing

For all envelopes, regardless of size, the return address and recipient's address appear in the same relative location and are keyed using a consistent format. Specifically, the return address (address of the sender) is placed in the upper left-hand corner of envelopes. In contrast, the recipient's address (person or firm to receive the envelope) is located in the lower middle section of envelopes. Both the return and recipient's addresses are always keyed block style and single-spaced.

There are two common envelope sizes for letters. The *personal-use* or *small* envelope is referred to as the 6¾ size (it is approximately 3.5 inches high and 6.5 inches wide). The larger envelope is commonly referred to as a *Number 10* envelope (it is approximately 4.25 inches high and 9.5 inches wide) and is known as a *business* or *large* envelope. Some Number 10 envelopes can include a window, and for this style of envelope, the letter is folded so that when the letter is placed in the envelope, the recipient's address displays in the window.

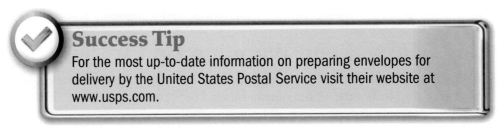

Success Tip

For the most up-to-date information on preparing envelopes for delivery by the United States Postal Service visit their website at www.usps.com.

Printing Envelopes

Word contains tools to help you print envelopes from previously keyed letters. Follow these steps to print an envelope from an existing letter:

1 Select the inside address of the letter.

2 Click the Mailings tab.

3 Click the Envelopes button in the Create group. Clicking the Envelopes button will launch the Envelopes and Labels dialog box. The selected recipient's address will appear in the *Delivery address* text box.

4 If your envelope does not include a preprinted return address, key a return address in the *Return address* text box. Otherwise, leave the *Return address* text box blank.

5 Click the Options button to open the Envelope Options dialog box.

steps continue

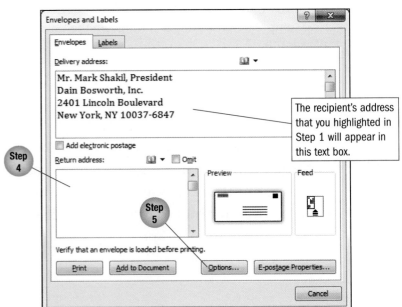

Complete two 3-minute timings on the timing text below. Timings 35.3 and 35.4 use the same passage.

Goal: 30 WAM and six or fewer errors.
SI: 1.47 syllables per word

Timings 35.3–35.4

Each spring thousands of gardeners declare war on one bothersome weed that seems to plague everyone. This weed is the lowly dandelion plant. In earlier times, people savored all the virtues of this many faceted plant. Rather than referring to it as a weed, folks utilized the very fine herbal qualities. Some broths and tonics were made and utilized to restore health to persons who were ill. Even now, modern pharmacies continue to use extracts of this springtime plant in quite a number of medicines on the market for our use.

As a food, the dandelion is a big source of nutritious, healthy, and delicious food. It is quite rich in proteins, calcium, and iron. The plant contains more Vitamin A than spinach or green peppers. The durable leaves, which may be used in many delicious salads, should be picked before the first blossoms appear. The tender leaves, although tangy in taste, are very nutritious. If you carefully dry the leaves and boil them correctly, you can make delicious teas. You might wish to consume the new blossoms and make wines, salad garnishes, and snacks made from blossoms that have been dipped in a very tasty batter.

 Ergonomic Tip
Vary tasks during the day to break up repetitive routines. This process improves your ability to concentrate.

Preparing Email Messages

The term *email* is a condensed form of the older term *electronic mail*. Email messages are prepared in much greater numbers than other business documents such as memos, letters, reports, and manuscripts. Most email messages are short and most are not printed. The recipient of an email message may print the message and has the option of deleting the message or leaving it stored on the computer.

The appearance and format of email messages varies according to the specific email program. An example of an email message produced with Microsoft Outlook is shown in Figure 35.1. Typically an email message contains the sender's name and email address, the date and time the email was sent, the subject of the email, and the name and email address of the recipient. If there is more than one recipient, the names and email addresses of all recipients are generally included at the top of the email. The ellipses (three periods) following the *To* and *Cc* fields indicate that the email address may be selected from a personal or business Address/Contact list. Also, emails may contain one or more attached documents, images, or videos.

Complete two 5-minute timings on the timing text below. Timings 43.3 and 43.4 use the same paragraphs.

Goals: 30 WAM and ten or fewer errors
SI: 1.40 syllables per word

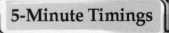

Timings 43.3–43.4

A letterhead creates an image for a business. It is possible to hire a person or a design firm to design a letterhead for you, or you may decide to use a computer to make your own. By making your own, you have the flexibility to make it a "true picture" of you and your firm. There are several things you should keep in mind while designing your letterhead.

Keep in mind that your letterhead will make a statement about your firm. It will give the reader vital data and also create an image in the reader's mind about your firm. Do you wish the reader to obtain the mental image that your firm is "solid-as-a-rock conservative"? Or, do you wish your firm to be seen as "active, flashy, and fast reacting"? You must decide.

Vital data that must be included on your letterhead is the name of your firm, address, phone and fax numbers, and website. There are certain placement guidelines that should be followed regarding the name and address of a business. For example, the firm's name, address, phone number, fax number, and website may be centered at the top of the page. Left- or right-justifying at the top of the page is also very popular. When displaying this data, you may simply block the lines, or you may wish to be more creative and try such things as separating the data by bullets, clip art, and so on.

Many businesses have logos and slogans that may be used on the page. These two items may be placed anywhere on the page. A popular location to display a slogan is across the bottom of the page with the logo placed on the left- or right-hand side of the page.

You may wish to use different fonts when displaying your firm's data. Experts warn, however, to not use more than two fonts when designing your letterhead. Consider using both bold and plain fonts for variety. When picking fonts, keep in mind the image you are trying to present. Don't select a "flashy" type font if you are attempting to appear conservative.

Ergonomic Tip

With legs straightened to the front, circle feet to relax ankle muscles.

Figure 35.1 An Email Produced with Microsoft Outlook

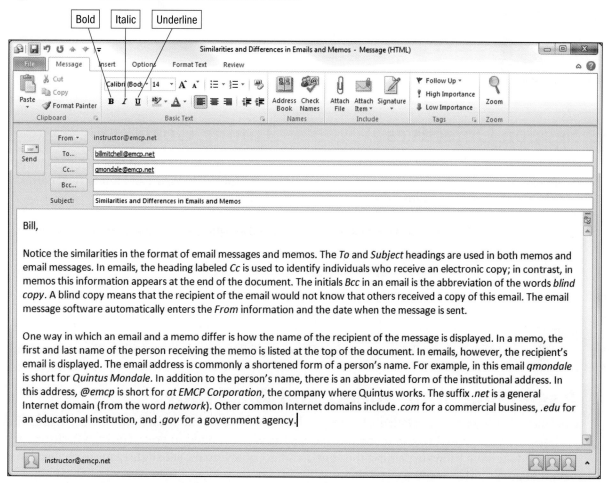

Different email software programs vary in the number of editing features available. For example, Outlook includes buttons that apply bold, italic, and underline formatting to text in an email message. As shown in Figure 35.1, these buttons appear in the Basic Text group on the Message tab. Word processing programs generally provide more formatting and editing features than email software. To take advantage of the features available in word processing software, some individuals create their email messages with their word processor, then copy and paste the text into their email software for transmission.

Creating an Email Message

Students use a wide variety of email programs at home, school, or work. In the following document activities, you will create email messages and then perform several basic editing functions. Rather than use one of the many commercially available email programs, the following document activities will be keyed in Word, which was introduced in Session 34. An additional advantage of preparing the activities in Word is that student work can be checked by the Online Lab.

Both Outlook and Word have features that allow you to bold, italicize, and underline text. As mentioned earlier in Outlook, the Bold, Italic, and Underline buttons are found in the Basic Text group on the Message tab. In Word, the buttons are found in the Font group on the Home tab. In both programs you can apply formatting as you key or key text and apply formatting after the text is typed. To apply formatting after keying text, select the text and then click the appropriate

Session 43 | Preparing Envelopes

Session Objectives

- Add recipient and return addresses to envelopes
- Fold and enclose letters into envelopes

Timing Goals

- 1 minute: 40 WAM and two or fewer errors
- 5 minutes: 30 WAM and ten or fewer errors

Getting Started and Warming Up

Exercise 43.1 If you are continuing immediately from Session 42, you may skip the Exercise 43.1 warm-up drill. However, if you exited the Online Lab at the end of Session 42, warm up by completing Exercise 43.1.

Exercise 43.2 Begin your session work by completing Exercise 43.2, a timed short drill, in the Online Lab.

Assessing Your Speed and Accuracy

Complete Timings 43.1 through 43.4 in the Online Lab. At the end of each timing, the Online Lab will display your WAM rate and any errors. Results will be saved in your Timings Performance report. If you have been surpassing the speed and accuracy goals, set slightly more challenging personal goals and strive to exceed them.

Complete two 1-minute timings on the timing text below. Timings 43.1 and 43.2 use the same paragraph.

Goals: 40 WAM and two or fewer errors
SI: 1.69 syllables per word

> **1-Minute Timings**

Timings 43.1–43.2   How the Internet came to be is an interesting story. The Internet actually is rooted in the Cold War. The researchers who established the network that was to become the Internet were inspired by a desire to begin a communication system that could survive an atomic attack. Following the launch of the Sputnik satellite by the Soviet Union, an agency was established to develop our first satellite. Next they established a system to run and control the missile system and strategic bomber fleet.

formatting button. To select text, position the insertion point at the first word, hold down the left mouse button, drag the cursor to the end of the text to be selected, and then release the left mouse button. Additional methods for selecting text will be described in Session 36.

Document **Email Message**

35.1

1 Read all instructions for this document activity, navigate to the Document 35.1 launch page in the Online Lab, and then click the Launch Activity button. The Online Lab will open **Doc035.01** in the activity window. The timer will start as soon as you begin keying the document.

2 Using the information in Figure 35.2, key the text for the *To, Cc,* and *Subject* lines. If the Word AutoCorrect feature sets an email address as a hyperlink (underlined blue type), position the insertion point immediately after the email address and press the Backspace key to remove the formatting.

3 Key the email message shown in Figure 35.2. Press the Enter key once at the end of the first and second paragraphs. *Note: Unless there is additional text after the last paragraph, such as a closing line or signature, do not press Enter at the end of the last paragraph.*

4 Proofread the document and correct any errors.

5 Save the document by pressing the Save button on the Quick Access toolbar or use the keyboard shortcut Ctrl + S.

6 Click the Check button to stop the timer and upload the document for checking. The Online Lab will report the WAM rate and number of errors for the activity.

7 If errors are reported, view the results document, correct the errors in the submitted document, save the document, and then click the Check button.

Figure 35.2 Email Message Content for Document 35.1

To…	Jhiggins@emcp.net
Cc…	Jlorenz@emcp.net
Subject:	Internet Literacy

Joel, we are missing the boat if we don't provide a more user-friendly website for our firm. For one thing, we have a variety of products that we can display in a much more dynamic way that would allow potential customers to review the products and services we sell. We have the technical expertise to design and implement such a site.

I have put together a proposal that includes the cost of a redesign and the annual costs to maintain such a website. Can you meet with me next Tuesday morning in Room 123 at 10:30? I'd like to go over the proposal with you.

Joan Lorenz was most helpful in pulling together some interesting ways that we could benefit from implementing a fancier website. If you can make the meeting at the time designated, Joan can also attend this meeting.

Figure 42.6 Memo to be Edited for Document 42.4

TO: Michael Chen, President
SUBJECT: Salary Adjustment Process

Many of the employees feel that the process for increasing our salaries is unfair. Some people seem to get salary reviews more often than others do. People get raises just because their manager likes them better. You've got to make some changes or the staff will get angry. They may even slow down their work and then you won't have products to sell.

A new system should be used that establishes a salary review schedule for all workers. You should also choose who will make the salary decisions and what factors they will use. A new process will make employees feel more satisfied.

Thank you for your consideration. I would be glad to discuss possible changes whenever you have the time.

Ending the Session

The Online Lab automatically saves the work you completed for this session. You may continue with the next session or exit the Online Lab and continue later.

Setting Text in Bold

One way to emphasize words or lines of text is to use the bold font style. Setting text in bold is commonly used to make key words and phrases stand out within a body of text. Bolding is also used in report headings to help set them apart from the text. Text can be set in bold as you key or previously keyed material can be set in bold.

To set text in bold as you key, complete the following steps:

1   Click the Bold button in the Font group on the Home tab (or press Ctrl + B).

2   Key the word or words to be bolded.

3   Click the Bold button to turn bolding off (or press Ctrl + B).

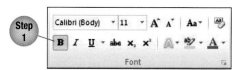

To set previously keyed text in bold, complete the following steps:

1   Select the text to be set in bold by pointing to where you want to begin the selection, holding down the left mouse button, dragging the pointer over the text to be bolded, and then releasing the left mouse button.

2   Click the Bold button in the Font group on the Home tab (or press Ctrl + B).

3   Click outside of the selected text to deselect the text.

The Bold button will appear selected when the insertion point is on a character that has bold formatting applied to it. It is correct to bold a space between words but it is not correct to bold a space that follows a bolded word.

■ Document Email Message with Bolded Text
35.2

1   Read all instructions for this document activity, navigate to the Document 35.2 launch page in the Online Lab, and then click the Launch Activity button. The Online Lab will open **Doc035.02** in the activity window. The timer will start as soon as you begin keying the document.

2   Using the information in Figure 35.3, key the information in the *To, Cc,* and *Subject* lines and then key the email message. Consider the following as you key the document:

   •   If the Word AutoCorrect feature sets an email address as a hyperlink after you key it, position the insertion point immediately after the email address and press the Backspace key to undo the formatting.

   •   Press the Enter key once at the end of the first paragraph.

   •   Bold the designation MIS 240 each time it appears. Do not set the space following the designation MIS 240 in bold.

3   Proofread the document and correct any errors. For example, confirm that the space following **MIS 240** is not bold by selecting the space using the mouse, and checking the Bold button in the Font group on the Home tab.

4   Save the document by pressing the Save button on the Quick Access toolbar or use the keyboard shortcut Ctrl + S.

5   Click the Check button to stop the timer and upload the document for checking. The Online Lab will report the WAM rate and number of errors for the activity.

6   If errors are reported, view the results document, correct the errors in the submitted document, save the document, and then click the Check button.

Reinforcing Writing Skills

A number of words in the English language have a negative effect on readers. Words such as *hate, argue, wrong, poor,* and *problem* are examples of words that tend to produce an undesirable reaction. Think about how you would react to the following statement in a proposal for automating operations in your organization:

> Our project team uncovered numerous problems in the day-to-day operations of your organization.

The terms *uncovered* and *problems* immediately convey a perception that may not be what you want to convey. Are workers or managers trying to cover up something? And, are there that many problems with our system? By rewording the sentence and eliminating the negative words, the reader is more apt to accept what is being presented and to think about it in neutral or objective terms. Here is a more positive way to say the same thing:

> Our project team has identified areas where changes can be made in the day-to-day operations of your organization that will make the work flow more smoothly.

When communicating with others, choose your words carefully. Decide what tone you would like to convey in presenting the information. Select language that helps achieve that mood or feeling. Put yourself in the position of the reader. Will you cause the reader to react negatively with what you are saying before the details are presented? If so, reword your material.

Document 42.4 — Editing a Business Memo for Tone

1. Navigate to the Document 42.4 launch page in the Online Lab and then click the Launch Activity button. The Online Lab will open **Doc042.04** in the activity window.

2. Read the memo shown in Figure 42.6.

3. Using the **Doc042.04** file, rewrite the memo using more positive language. You are trying to convince the president of your company that the salary adjustment process needs to be improved. Use the current date and use your name in the *FROM* field. Do not include reference initials, but do include the file name at the end of the memo.

4. Proofread the revised memo for clarity, correct grammar, spelling, and punctuation.

5. Save the document.

6. Click the Upload button to upload the document for instructor review.

Figure 35.3 Email Message Content for Document 35.2

To...	Gkingman@emcp.net
Cc...	Lmawson@emcp.net
Subject:	Addition of **MIS 240** General Studies

Dean Kingman,

Many faculty members of the School of Business are concerned that **MIS 240** is not included in the recently published list of additions to the general studies program. From past experience, we are convinced that selected courses offered in our school are beneficial to all students, regardless of their major. **MIS 240** is one of those courses. Its emphasis on general computer literacy and the use of the Internet to enhance learning is important to all students.

Please investigate the possibility of adding **MIS 240** to the general studies program. I am available to meet with you for 30 to 45 minutes any afternoon next week to discuss this issue in more detail and to provide a sampling of the information included in this course.

Italicizing Text

Italicizing is another feature available that can be used to make words stand out within a document. The italic font style is frequently used for book, newspaper, and magazine titles as well as key words such as names and headings.

To set text in italics as you key, complete the following steps:

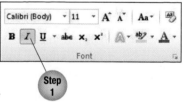

1. Click the Italic button in the Font group on the Home tab (or press Ctrl + I).
2. Key the word or words to be italicized.
3. Click the Italic button to turn italicizing off (or press Ctrl + I).

To set previously keyed text in italics, complete the following steps:

1. Select the text to be set in italics by pointing to where you want to begin the selection, holding down the left mouse button, dragging the pointer over the text to be italicized, and then releasing the left mouse button. *Caution: Be careful not to select/italicize the space after the text, since it will be marked as incorrect in the Online Lab.*
2. Click the Italic button in the Font group on the Home tab (or press Ctrl + I).
3. Click outside of the selected text to deselect the text.

The Italic button will appear selected when the insertion point is on a character that has italic formatting applied to it. It is correct to italicize a space between words but it is not correct to italicize a space that follows an italicized word. It is not correct to italicize a punctuation symbol that follows an italicized word.

7 At the Replace Font dialog box, click *Bold* in the *Font style* list box. Note the *Preview* box indicates how the text will appear with the selected formatting.

8 Click OK to close the Replace Font dialog box.

9 Confirm that the content of the Replace tab in the Find and Replace dialog box reflects the appropriate *Replace with* formatting request of *Font: Bold.*

10 Click the Less button to collapse the Find and Replace dialog box. (After clicking the button, it will change to the More button.)

11 Click the Find Next button and click the Replace button when each instance of *Blackhawk Technical College* is found in the document.

12 After all changes are made, click OK and then close the Find and Replace dialog box.

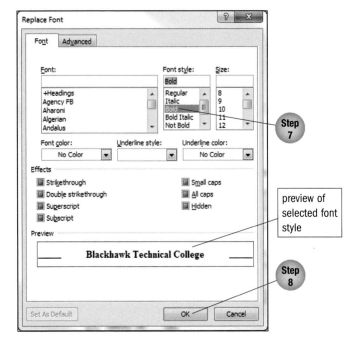

preview of selected font style

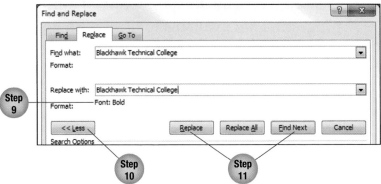

![Document icon] **Document** **Multiple-Page Letter Using Replace to Change Text and Formatting**

42.3

1 Read all instructions for this document activity, navigate to the Document 42.3 launch page in the Online Lab, and then click the Launch Activity button. The Online Lab will open **Doc042.03** in the activity window.

2 Search for all occurrences of *IDP Computing* and change them to *M & I Technologies* and bold those seven occurrences.

3 Search for and apply bold formatting to all occurrences of *Waedt-Steiner Investment Services* found within the body of the letter. (The company name appears in bold in the header of the first page of the document. You will be changing the four occurrences of the company name within the body of the document.)

4 Proofread the letter, paying special attention to the changes made in the file.

5 Save the document.

6 Click the Check button to stop the timer and upload the document for checking. The Online Lab will report the number of errors for the activity.

7 If errors are reported, view the results document, correct the errors in the submitted document, save the document, and then click the Check button.

Document

Email Message with Bold and Italicized Items

35.3

1. Read all instructions for this document activity, navigate to the Document 35.3 launch page in the Online Lab, and then click the Launch Activity button. The Online Lab will open **Doc035.03** in the activity window. The timer will start as soon as you begin keying the document.

2. Using the information in Figure 35.4, which continues on the next page, key the information in the *To* and *Subject* lines and then key the email message. Consider the following as you key the document:

   - If the Word AutoCorrect feature sets an email address as a hyperlink after you key it, position the insertion point immediately after the email address and press the Backspace key to undo the formatting.

   - Bold the names of the topics to be discussed as shown in Figure 35.4. Set the colons in bold but do not set the space following the colons in bold.

   - Italicize animal types as shown in Figure 35.4. If a punctuation symbol follows a word, such as a comma, period, or question mark, do not italicize the punctuation symbol.

3. Proofread the document and correct any errors.

4. Save the document by pressing the Save button on the Quick Access toolbar or use the keyboard shortcut Ctrl + S.

5. Click the Check button to stop the timer and upload the document for checking. The Online Lab will report the WAM rate and number of errors for the activity.

Figure 35.4 Email Message Content for Document 35.3

To...	bburkett@emcp.net
Cc...	
Subject:	Yellowstone Mammals

For your presentation to the school groups on the mammals of Yellowstone, please cover the following:

Bears: Discuss the difference in size, color, and habits of both *grizzly bears* and *black bears*. Include several photos of each type of bear.

Wolves: Please discuss the reintroduction program of *wolves* to Yellowstone. Provide estimates of the total number of *wolves* and which animals they most often hunt and feed on. Also compare *wolves* with their cousin, the *coyote*.

Bison: Discuss the size and group behavior of *bison* and how they deal with all the snow.

Mammal sightseeing: Discuss how easy it is for visitors to travel around Yellowstone and to actually see mammals. Can one see mammals from their car or do they have to hike on trails? How often does one see smaller mammals, such as *squirrels*, *marmots*, and *beavers*?

continues

Formatting with Find and Replace

The Find and Replace feature, which was introduced in Session 41, includes several options that allow you to customize your search, such as locating a name and changing its font appearance. For example, you might want to search for all occurrences of the words *Blackhawk Technical College* in an open document and change the font style of those words to bold. The following steps will guide you through this find-and-replace activity.

1. Click the Replace button in the Editing group on the Home tab. This will open the Find and Replace dialog box with the Replace tab selected.

2. Select any text that appears in the *Find what* text box and key **Blackhawk Technical College**.

3. Delete any text that appears in the *Replace with* text box and key **Blackhawk Technical College**.

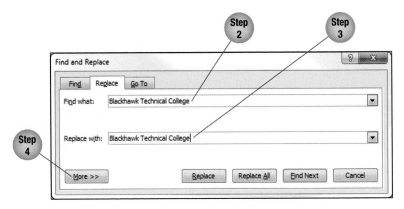

4. Click the More button to expand the Find and Replace dialog box.

5. Click the Format button in the *Replace* section. *Note: When the **Find what** text box is active, the section is labeled **Find**.*

6. Click the *Font* option to open the Replace Font dialog box.

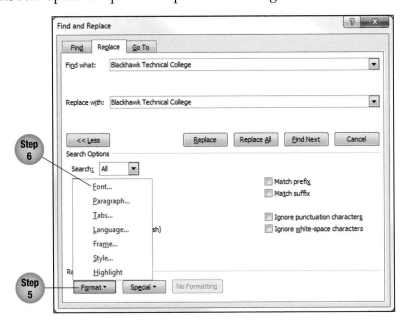

steps continue

Figure 35.4 Content for Document 35.3—Continued

> **Danger:** Discuss how dangerous it is if a park visitor comes across a *grizzly bear*, *black bear*, *bison*, or *wolf* while hiking on a trail. Can people use cell phones to call for help?
>
> Each middle school where you will talk has a classroom reserved for you. Your presentations will be on Wednesdays from 1 to 3 p.m. Expect 20 students in each class. Call Mike Baldwin at 4320 or send an email message to him (mbaldwin@emcp.net) if you have any questions or special equipment needs.

6 If errors are reported, view the results document, correct the errors in the submitted document, save the document, and then click the Check button.

Underlining Feature

Underlining is used for headings of a report or manuscript or to emphasize a word or phrase.

To set text in underline as you key, complete the following steps:

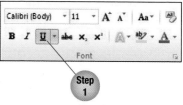

1 Click the Underline button in the Font group on the Home tab (or press Ctrl + U).

2 Key the word or words to be underlined.

3 Click the Underline button to turn underlining off (or press Ctrl + U).

To underline previously keyed text, complete the following steps:

1 Select the text to be underlined by pointing to where you want to begin the selection, holding down the left mouse button, dragging the pointer over the text to be underlined, and then releasing the left mouse button.

2 Click the Underline button in the Font group on the Home tab (or press Ctrl + U).

3 Click outside of the selected text to deselect the text.

The Underline button will appear selected when the insertion point is on a character that has underline formatting applied to it. It is correct to underline a space between words but it is not correct to underline a space that follows an underlined word.

Success Tip

The use of all capital letters in email messages is commonly interpreted as shouting. Thus, you should avoid using all capital letters to emphasize words, unless you want your reader to think that you are shouting.

Figure 42.5 Multiple-Page Letter Content for Document 42.2—Continued

my observations follow:

1. The sequence for the proposed textbook is oriented to one job occupation, the administrative services profession. If this is your market niche, then the proposal is right on target.

2. Units are not included in desktop publishing, office ergonomics, and email management.

3. The business communications chapter does not include anything about oral communications.

4. The emphasis is on legal and medical systems applications. However, a large number of administrative assistants today are working for manufacturing firms or in government offices. I recommend that the text include applications in these areas.

5. In the filing and records management chapter, nothing was mentioned about the cost of maintaining and disposing of recorded information or recycling. I believe this information should be added.

6. The principles of accounting chapter does not seem to cover the basics of electronic accounting. No mention is even made of the most popular accounting software packages.

7. The chapter on printers doesn't cover using copiers as printers as well as for sending and receiving faxes, making PDF files, and so on. There should be more emphasis on the range of equipment in use rather than how to operate specific machines.

8. The field of telecommunications is an important topic that should be discussed at length. Since this is a fast-evolving field, perhaps the text should be accompanied by online coverage of hot topics.

I hope these comments will help in your decision to publish in the office education area. I certainly would promote this venture and would be happy to help you in any way possible. If you have any questions, please write, or call me at (312) 555-5622. You may also email me at lmissham@emcp.net.

Sincerely,

Lorraine Missingham
Business Careers Editor

Reinforcing Writing Skills

Beginning with Session 35, most sessions include an optional writing activity intended to strengthen your writing and grammar skills while giving you an opportunity to compose at the keyboard. With practice, you will find that it is much easier to create documents directly at the keyboard. While these activities will be uploaded for instructor review, they will not be checked by the Online Lab.

Communicating with people in writing is much more difficult than communicating in person. On a face-to-face basis, the speaker knows immediately if the message is not being communicated correctly. Body language, facial expressions, and questions provide instant and ongoing feedback. A writer, however, does not enjoy those advantages. Instead, the writer must rely on clear sentences and carefully chosen words to convey the intended meaning.

One simple way to help the reader comprehend your message is to keep sentences at a reasonable length—15 to 25 words. Readers tend to get lost in sentences that are too long. In contrast, very short sentences create a "choppy" rhythm, which can annoy the reader.

Focus on creating sentences of the target length as you complete the next document. Compose the email message at the computer and then edit your document for clear meaning, correct punctuation, and accurate word choices. Check the sentence length and edit accordingly.

Document 35.4

Composing an Email Message

1   Navigate to the Document 35.4 launch page in the Online Lab and then click the Launch Activity button. The Online Lab will open **Doc035.04** in the activity window.

2   Using the downloaded document, compose an email message to your instructor with the subject *An Ideal Career*. The email message should contain at least two paragraphs. Describe your ideal career, the skills you have or would need to develop to succeed in the career, and the jobs you would expect to do as you travel the path of your career. Be sure to explain why you consider this career to be a good choice for you.

3   Underline at least one word in the message.

4   When you have finished the message, edit it for clear meaning, correct punctuation, and accurate word choices.

5   Save the document.

6   Click the Upload button to upload the document for instructor review.

Ending the Session

The Online Lab automatically saves the work you completed for this session. You may continue with the next session or exit the Online Lab and continue later.

If bulleted or numbered paragraphs are lengthy, improve the readability of the list by creating an extra line space between numbered paragraphs. To set this extra line space, press Shift + Enter and then Enter, rather than just Enter after each line.

⊞Document **Multiple-Page Letter with Numbered Paragraphs**

42.2

1. Read all instructions for this document activity, navigate to the Document 42.2 launch page in the Online Lab, and then click the Launch Activity button. The Online Lab will open **Doc042.02** in the activity window. The timer will start as soon as you begin keying the document.

2. Key the letter shown in Figure 42.5.

   a. Use March 20, 2014, as the date.

   b. This letter is being sent out of the United States, therefore a postal code is used instead of a U.S. ZIP code and the country to which the letter is being sent is keyed in all capital letters on the line below the city, province, and postal code.

   c. Allow the Word automatic formatting to format the numbered list.

   d. Do not format the email address as a hyperlink.

3. Add an extra line space between items within the numbered list by pressing Shift + Enter at the end of each numbered item, except the last item in the list. *Note: Make sure there is no space between the period at the end of the numbered paragraph and the Shift + Enter line break*.

4. Create a horizontal heading for the second page of the letter. Use the *Blank (Three Columns)* heading option and remember to click in each text placeholder to key the appropriate information.

5. After the title line, key the reference initials **hbr** and the file name.

6. Note the bad page break and insert an extra hard return (press Enter) after the date.

7. Proofread and correct any errors in the letter.

8. Save the document.

9. Click the Check button to stop the timer and upload the document for checking. The Online Lab will report the WAM rate and number of errors for the activity.

10. If errors are reported, view the results document, correct the errors in the submitted document, save the document, and then click the Check button.

Figure 42.5 Multiple-Page Letter Content for Document 42.2

Mr. Gary Wenner

Business Publications

510 Third Avenue

Toronto, ON M2H 2S6

CANADA

Dear Mr. Wenner:

Your letter regarding the proposal by Dr. Darlene Jones of Bailey College arrived while I was on vacation. I've reviewed the proposal carefully and

continues

Preparing Memos

Session Objectives

- **Explore basic features of memos**
- **Prepare and format memos**
- **Change alignment and indent text in a memo**
- **Practice composing a memo at the keyboard**

Timing Goals

- **1 minute: 35 WAM and two or fewer errors**
- **3 minutes: 30 WAM and six or fewer errors**

Getting Started and Warming Up

Exercise 36.1 If you are continuing immediately from Session 35, you may skip the Exercise 36.1 warm-up drill. However, if you exited the Online Lab at the end of Session 35, warm up by completing Exercise 36.1.

Exercise 36.2 Begin your session work by completing Exercise 36.2, a timed short drill, in the Online Lab.

Assessing Your Speed and Accuracy

Complete Timings 36.1 through 36.4 in the Online Lab. At the end of each timing, the Online Lab will display your WAM rate and highlight any errors. Results will be saved in your Timings Performance report. If you have been surpassing the speed and accuracy goals, set slightly more challenging personal goals and strive to exceed them.

Complete two 1-minute timings on the timing text below. Timings 36.1 and 36.2 use the same paragraph.

Goals: 35 WAM and two or fewer errors
SI: 1.33 syllables per word

1-Minute Timings

Timings 36.1–36.2

Rain is quite welcome when the land is dry. The earth's surface holds quite a bit of water, but in times of very dry weather it always seems to be in the wrong place, or it is of the type that can't be used. Normally, all regions of the United States receive adequate amounts of rain; however, there are particular periods when clouds don't release their moisture for long amounts of time.

Figure 42.3 Multiple-Page Letter Content for Document 42.1—Continued

M & I Technologies will pay the fees and expenses of its legal counsel; all printing charges relating to the registration, prospectus, and underwriting agreements; postage; SEC, state, and federal filing fees; and the reasonable costs of a due diligence meeting.

Following the conclusion of the public offering, M & I Technologies agrees to furnish quarterly unaudited financial statements to its shareholders and the underwriters with audited reports to be issued annually.

We look forward to working with you and your associates on the proposed public offering. This letter is accepted by M & I Technologies and Waedt-Steiner Investment Services as a statement of mutual intent to carry out the proposed transactions, but it does not constitute a firm commitment on the part of either the company or the underwriters.

If this letter sets forth your understanding of our arrangement, please contact us.

Sincerely yours,

Donald F. Steiner
Senior Vice President

Numbering Paragraphs

With Word you can create numbered paragraphs and lists similar to how you create bulleted lists. The Word default setting automatically formats a numbered list when a line begins with *1.* followed by a space. Word will indent the number and replace the space with a nonprinting Tab symbol. If the numbered paragraph continues to a second line, Word Wrap will begin the second line as a hanging indent. In other words, the run-over line will align with the text that follows the nonprinting Tab symbol, not with the number. To stop the numbering of paragraphs, press the Enter key twice.

Once a numbered list is formatted, you can remove the formatting by selecting the list and clicking the Numbering button in the Paragraph group on the Home tab (see Figure 42.4). Or, if you wish to change the formatting of a numbered list (for example, to change from a numbered list to a lettered list) click the Numbering button drop-down arrow and select the appropriate formatting option.

Figure 42.4 Paragraph Group

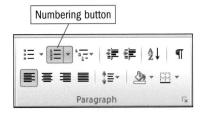

Numbering button

Paragraph

Complete two 3-minute timings on the timing text below. Timings 36.3 and 36.4 use the same paragraphs.

Goal: 30 WAM and six or fewer errors
SI: 1.33 syllables per word

Timings 36.3–36.4

Changes are often the cause of stress, whether you wanted these changes or they are thrust upon you. Change can be frightening and may call for some adjustment on your part. Change and stress are closely knit. You may experience stress as the result of changes that occur on a regular basis. These changes can be good or they can cause problems. Some of the common changes that cause stress are the death of a parent, the death of a child, the start of a new job, enrollment in a new school, asking someone for a date, or giving a speech.

You may also encounter stress by getting married or by having children. There are many other causes as well. It is best to confront stress when you have a problem managing it. Do not keep feeling bad about something that has happened to you on the job or at home. Work through the problems. Keep a positive outlook, and be prepared for the usual ups and downs in feelings. Work to handle your relationships with care. Learn to control stress.

Ergonomic Tip

With your fist facing down, press against the knuckles of the closed hand. Resist for five seconds on each knuckle. Repeat series five times. This exercise helps the circulation in your hands and fingers.

Preparing Memos

As discussed in Session 35, email is a commonly employed means of written communication. Other types of documents are also common, especially in business environments. These documents include memorandums, letters, reports, and manuscripts. This session will discuss memorandums (commonly shortened to memos). Memos are generally used to communicate within an organization. Memos can vary in length, but most are short. As we discuss memos, we will also introduce several additional features of Word.

Throughout this text, the term *memo* refers to internal documents that are keyed, printed, and delivered via the internal mail system of an organization. In contrast, an email is a message that is transmitted electronically. A document that contains a memo may, however, be distributed via email as an attached file.

Figure 42.3 Multiple-Page Letter Content for Document 42.1

Mr. Mark Shakil, President
Dain Bosworth, Inc.
2401 Lincoln Boulevard
New York, NY 10037-6847

Dear Mr. Shakil:

This is to record the mutual intention of M & I Technologies and Waedt-Steiner Investment Services to undertake a public offering of common stock of M & I Technologies (the "company").

It is our intention to form an underwriting syndicate to purchase up to 250,000 shares of new common stock from M & I Technologies and to reoffer the shares to the public at a price mutually agreed upon. This agreement is subject to the following:

The assurance that no materially adverse change in the affairs of the company and its prospects occurs which appears sufficient, in our opinion, to threaten the success of our effort.

The market conditions at the time of the offering.

The filing of a prospectus with the Securities and Exchange Commission (SEC) and its subsequent notification of effectiveness.

We will not be bound to receive and pay for your shares until Blue Sky qualifications have been met in a reasonable number of states of our mutual selection and a final underwriting agreement satisfactory to each of us is executed.

The exact terms of the underwriting will be set forth in an underwriting agreement to be entered into by M & I Technologies and Waedt-Steiner Investment Services. The underwriting discounts and commissions will not exceed 10 percent of the public offering price.

Except for any reimbursement provided for in this letter, Waedt-Steiner Investment Services will pay its own expenses and the expenses of its attorneys. The underwriters will also pay the expenses of running the customary advertisements in various publications following the offering.

continues

Formatting a Memo

Memos may be prepared on preprinted memo forms, letterhead, plain paper, or memo templates available in some word processing software packages. The standard format is the block style, with **guide words** (DATE, TO, FROM, SUBJECT) and the message starting at the left margin. The order and placement of the guide words may vary from one organization to another and among software packages that include preformatted document templates.

The traditional memo will be featured in this session. The order of the guide words for these memos is TO, FROM, DATE, SUBJECT.

The example of a memo in Figure 36.1 shows common formatting for a memo prepared on plain paper. Use the guidelines shown in the example in Figure 36.1 in preparing the memos in this book.

Figure 36.1 Sample Memo Format   *Note: Do not key this document.*

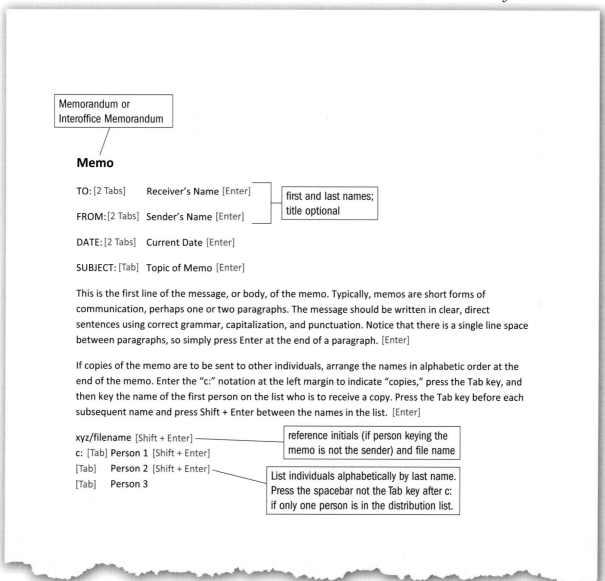

7   Key the date portion of the header by following these steps:

   a   Confirm that your insertion point is in the correct position. If keying a vertical header, press the Enter key so that the insertion point appears one line below the page number. If you are using the horizontal header style, click the right placeholder.

   b   Key the date as it appears on the first page of the letter. *Note: The date in a header must always match the date on the first page of the letter. If a letter is edited on a different date than it was keyed, be sure to change the date in the header, too.*

8   Click the Close Header and Footer button in the Close group or double-click in the body of the document.

If you need to make changes to the contents of a header later, double-click in the header to make it active, make your changes, and then double-click in the body of the document to make the document active.

Document 42.1 Multiple-Page Letter with Header and Bulleted Paragraphs

1   Read all instructions for this document activity, navigate to the Document 42.1 launch page in the Online Lab, and then click the Launch Activity button. The Online Lab will open **Doc042.01** in the activity window. The timer will start as soon as you begin keying the document.

2   Key the letter shown in Figure 42.3 as a block-style letter. Use April 8, 2014, as the date of the letter. The document has a different first-page header and footer, which consists of the company letterhead.

3   Create a vertical header on the second page.

4   Format paragraphs 3 through 5 in the body of the letter (the paragraphs that begin with *The assurance that no*, *The market conditions*, and *The filing of a prospectus*) as a bulleted list with standard black solid circle bullets.

5   After the title line, key the reference initials **jaf** and the file name. Also indicate that the letter is being copied to the Accounting Department Manager.

6   Proofread and correct any errors in the letter.

7   Save the document.

8   Click the Check button to stop the timer and upload the document for checking. The Online Lab will report the WAM rate and number of errors for the activity.

9   If errors are reported, view the results document, correct the errors in the submitted document, save the document, and then click the Check button.

Document Memo with Basic Formatting

1 Read all instructions for this document activity, navigate to the Document 36.1 launch page in the Online Lab, and then click the Launch Activity button. The Online Lab will open **Doc036.01** in the activity window. The timer will start as soon as you begin keying the document.

2 Key the guide words for the memo by completing the following steps:

   a Place the insertion point to the right of *TO:*, press Tab twice, key **Ron Decker, Editorial Department**, and then press Enter once to move to the next line.

   b Key **FROM:**, press Tab twice, key **Bill Walczak**, and then press Enter once to move to the next line.

   c Key **DATE:**, press Tab twice, key **October 26, 2014**, and press Enter once to move to the next line. *Note: Do not key the actual current date or the Online Lab will show this as an error.*

   d Key **SUBJECT:**, press Tab once, key **Seminar Outline**, and then press Enter once to move to the next line.

3 Key the body of the memo, shown in Figure 36.2, pressing Enter after each paragraph:

4 Indicate that the person typing the letter has the initials ctl and that a copy of the memo will be distributed to Juanita Jimenez, Ned Ostenso, and Bill Sauro by completing the following steps:

   a Key **ctl/Doc036.01** and then press Shift + Enter to move to the next line. Since Word automatically capitalizes the first letter of the first word in sentences, you will need to manually lowercase the first letter by pressing the Arrow key back and typing a lowercase letter. *Note: Do not key your actual initials or the Online Lab will show this as an error. Also, do not include the extension of the file name (e.g., "docx").*

   b Key **c:**, press Tab, key **Juanita Jimenez**, and then press Shift + Enter to move to the next line.

   c Press Tab, key **Ned Ostenso**, and then press Shift + Enter to move to the next line.

   d Press Tab and then key **Bill Sauro**. *Note: At the end of the memo do not press Enter or Shift + Enter or the Online Lab will show this as an error.*

5 Proofread the memo and correct any errors.

6 Save the document by pressing the Save button on the Quick Access toolbar or use the keyboard shortcut Ctrl + S.

7 Click the Check button to stop the timer and upload the document for checking. The Online Lab will report the WAM rate and number of errors for the activity.

8 If errors are reported, view the results document, correct the errors in the submitted document, save the document, and then click the Check button.

Figure 36.2 Memo Content for Document 36.1

Ron, attached is the revised seminar outline for the program on Organizational Communication.

Ned Ostenso, Bill Sauro, Juanita Jimenez, and I collaborated on this revision. Please note that we changed the name of the program. We feel that the new title describes the seminar content more accurately.

Please let us know when you are ready to review the program.

3 Click the appropriate header format option from the drop-down list. The *Blank* option is used for the vertical (three-line) header and the *Blank (Three Columns)* option is used for the horizontal (one-line) header.

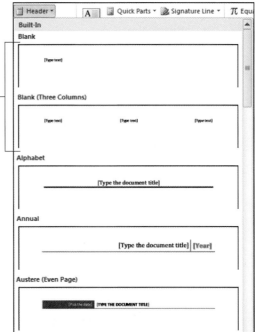

Step 3

4 Confirm that the *Different First Page* check box contains a check mark; if it is not already selected, click it to insert a check mark. If the *Different First Page* option is selected, the second and subsequent pages of a document have a different heading than the first page.

Step 4

5 Click the *[Type text]* placeholder and key the recipient's name. If you are keying the vertical header style and used the *Blank* header option, there will be one text placeholder. If you are keying the horizontal header style and used the *Blank (Three Columns)* option, there will be three text placeholders. Click the left placeholder and key the recipient's name. In either header format, you do not need to delete the placeholder; just click in it and key.

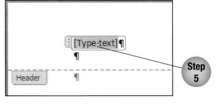

Step 5

6 Key the page number portion of the header by following these steps:

a Confirm that your insertion point is in the correct position. If keying a vertical header, press the Enter key so that the insertion point appears one line below the recipient's name. (The line spacing in a header is set for single space by default.) If you are using the horizontal header style, click the middle placeholder.

b Key **Page**, press the space bar, and then click the Page Number button in the Header & Footer group on the Header & Footer Tools Design tab.

c From the drop-down menu, point to *Current Position* and then click *Plain Number*.

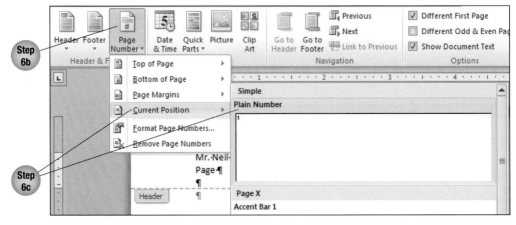

Step 6b

Step 6c

steps continue

Table 36.1 Selecting Words, Lines, Sentences, and Paragraphs

To select...	complete these steps with the mouse...
A word	Double-click the word.
A line of text	Click in the selection bar to the left of the line.
Multiple lines of text	Drag in the selection bar to the left of the lines.
A sentence	Hold down the Ctrl key and then click anywhere in the sentence.
A paragraph	Double-click in the selection bar next to the paragraph or triple-click anywhere in the paragraph.
Multiple paragraphs	Drag in the selection bar.

Selecting Text

As mentioned in Session 35, text can be selected using the mouse. Word provides many methods for selecting text with either a mouse or with the keyboard. Methods for selecting a word, a sentence, a paragraph, or one or more lines or paragraphs are listed in Table 36.1. In a document, the text that you select appears with a blue background.

Several additional methods for selecting text that you may find very useful include:

- Position the mouse pointer on the first character of the text to be selected, hold down the left mouse button, drag the mouse to the last character of the text to be selected, and then release the left mouse button.

- To select more than one word, double-click the first word, hold down the mouse button, and then drag over the additional words to be included in the selection.

- Pressing the Shift key and using the Up, Down, Left, or Right arrow keys on the keyboard.

To deselect text with the mouse, position the mouse pointer anywhere in the document outside the selected text and then click the left mouse button.

Changing Paragraph Alignment

In Word, the default setting for text in paragraphs is aligned at the left margin and ragged at the right margin (referred to as "left aligned" or "left justified"). Text alignment can also be set to have a ragged left margin and an aligned right margin ("right aligned" or "right justified"), to have both left and right margins aligned ("justify" or "fully justified"), or to have both left and right margins ragged ("centered"). Note that when text is fully justified, Word adds extra space to lengthen the shorter lines. The location of the paragraph alignment buttons in the Paragraph group on the Home tab is shown in Figure 36.3. The function of these buttons is summarized in Table 36.2. Text can be aligned as you key or preexisting text can be selected and then aligned. If you want to return paragraph alignment to the default setting (left aligned), click the Align Text Left button.

Figure 36.3 Paragraph Group on the Home Tab with the Align Text Left Button Activated

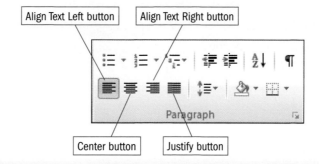

Figure 42.1 Pages Break Button in the Pages Group

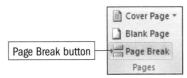

Inserting Headers

A letter that is longer than one page should include a header on the second page and on any subsequent pages. The header of a business letter contains three pieces of information: the addressee (recipient of the letter), the page number, and the date. Probably the two most commonly employed formats for headers are vertical style and horizontal style. As shown in Figure 42.2, the vertical style appears on three separate lines, whereas the horizontal style contains all the header information on one line.

Figure 42.2 Second Page Header Options   *Note: Do not key this document.*

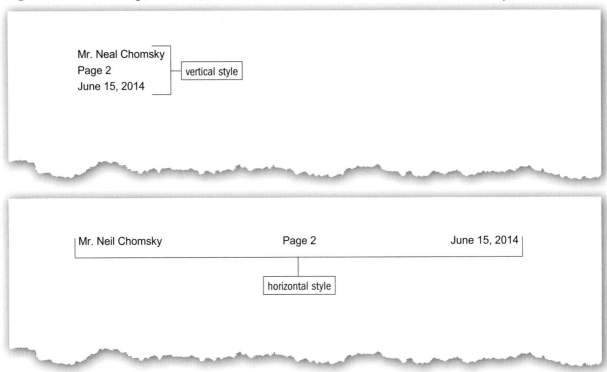

Word has automated the process of inserting headers. Headers may be inserted at any time; however, it is simpler to insert the heading after the document is keyed—or at least after you begin to key the second page.

After keying a letter that is more than one page long, place your insertion point in a location on the second page and then follow these steps to insert a header:

1 Click the Insert tab.

2 Click the Header button in the Header & Footer group.

steps continue

Table 36.2 Paragraph Alignment Buttons and Functions

Text Alignment	Button Name	Button
At the left margin	Align Text Left	
Between margins	Center	
At the right margin	Align Text Right	
At the left and right margin	Justify	

To change the alignment of existing text in a paragraph, position the insertion point anywhere within the paragraph and then click the button on the toolbar for the desired alignment. If you want to align multiple paragraphs, select the paragraphs to be aligned and then click the desired alignment button.

Document 36.2 Memo with Text Aligned at the Left and Right Margins

1. Read all instructions for this document activity, navigate to the Document 36.2 launch page in the Online Lab, and then click the Launch Activity button. The Online Lab will open **Doc036.02** in the activity window. The timer will start as soon as you begin keying the document.

2. Use the content in Figure 36.4 below and on the next page to key the memo. Be sure to apply correct formatting, as shown in Figure 36.1. *Hint: Remember to tab the correct number of times after the guide words.* Italicize where indicated, remembering not to italicize the punctuation symbol.

3. Justify the three paragraphs within the body of the memo so that they are aligned at both the left and right margins. *Note: The text provided in Figure 36.4 is not correctly justified.*

4. Include the reference initials sjc (remember to Undo Auto Capitalization and add a forward slash) and the file name, **Doc036.02**, at the end of the memo. Make sure that the reference initials and file name are formatted to align at the left margin. Note that there are no copies being sent in this activity.

5. Proofread and correct any errors.

6. Save the document.

7. Click the Check button to stop the timer and upload the document for checking. The Online Lab will report the WAM rate and number of errors for the activity.

8. If errors are reported, view the results document, correct the errors in the submitted document, save the document, and then click the Check button.

Figure 36.4 Memo Content for Document 36.2

TO: Leslie McKay, Training and Education

FROM: Pat Iverson, Human Resources

DATE: October 28, 2014

SUBJECT: Workplace Literacy

continues

Ergonomic Tip

Turn your head to look over your right shoulder, back to the front, and then over your left shoulder. This type of stretching helps your neck muscles to relax.

Preparing Multiple-Page Letters

Most business letters fit on one page. However, you may prepare complex letters that require a second page or additional pages. There are a few guidelines to consider when formatting multiple-page letters. For example, do not create a second page just for the complimentary closing, signature, etc. If this situation occurs, insert several hard returns (press Enter several times) before and/or after the date. This will force some content on the first page to spill onto the second page.

The Word default settings end each page approximately 1 inch from the bottom of the page. This automatic page break is called a ***soft page break***. The Word default settings also prevent undesirable breaks between pages such as dividing a paragraph so that only one line remains on a page by itself. This default setting is called *Widow/Orphan control*. Check your computer settings by following these steps:

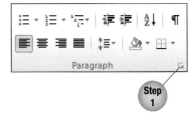

1. On the Home tab, click the dialog box launcher in the Paragraph group.

2. Click the Line and Page Breaks tab if it is not selected.

3. If there is no check mark next to *Widow/Orphan control*, click the check box to insert a check mark and to make the option active.

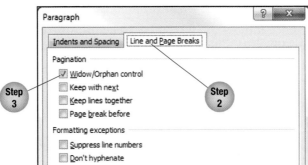

4. Click OK to activate the setting change and to close the dialog box.

Even with this default setting, it may be necessary to force a page break within a document. Forcing a page break is discussed in the next section.

Inserting a Hard Page Break

To insert a page break in a document, place the insertion point where you want the break to occur, click the Insert tab, and then click the Page Break button in the Pages group (see Figure 42.1) or press the keyboard shortcut Ctrl + Enter. A page break that is created using the Page Break button or the keyboard shortcut is called a ***hard page break***.

Figure 36.4 Memo Content for Document 36.2—Continued

How are you doing on the workplace literacy project? Workplace literacy appears to be an important topic for all businesses in the United States. Yesterday, I read an article in the August 2014 edition of *Training and Development Journal*. The author has some interesting thoughts.

With foreign competition challenging American businesses, U.S. industrial plants are pushing to improve worker productivity, often by using more advanced equipment. But many companies have introduced sophisticated, computer-driven machinery, only to find that workers do not have the basic reading and math skills required to operate the equipment.

Are you still on target with the project? I am anxious to read the final research results and the recommendations you will make.

Document 36.3 **Memo with Center Justification**

1. Read all instructions for this document activity, navigate to the Document 36.3 launch page in the Online Lab, and then click the Launch Activity button. The Online Lab will open **Doc036.03** in the activity window. The timer will start as soon as you begin keying the document.

2. Use the content in Figure 36.5 to key the memo. Be sure to apply correct formatting, as shown in Figure 36.1. *Note: The symbol ¶ is used to indicate a new paragraph break.*

3. Center justify the second paragraph in the body of the memo (begins *The National Business Educators Association (NBEA) is*).

4. Proofread and correct any errors.

5. Save the document.

6. Click the Check button to stop the timer and upload the document for checking. The Online Lab will report the WAM rate and number of errors for the activity.

7. If errors are reported, view the results document, correct the errors in the submitted document, save the document, and then click the Check button.

Figure 36.5 Memo Content for Document 36.3

TO: Ms. Pat Ganser, Business Development Department ¶ FROM: Amos Grant, Research Director ¶ DATE: October 28, 2014 ¶ SUBJECT: Abstracts of Office Research Studies ¶ The following announcement was published in an NBEA flyer: ¶ The National Business Educators Association (NBEA) is calling for abstracts of research studies that were completed in office systems during the past calendar year. Abstracts should be submitted to the attention of Oscar Byrnside, Executive Director of NBEA. ¶ All abstracts must reach NBEA headquarters within the next 30 days. Please indicate the specific topic area on the abstract form. ¶ sjc/Doc036.03

Complete two 5-minute timings on the timing text below. Timings 42.3 and 42.4 use the same paragraphs.

Goals: 30 WAM and ten or fewer errors
SI: 1.43 syllables per word

5-Minute Timings

**Timings
42.3–42.4**

A person who owns a home and wishes to sell it has to identify an asking price. Most people who want to sell their homes don't have the background for putting a fair market value on their home. Often, the sale price is based on the original cost plus added improvements to the home. In other cases, sale prices are based on what the owner thinks the property is worth. For most people, their home is their largest investment, and if they plan to sell, it is a good idea to contact a real estate agent or an appraiser for input on the fair market value of a home.

Many factors have to be taken into account when arriving at a property's fair market value. Some of the most important factors are location, size of home, energy efficiency, eye appeal, decorating, age, floor plan, and landscaping, as well as many other minor points. One of the best indicators of the market value of a home is comparable sales, as that is what the buying public is willing to pay. Recent sales of properties that have been sold that are the most similar in size, style, location, and condition are most helpful in establishing a realistic sale price on a home.

No two properties are alike; it is important to review the pros and cons of each property being compared. However, the positives and negatives are really up to the buyer to decide. There are other factors to be considered in setting a sale price on a home. For example, at the time the house is to be listed for sale, is it a seller's or buyer's market? When there is a shortage of homes in a particular category and there are people wanting to buy, this represents a seller's market. Many times, new firms entering or leaving an area will have a direct impact on the market value of homes.

People who are planning to sell their homes should also be aware that at least 90 percent of all buyers will require new financing. Those lending the money to homebuyers will require an appraisal on the property to ensure that the asking price is realistic. In the process of selling a home, the seller wants to get the highest possible dollar for the sale while the buyer wants to purchase at the lowest possible amount. No doubt supply and demand are critical factors in arriving at the sale price of a home.

Figure 36.6 Location of Word Ruler and Indent Markers

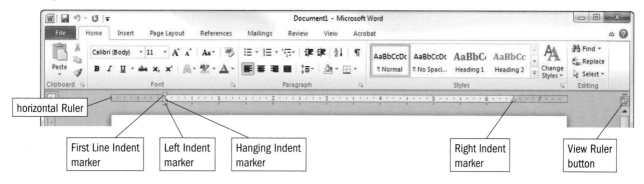

Word Ruler

When you open a blank Word document, the horizontal **Ruler** may appear just below the ribbon and just above the document, as shown in Figure 36.6. The Ruler can be hidden or displayed by clicking the View Ruler button on or off.

The numbers on the Ruler are measured in inches, from the left margin. The inches are divided into eighths of an inch (smallest tick marks), with half-inches shown by larger tick marks.

The width of the right and left margins of a document is indicated by the portion of the Ruler shown in white. There are several ways to change these margins, but a simple way is to select the left or right indent marker and drag the marker along the Ruler to the desired location. You will use this approach as you prepare Document 36.4.

Indenting Text Using the Ruler

Text in a paragraph may be indented from the right or left margin, or both, as you key or after text has been keyed. To indent the left margin of text as you key, drag the Left Indent marker to the right to the desired location and then key text. If, at a position later in the document, you want to return the margin to the original position, drag the Left Indent marker to the original position and then continue keying. To indent the right margin of the text as you key, drag the Right Indent marker to the left to the desired location and then key the text.

To change the left or right indent of previously keyed text, select the desired text and release the mouse button. With the text selected, drag the Left or Right Indent marker to the desired location and then click anywhere in the document to deselect the text.

Document **Memo with Text Indented from the Left and Right Margins**

36.4

1 Read all instructions for this document activity, navigate to the Document 36.4 launch page in the Online Lab, and then click the Launch Activity button. The Online Lab will open **Doc036.04** in the activity window. The timer will start as soon as you begin keying the document.

2 Use the content in Figure 36.7 to key the memo. Be sure to apply correct formatting, as shown in Figure 36.1. Watch for italicized and bolded words. *Hint: When two words are formatted, format the space between the words. Do not format the punctuation or the space following the last formatted word.*

3 Indent the second paragraph in the body of the memo (begins *Leaving the hospital after*) 0.5 inch on both the right and left margins by changing the indent markers on the Ruler. *Hint: Ensure that you are dragging the Left and Right Indent markers, not the First Line or Hanging Indent markers.*

steps continue

Preparing Two-Page Business Letters

Session Objectives

- Insert hard page breaks
- Create a header in a multiple-page letter
- Number paragraphs
- Find and replace formatting
- Choose positive words in writing a document

Timing Goals

- 1 minute: 40 WAM and two or fewer errors
- 5 minutes: 30 WAM and ten or fewer errors

Getting Started and Warming Up

Exercise 42.1 If you are continuing immediately from Session 41, you may skip the Exercise 42.1 warm-up drill. However, if you exited the Online Lab at the end of Session 41, warm up by completing Exercise 42.1.

Exercise 42.2 Begin your session work by completing Exercise 42.2, a timed short drill, in the Online Lab.

Assessing Your Speed and Accuracy

Complete Timings 42.1 through 42.4 in the Online Lab. At the end of each timing, the Online Lab will display your WAM rate and any errors. Results will be saved in your Timings Performance report. If you have been surpassing the speed and accuracy goals, set slightly more challenging personal goals and strive to exceed them.

Complete two 1-minute timings on the timing text below. Timings 42.1 and 42.2 use the same paragraph.

Goals: 40 WAM and two or fewer errors
SI: 1.56 syllables per word

1-Minute Timings

Timings 42.1–42.2   You are a consumer. Without you and millions of other consumers in the nation, businesses would have to close. There would be nobody to buy those goods and services that businesses produce. The impact of ceasing all operations would quickly affect every person. Workers would have no jobs and would have no money to continue living. There would be no hustle and bustle of daily life. Every family would have to supply all the necessities in life for themselves. Each family or group would have to grow food, produce clothing, and provide shelter.

4   Proofread the memo and correct any errors.

5   Save the document.

6   Click the Check button to stop the timer and upload the document for checking. The Online Lab will report the WAM rate and number of errors for the activity.

7   If errors are reported, view the results document, correct the errors in the submitted document, save the document, and then click the Check button.

Figure 36.7 Memo Content for Document 36.4

TO: Joshua Redmond, Public Relations Department ¶ FROM: Raye Dearborn, Human Resources Department ¶ DATE: October 27, 2014 ¶ SUBJECT: Nancy Rushmore's Retirement ¶ After 22 years as an employee at the hospital, Nancy Rushmore is retiring. For the past five years, Nancy has worked as the Personnel Director for the Human Resources Department. When asked about her retirement, Nancy stated: ¶ Leaving the hospital after 22 years is going to be very difficult. I have made wonderful friends over the years that I will miss *very much*. I haven't made any future plans, but I do hope to spend time reading, relaxing, and doing some traveling with my husband. We hope to visit **Switzerland** next summer! ¶ Please have one of your staff members write an article about Nancy's retirement for the next hospital newsletter. The above quote should be included. ¶ mtv/Doc036.04

Reinforcing Writing Skills

Some students, instructors, and office workers still print or handwrite documents and then key them at their computers. The process of preparing documents can be shortened if you can think and key at the same time—as you probably do in text messaging. You do not need to prepare the handwritten copy first. The average individual writes at the rate of 10 to 12 WAM. You can key at approximately two or three times this speed. With practice, you will find that it is much easier to create documents directly at the keyboard.

Document 36.5 Composing a Memo

1   Navigate to the Document 36.5 launch page in the Online Lab and then click the Launch Activity button. The Online Lab will open **Doc036.05** in the activity window.

2   Using the format shown in Figure 36.1, key the guide words for the memo. Address the memo to the director of your school and key your first and last names as the sender. The subject of the memo should be *School Evaluation*. (Do not set it in italic type.)

3   Compose two paragraphs in the body of the memo using the following information to assist you:

a   In the first paragraph, state your purpose (evaluating the strong and weak points about your school). Identify two or three things you like about the school (for example, the curriculum, the buildings, the computer software and hardware, the faculty, the students, the administration).

steps continue

Reinforcing Writing Skills

It is human nature to delay action whenever urgency is not apparent. This habit of "putting things off" is known as *procrastination*. For this reason, it is important that whenever you send someone an email or a letter that contains a request you must carefully include phrases that essentially "force" the reader to act promptly. For example, assume that you are sending someone a proposal to automate operations at a company, and you need that person's approval before you can move to the next phase of the project. Review the two sentences that follow. Which one is likely to produce action?

> After you've had an opportunity to review the attached proposal, please call me so that I can answer questions and get your reaction.

> Please review the attached proposal; I will call you on Monday between 10 a.m. and 11 a.m. to answer any questions you may have and to get your reaction.

In the first example, the person has the option of putting off reviewing the proposal. No sense of urgency is conveyed in the sentence. In the second example, the person knows that a call for the response will be made on a specific day at a specific time. The person can still put off the review, but chances are the review will be done. As you compose letters and memos that require action, do what you can to stimulate a response within a specified time.

Document 41.5 — **Composing a Business Letter that Requires a Response**

1. Navigate to the Document 41.5 launch page in the Online Lab and then click the Launch Activity button. The Online Lab will open **Doc041.05** in the activity window.

2. Key a letter to Ms. Lucy Allarie-Gosselin, Manager, Continental Weston Hotel, 400 Columbus Avenue, St. Paul, MN 55102. In the letter, dated November 13, 2014, explain that you are looking for a hotel at which to hold the annual state convention next fall of the *International Association of Administrative Professionals,* an organization with local chapters throughout Minnesota. You need to find out a number of things:

   - Are the dates of October 4 to 6, 2015 available?
   - Do they have sufficient space to accommodate 300 participants?
   - What are the single-occupancy room rates?
   - What do they have in the way of meeting room facilities?
   - Is wireless Internet access provided in the meeting rooms?
   - Would the manager be able to give a tour of the hotel to the three members of the Convention Site Selection Committee on December 15, 2014?

   Remember to use words that require a specific response by a certain time. The response could be a letter, email, or a phone call.

3. Indicate your name for the signature line. Because you have written and keyed the letter, do not include your initials below the signature line, but do include the file name.

4. Proofread and correct any errors in the letter.

5. Save the document.

6. Click the Upload button to upload the document for instructor review.

Ending the Session

The Online Lab automatically saves the work you completed for this session. You may continue with the next session or exit the Online Lab and continue later.

    b   In the second paragraph, note two or three things you would like to see changed. Be sure to explain how and when these changes can be made and their impact on the school.

4   Include the file name at the bottom of the memo. Note that the reference initials are not required since you are the author of the memo. When the author and typist are the same person, reference initials are not required.

5   After you have finished the message, edit it for clear meaning, correct punctuation, and accurate word choices.

6   Save the document.

7   Click the Upload button to upload the document for instructor review.

Ending the Session

The Online Lab automatically saves the work you completed for this session. You may continue with the next session or exit the Online Lab and continue later.

Figure 41.2 Business Letter Content for Document 41.3—Continued

year restrictive legend. ¶ Based on the two-year restriction as well as the speculative nature of Life Devices, Inc., it is our opinion that the fair market value, for the purpose of the stock option described above, would be a 50 percent discount from the market price. ¶ Life Devices, Inc. engaged in the manufacture and sale of neurological pain-relieving implant devices, has been in business less than five years, and has a limited sales and earnings history. The company's common stock is currently trading on the national over-the-counter market. On November 18, the stock closed at 14-5/8 bid and 15-1/8 asked. ¶ Please contact me at 720-555-4346 if you need further information. ¶ Sincerely, ¶ Donald F. Steiner ¶ Senior Vice President

Moving Text by Dragging

One method for moving text within a document is to select the text and then drag it to the desired location. After selecting the text you wish to move, hold down the mouse button on the selected text and drag it to the new location. When you release the mouse button, the text will be moved to the indicated location. If your text does not go where you expected, use the Undo command (Ctrl+ Z) and begin again.

Document 41.4 Business Letter Edited with Click and Drag and Replace

1 Read all instructions for this document activity, navigate to the Document 41.4 launch page in the Online Lab, and then click the Launch Activity button. The Online Lab will open **Doc041.04** in the activity window.

2 Move the third paragraph of the body of the letter (begins *Based on the two-year restriction*) so that it appears as the second paragraph in the letter.

3 In the first paragraph, delete *Mr.* before the name *Del Stewart*.

4 Using the Find and Replace feature, change the word *speculative* to *projected*.

5 Proofread and correct any errors in the letter, being sure to check the spacing between paragraphs in the letter.

6 Save the document.

7 Click the Check button to stop the timer and upload the document for checking. The Online Lab will report the number of errors for the activity.

8 If errors are reported, view the results document, correct the errors in the submitted document, save the document, and then click the Check button.

Production Progress Check: Email and Memos Part I

Session Objectives

- Review and practice word processing features presented in Sessions 35 and 36
- Produce documents at a rate of 25 WAM and in mailable form

Timing Goals

- 1 minute: 35 WAM and two or fewer errors
- 3 minutes: 30 WAM and six or fewer errors

Getting Started and Warming Up

Exercise 37.1 If you are continuing immediately from Session 36, you can skip the Exercise 37.1 warm-up drill. However, if you exited the Online Lab at the end of Session 36, warm up by completing Exercise 37.1.

Exercise 37.2 Begin your session work by completing Exercise 37.2, a timed short drill, in the Online Lab.

Assessing Your Speed and Accuracy

Complete Timings 37.1 through 37.4 in the Online Lab. At the end of each timing, the Online Lab will display your WAM rate and any errors made. Results will be saved in your Timings Performance report. If you have been surpassing the speed and accuracy goals, set slightly more challenging personal goals and strive to exceed them.

Complete two 1-minute timings on the timing text below. Timings 37.1 and 37.2 use the same paragraph.

Goals: 35 WAM and two or fewer errors
SI: 1.43 syllables per word

1-Minute Timings

Timings 37.1–37.2   A good keyboarder soon learns how to proofread. Glaring errors will mar the neatness and quality of a good report. Find all the mistakes before you key the final copy. Learn to watch for correct spelling, grammar, and word use. You might wish to examine your printed copy two or three times to make certain that it is without mistakes. In the long run, you will be pleased that you have carefully prepared an excellent copy. The person who reads your material will respect your ability to key and proofread. Aim for high-quality output.

Figure 41.1 Business Letter Content for Document 41.2

Dr. James Moline ¶ Metropolitan Professional Building ¶ 5991 Madison Drive ¶ New York, NY 10055-9110 ¶ Dear Dr. Moline: ¶ Truax-Vehlow Investment Services has been in the brokerage and investment banking business for over 35 years and specializes in growth companies. We firmly believe that such companies represent the greatest profit potential for individual investors. ¶ In recent years, we have devoted considerable attention to the medical industry through our research and investment banking activities. We have played an important role in the early stages of several emerging medical firms in the city of New York. ¶ Please give me a call whenever it is convenient, and I will be pleased to set up an appointment to discuss a mutually satisfying business partnership. ¶ Sincerely, ¶ Roberta E. Thomas ¶ Investment Consultant

Document 41.3 Business Letter Keyed, Edited with Find and Replace, and Justified

1   Read all instructions for this document activity, navigate to the Document 41.3 launch page in the Online Lab, and then click the Launch Activity button. The Online Lab will open **Doc041.03** in the activity window. The timer will start as soon as you begin keying the document.

2   Key the letter shown in Figure 41.2 as a block-style letter.

   a   Use January 6, 2014, as the date.

   b   After the title line, key the reference initials **mm** and the file name.

3   In the document, find all occurrences of *Life Devices, Inc.* and replace them with *Merrier Health Group*. **Hint: Be sure to include the period after Inc.**

4   Justify the four paragraphs in the body of the letter.

5   Proofread and correct any errors in the letter.

6   Save the document.

7   Click the Check button to stop the timer and upload the document for checking. The Online Lab will report the WAM rate and number of errors for the activity.

8   If errors are reported, view the results document, correct the errors in the submitted document, save the document, and then click the Check button.

Figure 41.2 Business Letter Content for Document 41.3

Mr. Howard Young ¶ West, Young & Stern ¶ 4200 Exchange Building ¶ New York, NY 10014-3728 ¶ Dear Mr. Young: ¶ On November 18, a nonqualified stock option was issued to Mr. Del Stewart for 2,500 shares of Life Devices, Inc. common stock. The mean between the bid and asked prices on November 18 was $14,875, resulting in our valuation of $4.44 per share. You have informed us that these shares, when issued, bear a two-

continues

Complete two 3-minute timings on the timing text below. Timings 37.3 and 37.4 use the same passage.

Goal: 30 WAM with six or fewer errors
SI: 1.43 syllables per word

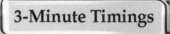
3-Minute Timings

Timings 37.3–37.4

Many people are growing herb gardens. The herb plants provide a variety of new seasonings, fragrances, and flavorings. Growing herbs is quite similar to growing a vegetable garden. You should select an area for your herb garden that is sunny, as herbs demand an abundance of sunlight to make them sweet and flavorful.

To supply enough herbs for a family of four, you would need a garden space of at least 12 to 18 square feet. If you do not have enough room, it is always easy to grow an abundance of herbs in an ordinary window box or in small clay flower pots. If grown inside, the herbs should be placed in a window that receives full sunlight at least half of the day. In cases where sunlight is not available, a fluorescent-light garden will give you a plentiful harvest of herbs. To promote compact growth, it is a good idea to snip the plants back on a regular basis.

Herbs placed with other plants add charm and grace with the rich foliage. Freshly picked herbs can either be dried or frozen for future use. Many good cookbooks offer directions for using a variety of herbs.

Ergonomic Tip
With arms hanging at your sides, gently circle shoulders forward and then backward. This movement helps relax your upper body muscles.

Checking Production Progress: Email and Memos

Sessions 35–36 discussed the procedures for preparing and formatting email messages and memos. In this session, you will be assessed on how quickly and accurately you can key these types of documents. Each completed document is to be "mailable," which means that it is properly formatted and contains no errors. A document that requires additional corrections is not considered mailable.

Your goal is to key each email and memo in mailable form and at a rate of at least 25 WAM. If your WAM rate is less than 25, or if you are missing errors that should have been corrected, your instructor may ask you to repeat document activities.

To help you succeed, carefully review the document instructions before keying it. If necessary, review the content of Sessions 35–36 if you are unsure how to complete a specific task.

To use the Replace feature, complete the following steps:

1 Press Ctrl + Home to position the insertion point at the beginning of the document.

2 Click the Replace button in the Editing group on the Home tab to open the Find and Replace dialog box with the Replace tab selected.

3 Key the search text in the *Find what* text box.

4 Key the replacement text in the *Replace with* text box.

5 Click the Find Next button to locate the first occurrence of the text in the *Find what* text box.

6 Click the Replace button to replace the found text with the text in the *Replace with* text box.

7 Continue pressing the Find Next button until no more occurrences are found, and then click OK.

8 Close the dialog box.

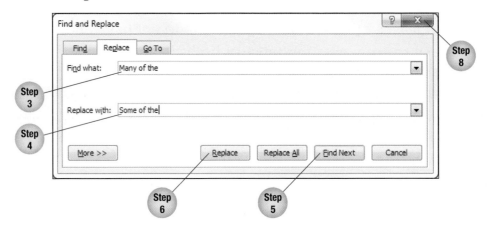

Document 41.2 Business Letter Keyed and Edited with Find and Replace

1 Read all instructions for this document activity, navigate to the Document 41.2 launch page in the Online Lab, and then click the Launch Activity button. The Online Lab will open **Doc041.02** in the activity window. The timer will start as soon as you begin keying the document.

2 Key the letter shown in Figure 41.1 as a block-style letter.

a Use February 12, 2014, as the date.

b After the title line, key the reference initials **ijt** and the file name.

3 Search the document for the word *partnership* and replace it with the word *relationship*.

4 Proofread and correct any errors in the letter.

5 Save the document.

6 Click the Check button to stop the timer and upload the document for checking. The Online Lab will report the WAM rate and number of errors for the activity.

7 If errors are reported, view the results document, correct the errors in the submitted document, save the document, and then click the Check button.

Document 37.1 Email Message

1 Read all instructions for this document activity, navigate to the Document 37.1 launch page in the Online Lab, and then click the Launch Activity button. The Online Lab will open **Doc037.01** in the activity window. The timer will start as soon as you begin keying the document.

2 Use the content in Figure 37.1 to key the email. *Hint: The symbol ¶ is used to indicate a new paragraph break.* Ensure that the email addresses are not set as hyperlinks.

3 Proofread and correct any errors.

4 Save the docment.

5 Click the Check button to stop the timer and upload the document for checking. The Online Lab will report the WAM rate and number of errors for the activity.

6 If errors are reported, view the results document, correct the errors in the submitted document, save the document, and then click the Check button.

Figure 37.1 Email Message Content for Document 37.1

To: Jerry.Adams@emcp.net ¶ Cc: Mark.Sanchez@emcp.net, Samantha.Beard@emcp.net, Eloise.Morgenstern@emcp.net ¶ Subject: Group golf lesson this Saturday morning ¶ Jerry and friends, ¶ Your group golf lesson is set for 10:00 in the morning, on Saturday, July 10, at Maple Park Golf Club. Please check in at least 15 minutes before the lesson. The lesson will last 60 minutes. The cost is $45 per person. You can pay with cash, check, or credit card. We will provide clubs and golf balls. However, if you have your own clubs, you are free to use them. Dress comfortably. ¶ Your golf teacher will be Ginger Smith. Ginger is our course professional and has taught and coached golfers of all different abilities. She has been a golf teacher for eight years. ¶ We believe you will enjoy the facilities at Maple Park. After your lesson you are welcome to use our practice facilities. Also, your lesson includes a complimentary round of golf.

Document 37.2 Memo with Italicized Words

1 Read all instructions for this document activity, navigate to the Document 37.2 launch page in the Online Lab, and then click the Launch Activity button. The Online Lab will open **Doc037.02** in the activity window. The timer will start as soon as you begin keying the document.

2 Use the content in Figure 37.2 to key the memo. Be sure to apply correct formatting for a memo.

3 Italicize *Office Systems Seminar* wherever it appears. *Hint: Do not format the space following the last word as italic.*

4 Proofread and correct any errors.

5 Save the document.

6 Click the Check button to stop the timer and upload the document for checking. The Online Lab will report the WAM rate and number of errors for the activity.

7 If errors are reported, view the results document, correct the errors in the submitted document, save the document, and then click the Check button.

Searching a Document Using the Find Feature

With the Word Find feature, you can search for specific characters, words, or formatting. One common use for Find is to locate a specific passage in the document where you want to modify, add, or delete text.

To use the Find feature, complete the following steps:

1. Press Ctrl + Home to position the insertion point at the beginning of the document.

2. Click the Find button in the Editing Group on the Home tab (or press Ctrl + F) to launch the Navigation pane at the left side of the screen. The third (or right-hand) tab is selected. The found words are also highlighted within the document.

3. Key the text you want to find in the Search text box. Text thumbnails will display in the Navigation pane showing the searched text and the instances will be highlighted in the document itself.

4. Click a thumbnail to move to that part of the document and then click in the document to position the insertion point.

5. Close the Navigation pane by clicking the Close button.

Document 41.1 Business Letter Edited with Find

1. Read all instructions for this document activity, navigate to the Document 41.1 launch page in the Online Lab, and then click the Launch Activity button. The Online Lab will open **Doc041.01** in the activity window.

2. Use the Find feature to find the words *We will not be bound*. (Do not key the period.)

3. Delete the paragraph that begins with the found words and then close the Navigation pane.

4. Check the spacing between the remaining paragraphs and correct if necessary.

5. Save the document.

6. Click the Check button to upload the document for checking. The Online Lab will report the number of errors for the activity.

7. If errors are reported, view the results document, correct the errors in the submitted document, save the document, and then click the Check button.

Finding and Replacing Text

You can also find specific characters, words, or formatting and replace them with other characters or formatting by using the Replace button in the Editing group. Some uses of the Replace feature include:

- Exchange a word or expression for another throughout a document—change instances of *Internet Explorer* to *Mozilla Firefox*, for example.

- Use abbreviations for common names when entering text and then replace the abbreviations with the actual text later.

- Set up standard documents with generic names and replace them with other names to create personalized documents.

Figure 37.2 Memo Content for Document 37.2

> TO: John Kearney, Editorial Director ¶ FROM: Frances Dalton, Administrative Assistant ¶ DATE: November 12, 2014 ¶ SUBJECT: Office Systems Seminar Outline ¶ John, next week I will be creating an updated copy of the Office Systems Seminar outline that we talked about yesterday. This program is offered through our department every quarter as a one-credit course. ¶ When I send you the outline, I will also send you a revised copy of the letter we will send to potential participants. I will ask you to review it and call me with any corrections or comments. ¶ I look forward to sharing the Office Systems Seminar outline with you and your staff. ¶ trt/ Doc037.02

Document 37.3

Memo with Bolded Words

1   Read all instructions for this document activity, navigate to the Document 37.3 launch page in the Online Lab, and then click the Launch Activity button. The Online Lab will open **Doc037.03** in the activity window. The timer will start as soon as you begin keying the document.

2   Use the content in Figure 37.3 to key the memo. Be sure to apply correct formatting.

3   As shown in Figure 37.3, set the names of the graduate assistants, the researcher, and the quarter-time faculty member in bold the first time their names appear in the memo. *Hint: Do not set the punctuation following the names or the spaces before or after names in bold.*

4   Key the reference initials **pmt** and the file name at the end of the memo.

5   Include a notation that copies of the memo will be sent to Kathy Joyce, Benjamin Disraeli, and Bill Bjorkman. *Hint: List the names in alphabetical order by last name.*

6   Proofread and correct any errors.

7   Save the document.

8   Click the Check button to stop the timer and upload the document for checking. The Online Lab will report the WAM rate and number of errors for the activity.

9   If errors are reported, view the results document, correct the errors in the submitted document, save the document, and then click the Check button.

Complete two 5-minute timings on the timing text below. Timings 41.3 and 41.4 use the same paragraphs.

Goals: 30 WAM and ten or fewer errors
SI: 1.53 syllables per word

Timings 41.3–41.4

One of the finest fruits on the market today is the mango, which is a fruit found in the tropics. The mango has become more popular all over the nation. The papaya is also a very good tropical fruit that has lots of vitamins and is good to eat. A carambola is quite a strange looking fruit. It has a waxy appearance and contains a solid meat. The cherimoya, or custard apple, is shaped like the strawberry and is green in color and oval in shape. The fruit is not very attractive, but it has a delicious and delicate flavor. Kiwifruit, the Chinese gooseberry, is grown in New Zealand; thus the name "kiwi" has been given to this fruit in honor of the native kiwi bird. The taste is mild and quite enjoyable.

The celery root has an ugly appearance. The outside of the root is deceiving; inside the ugly wrapping lies a great surprising flavor treat for vegetable lovers. Fine Jerusalem artichokes, also known as sunchokes, have lots of uses. The crispy, crunchy food has a nutlike flavor and makes a great finger food. A jicama is sometimes known as a Mexican or Chinese potato. The brownish vegetable looks like a raw turnip. The crispy and crunchy taste treat is quite good when served with a dip of some sort.

Although all of us seem to be creatures of habit, there is a new world of eating delights right in the produce bins, waiting for us to discover new taste treats. All it takes is some searching and a very sincere desire to try something new. Maybe a recipe or two would add to the variety of these exotic vegetables and fruits. Many cookbooks contain delightful recipes with which to vary our menus.

Ergonomic Tip
Blink often and take frequent opportunities to look away from your screen at an object farther away. Give your eye muscles a chance to relax.

Revising Business Letters

A common task in a business office is to use an existing letter as a starting point for creating a new, updated document. This session will introduce you to the Find and Find and Replace features, which are very useful tools when working with existing files. The session will also explain how to move text within a document using the click and drag method.

Figure 37.3 Memo Content for Document 37.3

To: Ben Goldstein ¶ From: Jim Albright ¶ Date: August 22, 2014 ¶ Subject: Office Assignments ¶ Attached is a list of the full-time faculty members in the Department of Office Administration and Business Education and their office locations. ¶ The department does not have any unfilled positions at this time. For the upcoming school year, in addition to the full-time faculty, our department will have two graduate assistants, **Ms. Jean Cannon** and **Ms. Diane Lawrence**, and one full-time researcher, **Mr. Mark Gomez**. We will have one quarter-time faculty member, **Dr. Rena Gibson**, who will be teaching courses in management information systems. ¶ Ms. Cannon and Ms. Lawrence will be using the office located in Room 420 of Emerson Business Hall. Dr. Gibson and Mr. Gomez will be in the adjacent office, Room 422.

Document 37.4 **Memo with Left and Right Indent and Underlined Words**

1 Read all instructions for this document activity, navigate to the Document 37.4 launch page in the Online Lab, and then click the Launch Activity button. The Online Lab will open **Doc037.04** in the activity window. The timer will start as soon as you begin keying the document.

2 Use the content in Figure 37.4 to key the memo.

3 Indent the paragraphs identifying the three training areas listed in the body of the letter 0.5 inch from both the left and right margins.

4 Underline the names of the three training areas. *Hint: Do not underline the colons that follow the training area names.*

5 Key the reference initials **gvo** and the file name at the end of the memo.

6 Proofread and correct any errors.

7 Save the document.

8 Click the Check button to stop the timer and upload the document for checking. The Online Lab will report the WAM rate and number of errors for the activity.

9 If errors are reported, view the results document, correct the errors in the submitted document, save the document, and then click the Check button.

Using Find and Replace in Business Letters

Session Objectives

- Use find and replace to edit text in a document
- Use click and drag to move text within a document
- Write a business letter that clearly prompts action

Timing Goals

- 1 minute: 40 WAM and two or fewer errors
- 5 minutes: 30 WAM and ten or fewer errors

Getting Started and Warming Up

Exercise 41.1 If you are continuing immediately from Session 40, you may skip the Exercise 41.1 warm-up drill. However, if you exited the Online Lab at the end of Session 40, warm up by completing Exercise 41.1.

Exercise 41.2 Begin your session work by completing Exercise 41.2, a timed short drill, in the Online Lab.

Assessing Your Speed and Accuracy

Complete Timings 41.1 through 41.4 in the Online Lab. At the end of each timing, the Online Lab will display your WAM rate and any errors. Results will be saved in your Timings Performance report. If you have been surpassing the speed and accuracy goals, set slightly more challenging personal goals and strive to exceed them. Note that with this session, the WAM goals for both the 1-minute and 5-minute timings have been increased by 5 WAM.

Complete two 1-minute timings on the timing text below. Timings 41.1 and 41.2 use the same paragraph.

Goals: 40 WAM and two or fewer errors
SI: 1.51 syllables per word

1-Minute Timings

Timings 41.1–41.2

At times a website will ask for approval to add a plug-in to the user's browser. A plug-in is a little program that extends the capabilities of browsers, usually by improving graphic, sound, and video elements. Most plug-ins are harmless, without any hidden features that may cause problems. However, as a general rule, it is a good idea to view a site before giving permission to load any plug-ins. If there are viewing errors, they are likely caused by missing plug-ins. If users think the site is trustworthy, they can hit the Refresh button on the browser to reload the site and cause the plug-in dialog box to reappear. The "Yes" box granting permission to install the plug-in can be selected, allowing improved web page performance.

Figure 37.4 Memo Content for Document 37.4

TO: Marilyn Donaldson, Computer Systems ¶ FROM: Jill Mersereau, Information Processing ¶ DATE: March 15, 2014 ¶ SUBJECT: Software Training ¶ I have talked with the employees of the Information Processing department about the type of computer training they would like to receive. The employees said they would like training in the following areas: ¶ Internet Browsers: The employees would like more training on the advantages of various browsers such as Internet Explorer, Firefox, and Chrome. ¶ Microsoft Applications: Please discuss the basic features of PowerPoint, Excel, and Access. I do not think that you need to discuss Word, as everyone is already familiar with that program. ¶ Desktop Publishing: One of the employees attended a half-day seminar on desktop publishing and thinks it would be valuable for the other employees of the department to attend a similar training program. Please discuss some of the features of programs such as Publisher and InDesign. ¶ Please consider these areas when determining the training budget for the Information Processing department.

Ending the Session

The Online Lab automatically saves the work you completed for this session. You may continue with the next session or exit the Online Lab and continue later.

PHILLIP C. COHN
2394 Emerald Drive
Seattle, WA 98102
(206) 555-3421
pccohn567@emcp.net

OBJECTIVE:

To secure a position as an in-house information systems consultant where I can use my skills to benefit the company.

EDUCATION:

In June 2013, I graduated with honors from the SeaTac Technical College with an Associate Degree in the Information Systems Program. The course of study for this degree included the following:

Word Processing (Word)	Office Layout and Space Design
Database Management (Access)	Business Communications
Keyboarding (50+ WAM)	Principles of Management
Business Mathematics	Telecommunications
PC Networking	Windows
Spreadsheets (Excel)	Office Automation Systems
Presentation Graphics (PowerPoint)	

PERSONAL QUALITIES:

Conscientious	Responsible
Cooperative	People-oriented
Detail-oriented	Hard-working

EXPERIENCE:

Office Assistant (Internship): Lowell Productions, Kent, Washington, fall semester 2012. Helped set up an electronic file-naming system, assisted in the design of their telephone auto attendant system, and conducted training sessions on PowerPoint.

Laboratory Clerk: Baxter Medical Center, Federal Way, Washington, summers of 2011 and 2012. Helped admit patients, recorded data, filed patient records, gave instructions to patients, and prepared specimen labels.

Baker: C & C Baker and Catering, Fife, Washington, part-time during school years 2010 and 2011. Prepared, baked, and decorated pastries, cakes, cookies, and pies; greeted customers, answered phones, and took orders; and supervised three employees.

References provided upon request

Ending the Session

The Online Lab automatically saves the work you completed for this session. You may continue with the next session or exit the Online Lab and continue later.

Unit 8

Business Correspondence Part I

Document   Composing and Editing a Cover Letter

40.4

1   Navigate to the Document 40.4 launch page in the Online Lab and then click the Launch Activity button. The Online Lab will open **Doc040.04** in the activity window.

2   In the downloaded file, compose a block-style business letter to an individual at a company where you would like to work. The goal of the letter is to highlight your skills and related work experience, to request an informational interview, and to provide a copy of your resume. When listing your skills, format them in a bulleted list. Include your contact information and suggest a specific time when you will follow up and arrange a meeting time. Include a reference to the enclosed resume both in the body of the letter and below the signature line (or below the signer's title line if one is included).

3   Proofread and edit your letter for wordiness and other language errors as well as punctuation and capitalization. Correct any errors.

4   Save the document.

5   Click the Upload button to upload the document for instructor review.

Document   Composing and Editing a Resume

40.5

1   Navigate to the Document 40.5 launch page in the Online Lab and then click the Launch Activity button. The Online Lab will open **Doc040.05** in the activity window.

2   In the downloaded file, compose a resume to accompany the cover letter created in the Document 40.4 activity. Review the sample resume shown in Figure 40.4 for ideas on how you will prepare your resume and what it will contain. (Do not key the sample resume.)

3   Use the formatting features presented so far to enhance the readability of your resume. The format is your choice, but keep the resume to one page in length.

4   Proofread and edit your resume for wordiness and other language errors as well as punctuation and capitalization. Correct any errors.

5   Save the document.

6   Click the Upload button to upload the document for instructor review.

Session 38

Preparing Personal Business Letters

Session Objectives

- Apply consistent formatting to personal business letters
- Vertically center text on a page
- Improve paragraph structure and readability

Timing Goals

- 1 minute: 35 WAM and two or fewer errors
- 3 minutes: 30 WAM and six or fewer errors

Getting Started and Warming Up

Exercise 38.1 If you are continuing immediately from Session 37, you may skip the Exercise 38.1 warm-up drill. However, if you exited the Online Lab at the end of Session 37, warm up by completing Exercise 38.1.

Exercise 38.2 Begin your session work by completing Exercise 38.2, a timed short drill, in the Online Lab.

Assessing Your Speed and Accuracy

Complete Timings 38.1 through 38.4 in the Online Lab. At the end of each timing, the Online Lab will display your WAM rate and any errors. Results will be saved in your Timings Performance report. If you have been surpassing the speed and accuracy goals, set slightly more challenging personal goals and strive to exceed them.

Complete two 1-minute timings on the timing text below. Timings 38.1 and 38.2 use the same paragraph.

Goals: 35 WAM and two or fewer errors
SI: 1.43 syllables per word

1-Minute Timings

Timings 38.1–38.2 Most clouds usually move from west to east as they cross an area of land. If there should be a high-pressure system holding around the West Coast, it will divert the clouds and moisture northward into the Canadian Rockies. Many experts think that the climate over the whole earth is becoming warmer and drier. These experts state that the one thing that will suffer most will be rainfall.

Business Letter Edited with the Cut, Paste, and Alignment Commands

1   Read all instructions for this document activity, navigate to the Document 40.3 launch page in the Online Lab, and then click the Launch Activity button. The Online Lab will open **Doc040.03** in the activity window.

2   Change the alignment of the inside address to align at the left. (It is currently aligned at the right margin.)

3   In the body of the letter, move the sentence that begins *The mean between the bid and asked prices* (the last sentence in the body of the letter) before the second sentence in the first paragraph (begins *You have informed*).

4   Move the second paragraph (begins *Life Tronic, Inc.*) to follow the third paragraph (begins *Based on the two-year*).

5   Key a new paragraph before the closing that reads *Please contact me at (720) 555-4346 if you need further information.* (Do not set the text in italics.)

6   Proofread and correct any spelling errors in the letter.

7   Save the document (Ctrl + S).

8   Click the Check button to stop the timer and upload the document for checking. The Online Lab will report the number of errors for the activity.

9   If errors are reported, view the results document, correct the errors in the submitted document, save the document, and then click the Check button.

Reinforcing Writing Skills

A letter of application, or cover letter, by itself generally doesn't get you a job. But if the letter is written well, it could get you an interview. The challenge is to prepare a letter that will make you stand out among all the job applicants. In planning the letter of application, think of it in three parts:

- **Introduction:** How did you find out about the job opening? Why is the job so interesting to you? What do you know about the company? What can you do for them?

- **Your qualifications:** What sets you apart from the crowd? Here you can identify educational qualifications, past employment, personal skills, achievements, and/or experience that make you especially qualified for the job opening. This may require two of three short paragraphs.

- **Next steps:** What can you do to create a positive reaction to your letter?

A resume is usually sent along with a cover letter. The goal of your resume is to highlight the skills and experiences that set you apart from others applying for the same job. If at all possible, try to keep the resume to one page. Develop the format with the reader in mind; make the resume easy to read, present the content in a logical order, and make sure it has a professional appearance.

When proofreading and editing your cover letters and resumes, it is critical that you take the time to delete unnecessary words. Make it a challenge to reduce your sentences to the essential words that convey your meaning clearly and completely. Also, because these documents will formulate a first impression, they must be completely free of errors.

Complete two 3-minute timings on the timing text below. Timings 38.3 and 38.4 use the same paragraph.

Goals: 30 WAM and six or fewer errors
SI: 1.40 syllables per word

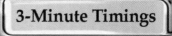

3-Minute Timings

Timings 38.3–38.4

To avoid consumer problems, some decisions should be made before buying a product. The first major point is to decide if you and your family really need that new product or new service. If the answer is yes, then the next step is to shop around and compare prices. A good library will have publications that give helpful comparisons among similar products. Check on the firm with which you are dealing; call the Better Business Bureau for more information. Make certain that a guarantee is in writing. Before you sign a contract, read it to make sure that you understand it fully. If you have any doubts at all, it would be wise to wait and think about the purchase a little longer.

When you buy a product or a service, be sure that you understand the method of payment if it is to be a credit purchase. Know exactly when each payment is due, how much interest is being charged, and how many months the payments are to be made. Read all tags and labels to learn all about the product before you use it. If you have any problems with the product or service, speak with the seller first. If you find that a seller does not give the proper satisfaction to a problem, there are many consumer protection groups and agencies you can contact.

Ergonomic Tip
Place fingertips on shoulders, bring elbows together in front of your chest, and lift them. Then allow elbows to swing open. This will help you relax your upper body muscles.

Preparing Personal Business Letters

A personal business letter is a letter written by an individual and sent to a business. Examples of personal business letters are the letters individuals write to companies requesting information or complaining about a product.

Figure 38.1 shows an example of a personal business letter. Note that the return address appears at the end of the letter, below the sender's name. The letter is printed on plain paper, not on company letterhead. Because Word automatically adds vertical spacing between paragraphs, press Shift + Enter at the end of the lines that do not require this extra spacing, such as in the address blocks.

Figure 40.2 Alignment Buttons in the Paragraph Group

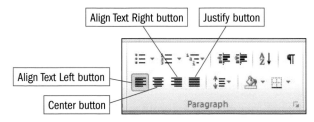

Business Letter with Justified Text

Document 40.2

1. Read all instructions for this document activity, navigate to the Document 40.2 launch page in the Online Lab, and then click the Launch Activity button. The Online Lab will open **Doc040.02** in the activity window. The timer will start as soon as you begin keying the document.

2. Key the text shown in Figure 40.3. Make the changes indicated by the proofreading marks and format the document as a business letter.

3. Justify the three paragraphs in the body of letter by completing the following steps:

   a. Select the three paragraphs in the body of the letter.

   b. Click the Justify button in the Paragraph group on the Home tab.

4. Proofread and correct any errors in the letter.

5. Save the document (Ctrl + S).

6. Click the Check button to stop the timer and upload the document for checking. The Online Lab will report the WAM rate and number of errors for the activity.

7. If errors are reported, view the results document, correct the errors in the submitted document, save the document, and then click the Check button.

Figure 40.3 Edited Business Letter for Document 40.2

December 17, 2014 Mr. Howard Young West, Young & Stern 4200 Exchange Building new York, NY 10014-3728 On November 29, *Dear Mr. Young:* a nonqualified stock option was issued to Mr. Del Stewart for 2,500 shares of Life Devices, Inc. common stock. You have informed us that these shares, when issued, bear a two-year restrictive legend. Life Devices, Inc., engaged in the manufacture and sale of neurological pain-relieving implant devices, has been in business less than five years and has a limited sales and earnings history. The company's common stock is currently trading on the national over-the-counter market. On November 20, the stock closed at 14-5/8 bid and 15-1/8 asked. Based on the two-year restriction as well as the speculative nature of ~~the company,~~ *Life Devices, Inc.* it is our opinion that the fair market value for the purpose of the stock option described above would be a 50 percent discount from the market price. The mean between the bid and asked prices on November 20 was $14,875, resulting in our valuation of $4.44 per share. *Sincerely* Donald F. Steiner Senior Vice President rmj/Doc040.02

Figure 38.1 Personal Business Letter

Note: Do not key this document.

February 13, 2014 [Enter]

[Enter]

Mr. Warren Chen, Manager [Shift + Enter]
New Age Electric Company [Shift + Enter]
4950 Scenic Heights Ridge [Shift + Enter]
Denver, CO 80219-1698 [Enter]

Dear Mr. Chen: [Enter]

My recent electric bill contains some errors that need correcting. For one thing, the bill shows a past-due balance of $59.98. However, I sent a check for that amount three weeks ago. Please review your records and make the necessary adjustment. [Enter]

Another error concerns the amount you charged for moving our underground service line. When I called to arrange this service, I was told that the charge would be $75. However, the bill includes a charge of $95. Again, please check your records and correct this mistake. [Enter]

I appreciate the prompt way you have dealt with my questions in the past, and I look forward to receiving a statement showing an accurate amount due for last month's electrical service. If you have any questions, you may reach me at (505) 555-0963. [Enter]

Sincerely yours, [Enter]

[Enter]

Ms. Maria Hill [Shift + Enter]
2350 Skyline Drive [Shift + Enter]
Denver, CO 80291

Figure 40.1 Edited Business Letter for Document 40.1

May 15, 2014

Mr. Mark Ogrel
Dain Bosworth, Inc.
1440 East McKinley Avenue
New York, NY 10037

Dear Mr. Ogrel:

This letter records the intentions of IDP Computing and Waedt-Steiner Investment Services to undertake a public offering of common stock of IDP Computing (the "company").

It is our intention to form an underwriting syndicate to purchase up to 250,000 shares of new common stock from IDP Computing and to reoffer the common shares to the public at a price mutually agreed upon. This agreement is subject to the following:

1. The completed filing of a prospectus for the common stock with the Securities and Exchange Commission.
2. The assurance that no change takes place in the company and in the common stock that would threaten success.
3. The market condition for common stock at the time of offer.

We will not be bound to receive or pay for your common shares until conditions for common stock have been met in several states and a final underwriting agreement concerning the common stock has been met.

We plan to work with management to obtain a distribution of the common stock that will be beneficial to the company, and we look forward to working with you and your associates on the proposed sale of common stock.

Sincerely yours,

Donald F. Steiner
Senior Vice President

rk/Doc040.01

Changing Text Alignment

The default text alignment in Word is to align the text in every paragraph at the left margin. Text can also be formatted (1) to align at the right margin, (2) to center align so that the text is centered between the left and right margins (which produces ragged left and right margins), or (3) to justify. When text is set with the justify formatting, extra space is added between words, as needed, to create smooth left and right margins. Magazine text is usually justified.

Change the alignment style of text by using the buttons in the Paragraph group on the Home tab (see Figure 40.2). When text is selected or when the insertion point is located in a paragraph, the alignment button corresponding to that format will be highlighted. Change the selected text alignment by clicking a different button in the Paragraph group.

Vertically Centering Text on the Page

Personal business letters are typically vertically centered on the page to make them more visually pleasing. Rather than adding extra hard returns above the date, use a setting in the Page Setup Dialog box to vertically center the letter text on the page. The following steps illustrate the process for vertically centering text on a page of an active document.

1 Click the Page Layout tab.

2 Click the dialog box launcher in the Page Setup group.

3 Click the Layout tab in the Page Setup dialog box.

4 Click the down arrow for the *Vertical alignment* setting and click *Center*.

5 Click the OK button to close the Page Setup dialog box.

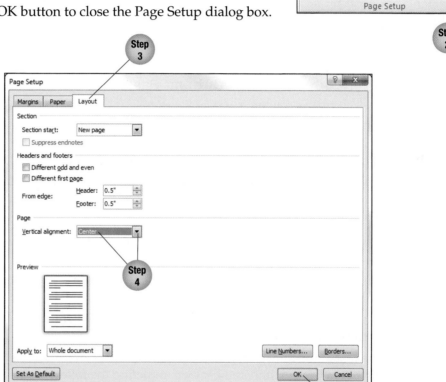

Personal Business Letter with Basic Formatting

Document 38.1

1 Read all instructions for this document activity, navigate to the Document 38.1 launch page in the Online Lab, and then click the Launch Activity button. The Online Lab will open **Doc038.01** in the activity window. The timer will start as soon as you begin keying the document.

2 Key the text shown in Figure 38.2. Use Word default formatting settings in the document and follow the style shown in Figure 38.1. Press the Enter key for paragraph breaks and the Shift + Enter key combination for line breaks. *Note: If Word formats the website address in the body of the document as a hyperlink (blue text with underline), press the Backspace key to remove the hyperlink formatting or right-click the hyperlink text and click* **Remove Hyperlink** *from the pop-up list.*

3 Vertically center the text on the page.

steps continue

Copying Text

To copy a block of text from one place to another, follow these steps:

1. Select the text to be copied.
2. Click the Copy button in the Clipboard group on the Home tab. You can also use the keyboard shortcut Ctrl + C.
3. Move the insertion point to the location where the copied text is to be placed.
4. Click the Paste button in the Clipboard group on the Home tab.

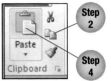

Deleting Text

As has been noted before, to delete text, select it and press the Delete key, press the Backspace key, click the Cut button, or press Ctrl + X. If you use the Delete key or the Backspace key to delete the text, the text is not available for pasting.

 Business Letter Edited with the Cut and Paste Commands

40.1

1. Read all instructions for this document activity, navigate to the Document 40.1 launch page in the Online Lab, and then click the Launch Activity button. The Online Lab will open **Doc040.01** in the activity window.

2. In the document, move the paragraph that begins *It is our intention to form* and the numbered list below it so that the paragraph and list appear before the paragraph in the letter that begins *We will not be bound* by completing the following steps:

   a. Select the text to be moved.

   b. Cut the text by pressing Ctrl + X or clicking the Cut button in the Clipboard group on the Home tab.

   c. Position the insertion point at the beginning of the second paragraph (the paragraph that begins *We will not be bound*).

   d. Paste the text by pressing Ctrl + V or clicking the Paste button in the Clipboard group on the Home tab.

3. Move the text of the third numbered paragraph that begins *The completed filing* so it appears as the first item in the numbered list by completing the following steps:

   a. Triple-click within the text of the third list item.

   b. Cut the text.

   c. Place the insertion point immediately to the left of the text of the numbered item that begins *The assurance that no change*.

   d. Paste the text.

4. Check your document against the document shown in Figure 40.1. Pay special attention to the spacing between paragraphs. Correct any errors created in cutting and pasting the text.

5. Save the document (Ctrl + S).

6. Click the Check button to stop the timer and upload the document for checking. The Online Lab will report the number of errors for the activity.

7. If errors are reported, view the results document, correct the errors in the submitted document, save the document, and then click the Check button.

4   Proofread the document and correct any errors.

5   Save the document (Ctrl + S).

6   Click the Check button to stop the timer and upload the document for checking. The Online Lab will report the WAM rate and number of errors for the activity.

7   If errors are reported, view the results document, correct the errors in the submitted document, save the document, and then click the Check button.

Figure 38.2 Personal Business Letter Content for Document 38.1

August 25, 2014 [Enter] [Enter]

Mr. Charles M. Reitnour [Shift + Enter]
BUY Credit Card Company [Shift + Enter]
12337 Lost Canyon Boulevard [Shift + Enter]
Los Angeles, CA 90723-7832 [Enter]

Dear Mr. Reitnour:

Please investigate the charge for $159.95 from Lorenzo Knitting Group shown on my July statement. My account number is 2155 0701 0125 3137.

I placed an online order from www.lorenzoknitting.emcp.net for specialty yarn on June 29. Later that same day, I received an order confirmation email with expected delivery within two to four weeks. When a month passed without the yarn arriving, I contacted Lorenzo Knitting Group by email. I was told on July 31 that the yarn had been on backorder, but I could expect to receive my order by August 10. Once again, I did not receive the yarn.

On August 15 I contacted Lorenzo Knitting by phone and requested that they cancel my order and refund my money. Robert in Customer Service refused to issue a refund and said the merchandise was on its way. On August 20 I sent an email asking them to cancel my order and refund my money. I still have not received either the yarn or my refund and would like this situation to be investigated.

Please provide me with a written statement of the outcome. Thank you for your attention to this frustrating situation.

Sincerely yours, [Enter] [Enter]

Kathy Martinez
17431 Buntline Drive
Glendale, AZ 85375-4671

Cutting, Copying, and Pasting Text

Some documents may need to be revised extensively, and those revisions may include deleting, copying, or moving blocks of text. This kind of editing is generally done by cutting and pasting. **Cutting** and **pasting** text means that text is deleted (cut) from its present location and moved and inserted (pasted) at a new location. **Copying** and pasting text means that a copy is inserted into a new location while the copied text remains in the original location. Thus, two copies of the text are now present in the document.

When cutting and pasting, you work with blocks of text. A block of text is a portion of text that you have selected. A block of text can be as small as one character or as large as an entire page or document.

Selecting Text

As discussed in Session 36, there are many ways to select text. Several of the most common methods are:

- Point in the document where you want to begin the selection, hold down the left mouse button, and then drag over the text to be selected.
- Move the insertion point to the left of the first character of the text to be selected, press and hold the Shift key, and then move the insertion point to the end of the text to be selected. Remember that you can move the insertion point by using the arrow keys, by using various keyboard shortcuts, or by clicking the mouse.
- To select a word, double-click on the word.
- To select a paragraph, triple-click a character within the paragraph. Alternatively, double-click in the left margin next to the paragraph.

Moving Text

To move a block of text from one place to another, follow these steps:

1. Select the text to be moved.
2. Click the Cut button in the Clipboard group on the Home tab. You may also use the keyboard shortcut Ctrl + X. (To help you remember this shortcut, think of scissors in relation to the letter X.)
3. Move the insertion point to the location where the cut text is to be placed.
4. Click the Paste button in the Clipboard group on the Home tab. You may also use the keyboard shortcut Ctrl + V.

Whenever you move text, make sure that the appropriate spaces remain where the text was cut and where the text was moved. Turn on the display of nonprinting formatting symbols to reveal the paragraph breaks and spaces in the text. To display nonprinting symbols, click the Show/Hide button in the Paragraph group on the Home tab.

Success Tip

Remember that Ctrl + Z will undo the last action performed. If you cut the wrong text or pasted it in the wrong place, undo the action with Ctrl + Z.

38.2

1 Read all instructions for this document activity, navigate to the Document 38.2 launch page in the Online Lab, and then click the Launch Activity button. The Online Lab will open **Doc038.02** in the activity window. The timer will start as soon as you begin keying the document.

2 Key the text shown in Figure 38.3. Use Word default formatting settings in the document and follow the style shown in Figure 38.1. Press the Enter key for paragraph breaks and the Shift + Enter key combination for line breaks. In the second paragraph of the letter, key two hyphens and allow Word to replace them with an EM dash. Do not press the space bar before, between, or after keying the hyphens.

3 Vertically center the text on the page.

4 Proofread the document and correct any errors.

5 Save the document (Ctrl + S).

6 Click the Check button to stop the timer and upload the document for checking. The Online Lab will report the WAM rate and number of errors for the activity.

7 If errors are reported, view the results document, correct the errors in the submitted document, save the document, and then click the Check button.

Figure 38.3 Personal Business Letter Content for Document 38.2

March 28, 2014

Larry Anderson
Director of Sales and Marketing
Sensational Software
259-A Research Boulevard
Raleigh, NC 27603

Dear Larry:

May I ask your advice and assistance? I was given your name by the Fuqua Alumni Office and am hoping to tap into your local network as I seek to return to the Raleigh area.

Since graduating from Fuqua and completing a 16-month MBA Enterprise Corps assignment in Ghana, I've spent an enjoyable five years in software marketing—developing strategy, evaluating marketing channels, and building strategic alliances.

I'm looking for a new challenge, where my proven strengths in strategic market planning can add value to a dynamic organization.

continues

Complete two 3-minute timings on the timing text below. Timings 40.3 and 40.4 use the same paragraphs.

Goals: 30 WAM with six or fewer errors
SI: 1.58 syllables per word

 Timings 40.3–40.4

When setting up a network, you will need to plug a cable into an adapter card to connect one device to another device to form a network. Cables are not needed for networks that have wireless ability. Network interface cards are available for desktop and mobile computers and take other forms.

Along with the physical, or hardware, aspects of setting up a network, there is also the software part. A network operation system is software that lets users and devices talk. The operating system installed must be able to support functions of a network like security access features and support for many users. The network style must also be thought about when choosing a network operating system.

Network design takes in the type of computers on the network and controls how network resources are handled. There are two common models used. One model uses each computer on the network as an equal in terms of tasks and resource sharing. The other consists of a group of computers connected to a server.

Physical topology refers to the arrangement of the nodes on a network. A node is a place on the network with a device able to process information, such as a computer or a printer.

 Ergonomic Tip
Take longer breaks from your computer every two hours—at least 15 minutes.

Revising Business Letters

In many cases, it is more efficient to reuse a document than to key new text from scratch. As we have discussed in previous sessions, it is easy to delete text with Word. However, Word also allows you to cut or copy text and to paste it elsewhere in a document. In this session, you will learn how to revise business letters by cutting, copying, and pasting text. These skills will allow you to work more efficiently.

Figure 38.3 Personal Business Letter Content for Document 38.2—Continued

If you know of an opportunity in strategic marketing for a technology company, a company that has aggressive growth plans and needs marketing leadership, or an individual at a technology or other high-growth company who would be interested in my background, I'd greatly appreciate hearing your ideas and referrals.

I welcome your advice and value your expertise as I look for the next exciting career opportunity. I'll phone you in a few days to hear your thoughts.

Sincerely,

Shawna Taylor
4540 Riverview Terrace
Covington, KY 41016

Document 38.3 Personal Business Letter with Proofreading Marks

1   Read all instructions for this document activity, navigate to the Document 38.3 launch page in the Online Lab, and then click the Launch Activity button. The Online Lab will open **Doc038.03** in the activity window. The timer will start as soon as you begin keying the document.

2   Key the text shown in Figure 38.4 and make the changes indicated by the proofreading marks. *Note: If Word formats the email address in the body of the document as a hyperlink (blue text with underline), press the Backspace key to remove the hyperlink formatting.*

3   Vertically center the text on the page.

4   Proofread the document and correct any errors.

5   Save the document (Ctrl + S).

6   Click the Check button to stop the timer and upload the document for checking. The Online Lab will report the WAM rate and number of errors for the activity.

7   If errors are reported, view the results document, correct the errors in the submitted document, save the document, and then click the Check button.

Session 40

Cutting, Copying, and Pasting Text in Business Letters

Session Objectives

- Select, cut, copy, and paste text
- Compose a cover letter
- Prepare a resume

Timing Goals

- 1 minute: 35 WAM and two or fewer errors
- 3 minutes: 30 WAM and six or fewer errors

Getting Started and Warming Up

Exercise 40.1 If you are continuing immediately from Session 39, you may skip the Exercise 40.1 warm-up drill. However, if you exited the Online Lab at the end of Session 39, warm up by completing Exercise 40.1.

Exercise 40.2 Begin your session work by completing Exercise 40.2, a timed short drill, in the Online Lab.

Assessing Your Speed and Accuracy

Complete Timings 40.1 through 40.4 in the Online Lab. At the end of each timing, the Online Lab will display your WAM rate and any errors. Results will be saved in your Timings Performance report. If you have been surpassing the speed and accuracy goals, set slightly more challenging personal goals and strive to exceed them.

Complete two 1-minute timings on the timing text below. Timings 40.1 and 40.2 use the same paragraph.

Goals: 35 WAM and two or fewer errors
SI: 1.52 syllables per word

1-Minute Timings

Timings 40.1–40.2   Computer hardware is notorious for becoming outdated soon after users take it home. Technology advances and gets cheaper at the same time. Planned obsolescence they call it. What can a computer buyer do to make sure a new machine lasts as long into the future as possible? Load up on two components either when you buy the new computer or as an upgrade in the future: hard drive and memory. A big hard drive will help you store more software, movies, music, and other data, while more memory will make for a smoother-running computer.

Figure 38.4 Personal Business Letter Content for Document 38.3

October 15, 2014

Ms. Michele Woggon
13643 N. Pima Spring Way
Tucson, AZ 85736-4891

Dear Michele:

Thank you for showing me the new homes being built in ~~the Vistoso Planned Community~~ *west* north ~~of~~ Tucson. I was especially impressed with the mountain view*s* and the way the new homes blended into the surroundings. The quarter-acre *corner* lot you showed me is my first choice. I hope it is still available.

Would you please send me a map that includes the street names and lots available in the new addition? I will be returning to Tucson on November 1*5* and would like to meet with you in the afternoon to discuss the purchase of a lot and to review the floor plan choices. I have some questions about changing ~~certain~~ *the size of the Arizona* room ~~sizes~~.

I will arrive in Tucson via American Airlines Flight 10*6* at 11:10 a.m., and I have rented a car ~~for~~ *to* use during my stay. I will be available ~~any time~~ after 1:30 p.m. on November 1*5*. Please ~~give me a call~~ at (612) 555-4320, or send me an email ~~message~~ at rsmith@emcp.net with the time I should meet you. *I look forward to working with you.*

Sincerely,

Robert Smith
2385 S. Universal Drive
South Holland, MI 49424

Reinforcing Writing Skills

Have you ever seen a document containing a paragraph that is half a page or more in length? Research demonstrates that most people will read a long paragraph quickly, paying little attention to detail. Yet those details frequently contain information that is important for the reader.

Technical reports, scientific research, and other academic documents commonly include long paragraphs due to the complexity of the information. However, general correspondence, business documents, and college assignments usually can be structured with shorter paragraphs of no more than nine or ten lines. As with short sentences, brief paragraphs tend to increase readability.

3   Navigate to the Document 39.4 launch page in the Online Lab and then click the Launch Activity button. The Online Lab will open **Doc039.04** in the activity window.

4   With the insertion point at the start of the document, press the Tab key and then key the paragraph shown in Figure 39.5, integrating the changes indicated by your proofreading marks.

5   Proofread the document and correct any errors.

6   Save the document.

7   Click the Upload button to upload the document for instructor review.

Figure 39.5 Paragraph to Edit for Document 39.4

The applicant's job interview went well. She had a difficult time finding a parking place. Within minutes after meeting the personnel manager, she began to ask thoughtful questions about the company. She was told that the company was previously located five blocks away. The personnel manager talked a lot about the company's history, its achievements, and its future plans. The applicant worried that someone else had already gotten the job. This company had been researching ways to recycle its products before most people had ever heard about recycling. It also won a presidential award for outstanding customer service. By the time the interviewer began asking her questions, she knew a lot about the company. This knowledge helped her answer the personnel manager's questions about her potential role in the company, and she got the job.

Ending the Session

The Online Lab automatically saves the work you completed for this session. You may continue with the next session or exit the Online Lab and continue later.

Typically, letters contain at least three paragraphs: an opening or introductory paragraph, the main content of the letter (which may be more than one paragraph), and a closing statement or call for action. As with all writing, but particularly when composing a letter, pay particular attention to your word choice and paragraph length. Are your words accurate and short? Are the paragraphs of average length? Is your message clear?

Document 38.4

Composing a Personal Business Letter

1   Navigate to the Document 38.4 launch page in the Online Lab and then click the Launch Activity button. The Online Lab will open **Doc038.04** in the activity window.

2   Using the downloaded file, compose a letter to a department manager of a company for whom you are interested in working. Your goals in writing this letter are to briefly introduce yourself, inquire if there are openings in the manager's department, and describe your qualifications.

3   Vertically center the text on the page.

4   Save the document.

5   Click the Upload button to upload the document for instructor review.

Ending the Session

The Online Lab automatically saves the work you completed for this session. You may continue with the next session or exit the Online Lab and continue later.

plan for automating office operations in a law firm. After reviewing the projects over the weekend, it was obvious that there was one area where all the groups seems to have difficulty and that was dictation/transcription systems.

On Monday morning I called Lynn Gullicksrud and asked her if there was any way that I could bring the class to Sacred Heart Hospital on a really short notice. I wanted her to explain and demonstrate how your dictation/transcription system functions. It was important for the class to see rather than just read about these systems.

Lynn came back to work on Monday evening at 6:30 p.m. and spent the next hour with our students demonstrating, explaining, and answering questions about your system. She did a fantastic job helping our students understand how these systems function and their value to an organization. Sacred Haert Hospital can certainly be proud of Lynn Gullicksrud. Please convey our thanks to Lynn.

Sincerely,

Jordan Leno, Chair Office Technology Division

tkl/Doc039.03.docx

Reinforcing Writing Skills

Well-written paragraphs begin with a topic sentence that presents the major point of the paragraph. Subsequent sentences expand on the topic sentence. Some paragraphs build to a clear conclusion. Each sentence will tie in with the one before and the one after it, creating a sense of *continuity*. Every sentence should also add information that helps explain or support the topic sentence.

Practice editing a paragraph of text in the next document activity.

Document 39.4

Editing a Paragraph

1 Read the paragraph of text shown in Figure 39.5. The paragraph contains both essential and unnecessary information. Read it carefully and decide which sentences can be omitted because they do not help explain the topic sentence. Use proofreading marks to mark your recommended changes to the paragraph. Do not omit essential information.

2 Read the paragraph again and look for weak word choices. Mark your recommended word changes to the paragraph using proofreading marks.

steps continue

Session 39

Inserting Bullets in Business Letters

Session Objectives

- Explore parts of a business letter
- Apply block-style formatting to business letters
- Use bullets in correspondence
- Practice building paragraphs

Timing Goals

- 1 minute: 35 WAM and two or fewer errors
- 3 minutes: 30 WAM and six or fewer errors

Getting Started and Warming Up

Exercise 39.1 If you are continuing immediately from Session 38, you may skip the Exercise 39.1 warm-up drill. However, if you exited the Online Lab at the end of Session 38, warm up by completing Exercise 39.1.

Exercise 39.2 Begin your session work by completing Exercise 39.2, a timed short drill, in the Online Lab.

Assessing Your Speed and Accuracy

Complete Timings 39.1 through 39.4 in the Online Lab. At the end of each timing, the Online Lab will display your WAM rate and any errors. Results will be saved in your Timings Performance report. If you have been surpassing the speed and accuracy goals, set slightly more challenging personal goals and strive to exceed them.

Complete two 1-minute timings on the timing text below. Timings 39.1 and 39.2 use the same paragraph.

Goals: 35 WAM and two or fewer errors
SI: 1.40 syllables per word

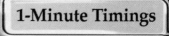

Timings 39.1–39.2   Roller blading can provide hours of exciting fun. If there is a nearby paved lot, you are ready. Roller blades and protective equipment are needed. Skating requires lots of energy or zest to keep moving for a long period of time. The beginning skater should only skate for a short time and not get too tired. After some time has passed, the skater should be able to skate for hours without ever getting tired.

Enclosed are your Transcontinental Gold membership credentials and your Gold Benefits Guide. Your Gold membership is valid for one calendar year. It will be extended for another full year when you accrue 50,000 credited Transcontinental actual flight miles between January 1 and December 31.

Transcontinental Gold was recently named the "Best U.S. Airline Frequent Flyer Program" by one of America's leading consumer reporting agencies and in the current issue of the *World Traveler* magazine. We appreciate your business and look forward to serving you often.

Sincerely yours,

Document 39.3 Block-Style Business Letter with Proofreading Marks

1 Read all instructions for this document activity, navigate to the Document 39.3 launch page in the Online Lab, and then click the Launch Activity button. The Online Lab will open **Doc039.03** in the activity window. The timer will start as soon as you begin keying the document.

2 Key the text shown in Figure 39.4 and make the changes indicated by the proofreading marks. Follow the style presented in Figure 39.1.

3 Proofread the document and correct any errors.

4 Save the document (Ctrl + S).

5 Click the Check button to stop the timer and upload the document for checking. The Online Lab will report the WAM rate and number of errors for the activity.

6 If errors are reported, view the results document, correct the errors in the submitted document, save the document, and then click the Check button.

Figure 39.4 Block-Style Business Letter Content for Document 39.3

December 11, 2014   (#)

Mr. Dale Egland, Division Director
Sacred Heart Hospital
900 Clairemont Avenue
Dubuque, IA 52003-0524

Dear Mr. Egland:

Lynn Gullicksrud, Director of Medical Records at Sacred Heart Hospital, is a "lifesaver." really helped us out on Monday evening, I teach Office Automation Systems at Bradford University. There are 36 students in the class, and *are* they were divided into teams of four each. They were to submit a strategic

continues

Complete two 3-minute timings on the timing text below. Timings 39.3 and 39.4 use the same paragraph.

Goals: 30 WAM and six or fewer errors
SI: 1.36 syllables per word

3-Minute Timings

Timings 39.3–39.4

Many of the metal articles in everyday use are made of brass. A bookend or candlestick made of brass is quite common. But no one has ever heard of brass mines, because there are none. Brass is a blend, or mixture, of metals. Copper and zinc are usually mixed when making brass. These two metals are heated to their melting points, at which time they are joined together. After the mixture cools, it begins to harden. The copper and zinc have blended and formed a new metal with which one can make many creations.

There are quite a few other alloys. In fact, almost none of the metal items we have are made of a single pure metal. The most common alloy by far is steel. Steel is chiefly iron. Since iron is not the strongest metal in the world, it must be combined with just the right amount of carbon for strength. The steel is then used to construct a number of objects such as cars, bridges, skyscrapers, and rails. The iron is also mixed with chromium and nickel to form stainless steel.

Bronze is another common alloy. Bronze is made from the mixture of copper and tin. We call our pennies copper, but actually they are made of bronze. Another alloy called pewter is made of tin.

Ergonomic Tip
Shifting position in your chair rotates stress between different muscle groups allowing some to rest and recuperate.

Preparing Business Letters

A variety of letter styles are used today for both personal and business letters. The letter format presented in this book is the *block style*. In the **block-style letter**, all parts of the letter begin at the left margin. The block-style letter is popular because it is easy to learn, and it is the fastest letter style to set up. Once you have mastered the block-style letter, you will have little difficulty adjusting to other letter formats.

As you learn to prepare letters, work toward the following goals:

- Prepare a document that conveys a favorable image. This requires following style and format guidelines.
- Prepare correspondence free from errors in spelling, punctuation, and word use.
- Prepare correspondence in mailable form at job-ready production levels of at least 25 WAM.

Document

Block-Style Business Letter with Bullets

39.2

1. Read all instructions for this document activity, navigate to the Document 39.2 launch page in the Online Lab, and then click the Launch Activity button. The Online Lab will open **Doc039.02** in the activity window. The timer will start as soon as you begin keying the document.

2. Key the text shown in Figure 39.3.

   a. Follow the style and format presented in Figure 39.1. The file already has the letterhead included. Press the Enter key for paragraph breaks and the Shift + Enter key combination for line breaks.

   b. In keying the bulleted list, select the arrow bullet style from the Bullets button options list. Be sure to press Enter twice at the end of the bulleted list.

   c. Do not format the space following the magazine title in italic.

   d. The person signing the letter is Jan Gould, Managing Director.

   e. Key the reference initials **ch** and the file name. Also include a reference to the fact that enclosures are included with the letter and that a copy of the letter is being sent to Jim Thornton.

3. Proofread the document and correct any errors.

4. Save the document (Ctrl + S).

5. Click the Check button to stop the timer and upload the document for checking. The Online Lab will report the WAM rate and number of errors for the activity.

6. If errors are reported, view the results document, correct the errors in the submitted document, save the document, and then click the Check button.

Figure 39.3 Block-Style Business Letter Content for Document 39.2

October 17, 2014

Ms. Teri M. Podgorski
140 Third Street South
West Orange, NJ 07052-2772

Dear Ms. Podgorski:

Congratulations! As one of Transcontinental's most loyal customers, you have qualified for membership in Transcontinental Gold. This elite membership entitles you to the following benefits:

➢ Unlimited domestic First Class Upgrades on any published Transcontinental fare, confirmable one day prior to departure.
➢ Periodic First Class Companion Upgrades that treat your traveling companions to the same luxury you enjoy.
➢ A 100 percent mileage bonus on credited Transcontinental mileage.
➢ First Class check-in and preboarding, even when you're traveling Coach Class.

continues

Parts of a Business Letter

Figure 39.1 shows the format used in a block-style business letter. This letter was produced using Word default settings. These defaults are Calibri font at a text size of 11 points, 1.15 spacing between lines, and 10 points of additional line space following hard returns. Figure 39.1 includes examples of the nine major parts of a business letter, which are described on the next page.

Figure 39.1 Format of a Block-Style Business Letter   *Note: Key this letter in the Document 39.2 activity.*

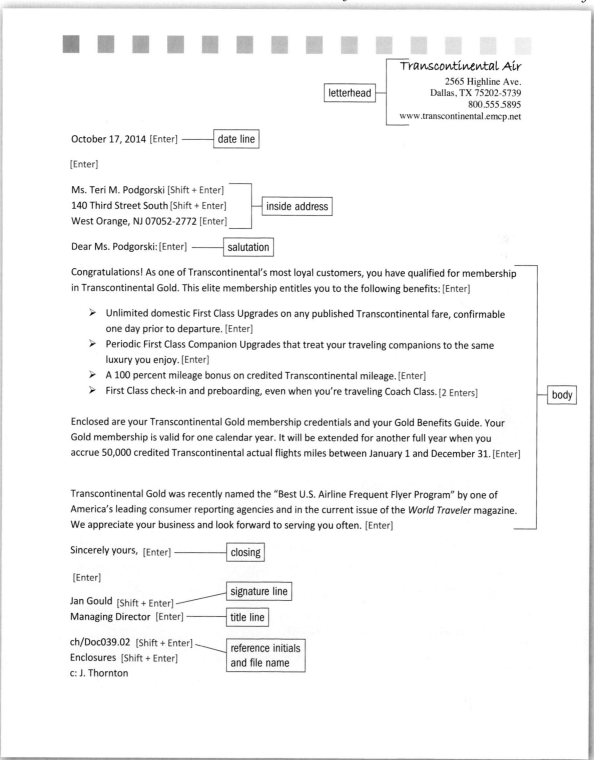

2   Key the text shown in Figure 39.2. Follow the style presented in Figure 39.1. The person signing the letter is Joan LaMavia, Administrator. Key the reference initials ttl and the file name. Indicate an enclosure is included and a copy is to be sent to Dr. Ross Byrd.

3   Proofread the document and correct any errors.

4   Save the document (Ctrl + S).

5   Click the Check button to stop the timer and upload the document for checking. The Online Lab will report the WAM rate and number of errors for the activity.

6   If errors are reported, view the results document, correct the errors in the submitted document, save the document, and then click the Check button.

Figure 39.2 Block-Style Business Letter Content for Document 39.1

October 24, 2014

Dr. Paul Mazza
140 Moloney Building
University of Kentucky
9868 Cooper Drive
Lexington, KY 40507-0235

Dear Dr. Mazza:

Thank you for coming to our school to conduct an in-service program for faculty and students on the "Impact of Technology on Business, Government, and Education." The evaluations of your presentation were absolutely outstanding. I have enclosed a summary prepared by my assistant.

We need your kind of guidance and expertise to help our students prepare for full-time employment. You can be sure that we will ask you to return to our school for a repeat performance.

Rosemary has told me a little about her discussion with you. We hope that your new endeavor will bring you the rewards and satisfaction that you anticipate. My staff members and I agree that you have the skills, knowledge, and dedication required for the new position.

We look forward to seeing you soon.

Sincerely,

- **Letterhead:** The letterhead usually includes the company logo, name, address, phone and fax numbers, and web address. The letterhead may be on preprinted stationery used for correspondence or it may be included in the electronic file used to create the letter and is printed when the letter is printed.

- **Date line:** The date line is the current date, with the name of the month, followed by the date (day of the month), and the year. A comma separates the date and the year.

- **Inside address:** The inside address includes the recipient's courtesy title, recipient's name, title, department, company name, and address.

- **Salutation:** The salutation is a greeting and includes the recipient's courtesy title. In the mixed punctuation style, a colon follows the salutation.

- **Body:** The body of the letter contains the message of the letter. The body consists of one or more paragraphs with one hard return (Enter) at the end of each paragraph.

- **Closing:** The closing is a short farewell In the mixed punctuation style, a comma follows the closing. In the open punctuation style, no punctuation is used after the closing. If the closing contains more than one word, e.g. Sincerely yours, then only the first letter of the first word is capitalized.

- **Signature line:** The signature line includes the first and last names of the sender. Avoid using initials for the first name, to more clearly identify the sender.

- **Title line:** The title line includes the sender's business or professional title.

- **Reference initials and file name:** The initials of the person who keyed the document (included only if this person is not the same as the sender) and the name of the saved file are included at the bottom of the letter. Separate the initials and the file name with a slash symbol (/). The reference initials should be set in lowercase letters. The AutoCorrect feature in Word may change the first lowercase initial to an uppercase letter. To change it back to lowercase, press Ctrl + Z (the shortcut for the undo command).

The goal is always to produce visually pleasing letters. If the letter is short, an additional hard return may be added after the date line. Do not vertically center business letters on the page.

Common Letter Notations

In addition to the major sections of a business letter, several notations are used if they are appropriate to a particular letter. Some of these are shown in Figure 39.1.

1 **Enclosure:** Indicates that a document or another item is included with the letter. If multiple enclosures are included, use Enclosures. Several styles are acceptable, including the abbreviation *Enc.*

2 **Attachment:** Similar to an enclosure but the item is actually attached (by tape or staple, for example) to the document rather than simply being enclosed. This notation is typically used for items included with memos as *Attachment* or *Att.*

3 **Copy Notation:** Lists in alphabetical order, by last name, any additional people who will receive copies of the letter. Either the word *copy* or the lowercase letter *c* followed by a colon is acceptable. *Note: Use Ctrl + Z to undo the AutoCorrect change from a lowercase to a capital C.* If only one person is receiving a copy, space once after the colon before keying the name. If multiple people are receiving copies, press the Tab key after the colon so that the other names will align correctly below the first name.

Success Tip

Pressing Ctrl + Z will undo the last command used. Learning to use keyboard shortcuts will increase your productivity (time on task).

Using Bullets to Highlight Items

Some letters include a list of items (words, phrases, or sentences) that are to be set apart from the body of the letter for special emphasis. These items can be numbered, in a **numbered list**, or they can be preceded by a bullet, producing a **bulleted list**. A bullet can take many shapes such as a circle, a square, a diamond, or an arrow.

When creating a bulleted list, by default, Word will include a nonprinting Tab character after a bullet. If the bulleted item is more than one line long, Word will begin the second line on a **hanging indent**. In other words, the start of the second line of the bulleted item will align with the first word of the bulleted paragraph rather than with the bullet.

You can create bullets of various types in Word using the following steps:

1   In the Paragraph group on the Home tab, click the down arrow on the Bullets button.

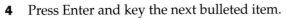

2   Click the desired bullet style from the options provided in the gallery. This will insert a bullet followed by a nonprinting Tab symbol.

3   Key the text of the first bulleted item.

4   Press Enter and key the next bulleted item.

5   To end bulleting, press the Enter key two times. This will place the insertion point at the start of the first paragraph following the bulleted list.

To make a bulleted list from text that has already been keyed, select the paragraphs or lines of text that you wish to include in the list, click the Bullets button down arrow, and then click the desired button style from the gallery. Word will insert a bullet at the beginning of each line that follows a hard return (where the Enter key was pressed).

To delete bullet formatting, select the bulleted text and then click the Bullets button.

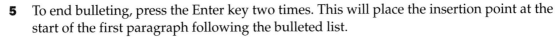

Success Tip

For lists with items that are sequential or should logically occur in a certain order, use a numbered list. In contrast, for lists with items that are not sequential or do not logically occur in a particular order, use a bulleted list.

Document **Block-Style Business Letter**

39.1

1   Read all instructions for this document activity, navigate to the Document 39.1 launch page in the Online Lab, and then click the Launch Activity button. The Online Lab will open **Doc039.01** in the activity window. The timer will start as soon as you begin keying the document.

steps continue

Index

H

Hanging indent, 229, 362–363
Hard copy, 177
Hard page break, 253–254
Headers
    changing header margin in memo report, 311–313
    inserting, 254–256
Headings
    APA style, 427–428
    CMS research paper, 402
    controlling pagination of in research papers, 405–406
Home tab, 177
Hyperlink, removing, 393

I

Indenting text
    hanging indent, 229, 362–363
    tabs, 336–338
    using Ruler, 206
Insert Footnote feature, 400–401
Insertion point, key commands for moving, 179
Insert proof reading mark, 183
Insert Table Dialog Box, 283, 284–285
Insert text, 179
Inside address, letter, 227, 228
In-text citations, 399
Italic text, 195–197

J

Justified text, 203, 204

L

Large envelope, 267, 268, 269–270
Left alignment, 203–204
Left Tab, 336
Lettered sublist, memo report formatting, 324
Letter head, 227, 228
Letter of transmittal, 351–352
Letters. *See* Business letters; Personal business letters
Line chart, 346–347
Line spacing, changing, 352–353, 387
Line Style Button Drop-Down Menu, 300
Lists
    bulleted, 229, 339–340
    lettered sublist, 324
    numbered, 229, 323–324, 339–340

M

Manuscript
    APA style for research papers, 425–428
    binding for, 333
    bound and unbound, 385, 386
    changing default font, 386–387
    characteristics of, 385

citing sources in research papers, 398–401
CMS format for research papers, 401–408
compared to business report, 311
compared to formal business report, 333
determining word count, 393
displays or exhibits for, 333
format for, 333
line spacing, changing default, 387
MLA format for research papers, 413–417
outline, 388–389
preparation steps for, 385
reference information, 333
remove hyperlink, 393
title page for, 392
Margins, page, for formal business reports, 334
Memo (memorandums)
    changing paragraph alignment, 203–205
    compared to email, 200
    defined, 200
    formatting, 201–202
    guide words in, 201
    indenting text, 206–207
    sample of, 201
    selecting text in, 203
    traditional format for, 201
    uses of, 200
    Word Ruler, 206
Memo business reports, 311–317, 322–330
    defined, 311
    fax cover sheets, 317–319
    Find and Replace feature, 328–329
    header margin changes, 311–313
    lettered sublist, 324
    numbered list formatting, 323–324
    sample of, 312
    setting automatic formatting options, 323–324
    undo and redo, 325
    Widow/Orphan control, 313–314
Microsoft Word. *See* Word documents
MLA (Modern Language Association) format, 398
    creating a works cited page according to, 416
    inserting in-text citations according to, 414–415
    overview of format guidelines, 413–414
Modern Language Association (MLA), 398, 413
Multiple-page letters, 253–262

N

Notations, letter, 228
Number 10 envelope, 267, 268, 269–270
Numbered list, 229
    changing indents for, in formal business report, 339–340
    memo report formatting, 323–324
Numbered paragraphs, 258–259

O

Orphans, 313–314

Appendix A

Keyboard Shortcuts

Feature	Keyboard Command
Bold	Ctrl + B
Center align text	Ctrl + E
Copy	Ctrl + C
Cut	Ctrl + X
Find	Ctrl + F
Find and Replace	Ctrl + H
Insert line space	Shift + Enter
Insert page break	Ctrl + Enter
Insert tab in a table	Ctrl + Tab
Italic	Ctrl + I
Justify align text	Ctrl + J
Left align text	Ctrl + L
Move insertion point one word to left	Ctrl + ←
Move insertion point one word to right	Ctrl + →
Move insertion point to end of document	Ctrl + End
Move insertion point to end of line	End
Move insertion point to start of line	Home
Move insertion point to top of document	Ctrl + Home
New document	Ctrl + N
Open document	Ctrl + O
Paste	Ctrl + V
Print	Ctrl + P
Right align text	Ctrl + R
Save	Ctrl + S
Select all	Ctrl + A
Show/Hide	Ctrl + *
Undo	Ctrl + Z
Underline	Ctrl + U

Appendix B

Proofreading Marks

Mark	Meaning	Example	Change Implemented
#	insert space	letter to the	letter to the
℘	delete	the commands is	the command is
(lc) /	lowercase	he is Branch Manager	he is branch manager
(cap) or UC ≡	uppercase	Margaret simpson	Margaret Simpson
¶	new paragraph	The new product	The new product
no ¶	no paragraph	the meeting. Bring the	the meeting. Bring the
⌐	line break	the dog and cat	the dog and cat
∨∧	insert	pens, clips	pens, and clips
⊙	insert period	a global search	a global search.
]	move right	With the papers	With the papers
[	move left	access the code	access the code
][[	center	Chapter Six	Chapter Six
∪∩	transpose	It is raesonable	It is reasonable
(sp) ◯	spell out	475 Mill Ave.	475 Mill Avenue
(stet) ...	stet (Latin for "Let it stand")	I am very pleased	I am very pleased
⌒	combine or close up	regret fully	regretfully
ss	single-space	The margin top is 1 inch.	The margin top is 1 inch.
ds	double-space	Paper length is set for 11 inches.	Paper length is set for 11 inches.
ts	triple-space	The F8 function key turns on Extend	The F8 function key turns on Extend

Mark	Meaning	Example	Change Implemented
bf ∿	boldface	*bf* Boldface type provides emphasis.	**Boldface** type provides emphasis.
(*ital*) ——	italic	(*ital*) Use <u>italic</u> for terms to be defined.	Use *italic* for terms to be defined.
(BL)	bulleted list	(BL) Start a bulleted list	• Start a bulleted list.
1/m	em dash	1/m Southeast⌣⌣even	Southeast—even
⨍ ⨍	parenthesis	⨍Figure 69.4⨍	(Figure 69.4)
=	insert hyphen	555=1212	555-1212
⟋	move text	⑫June, 2013	June 12, 2013
∿	run text in	John Smith, President	John Smith, President